MOVIE MAVENS

WOMEN AND FILM HISTORY INTERNATIONAL

Series Editors
Kay Armatage, Jane M. Gaines, and Christine Gledhill

A new generation of motion picture historians is rediscovering the vital and diverse contributions of women to world film history whether as producers, actors, or spectators. Taking advantage of new print material and moving picture archival discoveries, as well as the benefits of digital access and storage, this series investigates the significance of gender in the cinema.

A list of books in the series appears at the end of this book.

MOVIE MAVENS

US Newspaper Women
Take On the Movies,
1914–1923

Edited by

RICHARD ABEL

UNIVERSITY OF
ILLINOIS PRESS
Urbana, Chicago, and Springfield

© 2021 by the Board of Trustees
of the University of Illinois
All rights reserved
1 2 3 4 5 C P 5 4 3 2 1
♾ This book is printed on acid-free paper.

Library of Congress Cataloging-in-Publication Data
Names: Abel, Richard, 1941– editor.
Title: Movie mavens: US newspaper women take on the movies,
   1914–1923 / edited by Richard Abel.
Description: Urbana: University of Illinois Press, [2021] |
   Series: Women and film history international | Includes
   bibliographical references and index. |
Identifiers: LCCN 2021017187 (print) | LCCN 2021017188 (ebook)
   | ISBN 9780252043970 (cloth) | ISBN 9780252086045
   (paperback) | ISBN 9780252052903 (ebook)
Subjects: LCSH: Motion pictures—United States—Reviews. |
   Motion pictures—Press coverage—United States—History—
   20th century. | Silent films—United States—History and
   criticism. | Women journalists—United States—History—
   20th century. | Women and journalism—United States—
   History—20th century.
Classification: LCC PN1995.75 M565 2021 (print) | LCC PN1995.75
   (ebook) | DDC 791.4301—dc23
LC record available at https://lccn.loc.gov/2021017187
LC ebook record available at https://lccn.loc.gov/2021017188

For the Women Film Pioneers Project and
Women and Film History International

Contents

Acknowledgments   xiii

Introduction: Surveying a New Field for Newspaper Women   1

Chapter 1. Women Writers Lead the Way, 1914–1916   11

    Grace Kingsley, *Los Angeles Times*   13
        "Where the Movies Are Hatched: Universal City," August 23, 1914
        "Los Angeles the Globe's Moving Picture Center," January 1, 1915
        "Story's Well Told": *Shoes*, July 19, 1916

    Kitty Kelly, *Chicago Tribune*   21
        Advertisement, April 30, 1916

        "Flickerings from Filmland": *Wild Life*, March 2, 1915
        "Flickerings from Filmland": *The Woman*, May 3, 1915
        "Flickerings from Filmland": *Stolen Goods*, May 25, 1915
        "Flickerings from Filmland": *Birth of a Nation*, May 27, 1915
        "Flickerings from Filmland": *Carmen*, October 16, 1915
        "Flickerings from Filmland": Hugo Münsterberg, April 29, 1916
        "Flickerings from Filmland": *Where Are My Children?*, July 31, 1916

    Charlotta Bass, *California Eagle*   35
        "Thomas Dickson's Idea of American Liberty," January 30, 1915

    Louella O. Parsons, *Chicago Record-Herald*   36

"Seen on the Screen": *Birth of a Nation*, April 20, 1915
"Seen on the Screen": *A Fool There Was*, May 3, 1915
"Seen on the Screen": *Carmen*, October 16, 1915

Esther Hoffman, *The Day Book*   41
"My Movie Scrap Book," May 7, 1915

The Film Girl, *Syracuse Herald*   41
Advertisement, September 12, 1917
"Seen on the Screen by the Film Girl," June 22, 1915
"Seen on the Screen by the Film Girl," August 13, 1915
"Seen on the Screen by the Film Girl," December 28, 1915

Dorothy Day, *Des Moines Tribune*   44
"News of the Movies": *The Golden Chance*, January 28, 1916
"News of the Movies": *Where Are My Children?*, October 30, 1916

Mildred Joclyn, *Chicago Post*   47
"Movies Offer a New Field for Ambitious Women," September 2, 1916

Oma Moody Lawrence, *Chicago Post*   48
"Music in 'The Birth of a Nation,'" October 28, 1916
"The Etiquette of the Picture Show," January 13, 1917

Mae Tinee, *Chicago Tribune*   52
"Miss Mae Tinee," January 3, 1915
"Right Off the Reel": *Romeo and Juliet*, November 8, 1916
"Nazimova Makes Her Screen Debut," December 6, 1916
"'Idle Wives'—a Pictorial Goulash," December 7, 1916

Chapter 2. Women Writers during the Great War, 1917–1918   68

Mae Tinée, *Chicago Tribune*   69
"Miss Farrar's 'Joan of Arc' Splendidly Done," March 29, 1917
"'Her Greatest Love' Her Worst Film," April 5, 1917
"'The Divine Sarah' Divine Still in Tale of War and Woe," April 11, 1917
"Along Comes Constance and Proves a Riot," November 6, 1917
"The Best Picture Clara's Had in a Long, Long Time," March 15, 1918
"Griffith Shows Them How to Make a War Picture!," April 25, 1918
"Like Unto a Brown Brook or an Etching": *A Hoosier Romance*, August 19, 1918

Louella O. Parsons, *Chicago Herald* and *New York Morning Telegraph*   77
"How Fluffy, Flighty Keystone Beauties Proved They Had Brains," November 18, 1917
"In and Out of Favor," June 23, 1918

Dorothy Day, *Des Moines Tribune*   82
- "News of the Movies," January 8, 1918
- "Thrills of a Lifetime in Screen Picture": *Hearts of the World*, September 17, 1918

Kitty Kelly, *Chicago Herald and Examiner*   85
- "Flickerings from Filmland": *Weaver of Dreams*, February 16, 1918
- "Flickerings from Filmland": *The Bluebird*, May 6, 1918
- "Be Your Own Critic," May 26, 1918
- "The 'Very Best' Is Mr. Healy's Motto," July 28, 1918

Janet Flanner, *Indianapolis Sunday Star*   90
- "Comments on the Screen," June 30, 1918
- "Comments on the Screen," July 14, 1918
- "Comments on the Screen," July 21, 1918

Genevieve Harris, *Chicago Post*   97
- "Riley Poem Is Basis for a Fine Picture": *A Hoosier Romance*, August 22, 1918
- "A Visit to a Film Exchange," October 26, 1918
- "Two Views on Film Problems," December 7, 1918

Charlotte S. Kelly, *Indianapolis Sunday Star*   102
- "Comments on the Screen," September 22, 1918
- "Comments on the Screen," November 3, 1918
- "Comments on the Screen," November 24, 1918

Chapter 3. A Peak Period for Women Writers, 1919–1921   116

Marjorie Daw, *Cleveland Sunday Plain Dealer* and *Detroit Journal*   117
- "Favorite Stars Listed in Suitable Film Roles": *True Heart Susie*, June 15, 1919
- "Doug and Chas. at the Circus," November 11, 1919
- "Still Another Field for Girls," November 14, 1919

Mae Tinée, *Chicago Tribune*   120
- "Great Cast; Great Director; Great Picture!": *The Miracle Man*, September 15, 1919
- "Right Off the Reel," September 19, 1920
- "Alice as 'Kate' Comes Back into Her Own": *Cousin Kate*, January 15, 1921
- "O, Mary, Mary, and We Held Our Breath for This": *The Love Light*, January 25, 1921
- "Famous 'Best Seller' Makes a Fine Photoplay": *The Four Horsemen of the Apocalypse*, March 28, 1921
- "'Passion's' Players Do Not Act; They Live Their Parts," May 10, 1921
- "Whoops, My Dear! Do Bring on the Strait Jacket": *The Cabinet of Dr. Caligari*, May 15, 1921

"Here's Where De Mille Out–De Milles Himself": *The Affairs of Anatol*, August 15, 1921
"Take Your Hankie for You May Weep over 'The Blot,'" August 28, 1921
"The Ten Best Pictures of 1921—as Seen by Us," January 29, 1922

Charlotte S. Kelly, *Indianapolis Sunday Star*   130
"Comments on the Screen," January 26, 1919
"Comments on the Screen," February 9, 1919

Genevieve Harris, *Chicago Post*   134
"Mrs. Drew as Film Director," February 1, 1919
"Griffith Play Returns": *Broken Blossoms*, October 18, 1919
"Motion Pictures in Education," May 22, 1920
"Photoplays as Topics for Talk," August 20, 1921
"Photoplays": *The Blot*, August 24, 1921
"Photoplays": *Over the Hill*, September 5, 1921
"Second Thots on 'Four Horsemen,'" September 10, 1921
"Romance Factory," December 17, 1921

Virginia Tracy, *New York Sunday Tribune*   144
"The Dazzling Sameness of Douglas Fairbanks," January 26, 1919
"A Truce between Romance and Realism": *The Cheat*, February 9, 1919
"What Screen Comedy Owes the Drews," April 20, 1919
"Best of Griffith in 'Broken Blossoms,'" May 25, 1919
"Griffith's Hand Too Heavy on 'True Heart Susie,'" August 3, 1919

Dorothy Day, *Des Moines Tribune*   162
"News of the Movies": *Don't Change Your Husband*, February 18, 1919
"News of the Movies": *Mickey*, April 1, 1919
"News of the Movies," May 27, 1920

Rae McRae, *Des Moines Register*   166
"Breaking into the Movies," July 13, 1919

Virginia Dale, *Chicago Journal*   168
Advertisement, July 30, 1921
"Fox Studios Hive of Industry," December 17, 1921

Harriette Underhill, *New York Tribune*   171
"On the Screen," December 29, 1919
"On the Screen": *The Branded Woman*, September 6, 1920
"On the Screen": *The Mark of Zorro*, November 29, 1920
"On the Screen": *The Love Light*, January 10, 1921
"On the Screen": *The Cabinet of Dr. Caligari*, April 4, 1921

"On the Screen": *What Do Men Want?*, November 15, 1921

Alberta Hartley, *Des Moines News*   180
"At the Movies": *Midsummer Madness*, January 3, 1921
"At the Movies": *Why Trust Your Husband*, January 28, 1921
"Movie News," February 2, 1921

Chapter 4. Women Writers Carry On, 1922–1923   195

Grace Kingsley, *Los Angeles Times*   196
"Flashes: *Tol'able David*," January 23, 1922
"Day by Day Our Comedies Grow Sadder," January 14, 1923

Harriette Underhill, *New York Tribune*   199
"On the Screen": *Foolish Wives*, January 27, 1922
"On the Screen": *Smilin' Through*, April 17, 1922

Mae Tinée, *Chicago Tribune*   201
"Valentino Lova da Lady, Keela da Bull! Caramba!," August 23, 1922
"Real Life Reeled in Eskimo Land," September 2, 1922
"'The Merry Go Round' Worth All It Cost," September 25, 1923
"Introducing a Candidate for Vamp Honors": *Flaming Youth*, October 31, 1923

Elizabeth Kern, *Omaha World-Herald*   207
"This Week at the Movies," October 23, 1922
"This Week at the Movies": *Trailing African Wild Animals*, August 13, 1923
"This Week at the Movies": *Flaming Youth*, November 26, 1923
"This Week at the Movies": *Anna Christie*, December 3, 1923
"This Week at the Movies": *Little Old New York*, December 10, 1923

Virginia Dale, *Chicago Journal*   210
"At the Theaters": *Saturday Night*, January 21, 1922
"Moving Pictures," February 10, 1922
"Moving Pictures": *Smilin' Through*, March 29, 1922
"Moving Pictures," May 5, 1922
"Spendthrift Youth Owns Filmdom," February 17, 1923
"News of the Motion Picture World," October 25, 1923

Genevieve Harris, *Chicago Post*   218
"Screen Writing Distinct Craft," February 11, 1922
"Photoplays": *Polly of the Follies*, February 13, 1922
"Photoplays": *Foolish Wives*, February 14, 1922
"Woman Editor of Film Plays," March 18, 1922
"Photoplays": *Blood and Sand*, August 22, 1922
"Photoplays": *Nanook of the North*, September 11, 1922

"A French View of Film Art," December 16, 1922
"Films Add to Joy of Travel," February 17, 1923
"Film History to Be Shown," May 10, 1923
"Photoplays": *Ashes of Vengeance*, August 28, 1923
"French Films Show Artistry," December 29, 1923

Polly Wood, *Chicago Herald and Examiner* 234
"'Hollywood' Will Make Fans for Film Land," July 23, 1923
"'Zorro' Differs from Doug's Later Films," August 10, 1923
"Another Look at Year's Best Picture": *Enemies of Women*, August 22, 1923
"Maria Is Buffer for Mary in 'Rosita,'" November 26, 1923

Afterword 251

Appendix: Newspaper References 255

Index 257

Acknowledgments

This collection has come together during a period of deep loss followed by the COVID-19 pandemic. As a consequence, I owe many, many thanks to all those who offered such welcome support of and assistance on this unique project.

I am especially grateful to the staff and facilities of several archives and libraries: reference librarian Lesley Martin and her assistant Elizabeth McKinley at the Chicago History Museum Research Center; Carol Kirsch, supervisor of Special Collections & Publications at the State Historical Society of Iowa in Iowa City; state archivist Anthony Jahn and his staff at the State Historical Society of Iowa in Des Moines; and Eric Hoyt, director and web designer of the Media History Digital Library.

Three former doctoral students at the University of Michigan scanned crucial newspaper microfilm reels when I was unable to travel: Nathan Koob at the Chicago History Museum Research Center, Jim Carter at the Detroit Public Library, and Ben Strassfeld at the New York Public Library. Kris Lipkowski did some research at the Chicago Public Library, and Kaveh Askari shared a rare document listing the advisory council members of the New York Film Arts Guild. I myself relied heavily for online research on newspapers.com, genealogybank.com, Chronicling America (US Library of Congress), and Media History Digital Library.

Giorgio Bertellini, a close friend and silent cinema colleague, read the introduction in draft and shared several good ideas before I submitted the full manuscript to the University of Illinois Press. In their reader's reports, Christine Gledhill and Laura Horak were extremely enthusiastic, offering invaluable suggestions for making revisions, especially of the afterword, and querying numerous critical details in the texts and footnotes. I am very pleased that both thought the initial book proposal was ideally suited for the University of Illinois Press's Women and Film History International series.

At the University of Illinois Press, acquisitions editor Danny Nasset consistently offered strong support for this project, quickly arranged a contract, and kept me apprised of what I needed to do and when to do so for final approval of the manuscript, especially during the unusual constrictions of the pandemic. Assistant acquisitions editor Ellie Hinton efficiently handled preparation issues and questions about the massive number of text files as I readied the manuscript for submission. Managing editor Jennifer Argo coordinated the editorial and production process for the book with exceptional expertise and efficiency. Mary M. Hill handled the copyediting with timely, meticulous attention and suggested many felicitous revisions. Jessie Norris did consistently excellent work on the page proof. Designer Jennifer Fisher created a terrific book cover.

Throughout the writing and rewriting, Barbara Hodgdon hovered over my shoulder as a ghostly presence, quietly urging me here and there to elevate my prose, even if I could never match the unique elegance and wry intelligence of her voice.

MOVIE MAVENS

Introduction

Surveying a New Field for Newspaper Women

> Although few women do dramatic criticism, the motion picture field is virtually their monopoly. All over the country feminine by-lines go with cinema reviews. It has opened up a new crop of jobs. Many of the girls who are doing it have had no general newspaper experience.
> —Ishbel Ross, *Ladies of the Press*, 1936

In early 1914 the *Chicago Record-Herald* hailed the notion that "newspapers make picture-goers" with an ad in which a crowd of people are lined up to buy tickets to a movie theater whose entrance is framed by a full page from the newspaper itself.[1] The ad perfectly encapsulates what a few cinema historians have been arguing for more than a decade: newspapers are a rich, previously unexplored source for rethinking and rewriting early American cinema history. A leading figure, Paul S. Moore, advanced this argument recently in an essay in *The Routledge Companion to New Cinema History* (2019).[2] But others—for instance, Robert C. Allen, Kathryn Fuller-Seeley, Martin L. Johnson, Jan Olsson, and Gregory Waller—have been pursuing this kind of newspaper research as well, often exploring how the cultural and social are entangled in the history of the movies.[3] Even earlier, Anna Everett had done similar work, focused specifically on the Black press.[4] And I too have joined these colleagues, most notably in *Menus for Movieland* (2015).[5] During the research for that book I was surprised to discover so many newspaper women working as movie page editors, interviewers, gossip columnists, and/or film reviewers between 1913 and 1916. Since then, I have accessed as many American newspapers as possible beyond that book's scope, specifically from 1915 through the early 1920s.[6] This ongoing research reveals that newspaper women, particularly in the Midwest—Kitty Kelly, Mae Tinée, Louella O. Parsons, and Dorothy Day—continued to write about the movies after 1915.

Even more important, my research has turned up others, again mostly in the Midwest—Mildred Joclyn, Oma Moody Lawrence, Genevieve Harris, Janet Flanner, Charlotte Kelly, Marjorie Daw, Virginia Dale, Polly Wood, Alberta Hartley, and Elizabeth Kern.[7] Arguably, the work done by these women uncannily paralleled that of those increasingly brought into the spotlight not only as neglected filmmakers and scenario writers but also as production managers, continuity clerks, film cutters, and location finders among some "fifty different occupations [. . .] open to women in film work."[8]

In the conclusion to his recent essay in *Film History*, Louis Pelletier rightly urges early cinema historians to do further research "on the actual contributions of newspapermen to the rise of US cinema as a seminal form of vernacular modernity."[9] To be fair, "men" here may be taken as a generic term that includes other genders. But still, it is symptomatic of the long-outmoded assumption that men have been the main agents of history—let alone cinema history—and that women implicitly played a secondary role or even could be excluded. If, as *Menus for Movieland* argues, newspapers supported and sustained a mass audience of moviegoers as an American popular film culture emerged, then the editing and writing done by newspaper women demand our attention. Whether or not Ishbel Ross's claim is exaggerated, this collection means to write those women and their work, long "unremarked, forgotten, cast adrift," back into cinema history.[10] The only other collection that shares a similar claim about the significance of women writers is Antonia Lant's landmark edited volume, *Red Velvet Seat: Women's Writing on the First Fifty Years of Cinema*.[11] That volume, however, is admirably global in its choice of women writers and covers a lengthy half century. Moreover, one of its writers, Janet Flanner, appeared only very briefly in American newspapers in the 1910s. *Movie Mavens* may be focused more narrowly on notably white American newspaper women writing in English during a shorter period of time for the mainstream (white) press, but it aims nonetheless to offer an equally rich array of texts, with certain caveats.[12]

Among certain unavoidable restrictions is the collection's cut-off point of 1923. If 1914 can be justified as the starting point because that's when Mae Tinee and Kitty Kelly became an important movie page editor and film reviewer, respectively, for the *Chicago Tribune*, 1923 may seem arbitrary. Yet there are reasons, one having to do with legal issues. After that date (at least when I began this volume), reprinting newspaper columns in full potentially would require copyright permissions, which might be costly or difficult to obtain, especially if a newspaper no longer exists. Another restriction has to do with methodology, that is, with the limited accessibility of many newspapers, particularly when one is searching for women writers. In late 1919, for instance, *Motion Picture News* published its "First Annual Newspaper and Theater Directory," which compiled answers to its queries to the newspapers covering the movies in more than seven hundred cities of "over twelve thousand population."[13] Unfortunately, not all newspapers in major cities such as Chicago, Cincinnati, and Cleveland responded, and those that did respond offered incomplete lists of named photoplay editors, photoplay departments, and photoplay pages. Moreover, far too few of these newspapers turn out to be digitized and may not even survive on microfilm, and word searching those that are digitized too often leads to dead ends. Only half of the dozen writers with definite women's names appear in searches, and because many editors have only first-name initials, the actual number of women writers may be larger.[14] (For further information on this directory, see the introduction to chapter 2.) Similarly, although the advisory council of the New York Film Arts Guild in 1926 included six women out of fifteen columnists affiliated with newspapers, only one of those women definitely reviewed films.[15] Obviously, this collection's contracted page length presents its own restriction on the number of columns that can be reprinted. That said, I have sought to select those that are particularly representative of a writer's work, review important films and stars, are concerned with exhibition and the theater experience, or take up intriguing and sometimes unique issues.

To be more specific, let me sketch in broad outline what emerges as characteristic of these selected texts. Readers, of course, may find others equally salient. There are signs, for instance, that many but not all writers seemed to be addressing an audience or readership of women. First of all, particularly in the 1910s, daily columns—those of Kitty Kelly, Louella Parsons, Dorothy Day, and the Film Girl—usually appeared in the Society or Women's section of a newspaper. Second, several writers, such as Day, the Film Girl, and Polly Wood, followed Kelly in directly speaking to women, "girls," or "girruls." Third, both Mildred Joclyn and Marjorie Daw replayed Gertrude Price's 1912 claim that the motion picture industry had opened up a new field for women to pursue careers.[16] As further signs, Virginia Dale, Genevieve Harris, Alberta Hartley, and Elizabeth Kern all devoted individual columns to one or more women well known to the public as scenario writers. And Hartley lambasted one film as the ignorant product of, obviously, a male scenario writer. Harris even made a nearly forgotten woman the focus of a column on the invaluable work of a film editor. Several columnists praised Lois Weber, yet not unambiguously, as a major film director; and both Harris and Virginia Tracy surprisingly singled out Mrs. Sidney Drew as a little-recognized director of merit. Finally, to dissuade young women from thinking only of how to become a movie actress, Day printed Anita Stewart's tongue-in-cheek "ten commandments" of no-no's for pasting "over every girl's dressing table."[17]

Not unexpectedly, these women exhibited a wide range of writing styles that partly depended on their newspaper's readership. For the upscale *New York Tribune*, for instance, both Tracy and Harriette Underhill composed lengthy, serious, or somewhat formal columns—if ironic or satirical, in Underhill's case. But so did Harris in the *Chicago Post* (with its low circulation) and even Janet Flanner (who also deftly indulged in satire) and Charlotte Kelly in the *Indianapolis Star*. However, most of the writers—from the Film Girl and Day to Dale, Hartley, and Wood—adopted a colloquial, chatty style, presenting themselves as "ordinary" people talking to other "ordinary" people. The Film Girl even described herself as simply a "maid of the movies" or a fan like her readers. In her later columns for the *Chicago Tribune*, Mae Tinée began greeting readers like a friend or neighbor at the breakfast table with "Good Morning!" and signing off with "See you tomorrow." Dale used the tactic of concocting a "Chatty Person" (someone other than herself) to scatter dollops of gossip. In the *Chicago Tribune*, Kitty Kelly and Mae Tinée created distinctive writing personas. Kelly performed as an exuberant wordsmith whose love of language came close to "showboating." Mae Tinée's performance was no less flamboyant, with her snappy, idiomatic style, but she also verged on the "snarky," especially in her scorn for stars such as Theda Bara and Francis X. Bushman and in her disappointment with new films by Mary Pickford and Charlie Chaplin.

Nearly all of these writers shared movie fans' fascination with stars. They were far from unanimous in their praise, however, and could hold divergent opinions on major figures such as Douglas Fairbanks and Norma Talmadge. Parsons and Mae Tinée, for instance, were unusually harsh to Theda Bara. Fans' fascination is one reason for reprinting Esther Hoffman's weekly promotion in 1915 of star photos for movie scrapbooks. Many writers also highlighted the work of film directors, calling attention to them not quite as "authors" but certainly as the crucial figures in what were collaborative commercial projects or as relatively unheralded professionals at the time. And they were not always kind to famous names, finding fault with certain efforts of D. W. Griffith, Cecil B. DeMille, and Weber. By the mid-1910s, newspaper readers expected nearly all the writers to review newly released feature films. The columns included here, consequently, offered sometimes ambiguous and even contradictory judgments on familiar, even "canonical" films, from *The Birth of a Nation* and *Where Are My Children?* to *Foolish Wives*, *Robin Hood*, and *Flaming Youth*. Those judgments extended to the German imports that began impacting the American market in 1921–22. If the columns uniformly praised films directed by Ernst Lubitsch and starring Pola Negri, they were conflicted in the case of *The Cabinet of Dr. Caligari*. The task of reviewing led a few writers like Kitty Kelly, Parsons, Day, and Harris to ponder the principles one should use in evaluating a feature film and to share those as a means to "train" fans for thinking and talking more knowledgeably and persuasively about the films they like or dislike. As a corollary, Harris recommended a second viewing to confirm whether or not a film was as good as it initially seemed. Discussing specific stars and films is where intriguing differences arise between these women and their male counterparts. If "Wid" Gunning, unlike Parsons, frankly admired Theda Bara's "wonderful face" in the *New York Evening Mail*, the anonymous reviewers in the *New York Times* rarely mentioned Weber, and Carl Sandberg wrote nothing about her—at least according to the collection of his columns from the *Chicago News*.[18]

Although hardly uncommon, some of these writers took their readers behind the scenes of the movie industry. But their choices could be unusual. Grace Kingsley, for instance, offered rare studio tours of Universal City and other Los Angeles companies in the early years (1914–15); both Parsons and Dale visited studios in the New York City area, including Fox, in different years; and Dale briefly singled out Watterson Rothacker's company in Chicago not only for producing advertising and industrial films but also for developing and printing many Hollywood features. Kern surprisingly called attention to cameraman Alvin Wyckoff's practice of using "atmospheric lighting [. . .] to heighten the dramatic effect" in many of DeMille's features that fans would remember. And Wood took a whole column to reveal how cameraman Charles Rosher used a dummy named Maria to double for Pickford in the preparations for many of her films. In late 1918, Harris described in some detail the important yet unfamiliar operations of the new Famous Players–Lasky rental exchange in Chicago, crucial work that producers and exhibitors depended on for ensuring the quality of film prints, their promotion in posters and photos, and their standardized circulation in theaters. Revealingly, she highlighted the department responsible for inspecting and repairing prints, one that employed many women.

Writer after writer, in different ways, stressed the value of the theater experience for moviegoers. Some, like Day and Hartley, devoted columns to the splendor and comfort of new palace cinemas at their openings. Others, like the Film Girl, Flanner, Charlotte Kelly, Harris, and Kern, confessed that they either preferred the variety programs of shorter films in both neighborhood theaters and larger cinemas or else found short nonfiction films, including newsreels, sometimes the most attractive on theater programs. Underhill even praised Samuel Lionel "Roxy" Rothapfel's artistic stage settings, which contributed to the impact of *Passion* and *The Cabinet of Dr. Caligari* at the Strand Theater in New York. Kitty Kelly, Dale, and Harris chose to interview local exhibitors who had carved out a niche for themselves beyond the downtown Loop in Chicago. Intriguingly, several devoted columns to the music performed before, during, and after the films on a theater program. Lawrence, for instance, offered a detailed description of Joseph Carl Breil's perfectly arranged score for *The Birth of a Nation*. By contrast, Flanner satirized the overly "illustrative" cue sheets for the music in a Fox feature film. In September 1920 Mae Tinée asked moviegoers who complained that they wanted "to enjoy our picture in peace [. . .] without being annoyed" by the music what they thought after Chicago musicians went on strike.[19] As a corollary, Harris wondered if "the most important function of musical programs is educational," introducing the mass public to "the great music of the world."

Finally, a miscellany of columns prove amazingly unique. While Daw concocted a comic story about Chaplin and Fairbanks playing hooky at a nearby circus or carnival in Los Angeles, Rae McRae (a colleague of Day's) spun another about their visit to a fake acting school in Des Moines. During her first year, Kitty Kelly often ended her column with a rare record of the Chicago censors' demands for cuts in films and outright bans; she also wrote an intelligent review of Hugo Münsterberg's new book, *The Photoplay: A Psychological Study* (1916). Harris probably exhibited the most remarkable range of interests of them all. She noted that, according to librarians, films actually were increasing people's desire to read novels, and she reported on the film preferences of high school boys and girls as gathered in a National Committee for Better Films survey. In one column in May 1923, she described a visit to an exposition at the Chicago Palace of Progress, which advanced an early version of film history, listing the technical and artistic stages of motion picture development; in another column two months earlier, she summarized a "globe-trotting" clubwoman's observations about the spread of American styles and customs through the worldwide circulation of American films. Harris also was exceptional in her close contact with the French film industry and its cinéphiles. While she reported in 1922 on the "second annual 'Salon du Cinéma'" in Paris and quoted Léon Moussinac on film as "an independent art which must discover its own laws," one year later she also sketched significant differences between the American and French cinemas, citing one example of the French strategy of producing lengthy historical serials, standardized in eight episodes of at least an hour each in length. The status that some newspapers accorded these women writing about the movies was especially evident in the ads that promoted the columns of Kitty Kelly, Dorothy Day, and Virginia Dale as "required reading" for movie fans.

Although not its explicit aim, this collection of diverse columns also offers not only a different sense of what was going on in the American movie industry during this period but also a unique window onto what particularly interested women moviegoers, at least from the perspective of women writing in mostly midwestern newspapers. I have organized this collection of newspaper writings—at the time they were little more than ephemera—into four chronological and more or less equal chapters. The first, 1914–16, covers the period prior to the United States' entry into the Great War, when an equal number of women and men took advantage of the initial opportunity to write film reviews and other articles. Most of the nine writers selected here appeared in midwestern newspapers. The second, 1917–18, follows four of those women, who were joined by three others, all in the Midwest, up through the end of the Great War, during which time many potential male writers likely served as soldiers. The third, 1919–21, is marked by a surge in the number of newspaper writers, perhaps "freed" from the strictures of the war. Although male writers began to dominate the field, at least based on the *Motion Picture News*' directory, this period includes the greatest number of women, four of whom carried over from before, along with six new writers, two of them located in New York City. The fourth, 1922–23, adds two new writers, again in the Midwest, to five others—specifically, Virginia Dale, Genevieve Harris, and Mae Tinée in Chicago—who continued from earlier as potent rivals to what *Film Daily Yearbook* suggests were more numerous male writers. A short introduction heads each of these four chapters, offering some historical context; even shorter introductions provide relevant information for each writer; and most of the selected columns include further information and relevant commentary in endnotes. Most of the film review columns included cast lists, which I have deleted because the reviews usually talk about the main actors. In the end, all of these texts are assembled like "ingredients that will produce intellectual pleasures," as Barbara Hodgdon writes, whether for nourishing further research and writing or for "passing it on" in the back-and-forth of heady classroom conversations.[20]

Because countless newspapers may only survive on microfilm in public libraries and state historical society libraries scattered widely across the country, some of which continue to be digitized and made available on the internet, it is very likely that other researchers will find many more newspaper women than are highlighted here. In the future, may the yet-to-be-discovered columns of those newspaperwomen whet the appetite of those studying cinema history and/or women's history in the early twentieth century and lead them to lay out a smorgasbord of whatever new intellectual pleasures they choose to share. I'm guessing that even Martin Scorsese would approve of such a research agenda when he says: "If you're given the grace to continue working, then you'd better figure out something that needs telling."[21]

Two notes. First, I have listed the circulation figures of these writers' newspapers in an appendix. Second, I have not corrected any spelling (including variants), punctuation, or spacing in the texts, except for obvious typographical errors. However, I have added [?] where a word or line in a microfilmed newspaper copy is illegible, and I have occasionally added bracketed clarifications to the text. Ellipsis dots enclosed in square brackets are mine.

Notes

1. "Making 'Movie' History" ad, *Chicago Record-Herald*, February 16, 1914, 12.

2. Paul S. Moore, "'It Pays to Plan 'em!': The Newspaper Movie Directory and the Paternal Logic of Mass Consumption," in *The Routledge Companion to New Cinema History*, ed. Daniel Bilteryest, Richard Maltby, and Philippe Meers (New York: Routledge, 2019), 365–77. See also Moore, *Now Playing: Early Moviegoing and the Regulation of Fun* (Albany: State University of New York Press, 2008); Moore, "The Social Biograph: Newspaper Archives of the Regional Mass Market for Movies," in *Explorations in New Cinema History: Approaches and Case Studies*, ed. Richard Maltby, Daniel Bilteryest, and Philippe Meers (Malden, MA: Wiley-Blackwell, 2011), 269–79; Moore, "Advance Newspaper Publicity for the Vitascope and the Mass Address of Cinema's Reading Public," in *Companion to Early Cinema*, ed. André Gaudreault, Nicolas Dulac, and Santiago Hidalgo (Malden, MA: Wiley-Blackwell, 2012), 381–97; and Moore, "Subscribing to Publicity: Syndicated Newspaper Features for Moviegoing in North America, 1911–1915," *Early Popular Visual Culture* 12, no. 2 (2014): 260–73.

3. Robert C. Allen, "Relocating American Cinema History: The 'Problem' of the Empirical," *Cultural Studies* 20, no. 1 (2006): 48–88; Jan Olsson, *Los Angeles before Hollywood: Journalism and American Film Culture, 1905–1915* (Stockholm: National Library of Sweden, 2008); Kathryn Fuller-Seeley, ed., *Hollywood in the Neighborhood: Historical Case Studies of Local Moviegoing* (Berkeley: University of California Press, 2008); Gregory Waller, "Locating Early Non-theatrical Audiences," in *Audiences: Defining and Researching Screen Entertainment Reception*, ed. Ian Christie (Amsterdam: Amsterdam University Press, 2011), 80–95; and Martin L. Johnson, *Main Street Movies: The History of Local Film in the United States* (Bloomington: Indiana University Press, 2018).

4. Anna Everett, *Returning the Gaze: A Genealogy of Black Film Criticism, 1909–1949* (Durham, NC: Duke University Press, 2001).

5. Indeed, chapter 2 is titled "Newspapers Make Picture-Goers." Richard Abel, *Menus for Movieland: Newspapers and the Emergence of American Film Culture, 1913–1916* (Oakland: University of California Press, 2015), 73–129. See also Abel, "Reading Newspapers and Writing American Silent Cinema History," in Bilteryest, Maltby, and Meers, *The Routledge Companion*, 68–82.

6. For earlier research results, see Richard Abel, "Newspaperwomen and the Movies in the USA, 1914–1925," 2016, in the Women Film Pioneers Project, Columbia University Libraries, https://wfpp.columbia.edu; and Abel, "'My Goodness Gracious, Girls': Women Writers on the Movies in US Newspapers, 1911–1920," in *Presences and Representations of Women in the Early Years of Cinema, 1895–1920*, ed. Angel Quintana and Jordi Pons (Girona: Fundacio Museu del Cinema, 2018), 45–60.

7. The contracts under which these women worked for a newspaper might be found in business records, if those survive in archives of one kind or another.

8. Mark Garrett Cooper, *Universal Women: Filmmaking and Institutional Change in Early Hollywood* (Urbana: University of Illinois Press, 2010); Shelley Stamp, *Lois Weber and Early Hollywood* (Oakland: University of California Press, 2015); and Jane Gaines, *Pink-Slipped: What Happened to Women in the Silent Film Industries* (Urbana: University of Illinois Press, 2018). The quote is from "Not All Pretty Women in Film Business Are Actresses," *Richmond (IN) Palladium and Sun-Telegram*, June 26, 1922, 4.

9. Louis Pelletier, "From Photoplays to Movies: A Distant Reading of Cinema's Eventual Legitimation from Below," *Film History* 30, no. 2 (Summer 2018): 30.

10. I recontextualize the quote from "Little History of Photography," in *The Work of Art in the Age of Its Technological Reproducibility and Other Writings on Media*, by Walter Benjamin, ed. Michael W. Jennings, Brigid Doherty, and Thomas Y. Levin (Cambridge, MA: Harvard University Press, 2008), 285.

11. Antonia Lant, with Ingrid Periz, eds., *Red Velvet Seat: Women's Writing on the First Fifty Years of Cinema* (London: Verso, 2006).

12. But see Jean Voltaire Smith, "Our Need for More Films," *Half-Century Magazine*, April 1922, the only woman very occasionally writing about the movies that Anna Everett found in the Black press (*Returning the Gaze*, 154–57). Relatedly, Colin Gunckel cites no Spanish-language newspapers in Los Angeles during this period (*Mexico on Main Street: Transnational Film Culture in Los Angeles before World War II* [New Brunswick, NJ: Rutgers University Press, 2015]). Men and even women may have written about the movies in foreign-language newspapers, but I found none named in Detroit's Polish and Italian newspapers during research for *Motor City Movie Culture, 1916–1925* (Bloomington: Indiana University Press, 2020). In the future, researchers could consult one of these sources for potentially relevant newspapers: *African-American Newspapers and Periodicals* (Cambridge, MA: Harvard University Press, 1999); *Encyclopedia Directory of Ethnic Newspapers and Periodicals* (Littleton, CO: Libraries Unlimited, 1976); or *Hispanic Periodicals in the United States* (Houston: Arte Público Press, 2000).

13. "Motion Picture News First Annual Newspaper and Theater Directory," *Motion Picture News*, December 27, 1919, 156–68. Not unexpectedly, this survey excluded Black newspapers.

14. See, for instance, Ruth Cade writing a social column in the *Decatur (IL) Herald* and May Cameron covering court cases and sports in the *Evansville (IN) Press*.

15. I thank Kaveh Askari for sharing a copy of the 1926 Film Arts Guild Advisory Council. See also the list of newspaper film reviewers in "The Ten Best Pictures of 1924," *Film Daily Yearbook* (1925): 624–28. For more on that column, see the introduction to the last chapter of this book.

16. See also Constance Talmadge's 1922 series of weekly columns surveying seventeen of the industry's positions open to women, reprinted and analyzed in Richard Abel, "Opportunities for Women in the Movies," *Film History* 31, no. 2 (2019): 179–96.

17. Anita Stewart's "ten commandments" is an exception to my exclusion of ghostwritten columns from female stars, such as Daily Talks by Mary Pickford, written by Frances Marion and widely distributed through the McClure Newspaper Syndicate from early November 1915 to early October 1916. See the analysis of this column in Abel, *Menus for Movieland*, 160–65.

18. "Worth-While Feature Films Recommended by 'Wid,'" *New York Evening Mail*, July 23, 1915, 5; "Pavlova Dimmed in Film [*The Dumb Girl of Portici*]," in *The New York Times Film Reviews, 1913–1931* (New York: New York Times & Arno Press, 1971), 14; and Dale Fetherling and Doug Fetherling, eds., *Carl Sandberg at the Movies: A Poet in the Silent Era, 1920–1927* (Metuchen, NJ: Scarecrow Press, 1985). In the 1980s the latter book's editors may not have thought Weber important enough to include in their selection of columns.

19. However, she does not mention that "movie theatres were gutted with stench bombs" during the strike; nor do she and her colleagues refer to other criminal activity. See Gary B. Rhodes, *The Perils of Moviegoing in America, 1896–1950* (New York: Continuum, 2012), 131–33.

20. Barbara Hodgdon, "The Last Picture Show or Going to the Barricades," in *Teaching Shakespeare: Passing It On*, ed. Skip Shand (Hoboken, NJ: Blackwell, 2009), 116.

21. David Itzkoff, "Scorsese Knows How It Ends," *New York Times*, January 5, 2020, Sunday ed., special section, 26.

Women Writers Lead the Way, 1914–1916

Before 1914 at least two women were among an equal number of men who signed newspaper columns devoted to the movies.[1] For a brief time, between December 1911 and January 1912, Ona Otto wrote a page bannered "In the Land of the Photoplays and Players" in the *San Francisco Bulletin*.[2] But she was a kind of flaneuse, contributing columns on everything from window shopping and gardens to automobiles and real estate for several months thereafter. The more important figure was Gertrude Price, who, from October 1912 to April 1914, wrote a frequent column, first called "The Movies," for the Scripps-McRae newspaper chain, syndicated through the United Press.[3] Promoted as a "moving picture expert," she specialized in "personality sketches," primarily of movie stars and especially young, single, independent women, some of them playing leading roles in westerns. Among those sketches, however, were interviews with filmmakers Alice Guy Blaché and Lois Weber, as well as scriptwriter Nell Shipman (who later would produce and direct her own films); and one of Price's last columns encouraged readers to see "the movies as [a] great new field for women folk."[4] During the year and a half that her syndicated column appeared, Price likely was the signed newspaper writer most read by movie fans.

The period from 1914 through 1916 was marked by an explosion of pages and columns devoted to the movies across the country. Newspapers, from metropolitan areas to small towns, either assigned or hired at least a dozen male reporters to cover what had now become a major mass entertainment. Most of them served as editors or columnists of industry stories, star gossip, or fictional sketches: Gardner Mack of the *Washington Times*, Gene Morgan of the *Chicago Herald*, Britt Craig of the *Atlanta Constitution*, R. E. Pritchard of the *New Orleans Item*, George W. Stark of the *Detroit News-Tribune*, and N. D. Tevis of the *La Crosse (WI) Tribune*. Having relatively short tenures were James Warren Currie of the *Chicago Examiner* and Arthur C. Stolte of the *Waterloo (IA) Reporter*. Archie Bell and John DeKoven, one after the other, edited a special weekly supplement, the "Motion Picture Leader," in Cleveland. In the Black press, Lester A. Walton had been contributing a movie column to the weekly *New York Age* since 1909, and Juli Jones urged other African Americans to "join the ranks of the moving picture business" in a rare 1915 article in the *Chicago Defender*.[5] Four men, however, were known for their film reviews, including W. K. Hollander of the *Chicago News*, Richard F. Lussier of the *Birmingham Age-Herald*, and Philip H. Welch of the *Minneapolis Tribune*. The most important of all, however, was "Wid" Gunning of the *New York Evening Mail*, who left the newspaper in August 1915, eventually to edit *Wid's Daily*, which soon turned into *Film Daily*.[6]

Strikingly, as if propelled by Price's column on career opportunities for women, newspapers assigned or hired just as many female reporters and columnists to cover the movies. For a few exhausting months, Ruth Vinson wrote short reviews of as many pictures as she could "personally see" for the *Cleveland Plain Dealer*. Mary B. Leffler, the "circulation bragger" of the *Fort Worth Star-Telegram*'s "Sunday Sandwich," edited a weekly Sunday page bannered "In the Photoplay World," along with her daily "Flashes of Filmdom" column. Daisy Dean followed Price's model in concocting a syndicated column of personality sketches, which the Central Press Association distributed in the Midwest. The most influential of these undoubtedly was Mae Tinee, who in early March 1914 began editing a weekly Sunday page titled "Right Off the Reel" in the *Chicago Tribune*. Much imitated, this page had a centered feature, "In the Frame of Public Favor," with an exceptionally large publicity halftone (in a gilded frame) and profile of a current movie star supposedly chosen each week by readers. During this period, Mae Tinée served essentially as an editor and gossip columnist (and a recognized asset to the paper).[7] She began writing a film review column for the *Tribune* in late 1916.[8]

Nine other women writers were important enough that selections of their work are reprinted in the pages that follow. Strikingly, only three of those appeared in newspapers outside the Midwest. One was Grace Kingsley, best known perhaps as a drama critic and interviewer for the *Los Angeles Times*. Another was the Film Girl, who penned a daily film review column for the *Syracuse Herald*. A third was Los Angeles publisher Charlotta Bass, who wrote and/or edited unsigned columns in the *California Eagle*, the leading

Black newspaper on the West Coast. No fewer than four women besides Mae Tinée served as editors and columnists in three different Chicago newspapers, arguably making the city the initial center of newspaper film reviewing. Beginning in July 1914, Kitty Kelly, a major recent discovery, wrote trenchant daily film reviews and compiled rare censorship records for the *Chicago Tribune*, which promoted her in a large advertisement in April 1916. By early 1915 Louella O. Parsons was competing with Kelly with daily reviews, along with interviews, for the *Chicago Record-Herald*. At the same time, Mildred Joclyn began editing a movie page and writing columns for the *Chicago Post*; in late 1915 Oma Moody Lawrence replaced her as both editor and columnist. The last of these women was Dorothy Day, who, also in late 1915, was editing movie pages and writing review and gossip columns for the *Des Moines Tribune*.[9] One other not included here, however, was Anita Maris Boggs, a social reformer who in 1914 promoted films as an innovative form of visual education in *Pedagogical Seminary*, a specialist scientific journal.[10]

The short introductions that precede the selections of each writer's columns include more information.

Grace Kingsley (1873–1962)

Kingsley initially served as a secretary to superintendents in the Los Angeles school system, writing drama reviews and features on the side for the *Los Angeles Herald*. Hired by the *Los Angeles Times* in 1910, she became its motion picture editor in 1914. For the most part she contributed feature stories on the industry and conducted interviews with personnel at all levels. Her feature on Universal City in the summer of 1914 probably is the earliest description of the new studio facilities in a newspaper prior to its opening to tourists in the spring of the following year. Her column on the Los Angeles filmmaking scene in early 1915 is a rare survey of other major companies such as Famous Players–Lasky, Selig Polyscope Company, Bosworth Film, and Thomas H. Ince Film, as well as independents like D. W. Griffith of Reliance-Majestic Studios. Kingsley also wrote film reviews, such as the exemplary one on Lois Weber's *Shoes*, in which she showed some ignorance of the conditions ensnaring the film's shop girl heroine.[11]

"Where the Movies Are Hatched," *Los Angeles Times*, August 23, 1914, 3.1, 3.

"Biggest Thrill Factory in the World."
"Universal's New Picture Ranch"
"Zoo Where Animal Actors Stay"

A stock company of 2000 actors, the largest stock company in the world with a stage of 457 acres!

Universal City, the oddest city in the world, an Alice-in-Wonderland city, "where all the creatures do behave so queerly!"[12]

A vast stage is the new Universal City, nestling in the foothills edging San Fernando Valley, out there beyond Cahuenga Pass. The site is much larger than the old ranch studio at Oak Crest, and its ruler, political boss, Magician Merlin and General Pooh-Bah is Isadore Bernstein, manager of the Pacific Ocean studios of the Universal Film Company.[13] Mr. Bernstein avers the city will be "finished by December 1."

The army of 2000 employees and actors in the fifteen companies which work out there under the Universal management contains every sort of performer from the "artists," real hand-painted ladies and gentlemen, to the cook and fire department. Anyone who has a job at Universal City must be willing to drop into the phantom photos at a moment's notice. Wild mountain peaks, rushing streams, dark canyons, the whole city and the animal zoo—even the corner drug store—make up scenery and "props."

For this seemingly Rackety-Packety Town is just one big canned laboratory for the movies. Everything in it, from actors to architecture, is capable of being transformed in the twinkling of an eye into a performer or a background and setting for the silent drama. Even the big bridge to be flung across the stream will be only a foundation bridge, which can be hastily transformed into a Roman bridge or an S.P. crossing, as occasion demands.

CITY OF PARADOXES   A city of paradoxes is Universal City. Though not yet finished, it has the traditions of 1000 years. Its architectural façade of big buildings, facing on Lankershim boulevard, is an impressive and correct blending of mission and classic styles, yet scattered along its lovely boulevard are the ruins of an ancient city, and little bits of Spain, and, cheek-by-jowl with the cowboys' tents is a Greek temple, and there is the queer street composed entirely of front exteriors!

It has its own efficient lighting system, telephones, telegraph, post office; yet weird messages are carried long distances by naked runners and hurrying horsemen.

It is the most law-abiding city in the world. It has its own efficient police force, and noble deeds are as common as fly specks in July; yet beauteous maidens are imprisoned in tall towers and dark deeds are committed every day. It has a fire department, yet a whole tenement district in New York burns in "The Trye of Hearts," and nobody puts it out.

It will be an incorporated city as soon as all the buildings are complete, and its Mayor will probably be a cowboy or an expert (stage) safecracker, and its Chief of Police is Laura Oakley, sworn in last week.[14] Its society is the most democratic in the world. As we rode along the boulevard toward the gulley where the cowboys and girls were riding we viewed a hairy hermit drinking soda-pop under a tree in company with a lot of cow-punchers; a Roman senator was getting his shoes shined in front of the restaurant, and a smutty-faced slavey was borrowing a cigarette from a dolled-up duchess in an automobile!

BEAUTIFUL SETTING   No more beautiful spot was ever dreamed of than this Universal City ranch, with its wooded foothills, green canyons, its tiny springs under the chaparral, the willow-fringed river and the wonderful terrace of foothills and mountains viewed across the valley.

There under the giant eucalyptus trees, facing the Lankershim boulevard, beyond the ivy-covered arched entrance the big white buildings are to be placed. Already the hollow-tile framework of two of the buildings is erected, ready for the metal-lath and cement finish, and fronting them Japanese gardens, and a tiny artificial lake will soften the somewhat severe lines of the façade.

The administration building occupies the center. This contains Mr. Bernstein's office, offices of the directors, reception hall, telegraph and telephone booths, bank, business offices, library rooms for scenario writers and reader; while up above a lookout tower gives the manager a private retreat and also a place from which he may view nearly every spot on the ranch.

Fifty feet to the left is the huge factory, a laboratory for the building of every movie accessory imaginable, also containing three projecting rooms for showing the pictures to the assembled directors, developing-rooms, camera-rooms, etc.

WHERE THEY EAT   On the right of the administration building the restaurant will be erected, the foundation being already in. This will contain an open-air dining-room on a luxurious veranda, an inside dining-room, and a great cafeteria, a candy booth and immense soda fountain; also there will be a roof tea garden. Lawns and a picturesque Roman bath, with a pool and fountain will fill a big space back of these buildings. Across the City boulevard, which is to be of macadamized granite, a stadium will be built on a picturesque hillside. There is also to be a Roman forum.

The hospital will be built on the hillside. This will be a marvelous building, inasmuch as its efficiency is raised to the nth power by its adaptability to use in the moving picture plays. In the mission style of architecture, with big restful verandas, it will be a thing of beauty, and its excellent hospital equipment can be used in mimic scenes. There are two wards, one for the men, the other for the women, containing each four beds. There is a big operating-room, fully equipped. A doctor and nurse will be at all times in attendance. More than once, already, the Greek building up on the side of the hill has been used to restore a wearily fainting actress, a cowgirl overcome by the heat, a cowboy hurt in riding or in a scene with the wild animals, a too-fearless keeper, hurt in caring for bears or tigers, and recently it witnessed the tragic end of the man who was killed by the big lion Posey, who keeps lonely vigil in the big arena since the tragedy. For moving picture danger isn't the imitation danger of the regular stage by any means.

Across Lankershim boulevard, Mr. Bernstein plans to erect a big tourist hotel, which will also accommodate such of the moving picture actors as wish to live there.

Down the boulevard, there are four bungalows, equipped with billiard tables, shower baths and beds, in which are housed many cavalrymen.

THE BIG STAGE   On a big level stretch facing the river, the stage is to be built. This will be 200 x 400 feet, and will be fitted up with dressing-rooms, restrooms, prop rooms, etc. Six scene painters are at present employed and will probably be kept permanent on the staff.

Opposite the bungalows, of which several more will be built, is the mammoth zoo, containing twenty camels, two elephants, several lions, one with four cubs, seals, leopards, tigers, snakes, bears, wolves and monkeys. Here dwells Joe, the big chimpanzee. Joe, by the way, is a regular person, sleeps in a regular brass bedstead, and was skillfully plying a toothpick after breakfast, when we arrived.

The blacksmith and harness shop, already finished, with its quaint little dormer windows, resembles the pictures one sees of old English country homes, and doubtless will figure in many a romance.

Back of the zoo is the big arena, steel wired and barred, where some of the ancient Roman thrillers are staged, and from this lead several runways, connecting with a maze of tiny cages into which, in times of danger, the actor or camera man can flee for safety.

There is to be an arsenal building, 40 x 50 feet, in which guns, cannon, knives and all sorts of formidable hardware will be kept. And there will be tailor shops, carpenter shops, general stores and a post office.

A big corral with a hundred and fifty shelters and stalls house as many horses; and a garage will take care of the fifty machines which the company owns.

William Horsely the construction superintendent, pointed out and explained to us the sites for the reservoirs, and the six wells already dug; also explained the up-to-date sewer system, with its septic tanks, a system they state is large enough to care for a much larger population than that of the ranch.

And the pay roll? A fortune a week, no less than $26,000.

"Los Angeles the Globe's Moving Picture Center," *Los Angeles Times*, January 1, 1915, 146.

MILLIONS IN IT   Los Angeles, the moving picture stage of the world!

Imagine a theater whose stage contains thousands of acres, whose actors number ten thousand, and whose production of plays averages half a million a year. That's Los Angeles and environs, the biggest theater in the world.

Southern California is naturally suited to motion picture production, as its vast stretches of uncultivated foothill country, its big deserts and picturesque shore lines lend themselves ideally to the dramatic setting of great spectacular plays.

The climate, too, is especially propitious for the taking of pictures in nearly every season. In some cases, as in that of the Lasky Company, glass studios have been built in order that pictures may be taken at any time of year.

The growth of the industry has been almost incredible. Only three years ago there were but four or five companies, putting on inferior plays with nameless actors. Now there are about fifty studios in and about Los Angeles, housing anywhere from two companies to fifteen, as in the case of the Universal. In the days of the nameless pioneers all actors received $5 a day, no more, no less, no matter what the quality or scope of their work. Today the biggest stars in theaterdom are entering the field, the Los Angeles studios having secured many of them, with salaries that range dizzily into the thousands per week.

Vast strides have been made also in the sort of productions given. Whereas a few years ago the cheapest and wildest melodramas, badly acted and staged carelessly with faked scenery, was the rule, now great faithfulness to detail is the practice in the staging of pictures. When filming "The Rose of Rancho" the Lasky Company paid $18,000 for water-color sketches of costumes by an artist who made several weeks' careful research in order that the actors might be correctly dressed.

But it is not alone in taste and realism that the making of pictures has made great strides. All the domain of the dramatic has been invaded for artistic subject. Classic drama is staged elaborately, and even the realm of the psychological has been invaded, as in the case of David Griffith's adaptation of an Edgar Allan Poe poem in "The Avenging Conscience."

While the business departments have in most instances been located in the East, it is rumored that some of the largest companies with big producing plants in Los Angeles will also make their business headquarters here. The Selig company and the Universal are among those mentioned as intending to bring their entire business to this country.[15]

The great ranches where big pictures are produced are of unique interest. In a morning's drive across one of these you are likely to chance upon big armies of cowboys riding madly to the exigencies of a frontier tale, or you meet a band of fierce Indians, or glimpse a crowd of actors in quaint costume and make-up for a tale of bygone Spanish days, as in [the] case of Lasky's "Rose of the Rancho." Or you will come to life in a foreign country: for you may happen on an oriental village, complete in every detail, from the bazaars with their queer picturesque junk to the camels on the street, as was the case in the Cairo streets erected by the Selig company for the production of "The Carpet of Bagdad." Or it may be ancient Greece you encounter in the temple-crowned hills shown in "Damon and Pythias," produced by the Universal. Or you may find yourself on the battlefield of the Civil War, with thousands of soldiers fighting very realistically around you, as in the case of David Griffith's recent masterpiece, "The Clansman."[16]

The Lasky ranch, recently purchased, lies on the lovely slope of the San Fernando Valley foothills, and contains 500 acres of the most beautiful country in California. But the ranch really consists of 1500 acres, for the company has the right to range at will over a thousand additional acres of adjoining government land. Two well-known dramatists have charge of the directing on the big plays which are being produced, namely Messrs. Cecil and William De Mille. Only plays of the highest class are being done here, including the late Belasco successes, and some of the best known actors of the day, including David Warfield, Mrs. Leslie Carter, Edith Taliaferro, Maude Adams, Frances Starr, Dustin Farnum, Marguerite Clark and others are being negotiated with or have been secured for the production of their successes.[17]

With the recent entrance of Mr. Oliver Morosco into the moving picture world, it is said there is now no great theatrical success which cannot be secured for moving pictures.[18]

Universal City, out in the San Fernando Valley, about two miles beyond Los Angeles, owns 500 acres and is erecting great buildings of brick and cement, comprising factories, offices, a huge stage, hotels, restaurants, libraries and homes for the cowboys, Indians and ranch employees. Here the fifteen companies belonging to the Universal will do all their work. The place is a regularly incorporated city with its own Mayor, Chief of Police, police officers and other functionaries, most of whom are actors. There is a huge zoo containing several hundred wild animals and a specially patented cage with big runways and shut offs for the protection of actors and cameramen in the taking of wild-animal pictures.

The Selig company is the owner also of a unique plant consisting of a great park of forty acres almost in the heart of the city. Here handsome buildings of reinforced concrete in the rambling mission style house a great zoo containing some thousand wild animals, including elephants, camels, bears, lions, tigers, panthers, monkeys, snakes and others, many of rare breeds. Here a vast stage is erected and there are big stretches of lawn on any one of which an oriental or a classic city may be built at will. A big part of this park is to be opened to the public next year, and W. N. Selig is employing a sculptor to decorate the entrance and mold fountains and statuary. Besides this big park, the Selig company owns a large and artistically built plant in Edendale, Los Angeles, containing a stage and developing and printing rooms.

David Griffith's company, the Reliance, Mutual and Majestic, has some great improvements in contemplation so far as the physical aspects of the work are concerned.[19] Mr. Griffith is contemplating the building of a factory to do the entire positive developing and printing in the city.

One cannot speak of the development of moving picture production without speaking of David Griffith, whose genius has been universal in its results, and whose significance is far beyond the physical in motion pictures.[20] He was the first to conceive the idea of the five or six-reel production of great plays, featuring well-known artists of the stage. He was also one of the first to introduce realism instead of faked scenes. He it was who adapted the different modes of photography and applied them to moving pictures, such as the "close up," the fade-out, the cut-back, the silhouette and other effective picture methods.[21] And in his "Avenging Conscience" Mr. Griffith struck a new note and gave a new meaning to moving pictures, for it is a story of subtle psychological import and achieves what a few years ago would have been thought impossible, the laying bare of the workings of the soul and mind of a man.

The Bosworth Company, Inc. is the owner of one of the finest motion picture producing plants in the West.[22] The buildings and stage are entirely of reinforced concrete and the dark-rooms, stage, etc., are fitted with unusual mechanical appurtenances which make greatly for efficiency. The company is planning great things connected with the production of masterpieces in motion pictures, including all the Morosco successes, and involving the services of some of the greatest American stars.

The Thomas H. Ince Film Company has the largest moving-picture ranch studio in the world.[23] It is located at Santa Monica, at Port Los Angeles, and consists of eighteen thousand acres, mostly foothill country and beach. Its beautiful curving beach line is two miles long. Within the limits are wonderful canyons and streams, wooded hillsides, picturesque trails, and sheer cliffs. The plant consists of a huge stage, a carpenter shop, large property room, developing and printing rooms and houses for the cowboys and employees, while a village of tents houses the Indians, who live in their native state and according to their ancient customs. There is also a mission church faithfully reproduced and a Dutch village for picture purposes.

A hotel is to be built shortly for such actors as desire to live at the studio instead of going back and forth to the city.

The company is soon to incorporate as a town, the government already having given a permit for the establishment of a post office. There are 400 people at the studio, including actors, directors, Indians and other employees. The Masterpiece company, with Max Figman and Lolita Robertson as stars, and Mr. Figman as director, is considering the purchase of a fifty-acre ranch just outside Los Angeles, on which to stage the Williamson stories, which have lately been secured by the company.[24] The company already has a splendid plant and a large stage in the heart of the city.

The Favorite Players, with Carlyle Blackwell and Ruth Hartman as stars, are putting on the Richard Harding Davis plays, and have a fine plant in Edendale.[25]

The Balboa Company has a large picturesque ranch studio by the sea where are staged some of the loveliest of the sea film stories.[26]

From a business standpoint, Mr. Selig tells me that the motion picture industry is the fourth greatest industry in the United States. About 80 per cent of the motion pictures made in the country are made in and about Los Angeles.

Two million dollars are invested in Southern California in film-producing plants, and the annual pay roll is about $7,000,000. This includes the salaries of employees as well as directors and actors, and the running cost of plants. It is figured that the returns from sale of films made in and about Los Angeles amounts annually to about $25,000,000.

The biggest returns from any individual pictures made here are said to be those from "The Escape," made by Mr. Griffith, and "The Spoilers," made by the Selig company, the returns on each to date being about $350,000.

Thousands of people are employed in the crowds used in the production of the pictures, the largest number ever working in any picture produced in Southern California being those in Mr. Griffith's production of "The Clansman," who totaled up, including soldiers, negroes and Ku-Klux men, to the huge figure of 14,000.

"Story's Well Told: Lois Weber Photoplay Has Moving Appeal," *Los Angeles Times*, July 19, 1916, 13.

"Shoes," showing at the Alhambra, is the greatest photoplay which Lois Weber has ever produced. All praise to its perfection of acting, by Mary MacLaren and the others.[27] All praise to the fact that every atom of its fine-drawn drama grows out of the hearts, the lives, the motives of real human beings. And more praise yet that a stark story of poverty, stripped of every cheap trick of appeal, is yet so sincere, so gripping, that it holds you as no such simple screen tale perhaps ever has gripped before.[28]

Lois Weber is prone to juggle with the probabilities, to erect plausibilities on platitudes, in order to catch a sentimental and sensation loving public. But the strong and simple sincerity of "Shoes" proves she can look life fairly in the face when she chooses.

That there is the possibility of a flaw in the probabilities underlying the story of "Shoes" is the chief criticism. Would a pure young girl, apparently possessed of cool judgment, raised by a loving and unselfish mother, and possessing a brood of younger sisters whom she loved, deliberately go out one night, and give herself to a man she loathed in order to get a new pair of shoes, or for any other reason, except, possibly to procure food for a starving stomach? Would any such opportunity be a "temptation" to such a girl, weighing against the jewel of her purity?

Kitty Kelly (1888?–1965)

Kitty Kelly was the nom de plume of young Audrey Alspaugh, who graduated from the University of Iowa with an English degree in 1909 and two years later was hired as a book reviewer at the *Chicago Tribune*.[29] She very likely wrote the "Today's Best Photo Play Stories" column in the *Tribune*, beginning in February 1914, but the column only became "Photoplay Stories and News," signed by "Kitty Kelly," in early July. Usually located on the

Society or Women's page, Kelly's daily column of film reviews was innovative and influential, but her name disappeared from the *Tribune* in October 1916—only to reappear the following year in the *Chicago Examiner*.[30] In late October 1915 Alspaugh married the *Tribune*'s features page editor, Al Chase, and they announced their wedding in a comic film script dubbed a "reel romance."[31] It's possible that she and Mae Tinee could have had a disagreement of some kind, because the latter quickly took over the column within a week of Kelly's departure.

Kelly exhibited an exuberant style, spinning out tongue-in-cheek metaphors, neologisms, and syntactic tangles, and her evident love of language sometimes verged on "showboating." Yet her own sense of judgment and taste was always so perceptive that her criticism served to "train" fans in what to look for in watching movies.

These selected Kelly columns reveal several developments as she grapples with how to write about motion pictures.[32] The first column, from March 1915, evidences her unique interest in nonfiction features, specifically Edward Salisbury's *Wild Animal Life in America*, so unlike the popular *Rainey's African Pictures* (1912). The second and third columns, from May, exhibit the emerging critical principles that Kelly used to evaluate a fiction feature. Earlier, in her review of Lasky's *The Girl of the Golden West* (not selected here), she sums up those principles as "excitement and suspense of a logical sort, [...] heroism and humor and love, [...] stars, three in number, each one of them independently good, and [...] attractive atmosphere creating setting."[33] The second column on *Stolen Goods*, accordingly, singles out not only the quality of acting and characterization in the leading roles but also a film's narrative construction, atmosphere, and editing, which are attributed to the scenario writer and director. Intriguingly, like many other columns, it also closes with a list of what the Chicago censors ordered to be cut from eight films soon due for release. These lists first appeared in April, and Kelly continued to include them well into October 1915. They constitute a rare treasure trove of censorship data and presumably can be accepted as accurate; otherwise, the censors would have forced Kelly to discontinue them—and may have after that October.[34]

In late May Kelly argued against the Chicago censors' initial decision not to allow screenings of Griffith's *The Birth of a Nation*; although she praised the film, based on a viewing in Los Angeles, she also was ambivalent in her attitude toward the controversy over its evident racism.[35] Most of Kelly's columns, however, continued to offer her take on specific feature films and stars. In her review of *The Clue* (not selected here), she neatly caught the brooding and threatening sexual potency of Sessue Hayakawa's face in close-ups and in similar language to that Louis Delluc later used to describe his

Figure 1. Kitty Kelly advertisement, *Chicago Sunday Tribune*, April 30, 1916.

fascination with Hayakawa's face.[36] In reviewing *Carmen* in October, she was enthralled by Geraldine Farrar's performance and the "swift deftness" of Cecil B. DeMille's direction; but she also situated the film within the full program of prologue, scenic, newsreel, comedy, and solos staged by the Strand Theater. In July 1916 she defended Lois Weber's *Where Are My Children?*, a "problem play" about contraception and abortion, implicitly about class and gender relations, and within the unstated assumptions of the eugenics movement.

The most intriguing column is the unexpected intelligent review of Hugo Münsterberg's recently published book, *The Photoplay*. Kelly highlights his defense of motion pictures as a new medium of art that not only can achieve a harmonious form in and of itself but also creates an immersive psychological parallel to human consciousness. The mission of this new art, consequently, is the "aesthetic cultivation" of the new mass audience for motion pictures.

The *Tribune* thought so highly of Kelly that it took the unusual opportunity in late April 1916 to promote her columns with a rare half-page advertisement.[37]

"Flickerings from Filmland," *Chicago Tribune*, March 2, 1915, 10.

"WILD LIFE"   Many wonder pictures have come and gone, which with due measure of marveling accorded them have I said "Most wonderful!" But here are some that challenge that exclamation right out of my reluctant typewriter.

These close range camera glimpses of the wild life of our west coast, caught by Edward A. Salisbury and his company of investigators from various angles of opinion, stand out as most satisfyingly unique.[38]

They were taken primarily for scientific illumination, and their entertaining publicity is a mere by-product of their purpose. So it is they partake of scientific exactitude, but possess, nevertheless, enough vim and vitality to be of absorbing observational interest.

For three years Mr. Salisbury and his assistants waited around in mosquito infested swamps and trailed through mud and over rough country, enduring cold and wet and heat and dust, and running nameless risks of death from animals enraged, for the sake of securing these next to nature views. And the celluloid gives conclusive evidence that their efforts were not wasted. It isn't given to many folk to have such concrete testimony of achievement.

Seven reels is a long stretch, but so diversified are the subjects offered that they move by without wearying the observer. To my way of thinking the opening fish episode is a bit too biologic for general educational, let alone entertaining, consumption. It is clearly earmarked "scientific." Omission of some of it would not especially break the continuity of the film and would shorten it a trifle.

Many of the fishing scenes, including, incidentally, lovely bits of western falls and rivers, are of the sort to make a fisherman's heart go extra fast and to make nonfishers wish they might follow the trout line.

The many bird pictures are unusually effective, due to the close range the camera man was enabled to get by means of his blind hidden machine, with its cover incased turning mechanism ground down almost smooth, and so nearly soundless, and his hours of patient waiting. There is a tremendously effective pictorial preachment on the cruel waste of wild geese by some so-called hunters who kill for the mere exercise of it.[39]

In the animal pictures are thrills for the adventure seekers and photographic amazements for the captious. Subjects leaping wildly about from limb to limb of lofty trees are not ideal for cinematographic purposes, and occasionally the sequence is smashed when his bearship or cougarness elects to leap into the tree on which the camera is stationed.

But even so, there is a deal of fascinating film that makes one feel bravery is found not only on the battlefield. Some most ingratiating hunting scenes are shown also, featuring clever pointers.

The Studebaker screen brings out most happily the detail and depth of these pictures, demonstrating that they are of excellent photographic value.

"Flickerings from Filmland," *Chicago Tribune*, May 3, 1915, 18.

LASKY, "THE WOMAN"
George C. Melford, director[40]

That vivid play of graft grilling ruthlessly into private life, evolved for the stage once upon a time by William C. DeMille, pictures into a satisfyingly tense and sympathy arousing photoplay.[41]

It seems to me rather a directorial triumph, for the situations all have point, and they are crisp—cut off just before one begins to feel there is a touch too much. The adaptation of the play for the pictures gives opportunity for development of both character and atmosphere, and the observer follows the moods and emotions of the players as appreciatively as though they were appealing with the spoken word.

Mabel Van Buren, as The Woman and Lois Meredith as Wanda Kelly, the little telephone girl heroine, do some really convincing work—and they do it quietly with no ranting or wild gyrating in the effort to put the move in movies.[42]

Theodore Roberts emphasizes anew his ability as a significant character player in his portrayal of Jim Blake, the master wire puller.[43]

The handling of the scene in the legislative chamber, where Blake keeps his henchmen on the talk to gain time for chasing down the woman's name, is done with remarkable cleverness—attested to by the fact that every time the screen flashed it the audience rippled into amused laughter. The celluloid has possibilities as an adequate conductor of irony, and every situation of this sort strengthens general recognition of that fact.

The whole picture moves with well knit logicalness, outlining the story with perfect clarity, except in one instance. Perhaps the fault is mine and I missed the sequence, but I didn't quite get the pressure applied to Standish to make him call the woman on the telephone, thus establishing the link in the chain of pursuit and involving Wanda in her difficulties.

It is scarcely safe to make a criticism of that sort on one seeing of a picture, for the attention may have been distracted just at the critical moment, yet pictures are prone to slip up on some bits of subtlety, and they should always be as clear as crystal to the observer's understanding in order to be truly creditable.

This is, however, a good picture, well acted, well directed and adapted and happy consciousness all of the time, well set. With its pleasant surroundings and supplements at Orchestra Hall, it ought to please a large number of people through the coming week.

BREAKING IT GENTLY The following cutouts were ordered in films inspected by the municipal censor board at the city hall yesterday:

WITH SERB AND AUSTRIAN [Austro-Serbian Film Company]. Cast of characters and three part foreword; subtitle referring to giving commission to Prince Rudolph by Franz Joseph; [twenty-four subtitles deleted]; close view of stealing papers from vault.[44]

THE HIGH ROAD (Metro). Father throwing girl to ground brutally; paying money to thug to cause disorder in strike; Subtitles: 'We will start a fake riot to discredit the girls,' 'I mean she was Alan Wilson's mistress for three years'; two scenes of gang throwing missiles at police officers; shooting of policeman; shorten two riot scenes.

THEIR SOCIAL SPLASH (Kalem).[45] Man striking woman in stomach while she lies on couch.

THE ABSENTEE (Majestic). Flash two riot scenes; letter: I cannot stand the grind of poverty any longer—'I have chosen ease even with dishonor' appearing three times; three scenes of militia shooting strikers; foreman shooting girl.

THE VICTIM (Majestic). Two scenes of convict scaling prison wall; close view of plan showing method of tunneling under bank.

PAGES FROM LIFE (Gloria). Flash long gambling scene.

THE FAITH OF HER FATHERS (Gold Seal). Mob assaulting man; flash gambling scene; scene showing Cossack striking woman with butt of gun.

RENE HAGGARD JOURNEYS ON (Rex). Subtitles: And he broke his promise to marry; Ellmore to keep his silence demands his price.

THE TWO NATURES WITHIN HIM (Selig). Entrance of burglar; close view of loot.

"Flickerings from Filmland," *Chicago Tribune*, May 25, 1915, 18.

LASKY, "STOLEN GOODS" There is so much good in the picture feature at the Strand this week that it quite overshadows any efforts adequately to express it. In analysis it divides into some much elements: Blanche Sweet, alluring, heart warming, in spite of the gracelessness of much of her character heroine; Margaret Turnbull, interest impelling author; George Melford, shrewd director, and the artist behind the camera and in the dark room.[46]

"Stolen Goods" is a masterly story, written into pictures in masterly fashion. The full genius of both forms of expression can hardly be grasped at a single viewing. There is so much point to it, much careful manipulation of the suspense threads, such skillful selection of the high lights of interest, such compactness and yet such completeness, that one must put it down as a new member of that limited company of picture classics.

Miss Turnbull writes a well nigh perfect picture play and Mr. Melford picked out into settings its story thread so effectively that one forgets the matter is a picture. In it the observer comes as near to sharing the vital experience of any third person as he can come in life.

The story must not be too much revealed, for its procedure is so well knit and so well extended that to explain it would be to defeat in part its charm. But it deals with fate very humanly, manipulated according to human needs, and one does not know until the final hundred feet—devoted to a very beautiful bit of a love scene—just where the balance is going to rest. In the course of the story's telling the observer is taken into war rent Belgium, with some splendid scenes of war's business in the way of refugee making, property destroying, and body maiming. This is among the first of the inevitable flock of modern war pictures to come, and we may well be grateful that it sets so high a standard as a precedent.

And then, besides all of this, there is Blanche Sweet. In the course of the glamours of the other screen stars one may sometimes forget this young woman, but when she appears it is with a scintillation to put the great majority in the shadow.

In this picture her work is supreme in its personal appeal. She is herself, apparently, without a bit of effort or affectation, and she makes one's heart come up in one's throat from very sympathy. She is, moreover, one of those beings that transcend clothes; no matter what she wears, her personality shines out attractively.

Incidentally, some of the close up profiles are the most charming picture bits I have seen in a long time. All through the picture's progress Blanche Sweet carries your honest interest, not hectically or hysterically but as a commanding unfolding personality. Her final decisive bit at the telephone is just about the flower of her performance.

"Flickerings from Filmland," *Chicago Tribune*, May 27, 1915, 12.

"ANOTHER PLEA FOR 'BIRTH OF A NATION'" We have with us, and yet not with us, the so far ultimate achievement in motion picture making. The reels lay folded here waiting to speak their story to the city. David Wark Griffith's "The Birth of a Nation" is barred from Chicago's midst by the zealous efforts of those guardians of our civic welfare who permit the display of "The New Governor," adapted from the notorious "The Nigger," while discriminating against a work of artistic inspiration.[47]

"The Birth of a Nation" is acclaimed the country over, through all mediums of publications, magazines and newspapers, as the world's greatest picture. Chicagoans, only by commuting from the shades cast by the censorial dark lantern of their own town to the more enlightened regions of New York, Boston, Los Angeles, and San Francisco, may view this artistic triumph.

The picture was made by a master for the appreciation of intelligent people. It isn't going to attract the riotous, the hoi polloi, or the tumult stirrers, for the very price around it hedges it away. Its audiences in the east must be or the performance could not continue, and would not receive the general and continued commendation of thinking writers as it does.

They are orderly audiences because they are law-abiding citizens, doing their duty in the world, not vagrant street mobs, looking for a straw pointing excitementward.

The thrill is there because by the magic of pastoral reality the film takes one into the lives of people who figure in the tale. This has been done before in pictures, but never on so large a scale and with such perfect manipulation. In this it far exceeds "Cabiria," for it is a human thing—which "Cabiria" was not—along with its spectacular features, which it possesses in magnificent measure, striking the heart interest that makes it go home to our hearts.[48]

Mr. Griffith has used all of the threads of life—the love thread, the hate thread, the threads of passion, loyalty, patriotism, youthfulness, humor, sorrow, heroism, horrorism—in weaving his wonderful fabric.

The picture is melodrama, but melodrama translated means vitality, and it moves with the speed and the spring and the grace of a spirited horse. It shifts from every shade of feeling, the playfulness of carefree youngsters, to the heart mourning of a war-stricken family, the stirring tumult of battle in the quiet of home enduring, and it carries the observer with it through every second of dash and crash and whisper and echo of the story's progress, unconscious of the material fact of three hours and 12,000 feet of film used in the telling.

As a story of the civil war and the reconstruction period there is conflict in it of every sort, and there is villainy, both black and white, as well as heroism and faithfulness of each color.

The matter in supposed censorial disapproval shows the negroes as a people needing to be led and falling into the hands of false leaders—white ones, the film's traducers might notice.

Immense historical significance, handled with a fine and patriotic dignity of intent and achievement underlies the war tangled loves between the young folks of the north and the south, and the ultimate unraveling.

The picture is an interpretation of history in human terms and to audiences it carries distinctly a feeling of past, rather than present. True, the bias is southern, but biases untrammeled have been always the cherished possessions of free minded American folk; we like to argue one way or the other, for it is American doctrine that argument is good for the soul.

That this picture stirs in some the chord of controversy is no unprecedented experience, nor any necessarily fatal one. It is general American sentiment to prefer taking an experience first hand—risking that it be unpleasant—rather than suffer the protection of shielding by paternally minded censors.

Ah, well, this is a big picture, this "Birth of a Nation," a photographic marvel, a directorial wonder, and by missing seeing it we miss marking the greatest step in motion picture advancement.

"Flickerings from Filmland," *Chicago Tribune*, October 16, 1915, 14.

"CARMEN," PRODUCED BY LASKY, RELEASED BY PARAMOUNT   The Strand is in its new home and "Carmen," which has been so long in coming, has come and conquered. These two breath taking events in picturedom were commemorated last night amidst a glow of color and a warmth of music that, plus a capacity house, filled the walls of the old Globe with enthusiasm.

The performance last night was differentiated a bit from all successive ones by the Pagliacci prologue sung from the darkness by Burton Thatcher, symbolizing in Manager Cordner's intent the prologue of many things.

Thereafter followed the first edition of the regular Strand program, which is to continue day by day, a lovely Pathé scenic, "Gelthorn, a Rustic Venice," taking the place of the South American travel series, the regular Strand topics of the day, the conclusive comedy, soloing by Burton Thatcher and Naomi Nazor—and "Carmen."

And now to "Carmen," the vehicle with which the Lasky company captured grand opera for the celluloid, and Geraldine Farrar, the star they used to light up picture possibilities for the skeptical many.[49]

The result of their weeks of work and mountains of money is a high powered illuminator. "Carmen" is so good a picture that it scarcely seems a picture. It tells the Carmen story more coherently than does the opera for the common consumer, and the musical impression in large part is carried by the orchestral accompaniment gleaned from the Bizet score, for the Strand presentation.[50]

Cleancut directness of incident and action carries the tale through its course of hectic emotionalism to its pathetically beautiful tragedy. Most death scenes are bitter things to view. Farrar never looked lovelier, even at the climax of her hot-breathed enthralling, than when she lay limp in her blighted officer's arms.

But that is getting rather ahead of the story. One would say kind things of the settings, the supporting cast, the direction, the photography, but the "Carmen" of it, with all of Farrar's vigor and dominating personality, swings in, and the whole impression crystalizes into—"Carmen."[51]

She is a tremendous creature, this Carmen of the films. Except on the indispensable evidence of seeing, the existence of such vitality as Farrar embodies and its registration by the celluloid would be unbelievable. She is the livest collection of atoms imaginable. Every movement, every flicker of expression is instinct with vitality, and the slightest shades of change are caught by the camera.

In her love making, her shifting between toreador and officer, one reads her purposes without the need of subtitles. In her glowing, changing face are written the lines of the drama which the silent play does not permit.

And Miss Farrar has adequate support in her matador and officer. Pedro de Cordoba is a fine type of the bull fighter, while Wallace Reid as José is slim and good looking—thereby putting it over most of his operatic predecessors—and a lover to match Carmen's own vintage of emotion.[52]

It is no Sunday school play, this picture version of the classic heart bandit. There's a plentiful showing of emotion as they are, not as they are refined by civilization and the "what will people say" idea, but it is all done with a swift deftness that makes the point without the wearisome tediousness of other directors less artistic than Cecil de Mille.[53]

His long scene theory is satisfying evidence, too, giving the story stretches of pictorial narration that hold the interest and avoid the mental jerkings of frequent flashbacks.

Besides the lady of the picture, there's the bull fight, in itself quite worth seeing. One needn't jog into dangerous Tia Juana for this amusement, for there it is in all its glory and energy, minus its gore and tragedy, thrillingly reproduced by such clear photography that it scarcely seems a second hand medium, except for the lack of noise and smells.

One cannot do justice to "Carmen." It is a picture of finesse, encompassing the sincere efforts of a great player—even to the point of very rough treatment accorded the expressive person of a prima donna—of a great director and of a loyal studio support. It satisfies anticipations and it will go down on the records as a classic technically and histrionically.[54]

"Flickerings from Filmland," *Chicago Tribune*, April 29, 1916, 16.

"Handing One to the High Brows"   Mr. B.L.T., perhaps the most read man in the middle half of the country, has gratuitously come to the circulatory aid of Charles E. Whittaker in *Harper's Weekly* in his remark that "The movie is not art, because it is not literature; it has no persistence save for its illustration of daily news. . . . If it is necessary to find a definition for the movie, it would seem to be unrelated to art, of which it is not even the Cinderella. Myself, I regard it as the little cutey of the crafts."[55]

Which registers a curious state of mind. The movie is not art because it is not literature. So. That must then count out, on Mr. Whittaker's eeny-meeny-miny-mo-ing as non arts sculpture, music, drama, painting, for they assuredly are not literature. No more than they assume to be does the photoplay.

But the object of this column today is not argumentation. It is to scuttle "the cutey of the craft" that it may not obscure the vision of the stately ship of the photoplay just hoving over the horizon into people's consciousness. The attack is led by the submarine flotilla under the able commandership of Hugo Münsterberg, Harvard psychologist at large, who has looked into the photoplay and found it not only good but art. His U-boat is "The Photoplay" from the Appleton presses.[56]

Prof. Münsterberg is not writing from the basis of "the few moving pictures I have seen." He has studied the principles of the photoplay from the stroboscopic disks up, and he has gone out of the library into the picture theater and made first hand investigations. He is one of the first intelligent men of expression to take off the blinders of prejudice and write something of value in regard to the art that has come among us so recently as yet to be in the state of the prophet in his own country.

Prof. Münsterberg's whole discussion is brimful of informative material and interesting analyses. But it is mainly on his showing of the photoplay as a new art medium with which present concern is. He is not defending all present photoplays as being good; he is presenting the scientific possibilities of the photoplay that stamp it as a new art, suggesting there is infinite progress ahead of it.

"We want," he says, "to study the rights of the photoplay, hitherto ignored by esthetics, to be classed as an art itself under entirely new mental life conditions.... Photoplays are not and ought never to be imitations of the theater. They can never give the esthetic values of the theater; but no more can theater give the esthetic values of the photoplay. The one cannot replace the other; and the shortcomings of the one as against the other reflect only the fact that the one has a history of fifteen years, while the other has one of five thousand."

By elaborate scholarly induction Prof. Münsterberg finds that the object of art is "to remold nature and life so that it offers such complete harmony in itself that it does not point beyond its own limits, but is an ultimate unity through the harmony of its parts," an isolation that is achieved only by the artist.

Applying this criterion to the consideration of the conditions governing the photoplay, it follows that: "The richest source of the unique satisfaction in the photoplay is probably that aesthetic feeling which is significant for the new art and which we have understood from its psychological conditions. The massive outer world has lost its weight. It has been freed from space, time, and causality, and it has been clothed in forms of our own consciousness. The mind has triumphed over matter and the pictures roll on with the ease of musical tones. It is a superb enjoyment which no other art can furnish us."

That the photoplay of the present in many instances may be crude and common and unoriginal, Prof. Münsterberg grants, but so it need not always be, for "success has crowned every effort to improve photoplays."

There is comfort too, in the thought that though "the melodrama may be cheap, yet it does not disturb the cultured mind as grossly as a similar tragic vulgarity would on the real stage, because it may have the snowfields of Alaska or the palm trees of Florida as a radiant background."

And there is this, too: "Communities at first always prefer Sousa to Beethoven. The moving picture audience could only by slow steps be brought from the tasteless and vulgar eccentricities of the first period to the best plays of today, and the best plays of today can be nothing but the beginning of the great upward movement we hope for the photoplay.

"The greatest mission which the photoplay may have in our community is that of aesthetic cultivation. No art reaches a larger audience daily, no aesthetic influence finds spectators in a more receptive frame of mind."

So says Prof. Münsterberg. And the best words are these:

> Nobody can foresee the ways by which the new art of the photoplay will open, but everybody ought to recognize even today that it is worth while to help this advance and to make the art of the film a medium for an original creative expression of our time, and to mold by it the esthetic instincts of the millions.

It is curious to observe that almost invariably those who write as having authority derogatorily of the photoplay have self admittedly seen very few moving pictures. With the same basis of information, it is to be assumed they would hesitate at treatises on civil engineering or Sanskrit, but they rush in to damn the photoplay of which they know nothing.

There has been in the last two years since the movie has been depopulating the theaters and cutting into book and magazine circulation, more misinformation about it, written by men whose only qualification was a well known writing name, disseminated by standard publications than about any other subject.

To find a serious book by a clear-headed thinker who knows his subject, such as "The Photoplay," by Prof. Münsterberg, is almost as good as finding the pot of gold at the end of the rainbow.

"Flickerings from Filmland," *Chicago Tribune*, July 31, 1916, 11.

"WHERE ARE MY CHILDREN?"
Produced and released by Universal[57]

In the wake of the lurid "Little Girl Next Door," and on the wings of hectic advertising hinting at more sensationalism, out of the shadow of metropolitan amazement and national board of review disapproval, comes to the La Salle theater one of the most finely mannered photoplays yet produced.[58]

Those who pay their quarters seeking satisfaction for prurient tastes will find their measurement one of disappointment, unless the distinction of the picture can pierce their sordidness, for there is nothing more suggestive about it than the title itself, "Where Are My Children?"

It is a serious film, purposefully produced, but it bears no propaganda earmarks, nor is it pictured with the crude strokes usually employed when someone aims to make a celluloid preachment.

An artist worked skillfully with the materials of her expression and wrought a photoplay characterized equally by its strong purpose and its good dramatic and pictorial construction. If one is not interested in the theme, the story in itself, with its dramatic complications and its attractive directorial handling, is satisfying entertainment. It is, in fact, one of the few cinematic displays in which one loses thought of time.

The theme is that the wages of sin is death to happiness, the particular sin being the selfishness that abjures motherhood. In this it is an echo of an earlier production, American's "The Miracle of Life," but a much more finely and artistically done thing.

The district attorney, played most compellingly with a quiet, commanding dignity by Tyrone Power, longed for children in his beautiful home.[59] His wife, played with equal distinction and sureness by Helen Riaume, along with others of her set, frivolous fashionables, takes care to have no social engagements upset by interventions of nature.

Things go merrily, except for the attorney's father hunger, until a crisis is precipitated when the young brother of the attorney's wife seeks aid from her for the housekeeper's young daughter whom he has wronged.

Outraged at the occurrence—for she is a very nice woman, except for her selfishness—she gives the youth her doctor's name. The result is the girl's death, the doctor's haling into court, and a flurry of consternation amongst the local birds of paradise. From the doctor's ledger the attorney gleans much knowledge.

His wife, before his realizing his desire for children, and determining to bring him the happiness he sought, finds, as the subtitle puts it, that "she is no longer physically able to wear the diadem of motherhood," and all their lives together she must face that mute question, "Where Are My Children?"

The conclusion is impressively beautiful, with the lonely couple sitting before the fire while a fade-in brings visionary children playing about them. The years pass, and still they sit while the ghosts of children grown up come about them.

Everywhere the most exquisite delicacy rules every situation. How much may be accomplished by mere suggestion, how little need there is for suggestiveness in the relating of a powerful story on a delicate subject, is here convincingly demonstrated. This compares to a straight, clear-cut, well written newspaper story, containing facts and characterization and significance, in contrast with a murky Elinor Glynn novel.[60] It takes a problem of the day and looks at it honestly and cleanly instead of with the vice ventering[?] moral hypocrisy that produced "The Little Girl Next Door," playing up salaciousness for box office benefits.

Of course, here there may be no box office benefits, for the picture doesn't bear out some of the insidious announcements about it. It may be too fine a thing for the theater's clientele established through the past months. But for people who wish to see uniformly good acting, with never a bit of overdoing, a forceful story, forcefully, delicately, and humanly told, here is a rare opportunity. With the production of this picture Lois Weber has given power to her name.[61]

Charlotta Bass (1880?–1969)

Soon after leaving Providence, Rhode Island, for Los Angeles for health reasons, Charlotta Bass (née Spears) began working for the *Eagle*, a Black weekly newspaper owned by John Neimore.[62] When he died in 1912, one of his friends bought the *Eagle* at auction and made Bass the owner, with no strings attached. Charlotta and her new husband, Joseph B. Bass, changed the paper's name to the *California Eagle*, served, respectively, as publisher or "managing editor" and editor, and turned it into the most important Black newspaper on the West Coast.[63] Both were politically active in seeking to improve race relations in the city, which led them to protest *The Birth of a Nation*. The editorial selected here was part of a community effort in 1915 to get Los Angeles officials to deny the film's exhibition. Although that proved unsuccessful, Charlotta later claimed that the group did force Griffith "to cut some of the most vicious scenes."[64] In early 1916 she also reprinted several articles by Eugene Debs that denounced the film.[65]

After Joe Bass died in 1934, Charlotta continued to publish and edit the *California Eagle* until selling it in 1951. Long a local leader in the NAACP and a supporter of FDR in the 1930s, by 1950 she was a leading figure in the Progressive Party and was nominated as its vice presidential candidate in the 1952 elections.[66]

"Thomas Dickson's Idea of American Liberty," *California Eagle*, January 30, 1915, 4.[67]

Is it possible that Los Angeles will lower its dignity as one of the leading American cities by allowing even the picture play of the 'Clansman,' a picture in fiction that lowers the standard in the eyes of the people of the moral dignity of six millions of its faithful citizens by one Thomas Dixon, whose ability as a modern fiction writer has dwindled in insignificance in the eyes of the American people, because of his petty prejudices, hurled at a struggling people only fifty-two years up from slavery.

The American Negro has ever been ready to protect and defend the rights and interests of Americans. For more than three hundred years the Negroes of this country have been demonstrating a spirit of ready service without any hope of returns. But like every story or condition there is a crisis. And this is the chapter of Negro history that we are facing in this country today.

States and legislatures must reckon with the Negro as a component part of its citizenship.

The Negroes of Los Angeles have said that inasmuch as the 'Clansman' serves as an agency to stir up race hatred, and further inasmuch as it has been denied admittance by many of the Northern and the Southern cities of his country, we demand that it be denied theatrical recognition in Los Angeles.

Louella O. Parsons (1881–1972)

For three years (1911–14), Louella O. Parsons wrote scripts for Essanay, whose main office and studio were located in Chicago.[68] In December 1914 she parlayed that experience into writing a column, "How to Write Photo Plays," in the *Chicago Record-Herald*, which she then revised into a successful book, *How to Write for the Movies* (1915).[69] Much like Kelly, Parsons for several years wrote a daily column of film reviews, but increasingly her interest turned to interviewing movie personalities for a weekly column of profiles, "How to Become a Movie Actress" or "How to Become a Movie Star." She "honed an approach to newsgathering that was resourceful, shrewd, and, given the conventions of the era, highly unladylike," writes Samantha Barbas. "She sneaked into the theaters attended by stage and screen stars, loitered for hours in the lobby of the Blackstone Hotel, a popular hangout for actors, [...] eavesdropped in bathrooms, [and] learned to push through crowds of screaming fans to interview actors and to dash off thousand-word columns in an hour or less."[70]

Also located on the Society or Women's page, Parsons's film reviews often differed from Kelly's. To report on the protests against *The Birth of a Nation*, she interviewed Mrs. Louise de Koven Bowen of the Juvenile Protective Association, using Bowen's objections to Griffith's film on the basis of race prejudice to mask her pride in it, explicitly revealed in a later column: "We are going to recall when we saw it, where we saw it and how we wept and were overcome with emotion at the Little Colonel's daring."[71] Although entranced by the premiere of *Carmen*, she described not the program (as Kelly did) but the fairyland interior of the new Strand Theater. As a former scriptwriter she paid particular attention to story construction in feature films and celebrated their very skilled actors. This is noteworthy in her attention to William DeMille's scenario for *Carmen* (more than Cecil DeMille's direction) and the exuberant praise she shared with Kelly for Geraldine Farrar, "a revelation" who "makes the picture." Yet despite her praise for this "charming but cruel and wanton" Carmen, she also could exhibit a striking sense of moral approbation. The latter is quite explicit in her reviews of Theda Bara's overly "harsh" vampire and the illogical downfall of the family man, Joseph Schuyler, in *A Fool There Was* and of *Three Weeks*, based on "Elinor Glyn's salacious book" of the same title.[72] Unlike Kelly, she was conflicted about Weber's *Where Are My Children?* Although she found the director's "delicate" touch "wonderfully effective," she also worried that the subject (rather vaguely defined) was not suitable for a "mixed audience" and certainly not for adolescents.[73]

Supposedly, many readers of the *Chicago Record-Herald* told Parsons that "they valued her criticism as much as her gossip," but a male writer like Ben Hecht of the *Chicago Journal* was dismissive, once demeaning her as "the worst reporter the town ever knew."[74]

"Seen on the Screen," *Chicago Herald*, April 20, 1915, 8.

"'BIRTH OF A NATION' STIRS PROTESTS FROM CHICAGOANS" Protests against the showing of "The Birth of a Nation," which has been promised as a special attraction at the Illinois Theater next summer, are being registered daily.

"The Birth of a Nation," you will remember, is the film that David Griffith produced from Thomas Dixon's "The Clansman."[75] It took eight months to complete.

Mrs. Louise de Koven Bowen, president of the Juvenile Protective Association, is especially outspoken in her desire either to have the most harrowing scenes eliminated or else suppress the film entirely.[76]

"What is your chief objection to this picture?" I asked Mrs. Bowen.

"It is calculated to arouse race prejudice. In it the negroes are bestial and villainous, while the white men—especially those of the Ku Klux Klan—are uniformly heroes, performing magnanimous acts of chivalry and appearing always at the right moment to save the country from destruction. Such a presentation of this historic period will work great harm. It will stimulate and foster intense race hatred.

Miss Jane Addams saw it before she went abroad and she felt just as I do about its harmful influence."[77]

"But, I am told, the most objectionable parts have been cut out," I told her.

"The picture is remarkable and I should be glad to hear that all of those unpleasant scenes had been taken out of the film," said Mrs. Bowen. "You see our own Chicago censor board refused the picture a permit."

"Aside from the race question have you any other reasons for wishing the picture suppressed?" I asked.

"Yes," was the reply. "I think it would be exceedingly harmful for children. I should be sorry to have the children see it."

Mrs. Carter Harrison, who viewed the picture as a guest when it was shown in private exhibition, is of much the same opinion.[78]

It seems unfortunate that a picture in which the best efforts of the master producer, David Griffith, and one of the most talented screen actors, Harry Walthall, have been used to create this marvel should deal with a subject that can bring it under public disapproval.[79]

The Chicago "movie fans" have been greatly interested in this Broadway production and are hoping that the censors in some way may have the unwholesome scenes cut out so that they, too, may see the first $2 "movie."

"Seen on the Screen," *Chicago Herald*, May 3, 1915, 10.

"Finds No Excuse for Play Like 'A Fool There Was'" It is a mystery to me why producers will select such ghastly and unnatural subjects as "A Fool There Was," now running at the Ziegfeld, and produced by the William Fox company.[80]

There are so many wholesome, probable stories and plays whose adaptation would make an interesting and well balanced picture, that the photo-dramatizing of this play seems a pity and a waste of time.

I thought the stage production of the play wildly improbable, but the picture is appalling in its grewsome unreality.

In the first place no steady-going, level-headed business man, with a sweet wife and adorable "kiddie" would be led astray by a woman so palpably common. A more subtle, refined character might appeal to his senses, but never could this coarse creature lure a man of John Schuyler's responsibility away from his home.

The story was picturized by Roy McCardell with but few deviations from the play.[81]

Theda Bara, the vampire, while very handsome, gave almost too harsh an impersonation to this unpleasant character.[82] Edward Jose's downfall with his resultant gray hairs and wrinkled face was very well done.[83] He merged his own personality into the pitiful broken man who sacrificed everything for a vampire. The child, Runa Hodges, was a bit too "stagey" and sophisticated for the child she represented.

It is in no way a story for any one afflicted with troublesome nerves, for it makes you unhappy and irritated to think that such a seemingly strong man could leave his wife and child for such a creature.

My nerves and those of my companion had no chance to get unstrung, for we were entertained by a young woman and her escort, who insisted upon relating the story scene by scene. We could have shut our eyes and told every act of every character just from the conversation of this couple, who sat directly back of us. They kept it up from the first to the last scene.

"Seen on the Screen," *Chicago Record-Herald*, October 16, 1915, 8.

"CARMEN"   The Strand standard prevailed last night in the opening of the Strand Theater. The 1,500 guests were greeted by E. C. Divine, president of the Strand Theater Company; E. Q. Cordner, managing director; and A. J. Partridge and Joseph Interrieden, the officers of the organization, in their beautiful new home, Wabash Avenue and Seventh Street.

Standing out in harmony of color and beauty of decoration, the interior of the old panorama building, more recently known as the Globe Theater, presents a surprise for those who remember the former barnlike structure.

It was as if fairy hands had transformed dullness to magnificence. Japanese blue rugs cover the floor and upholster the Circassian walnut chairs. Scarlet hangings fall softly from the stage, with artistic lights shedding a subdued radiance here and there. The Strand Company has lived up to its reputation and given the public a theater in keeping with its program.

"Carmen" in opera is so popular that the thought of "Carmen" in motion pictures seems to many lovers of this tuneful opera a sacrilege. But when

Geraldine Farrar, as the beautiful, bewitching Spanish girl, pulsating with life and expressing every emotion known to Prosper Mérimée's heroine, smiled at the audience, all doubts were stilled.[84]

William De Mille, who prepared the scenario, describes Carmen of the novel rather than the opera. There is more latitude naturally in the film, and this Mr. De Mille uses to good advantage.

Geraldine Farrar is a revelation. Had she been a little extra girl chosen to enact this role she would have been just as remarkable. It is not the magic name of Farrar that compels one to admire the work of this artist. It is her portrayal, so real and so expressive. Miss Farrar looks like a slip of a girl of 18. Her vivacious and carefree air strengthens the youthful illusion, and we take Geraldine Farrar's Carmen straight to our hearts.

The story opens in the camp of the smugglers. We are introduced to Carmen's people—a band of desperate men who live and thrive on their illegitimate plunder. It is Carmen's duty to fascinate Don Jose, the handsome commander of the customs officers. This she does by every wile and art known to the feminine charmer. Jose steals and kills for her, and even then she spurns him.

Escamillo, the bold and fearless toreador, wins her attention through the clothes and luxuries he bestows upon her. She accompanies him to Seville and there watches him enter the arena to participate in a bull fight. There is a real bull, panting and snorting while he angrily paws the dust. He is ready to trample Escamillo beneath his hooves, though, of course, the toreador vanquishes the bull, but for humane reasons we are unable to see the actual finish of this maddened animal.

Then Don Jose follows her to Seville and plunges a knife into her breast. She dies in his arms, game to the last.

It is Geraldine Farrar who makes the picture. She is the irresistible Carmen, charming but cruel and wanton, full of whims, preferring always to be loved without giving of her love. Without Miss Farrar's radiant personality this picture would attract no unusual attention. From the standpoint of pictorial perfection Lasky has done even better things, but they have never brought to the screen a more delightful picture star than Geraldine Farrar.

Wallace Reid's Don Jose and Pedro de Cordoba's Escamillo are convincingly portrayed. There are some good scenic effects and frequent artistic touches that show the guiding hand of Cecil De Mille, Lasky's director in chief.

The music from "Carmen," with the Toreador song and other bits from the opera, accompany the picture, and are for those who know and love its score a necessary part of the entertainment.

Esther Hoffman

What little is known about Esther Hoffman can be summarized briefly. For a short time, beginning in 1914, as a "picture play reporter," she took over writing Gertrude Price's column of "personality sketches" in the Scripps-McRae newspapers. From July 1914 through September 1915 she also wrote a weekly "personality sketch" of "some popular film star" in the *Day Book*.[85]

"My Movie Scrap Book," *Day Book*, May 7, 1915, 4.

Have you started a Movie Scrap Book?

Perhaps not—it's such a brand new fad in movie land that some of the movie fans have not heard of it yet.

The Day Book will help you start your scrap book by publishing each week in the "My Movie Scrap Book" column the picture of some popular film star.

Get a book—any book will do, a scrap book bought in a department store is fine, but any good sized book—an old geography, for instance—will be just as good.

Clip the caption "My Movie Scrap Book" from The Day Book and paste it on the cover of your scrap book, then as the movie star's pictures appear in The Day Book cut them out and paste them in the book. Your book will be much more interesting if you also add stories of your favorite stars and names of plays in which you have seen them.

Number the pages and then index the book—making entries like this—Edna Mayo, page 1, etc.[86]

It will be great fun, this Movie Scrap Book, and it will be a very valuable record of doings in movie land.

The Film Girl

The Film Girl was an unassuming writer who addressed her readers in a colloquial, chatty, personalized style. After all, she was writing a "coly'um" simply as a "maid of the movies" or a fan much like those readers. Her daily column sometimes was paired with a piece of serialized fiction or nestled near a schedule of church events, but for nearly a year it frequently occupied the same page as the syndicated "Daily Talks with Mary Pickford." Neither was she concerned with films as art, nor did she "claim that they are instructive or that they benefit one mentally. [Instead] their mission is as a diversion—a relaxation."[87] So she could offer etiquette advice to moviegoers who wanted to relax on a rainy day, and she could praise really good feature films and stars in concise, impressionistic terms. She was well aware of her audiences of fans. While Vitagraph's *The Sins of the Mothers*, for instance, was "gripping and interesting [and] Anita Stewart singularly charming," what she noticed at an afternoon screening were the "many women who obviously had come because the name of the piece suggested something which they should see—and how greatly they enjoyed themselves once they were there."[88] And she shared their enjoyment of the "strange, distorted smiles across [Theda Bara's] cruelly beautiful face," as well as the "young whirlwind of energy" that marked Douglas Fairbanks, "a real comedian."

The name of this "film girl" finally was revealed as Miss Marjorie Dunmore Tooke when she was appointed a YMCA secretary in overseas service and set sail for France just after the end of the Great War.[89] Surprisingly, *Motion Picture News* took special note of her film reviewing, describing her as a "young lady of education and refinement who attends the showing of all pictures in the downtown section and gives her unbiased criticism of every program" and sometimes travels to New York City "to attend advance showings of the bigger and better pictures."[90] As one of her selected columns admits, however, she much preferred to frequent a variety program of short films at one or more neighborhood movie theaters in Syracuse.[91]

"Seen on the Screen by the Film Girl," *Syracuse Herald*, June 22, 1915, 9.

After I have seen a really good old-fashioned kind of a movie show consisting of a two reel feature and almost three good one reel photo plays, I am inclined to think that I'd just almost as soon go to the 5-cent theater as to the 15-cent one. And there are times which happen not infrequently when the many reeled feature does not appeal at all. I never remember seeing a better all around show than yesterday at the Crescent. To begin with there was Blanche Sweet, pretty and blonde, attempting to disguise herself in a black wig in "Judith of Bethulia," an Apocrypha story.[92] Well, I remember the "Judith" of my school days, for she and her sisters of an ancient line helped to make the study of the Bible and of little times interesting. There on the screen, beautifully done, was "Judith's" story. Then there was Marian Saix in a detective story, not at all bad, and Lillian Walker in a pretty piece entitled "The Little Doll's Dressmaker," and something else for which I, unfortunately, didn't have time to stay.[93]

[. . .]

Charlie Chaplin in "Work," and Edna Mayo in "The Little Deceiver," is the double header which the Crescent theater management hopes will interest the Syracuse movie fans to-day.[94] This is the first showing in the city of the celebrated Mr. Chaplin in "Work" and much is expected of it. Miss Mayo's photoplay is three reels in length and should be especially worth seeing. Bryant Washburn is cast in her support.[95]

"Seen on the Screen by the Film Girl," *Syracuse Herald*, August 13, 1915, n.p.

Aisles littered with protruding ends of wet umbrellas and paved with small rain water puddles through which run a succession of foot tracks both large and small, and a damp rubbery atmosphere—such was the condition which prevailed, I suspect in most of our movie houses yesterday. I do not think that the managers of motion picture theaters need bewail the rain. More people dash into the movies to escape it than fail to come downtown for a movie show. At the Novelty there was an audience which would have done credit to a sunshiny day. There they offered Hal Fords in a triple impersonation in a picture entitled "The Maker of Dreams," a title by the way, which absolutely had no connection with the play. Mr. Fords appeared as a young man, as the same young man grown old, and, finally, as his own son. It was a three-reel Broadway favorite Kalem picture, clever as to its plot. Then there was a Vitagraph picture somewhat heavy as to character, and Isabelle Rae, who used to be an ingenue at the Wieting [?] in one of the summer stock companies, was seen in "The Wanderer's Pledge." Miss Rae was not the wanderer; she was an adorable Westerner in a flannel blouse, short fringed skirt, leggings of leather and a flaxen braid.

I recommend a course of lessons on how to enter a motion picture show and sit down, and how to arise and leave without bumping against the heads of people in the row in front. With a little practice this may be done. It's done, however, alas, too seldom.

"Seen on the Screen by the Film Girl," *Syracuse Herald*, December 28, 1915, 5.

Should one search the country far and wide for authors who issue a positive money-back guarantee unless they put a thrill in every chapter—should one dig down among the musty melodramatic tomes of fiction of an elder day—even then one could scarcely find a more Fox like production than "Destruction," in which Theda Bara may be seen for the last time at the Eckel. There is always an appreciable difference in the size of an audience when Theda Bara is featured. How these audiences of yesterday must have enjoyed a production even more Bara-like than usual.

Truly Theda has never been so Bara as in "Destruction." Mephistophelian glee sends strange, distorted smiles across that cruelly beautiful face of hers as victim after victim is subdued. An extensive acquaintance with vampires of the movie variety convinces me beyond doubt that it is always necessary to look the part. Here Miss Bara makes it impossible for other vampires to achieve the fame which is hers. Her success lies not greatly in her ability, in which there is apparently no real depth, but in her beautiful face and body, which she can twist and contort into the most fiendish of postures.

The scenes of "Destruction" are, for the most part, managed with rare good taste, particularly those in a foundry where curious red-black shadows glance over the figures of the players. Extreme luxury characterizes the interior scenes. Did I not say Fox made the picture?

As refreshing as a cool dash of air in an overheated room is "Double Trouble," in which Douglas Fairbanks was seen yesterday at the Strand.[96] Here is a story improbable beyond all improbability, but offering so many delightful opportunities to its talented star that no one thinks of minding. The play is wholly enjoyable, and it provides opportunities for endless fun on the part of Mr. Fairbanks, who plays his dual character with equal ease.

In a dazzling manner he is changed from the president of the Sabbath Day society to "Eugene Brassfield," a young whirlwind of energy, who swoops down upon a hustling Western town, wrests a fortune from it, becomes its lion, buys its votes and becomes its mayor, all things which shock beyond measure the president of the Sabbath Day society to which identity he is returned at intervals by an extremely pretty sorceress. The reason for the two identities is that the young man was hit on the head by a thug and that when he awoke, he awoke a new man, totally foreign to this previous quiet existence. In Mr. Fairbanks we have a real comedian, one who is funny even in [?] scenes.

Dorothy Day

Dorothy Day was the nom de plume of Dorothy Gottlieb, apparently a family friend of A. H. Blank, who owned the largest circuit of movie theaters in Des Moines and elsewhere in Iowa.[97] She likely was the writer of the unsigned daily "News of the Movies" column, which in August 1915 the *Des Moines Tribune* began printing on the Society or Women's page. That November the *Tribune*'s coverage of the movies expanded to a weekly Saturday page; the daily "News of the Movies" was enlarged; and Day was given a byline for one of its columns, "What Do You Want to Know About the Movies," in February 1916. Within two months, she was identified as the editor/writer of all the material printed under the "News of the Movies" banner.

Day could be as chatty and colloquial as the Film Girl, sometimes addressing her readers directly, even jokingly, much like Kelly. Here she is describing a newsreel story: "Ladies, ladies, you are to be enabled to see just how the president's wedding cake was made and decorated. Think of it. A recipe for the cake and how to decorate it."[98] But she also could be serious in summarizing the essential elements she looked for when judging a movie. In praising *The Golden Chance*, she focused on the "uncommonly strong" story, with its "well constructed introduction" and "unexpected" twists that—in a domestic metaphor shared by several of these women writers—so neatly wove together the plot's three "threads" into the film's "exquisite texture." She shared Kelly's appreciation for Weber's *Where Are My Children?* and concisely posed its "two great questions" for viewers: Can a "good, conscientious physician" be justified in giving poor women "the secrets of birth control," and, by contrast, can "women, blessed with health and good homes," be justified in seeking an abortion because a pregnancy would inconvenience their "pleasure loving"? She also was impressed by the film's poignant ending.

"News of the Movies," *Des Moines Tribune*, January 28, 1916, 11.

[...]

"The Golden Chance," the Lasky Feature featuring Cleo Ridgley and Wallace Reid at the Garden today and tomorrow is a marvelous picture.[99] In the first place, the story is uncommonly strong. It is rich in dramatic material and replete with genuine pathos. It describes in pictures of super beauty and sublime simplicity the Golgotha of a woman's heart. The theme of the story is entirely modern life, but it takes the eye of an artist and dramatist to find it. The romantic element is of what can be extracted from modern life in the way of romance and sentiment if one has a real divining rod. The guile of a society woman aiding her husband in the exploitation of a young millionaire is the first thread in this exquisite texture. The next is the silly but tragic adventure of a well-bred young girl who marries a scoundrel. The third thread is supplied by the play of hearts—the heart of a woman so cruelly toyed with by fate and the heart of the young millionaire. Next the dramatic power found in [a] swift and well constructed introduction [that] wakes our sympathy and interest in the leading characters. The author has chosen, and chosen wisely, to depart from all conventional time-worn notions. The unexpected is happening all the time. The spectator is invited to guess at the next turn in the play and is delighted to discover that he has been wrong for the solution is far more dramatic, far more subtle and entertaining than he could ever have guessed by himself.

"News of the Movies," *Des Moines Tribune*, October 30, 1916, 7.

"WHERE ARE MY CHILDREN?" I crowded my weary way into the Palace last night to be shocked—yes, and all the rest of the crowd were going for the same reason. And I will bet that not one of the sensation seekers was shocked one whit more than I, and I was not shocked at all. I found a wonderfully well enacted, splendidly and carefully produced preachment on a subject that is usually discussed in whispers.

The production presents for serious consideration by the public two great questions:

Are women, blessed with health and good homes, justified in denying entrance to the world those fine, strong souls that would be a blessing to humanity?

Are doctors justified in denying entrance into this world those souls that would be marked as moral and physical defectives and bear the sign of the serpent?

THE PHYSICIAN ARRESTED The second question is taken up first and we find a good conscientious physician, one who practices much in the slums, and who knows the terrible conditions among the poor, arraigned in court for publishing a book, asking for the right to give these poor people the secrets of birth control—the secrets that are the property only of the wealthy, who do not need them.

This man and his work enlists the sympathy and the interest of the district attorney, Richard Walton. We see the terrible need of birth control among the poor as the doctor is making his testimony and with Walton are convinced of the truth of his statements.

AT THE ATTORNEY'S HOME Then we are taken into Walton's home, introduced to his wife, a pleasure-loving piece of humanity, surrounded with luxury and her dogs. We are introduced to her butterfly friends, women of the best families and of wealth. One of these is about to be blessed with a child, but because her friend is to have a house party the next month, she is persuaded by Mrs. Walton to consult her doctor, Dr. Malfit. Later Mrs. Walton's brother comes to visit her at the same time as the housekeeper's daughter comes to stay with her mother.

THE GIRL DIES   The brother is of a familiar type, the imitation of a man who finds his enjoyment in preying on the innocent young girls who cross his path. The girl is a beautiful flower of innocence and falls easily to his wiles. The wages of sin is death, however, and in seeking relief from her condition, on the advice of Mrs. Walton, Dr. Malfit blunders and she dies, after telling her secret to her mother.

The doctor is brought to trial, is convicted, and tells the district attorney to look into his own household before accusing others. In the doctor's books, he finds his wife's name many times along with her fashionable friends, and we leave the two to pass a dreary, childless life, since the wife when she really wishes to give birth to a child finds that nature has rebelled against being so long thwarted.

TYRONE POWER A STRONG FIGURE   Tyrone Power, who will be remembered for his powerful performance in "The Eye of God," is again a pillar of strength in the role of Walton. I know of no player who could have carried this difficult role as does Power. Helen Riaume is the heartless wife and at no time does she gain our sympathy. Marie Walcamp deserves to be placed second in her interpretation of the friend, who follows Mrs. Walton's advice.[100] Miss Walcamp seems to be able to carry any role well. You will remember her as "The Flyirt," Juan de la Cruz as Dr. Malfit has a small role, but he plays it well. He is with Morosco now and recently played with Edna Goodrich. Rene Rogers is the beautiful girl child who loses her life with her honor. The rest of the cast are unnamed but you will recognize Mary MacLaren as the maid. All do their work well under the careful guidance of Lois Weber.

Mildred Joclyn

Mildred Joclyn began writing a movie column in the *Chicago Post* at least as early as December 1915, a column that continued to mid-September 1916.[101] She was important enough that a few theater ads included snippets of her movie reviews, notably for *The Little Girl Next Door* and *Where Are My Children?*[102] Because the *Post* is long gone and not yet digitized, searching for further information about her is difficult. One news item in the *Chicago Tribune*, however, turns up a possible clue to her name's disappearance from the *Post*. In mid-July a "Miss Mildred Joclyn" was driving a car that struck a sixteen-year-old girl on Lake Shore Drive and, despite taking the injured girl to a hospital, was booked by the police "on a charge of assault."[103] She was "released on a $1,000 bond signed by Wilfred E. Gerry of Oak Park, whose machine she was driving." Her name is unusual enough that Joclyn could be that charged driver, but the *Tribune* seems not to have reported any plea agreement or trial.

The column selected here seems addressed directly to fans in the audience. It replays an argument that Gertrude Price had made more than two years earlier in the Scripps-McRae newspapers: the movie industry is a welcoming field for "ambitious women" among fans, and Joclyn specifically wants to see more women filmmakers like Lois Weber.[104]

"Movies Offer a New Field for Ambitious Women," *Chicago Post*, September 2, 1916, 6.

The photoplay industry has done much toward opening new fields of adventure for ambitious women. Women are to be found in the scenario department, in the sales department, in the publicity department, in the producing game, in the role of exhibitor, a few in the directorial field. But the latter to me would seem to offer broader opportunities than any of the others. Women, with their keen insight for detail, are in a position to better many a production. Woman is quick to detect faulty construction, for from time immemorial she has made it her business to sift causes for effects. There is not a picture that could not be improved upon by numerous little feminine touches that the average picture sadly lacks. A woman never would make the mistake of having her heroine receiving callers in the morning wearing an evening frock. Neither would she have her butlers in livery. She has made a life-long study of social requirements and ethics, and she wouldn't have any personal note signed "Lord or Lady So-and-So." She would never countenance a rescue from a watery grave with the hero or heroine perfectly dry and fresh as a daisy. She would see to it that if someone entered a doorway wearing one suit they would not effect a lightning change before reaching the other side. There are ever so many other little details which she would master successfully.

I long for the day when there will be many more able directors like Lois Weber, with so many artistic triumphs to her credit, and can see in such a move a higher standard of education for the photoplay-going public.

Oma Moody Lawrence

Information on Oma Moody Lawrence is difficult to find. She obviously was important enough as a columnist for the *Chicago Post*, from mid-September 1915 (replacing Mildred Joclyn) through mid-August 1918, to have snippets of her film reviews singled out for reprinting in downtown theater ads.[105]

Whether she was the same person as Oma Margaret Lawrence, married to a John James Rutter Lawrence, is tantalizing but improbable—"Oma" is such an unusual first name. In January 1917 the latter sued and divorced her husband for "wife and child abandonment."[106] In 1972, however, an eighty-three-year-old woman named Oma Moody Lawrence ("a 1909 graduate of the University of Chicago in classical languages") is shown with her daughter taking a calligraphy class in Salem, Oregon.[107] It is much more likely that she was the *Chicago Post* reviewer.

The column devoted to *The Birth of a Nation* does evidence a woman with an advanced education, and her attention to the specific musical score for the film is unique. In another column on the film (not included here), she accepts the ideology of the "Lost Cause" and describes African Americans in blatantly racist language.[108] A second selected column takes a rather snobbish position promoting a certain "etiquette" in attending a picture show, and here the chastised spectators are women of her own "well-bred and dignified" class.

"Music in 'The Birth of a Nation,'" *Chicago Post*, October 28, 1916, 8.

When piquant little Elsie Stoneman decides to become a nurse and solace wounded, gallant youths back to health, her goings and comings are accompanied in the score of "The Birth of a Nation" by a most catching little melody which she is supposed not only to sing but also to pick on the banjo. In the "close-ups" you can see the dainty lips fashioning the song's words, and in the full figure you can see her plucking away on the old banjo, while the handsome sufferer on the cot manages to turn his head far enough to get a glimpse of her. Many persons have asked what this tune is. It is Henry C. Work's "Kingdom Comin'," otherwise known as "Massa's Jubilee," one of the most fetching ditties that was ever picked on banjo or guitar.[109]

In the great war scenes there is a different sort of music. Thus no one is surprised that "In the Hall of the Mountain King," from Grieg's "Peer Gynt" suite, is used for the terrific pictures of the torch against the heart of Atlanta, that Wagnerian operatic crashes accompany the cannonading and infantry charges at Petersburg, and that even a national air like "Marching Thru Georgia" is elaborated into a great, overwhelming symphonic movement.[110]

In the scenes of Lincoln's assassination, in Ford's Theater, Washington, April 14, 1865, the appearance of the great emancipator is greeted, as it was on that occasion, by the familiar strains of "Hail to the Chief"; but the fatal crisis of the hour can only be rendered by such classical strains, as those of Belibri's Norma overture.

Three distinctive strains or motifs run thru the second half of the picture, emphasizing the contrast between the three elements of which it is composed. For the love of Ben Cameron, the little Confederate colonel, and Elsie Stoneman, the dainty northern heroine, there is Breil's "Perfect Song," an original composition, for this play.[III] It is heard again and again each time with peculiar and ever-increasing effectiveness. Perhaps it sounds sweetest when out in the open Elsie kisses the dove and Ben quietly tries to steal a few kisses himself.

Then there is the old, chaotic-seeming tune that marks the entry of the negro mobs—the yawp of the barbaric African—the racket of the rioters and the outcropping of the orgy in the master's hall, when ignorant negroes dominated the legislature of South Carolina in 1874. Perhaps D. W. Griffith, creator of this wonderful spectacle, got this from the semi-barbaric strains sung by the negroes on the old Kentucky plantation where he was born and raised. It is certainly original, as far as can be learned. It does not represent the negro of today, for a veneer of civilization has subdued and hidden the traits that wrought so much woe to the South in the days of reconstruction.

"The Etiquette of the Picture Show," *Chicago Post*, January 13, 1917, 6.

The "movie" has become such an institution and is so informal in its nature that many persons who would not think of talking in church have come to behave in the picture show as they would behave nowhere else on earth. It is useless to say that only the grossest of our audiences offend in any way while in the picture playhouse. Perhaps the middle classes are the majority of devotees of the screen drama, but I have found that many otherwise well-bred and dignified persons lost all their social veneer in the darkened neighborhood theater.

We can expect giggling schoolgirls to make pointed comments about the star and the production; they are at that age when self-consciousness takes the form of boldness, but I have sat in a seat next a gray-haired woman whom I had never seen before and been obliged to listen to the most breath-taking scandal about the star, whose replica was on the screen. A person whom I happened to know lived an unusually quiet and sane life in private. And I have often been obliged to listen to subtitles read in audible tones to a neighbor. There is, perhaps, not the objection to noises in the photo theater that there is in the domicile of the spoken drama or at the opera, but is it beyond imagination to reconstruct in the mind's eye any theater where every spectator is mumbling to himself? Would it be a pleasant place? I fancy not. And in these days of music with the play there is more than one reason why we should observe a courteous silence in the playhouse.

So much for the sins of the talkative; let us pass on to more usual and equally annoying foibles of mankind—or womankind, rather, since they are the chief offenders. Some of us are prone to forget that the seats behind us are occupied with persons that have just as much right to get their money's worth as we have. We ask everyone who is between us and the coveted vacant seat far in the center of the row to rise that we may pass in leisurely comfort to our chair. Of course, I know that it is not easy nor pleasant to have to crawl over everyone in the intervening space, but just think of the poor persons behind who have to lose the thread of the story while we settle ourselves. Yesterday I sat in a theater which was not entirely filled; a lady several rows in front of me edged into the very middle of the row, over about five persons, who all politely rose and obstructed the view of at least twenty-five other persons for the space of several seconds of the most exciting sequence of events. She stood while she removed a neckpiece and bulky wrap, took off her hat and arranged her belongings on the back of the seat; meanwhile the sufferers behind craned their necks. But that was not the worst—tho she had one of the best seats in the house, had not the slightest excuse, for changing, that anyone could see, she rose in a few moments, clambered over the same five patient and polite men, sought another seat in a similar situation, and seemed content. That sounds farfetched, but it is as true as gospel, and she looked daggers at a harmless youth who groaned when she stepped on his feet.

Then there is the group of friends who, having met in town, decide that it would be nice to take in a picture show, in reality desiring only a comfortable place in which they may chat about their friends and neighbors and husbands.

There are other types of bad manners. There is the well-known end-seat hog who finds few other opportunities for display of his peculiar form of selfishness. There is the sprawler, who occupies three seats when he should be comfortable enough in one, and there is the man who sits thru two or three shows just to kill time, even if the theater is "holding them out." There are other forms of selfishness that are more common, perhaps, but are not especially rife in motion-picture theaters. There is not space to devote to all of them, but one remark is in order. When you go to the theater, as when you go any place else, think whether you would like to have done to you what you are doing to others. "Put yourself in his place" is a good motto in or out of a motion-picture show.

Mae Tinee

Mae Tinee was the nom de plume of Frances Peck (1886?–1961), who worked briefly as a reporter at the *Denver Republican* before being hired at the *Chicago Tribune*. In February 1914 she established a Sunday page, "Right Off the Reel," devoted to motion pictures. It featured a large photo profile of a current star in "The Frame of Public Favor," several columns of industry news and gossip, and another column, "Answers to Fans." In early January 1915, in what likely was a promotional stunt, the *Sunday Tribune* editor supposedly "without her knowledge" put Mae Tinee in "The Frame of Public Favor" as that week's most "popular player." "Right Off the Reel" appeared in a number of other newspapers across the country through the *Tribune*'s syndicated service and was hugely influential.[112] In late 1916 she took over Kitty Kelly's film review column, soon making it her own by retitling it "Right Off the Reel."

From early on, Mae Tinee had cultivated a snappy, idiomatic style in her industry news reports and gossip columns, and she carried that over into her film reviews—as if wishing to one-up Kitty Kelly. This is especially the case when Tinee scorned stars such as Theda Bara and Francis X. Bushman in their separate, simultaneously released productions of *Romeo and Juliet*. But that style was also on display when she dismissed films such as *The Price of Fame* as a "waste of time," found *The Unborn*'s argument that birth control was wrong absolutely unconvincing, satirically retold the story of *The Devil's Double* (with William S. Hart) as if concocted by a "bunch of youngsters" playing in a barn, and tartly gulled Lois Weber's *Idle Wives* as a "pictorial goulash."[113] Although hypnotized by the dazzling spectacle of D. W. Griffith's *Intolerance*, in the end she had to admit: "Wasn't it wonderful—wonderful? But just what was it all about?"[114] Not all, however, was grist for her sarcastic wit. She praised Nazimova in her screen debut for sacrificing her beauty in order to look so "haggard, worn, unutterably sad" in Herbert Brenon's "tragic, tender probing of motherhood" in *War Brides*.[115]

The sometimes snarky tone of Mae Tinee's column often sharply contrasted with that of the other columns and articles on the Society or Women's page.

"Right Off the Reel," *Chicago Tribune*, November 8, 1916, 15.

Ah! But This Is Comedy Indeed.
"ROMEO AND JULIET"
Produced by Metro with Francis X. Bushman and Beverly Bayne.[116]
Produced by Fox with Harry Hilliard and Theda Bara.

Figure 2. Mae Tinee, *Chicago Sunday Tribune*, January 3, 1915.

    Francis—Wherefore art thou Romeo?
    Theda—Wherefore art thou Juliet?
    Or, if you must needs be Romeo and Juliet, wherefore not in the same picture? Ah, that would be comedy indeed.[117]
    There may have been worse Romeos than Francis X. Bushman's and there may have been worse Juliets than Theda Bara's; but certainly no funnier pair ever unwittingly made burlesque of tragedy. Metro's Romeo with his set sweet smile and biceps! Fox's Juliet with the experience of a hundred vampire roles writ large across her face; her leaded lashes and voluptuous mouth—Dear heaven! And producers cry out because we do not take them seriously! This Romeo and Juliet, I'm thinking, Shakespeare would willingly acknowledge Bacon's.[118]
    Let it not be thought for a moment that, so far as cleverness of conception, careful attention to detail, and lavishness of display, there is the least comparison between the two productions. Metro has put forth a beautiful

and creditable picture, beside which the Fox effort is scarcely worthy of mention.[119] The latter was apparently prematurely born, due to the shock received evidently by the knowledge that in the Metro studios something worth while had been thought of which Fox would have liked to think of first. Not having apparently thought first, those concerned saw to it that they released first, which is no doubt accountable for a lot of things—possibly Theda Bara.

The Metro production, eight reels long, is in many respects an artistic triumph. John W. Noble, who superintended the direction, knew his Shakespeare and gave, apparently, the greatest thought to the smallest details.[120] Where Fox has improvised to please the erratic fancy of somebody who thought he could do it better than the Bard of Avon, Metro has bowed to greatness and aspired to technical perfection. The death scene in the vault has been absolutely twisted about by the former, with an eye, no doubt, to the spectacular and to provide their heroine with a chance for the writhings that are peculiarly her own. Neither she nor Hilliard die nicely at all. It must be said for Mr. Bushman, on the contrary, that dying is the best thing he does in the picture. None of the Bushman pants and grimaces. He just stiffens and topples over and is quite horribly realistic about it.

Beverly Bayne was a surprise.[121] She made a most beautiful and appealing Juliet. This was not the surprise. The surprise was that throughout the piece she did some remarkably clever acting. Only once or twice did she seem to me to be out of the role. She was natural. She was unsophisticated, ardent, desperate, hopeless—tragic—and she carried you with her. If she keeps up after this fashion, should Fate decree a parting of the ways between her and her co-star, she need not worry, for she'll be quite worth while starring alone. All other parts in the Metro case are exceptionally well taken. Deserving of honorable mention is Adella Barker, the old nurse of Juliet. You know the devoted, irascible old soul true to life.

As regards Harry Hilliard—he might have been worse.[122] Poor soul, he was so awfully up against it! I've seen and liked him in other pictures.

But—

"Never was a story of more woe
Than Fox's Juliet and Metro's Romeo!"

"Nazimova Makes Her Screen Debut,"
Chicago Tribune, December 6, 1916, 18.

"WAR BRIDES"   Nazimova's screen debut, this picture with its tragic, tender probing of motherhood, which must give but never be consulted as to war, is one, I fancy, that will not soon be forgotten by those who see it.[123] Its strength lies in the marvelous simplicity with which the subject is treated by a cast scarcely one of the members of which has ever before worked to the clicking of a camera. Adapted from the vaudeville sketch, it has gained rather than lost in transit. Not a pretty picture, nor a pleasant one, but distinctly worth while from the standpoints of production, photography, and dramatic artistry. It is not unlikely that Nazimova, witnessing herself and holding in the back of her brain the memory of salaries she has heard of, may turn a supple back on the spoken drama and devote her energies to the shadow stage.

As Joan she marries the eldest brother of a large family of boys and girls. No sooner is the wedding over than war is announced. A fleeting, shadowed honeymoon is hers, and then her husband departs for the trenches, from which he never returns. He is followed by the other brothers. The splendid, stalwart mother, the sisters, and the new sister-in-law, who already knows she is to become a mother, are left desolate.

As regiment after regiment leaves, the government makes an impassioned appeal to loyal women to marry the soldiers before they go, that from the ranks as they fall may still rise the children of the future. Carelessly, they marry and part, until Joan, horrified by what she considers sacrilege, begins to protest. Silenced for a little by the threats of the captain on hearing of the death of the sons, her husband among them, she becomes crazed with grief. Rushing into the church where the priest is still at his business of marrying, she shrieks protest at the loveless wedlock which will result only in "cannon food for other wars."

"'War Brides'—nah! Brood mares—ha!" The censors cut the caption. But her philosophy is contained in it.

She is, of course, arrested, to be shot—after the birth of her child. Escaping from prison, she leads a mob of women bearing their children in their arms and otherwise confronts the king as he motors into the capital.

"Promise us there shall be no more wars!" she demands, confronting him, a tragic, mad, tearless creature, grimacing in agony.

"Impossible. There will always be war," his majesty replies. Whereupon, Joan, producing a pistol she has had concealed, announces with cold finality:

"Then we women will bear you no more children." And the bullet does its work. The women lift her, a dead weight, high on the palms of their hands, and stand there silent, and the curtain goes down.

Although I have said little about her, the mother of the boys who fight and die is a vital part of the picture. If there is one person who can witness her renunciation, the royal sacrifice she makes and the royal way in which she makes them, without at least swallowing a quick uprising of emotion, I am not that one. Here is finished acting, in that you can never believe that it is only acting.

Nazimova is beautiful only once, to my way of thinking. Most of the time she is haggard, worn, unutterably sad. She is one of the few, however, who sacrifice mere prettiness to effect.[124] You and I might grimace and grin and writhe as she does were we to be told that the one we loved most was gone forever. But they seldom do it that way on the stage or in pictures.

"'Idle Wives'—a Pictorial Goulash,"
Chicago Tribune, December 7, 1916, 14.

"IDLE WIVES"[125]   I come forth humbly to announce that I haven't an idea what "Idle Wives" is all about. I saw it from start to finish, and once or twice I could have sworn I spotted a clew. Alackaday, no! True, the picture deposes that if your wife is idle and not allowed to lift her hand she is unhappy and apt to be driven into charitable work. On the other hand, you are graphically shown a busy mother, haggard under the strain of housework and baby tending. Her daughter goes wrong and she breaks down under all the work and worry. There is a lot of good acting, helter skelter, here and there; some pathos; the occasional glimmer of an idea from chaos. But—

There's no use trying to tell you about it. I acknowledge myself helpless, for I never saw such a pictorial goulash. Never—in all my life!

Notes

1. The pioneer was Ralph P. Stoddard, the "Photo-Plays and Players" page editor at the *Cleveland Sunday Leader* from late 1911 through late 1912. Another was J. Willis Sayre, who in 1913 expanded coverage of the movies to a full Sunday page in the *Seattle Times*. Also, between 1909 and 1919 Lester A. Walton increasingly devoted his amusement column to the movies in the *New York Age*. See Anna Everett, *Returning the Gaze: A Genealogy of Black Film Criticism, 1909-1949* (Durham, NC: Duke University Press, 2001), 18–34.

2. Although focused on stage performances, between 1911 and 1914 Minnie Adams made rare comments on the movies in the weekly *Chicago Defender*. See Everett, *Returning the Gaze*, 41–44.

3. Among the dozens of newspapers in the Scripps-McRae chain were the *Day Book* (Chicago), the *Cleveland Press*, the *Des Moines News*, the *Detroit News*, the *New Orleans Statesman*, the *Reno Gazette*, the *St. Paul News*, and the *Toledo News-Bee*.

4. Gertrude Price, "Sees Movies as Great New Field for Women Folk," *Toledo News-Bee*, March 30, 1914, 14. For further information on Otto, Price, Stoddard, and Sayre, see Richard Abel, *Menus for Movieland: Newspapers and the Emergence of American Film Culture, 1913–1916* (Oakland: University of California Press, 2015).

5. See, for instance, Lester A. Walton, "Negroes in New York Theaters," *New York Age*, November 18, 1909; and "New Yorkers Have Gone 'Dippy' over the Movies," *New York Age*, May 4, 1914. Juli Jones, "Moving Pictures Offer the Greatest Opportunity to

the American Negro," *Chicago Defender*, October 9, 1915, quoted in Everett, *Returning the Gaze*, 54. A production company owner and filmmaker, William Foster used the pseudonym Juli Jones as a writer.

6. For further information on these newspaper men, see Abel, *Menus for Movieland*. Rob Reel (likely male) also wrote reviews for the *Chicago American*, while Columbus Bragg sometimes offered advice on acting for the camera in the *Chicago Defender*. See Everett, *Returning the Gaze*, 44–46. Between 1913 and 1924 anonymous writers (also likely male) wrote increasingly frequent reviews in the *New York Times*. See Vincent Canby, introduction to Amberg, *The New York Times Film Reviews*, n.p.

7. Two ads listed "Right Off the Reel" as a top weekly feature in the *Tribune*'s Sunday edition: "Tomorrow's Sunday Tribune" ad, *Chicago Tribune*, May 22, 1915, 14, and July 17, 1915, 5.

8. For further information on these newspaper women, see Abel, *Menus for Movieland*.

9. For commentary on Dorothy Day, the "Film Girl," Kitty Kelly, and Louella Parsons, see ibid.

10. A. M. Boggs, "Visualized Opportunity," *Pedagogical Seminary* 21 (January 1914): 445–53. For an informative essay on Boggs, see Laura Isabel Serna, "Anita Maris Boggs: Historical Invisibility and Gender in the History of Sponsored and Educational Film," *Feminist Media Histories* 1, no. 2 (2015): 135–43.

11. See Shelly Stamp's excellent analysis of *Shoes* in *Lois Weber in Early Hollywood* (Oakland: University of California Press, 2015), 101–18.

12. Universal City opened to tourists in March 1915 as a prototype of the movie industry's later popular amusement parks. Kingsley's is an early, lengthy description of the sprawling studio space. Kitty Kelly wrote of her experience there in "Flickerings from Filmland," *Chicago Tribune*, March 17, 1915, 14, and March 20, 1917, 12.

13. Isadore Bernstein (1876–1944) not only served as general studio manager at Universal City but also wrote many screenplays, including for *Tarzan of the Apes* (1918).

14. For several years Laura Oakley (1879–1957) acted in scores of short comedies at Keystone. Lois Weber also replaced manager A. M. Kennedy as mayor.

15. William Selig (1864–1948) founded the Selig Polyscope Company in Chicago in 1900 and established a second studio in Los Angeles in 1910. Despite successful films like *The Adventures of Kathlyn* serial and *The Spoilers* (both 1914), the company ceased film production in 1918.

16. Griffith adapted Thomas Dixon's novel *The Clansman* for *The Birth of a Nation*.

17. Often called the American Sarah Bernhardt, Mrs. Leslie Carter (1857–1937) reprised her stage roles in *DuBarry* and *The Heart of Maryland* (both 1915), neither of which was a success. The sister of Mabel, Edith Taliaferro (1894–1935) performed in only three films after her starring stage role in *Rebecca of Sunnybrook Farm* (1910) and continued to work mostly in the theater. A very popular stage actress, Maude Adams (1872–1953) was best known for her leading role in J. M. Barrie's *Peter Pan* (1904) but never appeared in films. A well-known stage actress, Frances Starr (1886–1973) later appeared in a few films, most notably in *Tiger Rose* (1923) and *Five Star Final* (1931).

A successful stage actor, Dustin Farnum (1874–1929) starred in *The Squaw Man* and *The Virginian* (both 1914), which led to many leading roles in westerns, among his dozens of silent films. A notable stage actress playing "little girl" roles, Marguerite Clark (1883–1940) joined Famous Players–Lasky in 1914 and first garnered attention in *The Goose Girl* (1915) and *Snow White* (1916). Sometimes, like Pickford, she also played boy and tomboy roles. After *Scrambled Lives* (1921), which she produced and directed, she retired.

18. A successful theater impresario, Oliver Morosco (1875–1945) produced Broadway plays in New York and between 1914 and 1917 financed half a dozen feature films.

19. An early "independent" company founded in 1910, Reliance merged with Majestic in 1913. Reliance-Majestic was the chief studio for Griffith after he left Biograph, with films distributed by Harry Aitken's Mutual Film until it became part of the Triangle Corporation in 1915. Founded in 1912, Mutual Film was a major film distribution rival to the General Film Company. After Aitken and Griffith left the company in 1915, Mutual resumed distribution of short films, most famously a series of Chaplin comedies (1916–17).

20. An unsuccessful playwright and stage actor, D. W. Griffith (1875–1948) joined the Biograph company in 1908 and soon became a major influential American filmmaker. Leaving Biograph in 1913, he joined Reliance-Majestic Studios and achieved notorious fame with *The Birth of a Nation*, which is available in many different versions on DVD.

21. Griffith himself had claimed that he originated these film techniques or devices in a full-page ad published in *Variety*, November 28, 1913, 23.

22. After acting and directing films for Selig, Herbert Bosworth (1867–1943) established Bosworth Film in 1913 to produce features based on Jack London novels. A year later he turned production briefly over to Weber.

23. After directing short films for Laemmle's IMP, Thomas H. Ince (1880–1924) was hired by New York Motion Picture in 1911 and established a sprawling set of studios that became known as Inceville just northwest of Santa Monica. There he produced Indian pictures and Civil War films, including the lost five-reel *Battle of Gettysburg* (1913), and other features such as *The Italian* (1915) and *Civilization* (1916), released through Triangle.

24. As husband and wife, Max Figman (1866–1952) and Lolita Robertson (1888–1959) were a well-known duo onstage who acted for a few years in films.

25. In the 1910s Carlyle Blackwell (1884–1955) was a popular actor in Vitagraph shorts and then in a series of feature films. His wife, Ruth Hartman, also acted in films. Richard Harding Davis (1864–1916) became famous as a war correspondent and author of *Soldiers of Fortune* (1897), a novel later made into a 1914 film starring Dustin Farnum.

26. Balboa Film was best known for its serials with Ruth Roland, distributed by Pathé Exchange.

27. After *Shoes*, Weber continued to star Mary MacLaren (1896–1985) in other feature films through 1917. As an independent actress, MacLaren then failed to find suitable movie roles but worked as a bit player from the 1930s into the 1950s.

28. Margaret I. MacDonald also praised the film highly but found the scenes in which the shop girl cuts out cardboard insoles to put inside her worn shoes "repetitious" ("Shoes," *Moving Picture World*, June 24, 1916, 2257–558). By contrast, Philip H. Welch was fascinated by such "concrete objects," often shown in close up ("Motion Pictures by Philip H. Welch," *Minneapolis Tribune*, October 27, 1916, 11). The EYE Museum (Amsterdam) restored its 35mm print of *Shoes* for a 2018 Milestone release on DVD.

29. "Iowa Girl to Review Books," *Ottumwa Courier*, January 19, 1911, 9.

30. For more information on the development of the newspaper woman's page, see Sandra Gabriele, "Gendered Mobility, the Nation, and the Woman's Page," *Journalism: Theory, Practice & Criticism* 7, no. 2 (2006): 174–96.

31. "It Can Be Done: A Reel Romance," *Chicago Sunday Tribune*, October 31, 1915, 2.3. Well into the 1950s, Chase served as the *Tribune*'s financial and then real estate editor.

32. In her early columns, Kelly seemed to rely on or even reproduce a company's publicity material for a particular film. In her review of Kalem's *The Rival Railroad's Plot*, however, she frames a plot summary with her own commentary. See Kitty Kelly, "Photoplay Stories and News," *Chicago Tribune*, July 22, 1914, 11. Throughout the rest of 1914, the reviews increasingly presented her own responses, a characteristic that later marks all of the other writers and their columns as well.

33. Kitty Kelly, "Flickerings from Filmland," *Chicago Tribune*, January 6, 1915, 10. A successful theater producer, Lasky (1880–1958) formed the Jesse L. Lasky Feature Play Company in 1913, together with Cecil B. DeMille, Samuel Goldfish, and Oscar Apfel. Born in Austria-Hungary, Adolph Zukor (1873–1976) was a successful furrier who used the profits, in the early 1900s, to invest in an expanding circuit of penny arcades, vaudeville houses, and movie theaters in the Northeast. A hard-driving entrepreneur, in 1912, he founded Famous Players Film Company, merged it with the Jesse L. Lasky company to create Famous Players-Lasky, and co-founded Paramount Pictures to distribute its films. Shedding partners along the way, in 1919 Zukor had Paramount begin to buy a circuit of movie theaters and to erect palace cinemas, establishing a vertical corporation that handled production, distribution, and exhibition.

34. See Richard Abel, "Chicago's 'Censorial Casualties' and the Provenance of Archive Prints," in Joanne Bernardi, Paolo Cherchi Usai, Tami Williams, and Joshua Yumibe, eds., *Provenance and Early Cinema* (Bloomington: Indiana University Press, 2020), 169–178. For a discussion of Selig and Essanay films listed in Kelly's censorship columns, see Michael Glover Smith and Adam Selzer, *Flickering Empire: How Chicago Invented the U.S. Film Industry* (London: Wallflower, 2015), 161–64, 193–95.

35. The *New York Age*, *Chicago Defender*, and *California Eagle*, not surprisingly, strongly condemned the film and supported its censorship. See Everett, *Returning the Gaze*, 71–105.

36. Kitty Kelly, "Flickerings from Filmland," *Chicago Tribune*, July 6, 1915, 18. A Japanese American, Sessue Hayakawa (1886–1973) achieved fame as the villain opposite Fannie Ward in *The Cheat* (1915), after which he became one of the industry's highest-paid actors. "Wid" Gunning had called attention to the power of close-ups in "'Close-Ups' Are Very Important," *New York Evening Mail*, January 9, 1915, 5. Louis

Delluc, "La beauté au cinéma," *Le Film*, August 6, 1917, 5, translated as "Beauty in the Cinema," in Abel, *French Film Theory and Criticism, 1907-1939, Volume 1, 1907-1929* (Princeton, NJ: Princeton University Press, 1987), 139.

37. In an otherwise thorough analysis of exhibition venues and programs in Chicago, Moya Luckett often cites Louella O. Parsons but never mentions Kitty Kelly. See *Cinema and Community: Progressivism, Exhibition, and Film Culture in Chicago, 1907-1917* (Detroit: Wayne State University Press, 2014).

38. Salisbury was a millionaire filmmaker, writer, and world explorer whose articles frequently appeared in the *National Geographic* and who had some kind of relation to the University of California. In an interview a week later, Salisbury claimed that his scientific purpose was to "hunt with the camera" and admitted that he "never expected to show these pictures for public exhibition." See Kitty Kelly, "Flickerings from Filmland," *Chicago Tribune*, March 12, 1915, 12.

39. A few years ago, searching the New Zealand Film Archive, the National Film Preservation Foundation found and restored a surviving fragment of Salisbury's *Wild Animal Life in America*. The last half of the fragment is devoted to this "Hunting Wild Geese for Market," and another intertitle argues for legislation "to eliminate this work of destruction and conserve our wild life."

40. George Melford (1877-1961) directed more than thirty short films for Kalem between 1909 and 1915, when Lasky hired him. His most famous film was *The Sheik* (1921), starring Valentino. Born in Italy, Rudolph Valentino (1895-1926) first found work as a waiter, dancer, and touring stage actor. By 1919, he was playing secondary roles in the movies, where June Mathis noticed him and cast him as Julio Desnoyers in *Four Horsemen of the Apocalypse* (1921). An immediate star sensation, Valentino made *The Sheik* (1921) and *Blood and Sand* (1922) very successful films. Although he remained a popular sex symbol, none of his films measured up until *Son of the Sheik* (1926), released shortly after his unexpected death from an operation for a perforated ulcer. Huge throngs of fans made his funeral a major news event.

41. William DeMille (1878-1955), the elder brother of Cecil, was a successful playwright with *The Warrens of Virginia* (1907) and *The Woman* (1911). He became an even more successful scenario writer for Lasky, notably *Carmen* (1915), and director for Famous Players-Lasky.

42. Mabel Van Buren (1878-1947) had been a lead actress in *The Virginian* and *The Squaw Man* onstage, and DeMille hired her to perform in Lasky features. Lois Meredith (1897-1967) was an American movie actress of some note between 1914 and 1918, when she left for France to star in Tristan Bernard's *Le secret de Rosette Lambert* (1920).

43. A well-known stage actor, Theodore Roberts (1861-1928) joined Lasky in 1914.

44. Does the absence of names (even in this American feature) identifying who was fighting and where perhaps suggest that the censors did not want the film to promote either side in the war and thus create controversy within audiences?

45. Founded in 1907, Kalem eventually had permanent studios in New York / New Jersey, Florida, and California. The company trained directors Sidney Olcott

and Marshall Neilan, as well as actors Gene Gauntier, Alice Joyce, Ruth Roland, and Helen Holmes.

46. At a very young age in 1909, Blanche Sweet (1896–1986) joined the Biograph company, where Griffith featured her in *The Lonedale Operator* (1911), *Enoch Arden* (1911), and *The Painted Lady* (1912). Following Griffith to Reliance-Majestic, she starred in early features such as *Judith of Bethulia, Home Sweet Home*, and *The Avenging Conscience* (all 1914). An accomplished actress, Sweet was a major star for Lasky and then Famous Players–Lasky from 1915 on. A Scottish-born playwright, Margaret Turnbull (1872–1942) joined Lasky as a scenario writer in 1915, helped establish Hayakawa's star image, and wrote an early novel about the industry, *The Close-Up* (1918).

47. *The New Governor* was adapted from Edward Sheldon's melodrama *The Nigger* (1909).

48. Directed by Giovanni Pastrone, *Cabiria* (1914) was a spectacular Italian epic film set during the Second Punic War. It equaled the earlier success of *Quo Vadis?* (1912) in the United States.

49. Already a famous soprano opera singer in Europe, Geraldine Farrar (1882–1967) debuted at the New York Metropolitan Opera in *Romeo et Juliette* in 1906. Extremely popular among young women (dubbed "Gerry-flappers"), she also sang for phonograph recordings and was an early performer on radio. *Carmen* made Farrar an immediate star, and she went on to appear in other DeMille features such as *Joan the Woman* (1916) and *The Woman God Forgot* (1917).

50. A brilliant French pianist, Georges Bizet (1838–75) was unsuccessful as a composer until the 1875 premiere of *Carmen*. But he died of a heart attack before critics declared it a masterpiece.

51. The anonymous *New York Times* reviewer also praised Farrar: "She brings to the richly colorful performance a degree of vitality that animates all the picture" ("Geraldine Farrar Seen but Not Heard," in *The New York Times Film Reviews, 1913–1931*, 7.

52. Wallace Reid (1891–1923) became a movie star acting for Vitagraph and then Famous Players–Lasky; he was often described as a matinee idol par excellence. In 1919, recovering from a train wreck injury on location, Reid became addicted to morphine and died in a sanitarium in early 1923. Founded in 1897, Vitagraph was a major film producer between 1906 and 1915, with stars such as Florence Turner, Maurice Costello, John Bunny, Norma Talmadge, and Clara Kimball Young. See Anthony Slide, *The Big V: A History of the Vitagraph Company*, rev. ed. (Metuchen, NJ: Scarecrow Press, 1987). Pedro de Cordoba (1881–1950) first appeared on the screen in *Carmen*, went on to have a long career as a character actor because of his basso voice, but much preferred acting onstage.

53. Like his brother William, Cecil B. DeMille (1881–1959) was a successful playwright and stage director before joining the Lasky company to direct feature films in 1913. *The Squaw Man* (1914), *The Virginian* (1914), and *The Cheat* (1915), along with *Carmen*, elevated DeMille to become one of the top three filmmakers in the industry, rivaling Griffith and Lois Weber.

62 ○ CHAPTER I

54. Video Artists International's DVD release of *Carmen* (2006) is available for purchase online.

55. Bert Leyton Taylor wrote "*A Line o' Type or Two*' by B.L.T.—the humorous and sarcastic 'Colyum Conductor' who is the tabasco sauce of The Tribune's editorial page six days a week" (see the half-page advertisement in the *Chicago Sunday Tribune*, March 12, 1916, 7.7). *Harper's Weekly* was an influential political magazine between 1857 and 1916. Particularly known for its illustrations, its featured caricaturist was Thomas Nast. Whittaker may have been the weekly's circulation manager before it ceased publication.

56. Long after receiving a doctorate in physiological psychology in Germany, Hugo Münsterberg (1863–1916) was invited to Harvard, where he pioneered the study of applied psychology. He became a controversial figure for his pro-German position at the outbreak of the Great War. For an extensive study of *The Photoplay: A Psychological Study* (New York: D. Appleton & Co., 1916), see Allan Langdale, *Hugo Münsterberg on Film* (New York: Routledge, 2002).

57. Owner of a big film rental service in Chicago, Carl Laemmle (1867–1939) formed his own production company (IMP) in 1909; in 1912, with half a dozen others, he founded Universal Film, soon a major independent corporation. In 1914 Laemmle, now Universal's president, opened Universal City in Los Angeles, then the largest studio complex in the world. The National Film Preservation Foundation included the Library of Congress's surviving 35mm print of this film on its *Treasures III: Social Issues in American Film, 1900–1934* (DVD, 2007).

58. *The Little Girl Next Door*, a white slave film, was banned in many states but approved in Illinois, where two hundred thousand people reportedly saw the film in Chicago. Louella Parsons condemned it as a sensational "picturization of vice with all its trimmings" ("Seen on the Screen," *Chicago Herald*, May 8, 1916, 8).

59. Born in London, Tyrone Power Sr. (1869–1931) had a long, very successful stage career in the United States. In 1914 he began acting in films and then alternated between screen and stage roles.

60. Elinor Glyn (1864–1943) was a popular British-born novelist best known for risqué romantic fiction, especially *Three Weeks* (1907) and its promotion of a woman's "It." In 1919 she joined Famous Players–Lasky as a scenario writer, working particularly with Gloria Swanson.

61. After a minor stage career, Lois Weber (1879–1939) and her husband, Phillip Smalley, began working at Rex and then Universal, for which she wrote, directed, and starred in the stunning thriller *Suspense* (1913). By 1916 Weber rivaled Griffith and DeMille as one of the highest-paid directors in the industry, based on features such as *Hypocrites* (1915), *The Dumb Girl of Portici* (starring Olga Pavlova), *Shoes* (introducing Mary MacLaren), and *Where Are My Children?* (all 1916). In 1917 she formed her own studio, Lois Weber Productions.

62. For the best information on Charlotta and Joe Bass, see Douglas Flamming, *Bound for Freedom: Black Los Angeles in Jim Crow America* (Berkeley: University of California Press, 2005), 17–20, 26–34, 86–89.

63. Thanks to Ellen Scott for informing me that selected microfilm reels of the *California Eagle* can be found digitized on the Internet Archive. Most are from later years, but one covers issues, some in fragments, from February 1914 to December 1915.

64. Charlotta Bass, *Forty Years: Memoirs from the Pages of a Newspaper* (Los Angeles: California Eagle Press, 1960), 35–36.

65. "Eugene V. Debs Flays Big Movie," *California Eagle*, January 29, 1916); and "Debs Flays Big Movie," *California Eagle*, March 18, 1916, both cited in Everett, *Returning the Gaze*, 91.

66. Flamming, *Bound for Freedom*, 211, 367–71.

67. This week's issue of the *California Eagle* carried a large first-page headline: "The Afro-Americans of Los Angeles Demands The Clansman in Moving Pictures Be Denied Admittance." "Correct" spelling, syntax, and punctuation were not always a priority for the weekly.

68. Founded in Chicago by George Spoor and Gilbert Anderson in 1907, Essanay soon became one of six major American production companies. After opening a studio in Niles, California, in 1912, Anderson starred in a popular series of *Broncho Billy* films. Although best known for its series of Chaplin comedies in 1915, Essanay faltered once he left for Mutual and went out of business in 1917.

69. Along with other prominent female scenario writers, Parson is excluded from a recent book about five male writers: Stephen C. Curran, *Early Screenwriting Teachers, 1910–1922: Origins, Contribution and Legacy* (Accelerated Education Publications, 2019).

70. Samantha Barbas, *The First Lady of Hollywood: A Biography of Louella Parsons* (Berkeley: University of California Press, 2005), 54–55. Parsons also reported that "not all the attractive picture theaters are in the Loop," briefly describing several of those in "Exhibitors' Notes," *Chicago Record-Herald*, August 10, 1915, 8.

71. Louella O. Parsons, "Seen on the Screen," *Chicago Record-Herald*, October 15, 1915, 10.

72. Louella O. Parsons, "Seen on the Screen," *Chicago Record-Herald*, April 16, 1915, 8. Her responses here conform to the then current sense of middle-class white women's respectability and to the moral reform uplift movement.

73. Louella O. Parsons, "Seen on the Screen," *Chicago Record-Herald*, July 31, 1916, 7.

74. Barbas, *The First Lady*, 54–55.

75. Thomas F. Dixon Jr. (1864–1946) was an ardent promoter of white supremacy and the "Lost Cause" of the Confederacy and an opponent of women's emancipation. Among his twenty-two novels besides *The Clansman* (1905) was *The Fall of a Nation* (1916), also made into a movie.

76. An influential reform movement figure in Chicago, Mrs. Louise Koven Bowen led the Juvenile Protective Association and wrote *Five and Ten Cent Theatres: Two Investigations* (1909/1911).

77. A pioneering social reformer and author of *Twenty Years at Hull House* (1910), Jane Addams (1860–1935) had run a short-lived theater for children in 1907 to counter the South Halsted nickelodeons surrounding her famous settlement house.

78. However, Mrs. Carter Harrison actually did not support Koven Bowen, for she was partly responsible for lifting the film's censorship in Chicago. See Everett, *Returning the Gaze*, 86–87.

79. Harry (or Henry B.) Walthall (1878–1936), a stage actor who was hired at Biograph in 1909, became a crucial actor for Griffith, appearing in such films as *The Informer* (1912) and *The Avenging Conscience* (1914) before his starring role in *The Birth of a Nation*. In *Art of Moving Pictures* (1915), Vachel Lindsay (1879–1931) singled out Walthall for special praise.

80. Hungarian-born William Fox (1879–1952) drew on his experience as a successful vaudeville, movie theater, and rental exchange entrepreneur to found in 1914 Box Office Attractions, which turned into the Fox Film Company in 1915. This film is readily available on DVD.

81. Roy McCardell (1870–1961) edited the *New York Sunday World*'s comic supplement, featuring "The Yellow Kid." A prolific scenario writer, he was best known for American Film's serial, *The Diamond in the Sky* (1915), as well as *A Fool There Was*.

82. A minor stage actress, Theda Bara (1885–1955) became Fox Film's biggest star with this film. Although she also played more wholesome heroines, as in *Romeo and Juliet* (1916), she soon was typecast as an exceptionally popular "vampire" or vamp character.

83. Belgian-born Edward Jose (1880–1930) also directed some forty-two films between 1915 and 1925.

84. Prosper Mérimée (1803–1870) was a French writer best known for his pioneering work in the novella. The most enduring was *Carmen* (1845), later the basis for Bizet's opera in 1875.

85. E. W. Scripps published the *Chicago Day Book* as a thirty-page tabloid without ads that served to announce ideas and developments in his newspapers. It ran from November 1911 to July 1917. For further information and analyses of early movie scrapbooks created by young women, see Diana W. Anselmo, "Bound by Paper: Girl Fans, Movie Scrapbooks, and Hollywood Reception during World War I," *Film History* 31, no. 3 (2019): 141–72; Leslie Midkiff DeBauche, "Memory Books, the Movies, and Aspiring Vamps," Observations on Film Art, http://davidbordwell.net/blog/2015/02/08/memorybooks; and Abel, *Menus for Movieland*, 257–73.

86. Edna Mayo (1895–1970) starred in twenty-six films between 1914 and 1916, mainly for Essanay, and retired from acting in 1918.

87. "Seen on the Screen by the Film Girl," *Syracuse Herald*, November 22, 1915, 9.

88. "Seen on the Screen by the Film Girl," *Syracuse Herald*, June 29, 1915, 11.

89. "Herald 'Film Girl' for Overseas Duty," *Syracuse Herald*, October 13, 1918, 1; and "Sails for France," *Syracuse Herald*, December 11, 1918, 3.

90. "The Press, Press Representative and the Picture—VI," *Motion Picture News*, November 20, 1915, 46.

91. See also "Seen on the Screen by the Film Girl," *Syracuse Herald*, July 14, 1915, 14; July 15, 1915, 11, September 10, 1915, 10, September 29, 1915, 9, and October 22, 1915, n.p.

92. Griffith's *Judith of Bethulia* is readily available on DVD.

93. An artist's model, Lillian Walker (1887–1975) was hired in 1909 at Vitagraph, where she became a successful actress during the 1910s. In 1916 *Photoplay* described her as "a feminine confection composed of dimples, golden hair, and curves."

94. By 1915 Charlie Chaplin (1889–1977) already had achieved immense popularity with movie fans and left Keystone to make a series of short comedies for Essanay. Chaplin's *Work* is readily available for purchase online.

95. Bryant Washburn (1889–1963) appeared in hundreds of films from 1911 on. During this period, he worked primarily at Essanay, including in *Graustark* (1915).

96. After becoming a popular stage actor on Broadway, Douglas Fairbanks (1883–1939) joined Triangle Pictures in 1915 and quickly became a major star. The Film Girl's description of *Double Trouble* nicely catches the impact Fairbanks had on movie fans.

97. A. H. Blank opened his first picture palace, the Garden theater, in early 1914. Later that year, Gottlieb and Mrs. Blank won top prizes in a card game involving forty paired players. See "This Page of Special Interest to Women," *Des Moines Capital*, September 14, 1914, 8.

98. Dorothy Day, "Real Fire, Thrilling Escapes, Give This Film Real Thrills," *Des Moines Tribune*, March 21, 1916, 4.

99. Cleo Ridgley (1894–1962) first acted for Kalem in the early 1910s, became a movie star for Famous Players–Lasky, and also directed a number of feature films. Image Entertainment's 2005 DVD release of this film, along with *Don't Change Your Husband*, is available online.

100. Marie Walcamp (1894–1936) began working at Universal in 1913 and acted in scores of films, mostly in westerns and serials. Rarely was she in a serious feature like *Where Art My Children?*

101. The *Chicago Post* boasted more lines of automobile advertising than any other paper in the city. It targeted middle- and upper-class readers. See *Chicago Post* ad, *Editor & Publisher*, January 15, 1920, 28. Joclyn's column appeared on a variety of pages, from the Saturday amusements to the daily comics (at least into May).

102. La Salle ads, *Chicago Tribune*, May 14, 1916, 8.3, and, August 29, 1916, 15.

103. "Miss Eloe Cherry Struck in Lincoln Park by an Auto Driven by Woman," *Chicago Tribune*, July 19, 1916, 1.

104. Gertrude Price, "Sees the Movies as Great New Field for Women Folk," *Toledo News-Bee*, March 30, 1914, 14.

105. The *Post* consistently placed Lawrence's weekly column on the Saturday Amusements pages. See, for instance, the Colonial ad for *Joan the Woman*, *Chicago Tribune*, April 24, 1917, 11; and the Playhouse ad for *Revelation*, *Chicago Tribune*, May 15, 1918, 15.

106. "Partings," *Chicago Tribune*, January 23, 1917, 11.

107. "Variety's a 'BIG' Thing at Chemeketa," *Sunday Capital Journal*, May 6, 1972, Photo, 4.

108. Oma Moody Lawrence, "'The Birth of a Nation'—an Appreciation," *Chicago Post*, September 30, 1916, 9. For an analysis of Civil War films prior to *The Birth of*

a Nation, many of which accepted the tenets of the "Lost Cause," see Richard Abel, "The 'Usable Past' of Civil War Films: The Years of the 'Golden Jubilee,'" in *Americanizing the Movies and "Movie-Mad" Audiences, 1910–1914* (Berkeley: University of California Press, 2006), 141–67.

109. An active abolitionist and Union supporter, Henry C. Work (1832–84) was a self-taught song composer. Along with "Marching Through Georgia" (1865), "Kingdom's Coming" (1862), which used slave dialect, made him at the time a more popular songwriter than Stephen Foster.

110. The Norwegian composer Edvard Grieg (1843–1907) was best known for his incidental music for Henrik Ibsen's *Peer Gynt* (1867), first performed in 1876.

111. Joseph Carl Breil (1870–1926) was one of the first composers to write scores for the movies, beginning with *Queen Elizabeth* (1912). He also would arrange the score for *Intolerance* (1916).

112. For further information on Mae Tinee, see Abel, *Menus for Movieland*, 92–94, 148–52, 237–39, 241–42.

113. Mae Tinee, "Right Off the Reel," *Chicago Tribune*, November 20, 1916, 14; Tinee, "Flickerings from Filmland," *Chicago Tribune*, October 17, 1916, 15; Tinee, "Right Off the Reel," *Chicago Tribune*, November 25, 1916, 14.

114. Mae Tinee, "Right Off the Reel," *Chicago Tribune*, November 29, 1916, 14. The *New York Times* reviewer shared some of Mae Tinee's misgivings: despite the film's "utter incoherence, the questionable taste of some of its scenes and the cheap banalities into which it sometimes lapses," it was "a stupendous spectacle" ("'Intolerance' Impressive," in Amberg, *The New York Times Film Reviews*, 20–21). After denouncing *The Birth of a Nation*, the *California Eagle* praised *Intolerance* in a front-page article written by C.A.S. Cited in Everett, *Returning the Gaze*, 99–100.

115. Irish-born Herbert Brenon (1880–1958) became a major American filmmaker with features such as *Neptune's Daughter* (1914), starring Annette Kellerman. He later directed Pola Negri in *The Spanish Dancer* (1923) and *Shadows of Paris* (1924), as well as the first adaptation of *Peter Pan* (1924). The 1918 rerelease of *War Brides* was censored as propaganda for "peace at any price."

116. A body builder and sculptor's model, Francis X. Bushman (1883–1966) was an unusually popular star from the early 1910s through the early 1920s. He and Beverly Bayne began working together for Essanay and then at Metro. They costarred in many films, from features like *Romeo and Juliet* (1916) to serials like *The Great Secret* (1917); once their long affair had become a scandal, they married in 1918. After their divorce in 1925, Bayne's film career waned, but Bushman had some success in radio serials and later in guest appearances on television.

117. In contrast to Mae Tinee's disdain, the *New York Times* reviewer judged the two films excellent and simply enumerated the ways each was better than the other in relation to Shakespeare's play. See "Shakespeare Movie Way," in Amberg, *The New York Times Film Reviews*, 22.

118. Many Shakespeare skeptics believe Francis Bacon was the actual author of his plays.

119. Founded by Richard A. Rowland and Louis B. Mayer as a rental exchange in 1915, Metro Pictures soon was producing films with the star teams of Bushman and Bayne and Harold Lockwood and May Allison. Investing in penny arcades, nickelodeons, and vaudeville theaters, by 1913 Marcus Loew (1870-1927) was operating a large number of theaters in New York City and elsewhere in the East. In 1920 he bought out Metro, gained control of Goldwyn, and formed Metro-Goldwyn-Mayer in 1924, with Louis B. Mayer as studio director and Irving Thalberg as head of film production.

120. As the professional name of Winfield Fernley Kutz (1880-1946), John W. Noble began working at Thanhouser in 1910 and then served as a screenwriter and director for a number of companies, including Metro through the 1920s.

121. In 1912 Beverly Bayne (1894-1982) joined Essanay in Chicago, where she soon partnered with Bushman and moved with him to Metro for a series of films between 1916 and 1918. Although her movie career declined in the 1920s, she turned to perform on Broadway throughout the 1930s and 1940s and briefly appeared on radio as well.

122. Although sometimes starring opposite Theda Bara, Harry Hilliard (1886-1966) performed chiefly as a character actor for Fox Film and then Metro.

123. Born to Jewish parents in Crimea, Alla Nazimova (1879-1945) became a major stage star at the Moscow Art Theatre. In 1905 she moved to New York City and found critical and popular fame in Ibsen and Chekhov productions. The success of *War Brides* led to a series of films for Metro, including *The Brat* and *The Red Lantern* (both 1919) and then *A Doll's House* (1922) and *Salomé* (1923), the latter two box-office failures. Between 1918 and 1926 she owned a Hollywood mansion known as the Garden of Allah, where lesbian and bisexual actresses could meet in what she called a "sewing circle." For further information, see Jennifer Horne, "Alla Nazimova," Women Film Pioneers Project.

124. The *New York Times* reviewer agreed that Nazimova's "marvelously mobile face [was] a priceless asset [. . .] capable of indicating varying shades of emotion" ("Nazimova in Film of War Brides Play," in Amberg, *The New York Times Film Reviews*, 23).

125. Only the first reel of this film survives in the New Zealand Film Archive.

o 2 o

Women Writers during the Great War, 1917–1918

The task of locating newspaper pages and columns devoted to the movies from 1917 through 1918, a period that largely overlapped with the United States' entry into the Great War, can be daunting. One may find a few names of known editors and writers in digital databases, but random word searches of "photoplays," "motion pictures," and "movies," for instance, yield limited results. Most of the women writing columns that reviewed films or took up other relevant subjects by late 1916 continued their work well into 1918: Kitty Kelly, Mae Tinée, Louella Parsons, Dorothy Day, Oma Moody Lawrence, the Film Girl. But how many more—other than Janet Flanner and Charlotte S. Kelly of the *Indianapolis Star* and Genevieve Harris of the *Chicago Post*—joined them is difficult to pin down. Although it appeared in late 1919, the "First Annual Newspaper and Theater Directory," published in *Motion Picture News*, despite the problems enumerated earlier in the general introduction, does promise access that can be more specifically targeted.

Motion Picture News organized this directory according to the alphabetical order of cities and towns that responded to its query, making no distinction between the megalopolis and the smallest rural town. To make the best use of this directory, it seems productive to rearrange the information provided by all these newspapers into the following five categories. First, many newspapers list a managing or advertising editor, the likely source of information, but make no mention of a photoplay editor, photoplay page, or review column.[1] Second, more than fifty newspapers name a photoplay editor but say nothing about photoplay pages and/or reviews. Of the five photoplay editors who definitely are women, Mary B. Leffler actually had been editing a motion picture page of news and gossip for the *Fort Worth Star-Telegram* since 1914.[2] The second woman, Virginia Dale, appears in chapter 3. The other three women are in newspapers not yet digitized.[3] Third, more than a hundred newspapers claimed they had photoplay departments or photoplay pages but did not list a photoplay editor. Here, only two women are clearly identified, and Harriette Underhill, who appears in chapter 3, held neither position at the *New York Tribune*.[4] Fourth, more than thirty newspapers named a photoplay editor responsible for a photoplay department and/or photoplay page. Of the three identifiable women editors, the most important was Charlotte S. Kelly of the *Indianapolis Star* (which is digitized and accessible), who initiated a Sunday column in September 1918.[5] Fifth, at least ten newspapers had photoplay editors yet only reported that they "conducted their "own reviews," sometimes by a staff member. None of these latter editors can be identified definitely as women. Yet there is an important caveat in deciding the gender of these editors and writers, for most have only initials rather than full first names. Given that Kelly and Underhill are listed as C. Kelly and H. Underhill, one has to wonder how many other women remain "hidden" under such initials.

The directory proves no more useful, however, in determining how many men were editing newspaper movie pages and writing reviews. At least one continued from earlier—W. K. Hollander, *Chicago News*—and another took over from "Wid" Gunning—T. Oliphant, *New York Mail*. But many of the listed names do not appear in digitized newspapers, and whether they might be found in newspapers yet to be digitized remains to be seen. Even in a digitized black newspaper like the *Chicago Defender*, a rare article on Noble Johnson's Lincoln Motion Picture Company went unsigned.[6] Could the Great War also have had an effect? Had recruitment reduced the number of men staffing newspapers, as it had in other businesses?

Despite these uncertainties, what can be said generally about the following selected columns written by women? Although the majority do review specific films, others explore an even wider range of interests. While some extend writers' concerns for what occurs "behind the scenes," whether in film production, distribution, or exhibition, a few begin to seek answers to what really appeals to fans in the moviegoing experience and to invite their participation in an ongoing dialogue about the worth of motion pictures.

Mae Tinée

This second selection of Mae Tinée's columns represents at least three threads of interest. The first calls attention to *Mothers of France*, starring the aged and ailing Sarah Bernhardt as a mother who loses her husband and only son in the war.[7] That film, released in conjunction with the US declaration of war to promote support on the home front and perhaps to encourage military recruitment, likely prompted the new French accent in Tinée's name.[8] The second thread unites her reviews praising a variety of feature films. Two related to the war might be expected: Cecil B. DeMille's *Joan the Woman*, starring Geraldine Farrar, and D. W. Griffith's *Hearts of the World*, with Lillian Gish, Robert Harron, and Dorothy Gish.[9] Others, however, offer a kind of relief from the war and single out the stars Tinée liked: Douglas Fairbanks in *Down to Earth*, Constance Talmadge in *Scandal*, Clara Kimball Young in *The House of Glass*, and Colleen Moore in *A Hoosier Romance*.[10] The third thread bundles together her persistent, scathing attacks on stars and films she disliked. Theda Bara she found "an unintentional comedienne" in *The Greatest Love*, which came across as a burlesque "jumble of improbable situations." The "poor defective" film *S.O.S.* simply provoked either a call for "HELP" or a "speedy death."[11] Missing is any reference to the influenza pandemic, except for a humorous exchange with the *Tribune*'s drama critic, Percy Hammond, who was all gloom because he could not write his usual column: "If there are no theaters there are no writings."[12]

In early 1917 Mae Tinée's fellow columnist Ring Lardner concocted a column telling friends how to pronounce her name as "May Tin-ay" (just weeks before she added the French accent) but then kept caricaturing her as "Mae Tiny," "Mae Tinney," "Ma Tin-eeeee," and "Miss Teeny-weeny," who "speaks and writes broken English."[13] More seriously, several industry figures took exception to the frequent sarcastic reviews that sometimes seemed intent on her own showy performance. Not long after Lardner's column, Sydney E. Abel, a Vitagraph branch manager, castigated one review as "narrow minded, bigoted," and counterproductive, given the company's extensive paid advertising in the *Tribune*.[14] Nearly a year later, even the Chicago Motion Picture Owners' Association protested what it described as her "frivolous treatment" of motion pictures.[15] But those claims of bigotry and protests of frivolity did not keep Mae Tinée from turning a discourteous usherette into a blackface caricature.[16] She called *The Fires of Youth* so laughable that she composed her review in the form of a comically rhymed doggerel.[17] Could columns like these have been just what readers wanted?

"Miss Farrar's 'Joan of Arc' Splendidly Done," *Chicago Tribune*, March 29, 1917, 10.

"JOAN THE WOMAN"   "Joan the Woman," like "The Birth of a Nation" before it, has the great asset of timeliness, coming as it does, when the world is full of war and rumors of war, and across the seas another girl is declaring raptly that she, like the Joan of old, "hears voices" and is the destined savior of the French people.[18]

With patriotism and feeling at high tide, a first night audience last evening paid enthusiastic tribute to the production. I venture to say, however, that the enthusiasm would have been there, backed perhaps by not quite so much fervor, had the picture appeared in times of peace, for it is a work of art and as such worthy.

While there is practically everything good to be said of the action, staging and the hundred and one matters of detail that go toward making perfect a picture as complete as this one, Geraldine Farrar is the big white light about which all the other lights revolve. There was no doubt in the mind of a learned lady near me, apparently appointed by heaven to check up on the picture regarding its adhesion to historical fact, as to whether or not Miss Farrar was the type of Joan. Joan, as she remembered reading, was "a mere slip of a girl." Well, perhaps. But to me the Joan of the picture made perfect the illusion of the Joan she portrayed. She was strength, chastity, renunciation, power, martyrdom. She had a big part to play and she merged herself in it completely, allowing no tricks or affectations to intrude. Much credit for this is no doubt due to her director, Mr. De Mille, for his finely calculating presence is apparent every minute.

Was there an Eric Trent in history who loved Joan? If so I have forgotten. At any rate there is such a person in the picture, and he is Wallace Reid. Mr. Reid has done much good acting in his life, but he has never done anything better than the role of the English officer who is saved from death by Joan, loves Joan and betrays her—still loving her. He is not afraid of his emotions. He lets them have their sway despite the fact that he is handsomer far when he is smiling, thereby placing himself in a niche all his own far and above the rank and file of so many of the handsome heroes.

Other splendid bits of work were done by Theodore Roberts as the rascal bishop, Cauchon; by Raymond Hatton as Charles VII, by Tully Marshall as L'Oiseleur, and by Lillian Leighton as the mother. Charles Clary as La Tremouille, the bad genius of Charles, was a wonder.[19]

Costumes, photography, music—all combine in making "Joan the Woman" a masterpiece.

The gentleman who, writing fretfully, declares that his principal objection to the movies is that they move, will certainly have a large sized "kick" to register as regards this Lasky's latest. It has moved beyond his comprehension and he is going to have an awful time catching up.

"'Her Greatest Love' Her Worst Film," *Chicago Tribune*, April 5, 1917, 10.

"HER GREATEST LOVE"   Daring the ire of those who always abuse me when I have naught but praise to tender Miss Theda Bara, I must say that in "Her Greatest Love" I believe I have beheld her worst picture. Not only is Miss Bara terrible—she is constantly and awfully supported by the rest of the cast, excepting Alice Gail. The latter, as the aged governess, is the only one to reflect credit on the production, which is supposed to be a drama, but can only be reviewed as burlesque.

Taking it as burlesque, I may say that as an unintentional comedienne I think Miss Bara has Charlie Chaplin backed off the boards. On second thought, maybe she is not an unintentional comedienne. Perhaps she realizes how funny she is, and is, therefore, a great artist. Perhaps that is why she let them dress her up in the short frocks of the simple little schoolgirl and put words of innocence and wonder into her heavily rouged mouth. If you ever in your life saw anything funnier than Theda Bara so garbed, rolling around her beblackened eyes in horror at the sight of her harridanlike mother lighting a cigarette, of Theda Bara staggering naively about in her first high heeled slippers, I miss my guess.

Thinking back over the picture, I can remember it only as a jumble of improbable situations, false whiskers, false women—none more palpably false heav'n knows than the masquerading Theda—and a hero reminiscent of the lavender afflicted Bushman pathetically endeavoring not to look the camera in the eye.[20] Even the subtitles carried misspelled words. Ah, well—It made me laugh!

"'The Divine Sarah' Divine Still in Tale of War and Woe," *Chicago Tribune*, April 11, 1917, 14.

"MOTHERS OF FRANCE"[21]   Since there must be, it seems, universal war to insure universal peace and the liberty we all hold dear, "Mothers of France" or, as it should be called, "Mothers of the World" comes as an incentive to sacrifice. If it is active service that is demanded let us serve with the assurance that not even death can render service futile. If by giving we can help, then let us give, gladly and with thanks that it is within our power to give. And if we can only watch and wait, why, let's do that with a high courage that cannot fail to be an inspiration. This is the message Sarah Bernhardt brings to us in the waning light of her marvelous career, at a time when the world stands greatly in need of just such a message.[22]

Mme. Bernhardt proves worthy the sobriquet of "the Divine Sarah."[23] She is noticeably feeble and the loss of her limb places her at a disadvantage. But she overcomes both weakness and lameness remarkably and acts with much of her old fire. And her pathetic, eloquent, lace draped old hands!

Much of the picture was filmed, we are told, on the actual firing lines of France, and this is easy to believe, for the trenches, landscapes and exploding bombs are very real. Mme. Bernhardt as Madame Jean Marsay, having sent her husband and beloved only son to war, where they are eventually killed, becomes a matron in the hospital at Reims, where her work with the Red Cross brings her into brutal contact with the horrors of war as they are. A thread of romance woven in the tale of sacrifice brightens it and sends you out of the theater not too sad.

It is a picture, I should say, we might all do well to see. War is upon us. However much we are against it—we have it. Let us accept it then in the same spirit as do "The Mothers of France."

[And the management of the theater should have shown better taste than to run a Mutt and Jeff comedy with its accompaniment of blatant ragtime on the same bill with so patriotic and reverent a feature.][24]

"Along Comes Constance and Proves a Riot," *Chicago Tribune*, November 6, 1917, 14.

"SCANDAL"   And now we have Constance Talmadge, Norma's little sister, starring all by herself—and making a mighty good job of it, too.[25] She is one of the most refreshing personalities that has come to the screen for a long time, a lithe, buoyant, clean limbed girl, as graceful as Mrs. Castle, charmingly gracious as to manner, suggesting always reserve force and boundless vitality. She's like a fresh, cool wind. The popular Norma will have to look to her laurels.

The picture in question was taken from a story by Cosmo Hamilton and we find Miss Talmadge as the beautiful and unconventional daughter of an old and aristocratic family.[26] She commits the indiscretion of visiting a rather notorious painter in an apartment building. When confronted by her enraged relatives, at bay, she answers thoughtlessly:

"How do you know I went there to see him? There are other people living there. As a matter of fact I had a perfect right to pay midnight visits to the man I had secretly married."

The man in question appearing on the scene, she throws herself into his arms and on his mercy, dealing out information to him in frantic whispers while her arms are about his neck.

The match which has apparently taken place is one that has been most ardently desired by relatives of both the young people. Blessings are showered upon them. They are finally affectionately left at the supposed bride's bedroom door. You can see there is much opportunity for many complications, and indeed they complicate thick and fast. The man, loving his new incumbrance, begs to be really and truly married. The incumbrance, however, is obdurate.

The story was more interesting as a story than as a picture. But at that "Scandal" is a most creditable production. Harry C. Browne as the bridegroom in name only is manly and likable.[27] The supporting cast is a good one.

And—don't forget to keep your eye on little Constance!

"The Best Picture Clara's Had in a Long, Long Time," *Chicago Tribune*, March 15, 1918, 14.

"THE HOUSE OF GLASS"
> Produced by Clara Kimball Young Corp. Directed by Emile Chautard.[28]

This is by far the best picture in which Clara Kimball Young has appeared lately—best story, best acting.[29]

The picture, taken from the play by Max Marcin, is exceedingly well directed and the types have been well chosen.[30] You know the adage that "those who live in glass houses should not throw stones"? The stone throwing is being done by Harvey Lake, husband of a beautiful wife whom he had known as Margaret Stanton, never dreaming that she was in reality a Margaret Case wanted by the police for having broken parole—though as a matter of fact she had been unjustly sentenced to prison on circumstantial evidence. In her trunk as she was preparing to leave town had been found valuable jewelry stolen from a prominent New York woman.

True Margaret had known it was there, but she had supposed it her own—gifts from her fiancé, who had informed her that the week before his father had died leaving him $100,000. A thief, but rather a decent chap at that, who had intended to reform after this "haul," go west with his bride, and start anew.

Harvey Lake, general manager of a railroad, vigorously bent on prosecuting a case against a young man, caught making light with the company books, only desists when the truth comes home to him through a detective who had long been on the trail of Margaret Case, and discovers her. Even the governor of the state has been interested in obtaining mercy for the boy.

By skillful juggling a treaty is made. The boy is freed and nobody opens the closet door on the Lake skeleton.

I was much interested in the work of Pell Trenton as the thief and hope next time he will have greater opportunity in which to demonstrate his ability. Corliss Giles as the husband, Edward Kimball as an attorney, and Norman Selby, detective, all played up beautifully.

And the large-eyed Clara gave demonstration of her sincerity.

"Griffith Shows Them How to Make a War Picture!," *Chicago Tribune*, April 25, 1918, 14.

"HEARTS OF THE WORLD"[31]   And now, after they've all had a try at the war picture, along comes D. W. Griffith and shows them how!

This long heralded production, made with the assistance of British and French governments, one-half the proceeds of which are to go to British charities, came to the Olympic last night and proved true in the main all that has been claimed for it. At any rate, the playhouse, bravely decorated with the allied colors, rocked with the enthusiastic applause of a representative audience of first nighters.

Unlike "Intolerance" and like "The Birth of a Nation," the strength of "Hearts of the World" lies in its simplicity. From out of the world of stories being lived these days in Europe the author has woven a simple little romance—the love affair of a boy and girl separated by war on the eve of their wedding day—carried them through the grilling business of battle to reunite them on that happy day when the allies overcome the Hun.

No one understands so well as Mr. Griffith the value of contrasts, nor how so effectively to present them. He carries you from sunny slopes, contemplative cows, and clucking hens to massed battlefields with their bursting bombs, ominous, slow-moving tanks, and hideous, devastating fires, back, perhaps, when the strain is becoming too great, to graceful swans swimming in a placid pool. So it is in this picture. There's plenty of emotional strain, but it is broken by exquisite scenic bits and the introduction of comedy that brings you swiftly from fears to smiles.

There is bound to be a diversity of opinion as to the acting of Lillian Gish.[32] She has peculiarities of manner and expression that to some are appealing and to others grotesque. But she certainly has her moments in the present role. It's sister Dorothy, however, who's the favorite.[33] As a strolling singer she may be described as a cute trick, and nothing breaks her spirit. Let the Hun rave—he can't prevent her making a face at him behind his back.

The soldier lover is Robert Harron, that nice boy who worked so well with Mae Marsh. He is always to be depended on. Always a gentleman, he proves this time that he can fight like a divil, too, and in some of his hand to hand encounters in the trenches he holds you breathless.

Speaking of encounters there are a lot of zipping ones. And there are so many human touches. The freckled face baby boy who hero-worships his brother, looking into his brother's face, touching with awe that brother's mustache, polishing with devoted little hands that brother's shoes; the mother whose daughter is to be taken from her the next day, with her still, hopeless face; the poilu (George Fawcett—funny old thing) taking a moment's respite from battle to sew a patch on his sock![34] These are the things that make the picture.

Of course, many of the wide area scenes with their panoramic visions of battle were staged in California. But the European battlefields themselves, guns, men, and all, were photographed for as many more. One can say of the supers that most of them were not supers at all. They were the people of the land assembled by Mr. Griffith to give to his picture the last touch of realism. The cast throughout is excellent.

The title, I think, is a weak one. The production itself is a super-picture.

There were many society folk and army officers present at the opening performance.

"Like Unto a Brown Brook or an Etching," *Chicago Tribune*, August 19, 1918, 10.

"A HOOSIER ROMANCE"   If you must have paprika and the heavy wines of excitement in your photoplay menu, I don't suppose "A Hoosier Romance" is at all what you are looking for. It hasn't any more punch than a translucent brown brook or a delicate etching. It has the cleanness of one and the exquisiteness of the other.

When they first began making pictures nobody would ever have dreamed of selecting this whimsical and delightful ode of the whimsical and delightful James Whitcomb Riley for picturization.[35] Reason, its lack of the aforementioned punch. Times have changed since then, however, and directors realize that once in a while a whiff of apple blossoms and a brief journey to the old homestead come as a blessed relief after much agonizing.

The story is, after all, none other than the old tale of a girl egged on by an avaricious guardian to wed money, who after all, rebels and marries the man she loves. Nothing extraordinary about the story, is there? But the joy of this picture lies in the beautiful scenery and the very excellent characterizations maintained throughout.

I've conceived a great liking for little Miss Colleen Moore.[36] She looks like a kitten, but has all the spunk of a small and healthy bull terrier pup. She's a human little imp and you're with her through smiles and tears.

Thomas Jefferson, one of the best of the older actors, is the "cruel guardian," a regular church member and a regular sonofagun. Frank Hayes is the walking sarcophagus, the pickled herring, who would wed the beauteous Patience. (What's in a name?) He is creaky in bone and rickety of muscle, every move and glance suggestive of embalming fluid. In the role, his delineation of the part is wonderful.

Harry McCoy as the lover is rather a silly pudding—but the lady loved him, so—?[37] An old squire and his white haired wife are admirably played by Edward Johnson and Eugenie Besserer.[38]

I enjoyed practically every moment of those five reels. But then, you know, you and I sometimes do differ so![39]

Louella O. Parsons

During this period Parsons wrote fewer and fewer film reviews and instead immersed herself in reporting studio news and interviewing stars for gossip. She confirmed that shift when the *Chicago Herald* sent her to New York to cover "the nationwide meeting of the Motion Picture Theater Owners of America" in November 1917.[40] While there she visited several studios and reported her findings in the first column selected here. In it she tells the story, with lots of partly fictional dialogue, of the day (resulting from a bet) that women took over the production of comic shorts at the Keystone studio; another (not included here) praises Herbert Brenon's directorial practice in his studio, located across the Hudson River in New Jersey.[41] Not long after William Randolph Hearst bought the *Herald*, Parsons left the paper, could not find a suitable position in Chicago, and heard that the *New York Morning Telegraph* "might be looking for a movie columnist."[42] Her initial column of "In and Out of Focus" in the *Morning Telegraph* promised that she would now compile the "choicest tid-bits of news and gossip" for her readers, "conduct a question and answer department," and only "review the special features," leaving most of the film reviewing to the paper's other staff.[43] Parsons would keep that promise, with variations, for the rest of her career.

"How Fluffy, Flighty Keystone Beauties Proved They Had Brains," *Chicago Herald*, November 18, 1917, n.p.

The Keystone studio has solved the problem of war elimination.[44] When the camera men, villains, heroes, carpenters, stage hands, directors and the rest of the masculine equipment of this studio step out of the moving picture lines to join Uncle Sam's ranks, there is not going to be the slightest show of consternation in the Keystone staff.

All because each branch of picture-making was put in charge of the Keystone beauty brigade for a day last spring, just to prove mere man is useless when and where feminine brains chose to reign. It all came about through an argument. One day, in a wagering mood, a certain Keystone comedian stated in the presence of Juanita Hansen, the blond Keystone beauty, the second draft would find the doors of the Keystone studios closed.[45]

"But why?" asked Miss Hansen. "We will still be here keeping shop at the old stand."

"Yes, but you couldn't build a set; you couldn't paint a drop; you couldn't direct a picture nor grind a camera or do any of the hundred and one things demanded of the men drawing money from the Keystone company."

"Is that so?" put in Gloria Swanson.[46] "You wait and see. I bet you a box of cigars against six pairs of gloves the girls on the lot can do anything the men can."

"You're on," he said. "When do you start proving you can do more than wear a pretty frock and do a bit of slapstick?"

"Just the minute I get permission from Mr. Sennett to put every man off the lot."

Mack Sennett wasn't easily convinced that the idea of having his Keystone beauty brigade in charge was a good one.[47] He looked dubious, but after the pleading of ten fair damsels assured him their honor was at stake he relented and said very doubtfully:

"Well, go ahead, but promise not to do any more than $2,000 damage, and, oh, for heaven sake, don't any of you get more than one arm or leg broken, and if death is to be the penalty please have it take place outside the studio gate."

So it was arranged that on a certain Friday, when the work was slack, the girls were to be put in charge and proceed to make a picture exactly as if the entire staff were at work in their own particular craft.

And discussing the situation calmly the girls each decided which niche they would occupy. Marie Prevost, because, as she said afterward, she was feeling specially humble and wanted to prove to the men she would do any kind of work when they were gone, cast herself as the janitor.[48]

A pair of dark blue overalls, a blue gingham checkered shirt and a cap didn't produce the desired effect, so Miss Prevost, who is nothing if not realistic, plastered on a black mustache, so completely transforming her pretty self she would have needed an introduction to her own mother.

Maude Wayne, who had helped grind the camera on other occasions, was put into the role of camera man, as being, so she herself announced, the best fitted for the job. Mary Thurman disputed her word, and so to avoid any argument it was then and there decided two camera men were an absolute necessity.[49]

Gloria Swanson decided she would keep her own feminine clothes and play leading lady. Director Polly Moran had another idea.[50] She said Miss Swanson looked into the camera, so the young lady was put off the floor.

But Miss Swanson is no quitter. She originated the idea of masquerading in men's attire and stayed on in the capacity of stage hand. Hurrying back to the wardrobe mistress, she was soon decked out in clothes befitting a stage hand, or, in the parlance of the moving picture world, a property man.

Peggy Pearce insisted she could do any sort of manual labor.[51] She was taken at her word and assigned to a place as carpenter. Miss Pearce became very proficient with the saw and proceeded to carve most amazing designs.

Eleanor Fields and Vera Stedman, being artistic in nature, were chosen as scene painters.[52] It matters not that they spilled more glaring red paint on themselves than on the canvas, or that a wagon supposed to be yellow came out a violent green. They stuck in the ship and went home that night as tired as two day laborers.

Edith Valk was cast as the snaky eyed villain. In a riding habit, with a Desperate Desmond high hat and a long, silky mustache, Miss Valk did a "meet me at the old mill" melodrama that has seldom been equaled on stage or screen.

So well and so glibly did she commit her villainy a special scenario was written for her in which she had to try and steal the handsome hero's bank roll.

The mortgage on the old homestead fell due and was being held up by the villain, who was determined to marry the beautiful heroine of the melodrama. Ethel Teare played the heroine, and in the dead of night crept out of her home to elope to the city with the wicked man.[53] When she returns with a plain shawl tied under her chin there is an infant in her arms, and here her suffering is so intense camera men, director, carpenter and the stage hands all stopped work to weep audibly at the scene they had woven.

Juanita Hansen, wearing the most vampish gown on the set, was appointed to play first aid to the villain. Assisting him in all his nefarious deeds, she helped him turn the heroine's father out of his humble home. In the closing scenes the police were called in, and because no one had had the foresight to produce the necessary screen greenery Marie Prevost, the janitor, had to be turned into service and arrest the erring men.

Eleanor Fields, being versatile, played the bewhiskered father, and so well she is now thinking of imitating Kathleen Clifford by putting boy roles on the screen.[54]

This day proved how little mere men actually count. The girls all started in fun, but each one of them had a feeling perhaps when the men march away their day's experience will not have been in vain.

Women are being substituted in every profession and occupation—in the hotels as bellboys, running elevators, and it does not seem at all unlikely that such a thing will come in the studios. If so, the Keystone force, believing in preparedness, will be one day ahead of all of the other film companies.

"The funny thing," said Marie Prevost after it was all over, "despite the usual pettiness of women, we really got along beautifully. Women are said to be petty and small, but I think we have proved we can rise to any great occasion and bury our jealousy for a great cause. With the world's war at stake I do not believe there is a woman in the world who would not put her shoulder to the wheel and give all the best she has in her to such a critical moment. It will be our way of doing our bit.

"And," she added, "Gloria Swanson won her bet."

"In and Out of Favor," *New York Morning Telegraph*, June 23, 1918, 5.2.4.

All the way on the train from Chicago to New York I kept thinking of the initial article I would write for The Morning Telegraph. I had in mind a lot of flowery phrases and well put words of greeting, but when I look at this stack of telegrams, letters and good wishes piled high on my desk I cannot remember a single one of the cunning sentences I coined to the music of the car wheels.

Even the brilliant ideas that soared so sky high when I decided to come to New York and be a Telegrapher have forsaken me, and as I sit looking at my shiny new typewriter I feel the warmest little glow in the region of my heart and the first thought that comes to me is:

"My! but I am glad to be here."

Those letters; I wish there wasn't so much to chat about. I should like to let all my readers—the old ones and new ones I hope to make—read them. Here is a wire from Adolph Zukor, one from David W. Griffith, Carl Laemmle, and Thomas H. Ince. Here are letters from Lewis J. Selznick, Jesse Lasky, Winfield Sheehan, Samuel Goldfish, Harry MacRae Webster, Aaron Jones, James Quirk, Julian Johnson, Tom North, Joseph Brandt, William Sherrill, John E. Flinn and many others.[55] The stars, too, have most of them sent me a line of welcome.

But being glad to be here isn't all. Now that I have washed the grime and soot from my face, and taken possession of this cosy office, I expect all of our readers to help me keep the ball of news activity rolling by sending me all their choicest tid-bits of news and gossip.

FOR THE LAITY AND THE ELECT   This department will be conducted for the laity as well as for those in the inner circles of picturedom. I have a number of letters here now from former readers—asking if we will conduct a question and answer department. We will be glad to answer any questions on moving picture subjects. Enclose a self-addressed, stamped envelope and send it to me care of The Morning Telegraph.

It will interest the exhibitors who have written and asked my opinion about various pictures during the past year to know I shall be here in New York and will review the special features. Besides this, the helpful reviews published in this paper each Sunday by the staff of reviewers in advance of the releases, will help them greatly to book their attractions.

WAR, PATRIOTISM AND PICTURES   And now about my first impressions of New York. The moving picture war work with so many big men commuting between here and Washington to be on hand to help greatly impresses me. The activities extended by the film men to help the Government is real evidence of their sincerity and patriotism. As the war progresses, and we get a firmer hand on the threat of the Hun, the ingenuity and efforts of these men aiding the Government at Washington seems to increase. Aside from the film propaganda pictures, which have illuminated the way for the unenlightened ever since President Wilson made his declaration of war, there is the continual spirit of "being on the job" personally to do whatever there is to help Uncle Sam bear his war burden.

The Associated Motion Pictures have planned to signalize the war work of the moving picture industry at a dinner given at Delmonico's on Wednesday, July 22. Such men as James Gerard, Senator J. Hamilton Lewis, George Creel, Edward Hurley, Charles Schwab and others will show their appreciation of the war work, accomplished by the industry by being present and voicing their sentiments in addresses to be given at the dinner.[56]

Dorothy Day

In September 1917 the *Des Moines Tribune* promoted Day as such "an authority on photo plays" that "her name is a household word in nearly every home in Des Moines and Iowa." Although not as large as that for Kitty Kelly the year before, this ad came shortly after what the newspaper titled an "editorial," in which Day urged everyone to see the CPI's patriotic feature, *Pershing's Crusaders*, and not only parents who anxiously watched for "a glimpse of their son."[57]

Among her reviews during these war years, two are selected here. The first begins with Day at the premiere of Griffith's equally patriotic *Hearts of the World*, joining the "hundreds of enthused, enraptured, tear-stained, shouting men and women who rose to their feet in one mass at the thrilling

Figure 3. Dorothy Day advertisement, *Des Moines Tribune*, September 12, 1917.

climax."[58] So powerful and moving was the film that she thought those who saw it should rush right out to buy "a slew of Liberty Loan bonds." The second, by contrast, follows Kitty Kelly and the Film Girl in directly addressing her readers as "girls—gurls—girruls!" and claiming that they might prefer a more ordinary player like Herbert Rawlinson to such familiar stars as William S. Hart and Douglas Fairbanks.

Another column (not included here) offers one of the earliest newspaper listings of the best films of the past year.[59] First, Day asked her readers to choose those films released in 1918 and, to help them, named the titles of those already "held up as best [. . .] by a certain publication" in 1917. A month later, she had found it impossible to compile the twelve best from the hundreds of readers' answers, so she simply listed the dozens that Des Moines fans "have liked especially well." She did report, however, that everyone chose *Hearts of the World* and that Nazimova, Fairbanks, Norma Talmadge, and Elsie Ferguson were favored stars—unlike Hart and, surprisingly, Mary Pickford.[60]

"News of the Movies," *Des Moines Tribune*, January 8, 1918, 5.

Oh, girls—gurls—girruls!

If you are a bit bored with Hart and his gun play, a bit tired of Doug and his smile, hie yourselves to the Royal tonight and take a look at Herbert Rawlinson.[61]

Rawlinson is anything but a newcomer to the screen, but Des Moines has seen him but comparatively few times, and for the majority of picture patrons he is a spic and span, new idol.

He's in "Come Through," another up and coming melodrama full of surprises galore. You think you know what's coming, maybe, but it never happens the way you have it doped out—and the result is you are always on the edge of the seat with wide eyes waiting for the outcome of this new wrinkle.

Rawlinson is not introduced until almost the third reel. He plays the part of a clever gentleman crook. A splendid cast has been chosen for support.

I'm not saying a word about the story except that it is a corker. The production is fine, and there's Herb to get acquainted with.

"Thrills of a Lifetime in Screen Picture," *Des Moines Tribune*, September 17, 1918, 5.

I have seen D. W. Griffith's screen triumph, "Hearts of the World." I never knew the deep thrill of being an American until I saw the sturdy, smiling faced boys of the S.A. swinging past the window of a little French restaurant, coming to the aid of torn and bleeding France and Belgium.

The hundreds of enthused, enraptured, tear-stained, shouting men and women who rose to their feet in one mass at the thrilling climax of "Hearts of the World" at the Rialto last night were not the same expectant, tired-of-the-war men and women who entered the Rialto at 8 o'clock.

LEARN OF WAR'S HORRORS   The people who saw the Des Moines premiere of "Hearts of the World" have lived and learned of the horrors and the sorrows, the joys and the happiness of this war. Through the wonderful power of a man and a little black box on a tripod, the curtain has been torn away and France, bleeding, suffering, but grimly smiling and cheerily carrying on, has been revealed.

Through this indescribable magic of the screen, the joyousness, the brightness and the peacefulness of that never-to-be-forgotten summer before the war is for a time brought back. A little group of delightfully human people of a small village in France are brought to our attention and we come to know them and love them—to weep with them, to smile with them.

Then comes the war with its heart wrenching parties and its tears masked in smiles. Our friends of the village are mangled and bruised under the iron heels of militarism. Through the hideous tortures, the blood-congealing scenes, the mind-unbalancing experiences of the millions of French and Belgian people, we weep and stare and sob our way.

You say, right here, "I know too much of this frightful war already. I don't want to see any more of it." Yes, you live in your comfortable home, with clothes and food and your loved ones about you. You, perhaps, kneel every night and thank God that you have been spared the horror of war. But you don't know what it is to be thankful. Not until you have lived through the poignant bliss of smiling with Marie and the Little Disturber and the littlest brother do you know how to be thankful.

FRIGHTFUL SCENES   Not until you have seen Marie's grandfather lying before you, his head and shoulders—only—staring up at you; not until you have seen the boy pull his fainting companion to his feet and kiss him back to courage; not until you have seen millions of men fighting; not until you have seen the bursting of scores of shells, the attack of dozens of clumsy tanks, the gallop of hundreds of cavalrymen; not until you have seen the wreck of once happy homes; not until then, do you know how to be thankful.

After you have seen "Hearts of the World"—for you must see it, if seeing it means going without a square meal for three days—you will feel faint—you won't know what you feel. You will come out of the Rialto and look up and down Locust street with its shining lights, its hurrying people, its peaceful every day life—and you will want to drop upon your knees, right there, with all the people about you, and sob out your thanks that you are an American.

DESIRE TO CRUSH HUN   You will want to rush to the nearest Liberty loan booth and buy until your last penny is gone and then contract for more. You will want to work your fingers to the bone to do—do—do to bring this Hun and his hordes to their knees.

You don't realize there is a war until you have seen "Hearts of the World." You think you do, but you don't. The cast? Oh, you never think of the cast in the unfolding of this magnificent cinema creation.

Kitty Kelly

A few months after leaving the *Chicago Tribune*, Kitty Kelly and her daily "Flickerings from Filmland" column resurfaced, sometimes again on the Society page, in the *Chicago Examiner*.[62] For a year or so, she stuck to reviewing new films, but by mid-May 1918, after Hearst merged the *Examiner* with the *Herald*, she also was editing a page titled "The Screen" in the new Sunday edition, which had the largest circulation in the city. The *Herald and Examiner* is not digitized beyond April 1918, so it is difficult to research Kelly's work beyond that date, but quotes from her reviews in *Tribune* ads indicate that one could still find her column at least through April 1919.[63]

Whether Kelly continued writing regularly in Chicago newspapers on the movies or other subjects is unclear. The *Tribune* did print a photo of her displaying the official city flag in 1921, and at least two columns devoted to the Goodfellows' Christmas gifts to needy families appeared under her name in 1924 and 1925.[64] Chase later served as the *Tribune*'s financial and then real estate editor; once he retired, they moved to Willow Brook farm near Glen Ellyn, Illinois. There she wrote a column reminiscing about her childhood when she "lived in a small Iowa town."[65] In 1956, either before or shortly after Chase died, perhaps as a tribute to her longtime love of American wildlife, Alspaugh bequeathed their forty-three-acre farm to the Du Page county forest preserve, which converted the tract into a wild animal refuge.[66] When she herself died in November 1965, she had been living with friends northwest of San Antonio, Texas. In a brief obituary, the *Pittsburgh Press* referred to her as "the nation's first movie critic . . . under the pen name of 'Kitty Kelly.'"[67]

Kelly's columns included here include reviews that reveal that her skill as a wordsmith had not faded. One review praises, with minor reservations, *A Weaver of Dreams*; its director, John Collins; its lead actress, Viola Dana; and the story and atmosphere, so "delicately done that it is gossamer-like in its gracefulness." Another describes a matinee program at Orchestra Hall, where Kelly seemed spellbound by Maurice Tourneur's *The Bluebird*, a magical fairy tale whose "delicacy and charm" she found even better than Maeterlinck's play. Two other columns introduce something new in her repertoire. One appeals directly to movie fans by inviting them to submit short reviews on the film she has chosen for the week; each of the winning reviews would be printed in the weekly "Lay Critics' Corner" and the writers paid a dollar.[68] The other column interviews the manager of a small movie theater on South Halsted in Chicago and makes him an example of how a "progressive" exhibitor can make a success of it in "a 5-cent neighborhood."

"Flickerings from Filmland," *Chicago Examiner*, February 16, 1918, 6.

"WEAVER OF DREAMS" Here's one of the rare and lovely pictures that give a brace to tottering filmdom—tipping from portraying horrors and sensations—and revives the feeling that the celluloid is a medium for fine story telling.[69]

And it makes John Collins stand out as an inspired director, one who works creatively, with his elements, and builds as originally as he does beautifully.[70]

Also it demonstrates that so far as he is concerned, Metro doesn't need an art director. The lovely rooms of the houses in this photoplay are so graciously soothing to the vase-worn and statue-rumpled spirit that it actually rests one to observe them. There could be no happier dream come true than to do one's abiding in any of the three.

The tale itself, as Myrtle Reeders know, is a-brim with sentiment, but so sweetly, delicately done that it is gossamer-like in its gracefulness.[71]

The picture, with its lavender and old lace atmosphere, must satisfy Myrtle Reed's spirit.

Viola Dana, as the Judith who sacrifices everything but her memories, is an enchanting little person in her pretty playfulness and her restrained grief.[72] When her exquisite throat quivers, the tears sting into the see-er's heart, if they don't seep through the lashes.

He was a foolish lover, one cannot help thinking, for all the little other girl is sweet, and it seems as if he must weary of his peach parfait, but "The End" flashes before he does. Margorie Gordon, who plays the other girl, is an excellent screen subject and does very well with her girlish role. And Miss Dana and Mr. Collins give her opportunities without grudging, which is a nice thing to see.

The older players, Clarissa Selwyn, who does Miss Bancroft, and Russell Simpson, who does Martin Chandler, do splendid gracious work, and beside them there is the collie, irresistable, realistic.

Two things ring false about the picture—one, the vast affectionateness of the two girls, when they scarcely know each other; two, Judith's suggestion that her fiancé give away his dog.

Nobody who knows a collie's love is going to suggest his giving away, for a collie is a regular member of the family. Maybe all of Judith's woes arose because she didn't sense this fact. One must be as tender of one's dog as of one's brother.

Except for that, "A Weaver of Dreams" is a lovely, poignant picture, handled in a poetically beautiful way.

"Flickerings from Filmland," *Chicago Herald and Examiner*, May 6, 1918, 5.6.

"THE BLUEBIRD"[73]   To-day is like going back to the old days, for Orchestra Hall's cool auditorium again invites one in to a carefully presented picture program. It is a rather special affair to-day with a matinee performance this afternoon at 2:30 and an evening showing at 8:15, with invited celebrities and all that.

To read the program of anticipated pleasure makes one want to put on one's hat immediately and set forth for the vicinity of Adams and Michigan.

Arthur Duncan will be back with his baton, and to-day he leads off with the overture to "Oberon," giving as prelude to the photoplay itself the "Danse des Sylphes." A glimpse of far fields is offered in a Burton Holmes travelogue, which takes the seer into Atlin, the Switzerland of British Columbia.[74]

A few minutes are given over to the news of the day, gleaned from animated weeklies and the Paramount Pictograph, and then we will dip into one of the loveliest stretches of celluloid ever camera-captured.[75]

"THE BLUEBIRD"   In translating Maeterlinck's fanciful, inspiring story to the celluloid, Director Tourneur, instead of losing values, has emphasized them.[76]

His artist sense extracted the quintessence of the poetry from the print, and cloaking it in concrete tangibility retained its delicacy and charm. Even of more poetic appeal than the play is the appreciative interpretation of it, for in the half realm of things that are and that aren't, there is no medium of expression superior to the camera's.[77]

By clever tricks it brings the fairies out of the nothingness, spirits out of such commonesses as bread and sugar and fire, beauty out of ugliness.

So in "The Bluebird," as Hytyl and Tytyl roam through wondrous places seeking the elusive bird of happiness, there is a constant succession of the most magic that any folks, grown-up or small, could imagine.

One cannot help going away from the photoplay refreshed in spirit, transformed in perspective. It shows there are so many things in life so very essential to which we have given such small care.

Eventually it is a fairy tale for the youngsters, and just as essentially it is delicate preachment for the grown-ups, and on every turn it is entertaining, for along with the beauty and the imaginativeness of it goes a simple humanity and a dash of comedy that relieves it from the stickiness of perfection.

There will be music with the picture, of course, and during the baby scene a hidden chorus will give the Song of the Mothers.

Other days there will be full orchestral performances at 2, 7:30, and 9:30, and at 12, 4, and 6 organ accompaniments with Mildred Fitzpatrick presiding. On Sundays during May there will be only matinee performances.

"The Bluebird" is something good, not to be missed. As a picture of inspiration, a piece of entertainment, a remarkable illustration of camera mechanics, a stretch of captured beauty—from some angle it must cast its spell over the seer.

"Be Your Own Critic," *Chicago Herald and Examiner*, May 26, 1918, 5.6.

Here is the Something New predicted last Sunday.

It's a "Lay Critics' Corner," and you can be in it if you want to go to a little trouble.

Everybody who sees a photoplay thinks about it afterward—at least we all should hope everybody does. Photoplay reviewers do it as a matter of their job, though unfortunately sometimes they have too little time to think before they must put their think into type. And seers in general do it, though sometimes they never get their thoughts expressed to their friends even.

But we all ought to think and think out loud, for the future of the motion picture is in the hands, not of the producer, or the exhibitor, or the professional writer, but of the public, and if the public wants certain kinds of pictures it is up to it to say so. The best way is by the concrete process of saying what it thinks about certain pictures that are already made—what it likes and what it dislikes.

With the coming of Summer the town is full of big, pretentious photoplays which have cost a lot of money and effort to produce. Does the public like them or are they just thrust down its throat?

This is where we get to the "Lay Critics' Corner."[78]

Let's everybody concentrate on one photoplay this week, see it, think about it and write about it.

Send your letters in and we'll print some of them right here in this corner of the paper, for each one published paying a dollar, which will cover the wear and tear on the ink, stationery and postal department. If not on your gray matter, and pay your way to some other show for recreation.

The letters must be brief because space is—write 200 words or less and address them to Kitty Kelly, Chicago Herald and Examiner.

Oh, yes. There's the picture. Let's make it "Over the Top" beginning at the Auditorium to-day.[79]

Come on into the corner—and do it early in the week too. Your letters must be in by Thursday noon.

"The 'Very Best' Is Mr. Healy's Motto," *Chicago Herald and Examiner*, July 28, 1918, 5.6.

But in the heart of South Halsted where there is no lake front and where electric fans are some luxury Mr. R. A. Healy of Texas conducts the Monogram Theater. This is at No. 3520. Healy belongs to the progressive party of motion picture exhibitors.

To the right, to the left and all around him there are 5-cent houses with their lurid lobby display and their cheap pictures.

"That's the way the Monogram was run when I took it over," said Healy, "and the first thing I did was to put in the best pictures I could buy and raise the price to 10 and 15 cents. People laughed at me and said it couldn't be done, but like the story of the [man] who couldn't be put in jail it is done. I have succeeded. I run the highest priced Paramount pictures—Bill Hart, Mary Pickford, Douglas Fairbanks and all of them just as soon as I can get them from the loop.

"One of the first things I did was to put in a $5,000 organ and for that, too, I was put down as an extravagant idiot. I have 432 seats and play to capacity almost every afternoon and night."

To-day the Monogram is showing the great official war film "Pershing's Crusaders" and in addition to that the first episode of Vitagraph's thrilling picture, "A Fight for Millions," with William Duncan.[80] That is just a sample of what Mr. Healy is offering in what was considered a 5-cent neighborhood. More power to him and to men like him.

Janet Flanner

Janet Flanner (1892–1978) is best known as the American expat journalist who, from 1925 on, contributed a popular "Letter from Paris," signed "Genet," to the *New Yorker*. Born in Indianapolis, she attended the University of Chicago for two years and in June 1918 began writing a weekly column for the *Indianapolis Star*, "Comments on the Screen," which appeared on page 1 of its Sunday section devoted to the theater and photoplay. Later that year she married an artist friend living in New York and left her hometown. The marriage did not last long, and Flanner became involved in a lifelong relationship with Solita Solano, the *New York Tribune*'s drama editor, and joined the writers and artists who were part of the Algonquin Round Table. They included the *New Yorker*'s Harold Ross, who gave her the assignment in Paris.[81]

Flanner's "Comments on the Screen" column ran for only two months, from early June to early August 1918, and already evidenced her talent as a stylist.[82] Her initial columns echoed the earlier attitude of the Film Girl in claiming that she much preferred a variety program of short films.[83] She cited not only "Roxy" Rothapfel's experiment in programming at the New York Rialto (it proved unsuccessful) but also the pleasure of seeing Fairbanks in "a gem of a concise story" rather than in "7,000 feet of dragged out, too-heated Mexican brigandage." That sarcasm is on display in her tongue-in-cheek "celebration" of film melodrama, especially in westerns, with their omnipresent dance halls and bars—where Hart "is the hardest drinker on the screen." The irony is even richer in her informative satire on film music cue sheets, specifically in her over-the-top account of an overtly "illustrative" cue sheet for *Her One Mistake* (1918).

"Comments on the Screen," *Indianapolis Sunday Star*, June 30, 1918, 6.1.

S. L. Rothapfel, of the Rivoli and Rialto Theaters in New York city, is trying out at the Rivoli.[84] He is including no cinema in his program, substituting instead various one or two-reel incident pieces, whose bulk, added together, makes up in time—or should—the requisite number of minutes of entertainment for the spectator.

He mildly replied, it would appear, when interviewed, that he thought he was doing nothing radical in making this change. He said he could see no reason why there should be any set length to a feature and that he even strongly suspected that many features, if they had footage according to the volume of a real story inherent in them, would be reduced materially. They are too long. He also says that what is ordinarily referred to as the feature of a cinema program often fails to be the feature at all. Today, he continues, he finds that the most important portion of his program are such portions of the news weeklies that contain the latest visualizations of the war news. He knows there is not in the market enough small stuff to make up his programs of short-length subjects, but thinks that in the event of the success of his experiment at the Rivoli there may be a general tendency to return to the production of shorter-length dramas. These, he believes, are sadly needed.

It would be hard to admit that a solid program of mere war features would hold the interest of the patron who had entered a motion picture house firmly resolved to be amused. If war scenes were what he wanted, assuredly war scenes would satisfy, nor would there be any lack of opportunity today to see belligerent films; the trenches are being photographed everywhere from France to California, where several studios keep trenches already made in case anything needing an "on the battlefields of the Marne" ending turns up in the week's work. But the information about the great fight, as patriotic as we are, would not satisfy if it were all one got, no matter where one turned. It is likely war incidents are small, but poignant features for Mr. Rothapfel. They can not take the place of emotional relaxation to be got from viewing a pictured story of love and adventure, however.

One must pause and salute with appreciation and gratitude the two-reel comedies made by those talented and genuine artists, Mr. and Mrs. Sidney Drew. Their films are sketches of psychology and domesticity, enchanting and thoroughly satisfying the discriminating spectator and amusing the less critical by their humorous appeal. In their particular line they are pioneers. William Parsons, one time insurance agent in this city, is now making two-reel comedies, using his large and smiling face and his ability to be attracted to pretty girls as his capital.[85] His comedies, like those of the Drews, are short affairs. They are in fact, the short stories of film life.

America, on the whole, is a nation devoted to short stories. In the absence of statistics and in order to make the point perfectly clear, we will say that some fifty different short story magazines are maintained and consumed by the reading public constantly. We like the variety in menu we get from such periodicals. We like a tale of Honolulu concerning emeralds, we relish a yarn about whale fishing when sandwiched in between a charming and satisfying plot devoted to the ultimate emotional and national victory of a young second lieutenant some place in love over there. Why should we not like short picture stories on the screen? It is only in accord with our national tastes that we should.

It is rumored certain stars are bound in contracts which specify six-reel features only. It is rumored that the precinct exhibitor buys by the basketful rather than by quality, preferring in his purchase lots of spools of celluloid of one subject, much advertised, than several on different subjects. Pickford and Fairbanks are as good a guarantee, so, at least some exhibitors appear to believe. The small exhibitor who is, after all, the ultimate consumer for the feature, has wanted something customary that he could be sure of as an investment. Six and seven reels were accordingly in demand. Now conditions are changing. The short reel subject is coming into its own.

Who would not rather see Douglas Fairbanks in a gem of a concise story, where room was not afforded him to make fun of the plot through the medium of his own exuberance, than to see 7,000 feet of dragged out, too-heated Mexican brigandage? Who would not rather see, on the same program, Mary Pickford in a short and delightful love story, where her ability to be, as is claimed, "America's sweetheart," satisfies even the young and scoffing, than Mary Pickford in a flat, thin tale spun to six reels, regardless of value?

We probably would have more short-reel pictures if the producing studios were not so involved with contracts hastily entered into as to prevent a change of policy. The Packard manufacturers would not adjust their factory to the making of Fords. No more can the leading producing companies adjust their factories to the making of one, two and three-reel pictures. That is, not quickly. One or two firms have tried to do so. Here, locally, however, the better plan prevails no doubt in the establishing of the Capital Company for the specific purpose of producing only the short subjects.[86] It will produce these, and none of more than three reels. This shows "how the wind blows."

Let us confess that, very often, the long feature bores us nowadays and that the short pictures catch and hold our interest.

"Comments on the Screen," *Indianapolis Sunday Star*, July 14, 1918, 5.33.

How much most of us owe to the cinema melodrama! What would we know of kidnapping the heroine on a fleet-footed horse, for instance, if it were not for the motion picture "Western!" What would we know of that flip use of two guns at once—the last word in ambidextrous efficiency—if it were not for W. S. Hart, Tom Mix and other kind of men who have apparently made it their life work to see that fast riding and hard drinking never die?[87] In our home life we know naught of brigandage, holdups, kidnappings, even for love, and the like. We have been kept completely ignorant of the pleasant use of firearms when shot from both hips owing, likely, to our parents' timorous dispositions and the fact that our neighbors' houses and yards set close to the right and left of us as we go down the cement walk.

Three meals a day, an honest clerkship, and an occasional "see-America-first" trip are about all we know from actual experience. But we have learned enough from the Western cinema to feel that, emotionally, we have lived a rich life indeed.

Most thankful of all are we for the Western cinema bar.

In this day of limited taste, with sarsaparilla and a chocolate soda the extreme outer edges of the government's answer to our thirst, the barroom scene assumes a new responsibility as an entertainer. It has always been a rich field. The chief brigand and his coteries of friends, on whom we Easterners—to a Californian all things are East, even Indians—have turned rapt eyes at least once a week ever since we were old enough to go to the precinct motion picture house alone, have swaggered up before its wooden counter 100,000 times, surely, and for our entertainment rapped for whiskey straight. After drinking down theirs cold they have turned—this they never fail to do—and rested the elbows away from the camera on the bar's edge while they handled the plot. Then they, meaning the hero and his confrere, would stride away from the bar and the hero's mind would be made up. It was always made up when he left the bar with a long, swinging stride.

Of course, if he wobbled pitifully on leaving the counter, the barroom scene became a little sadder and not so invigorating, for one realized that it indicated the heroine was going to be forced into taking some temperance and reform steps before the end of the sixth reel. The way a hero acted before the bar indicated fairly enough what responsibilities were cut out for him in the play. If he drank recklessly, he was a bad man—see W. S. Hart for details—and would please you for 689 feet with bad-man carryings-on of heart. If he drank, steely-eyed and quiet, he was going to be desperate, maybe, but always just in his shooting. He would look out for the poor and innocent and disdain, even at the last moment, perhaps, actually to kill the villain. The steely-eyed drinker was self-controlled. He took his pleasure sparsely.

The "supers" in a "Western" could drink at the bar any way they pleased, just as they did not thump the wooden counter. They might stick their feet up but thumping was reserved for the leading man.

Cinema bars come in two sorts. There are close-ups and what is called long-shots. The close-ups show the glittering glasses and accompanying bartender's cheery face. The long-shots show the backs of the drinkers and produce atmosphere rather than indicate action. They have nothing to do with the plot, but are a customary courtesy.

William Hart, of course, is the hardest drinker on the screen. If the public ever becomes completely in sympathy with the white ribbon movement poor Mr. Hart will have a tight squeeze to earn his living. William Farnum is an occasional taster, but a tendency always to be an older and long-suffering brother, whose younger kin has the privilege of doing all the riotous living, has restricted him in his habits.[88] He appeals to a different class of people in consequence—those who enjoy a steady pillar of virtue, which advances day and night without an interesting falter.

Fairbanks does not drink at bars in the pictures at all any more. He has got to be a healthy ideal of late and has stinted his fullest powers of self-expression. Back in the early days, though, when he did not need to be so cautious, he was known, in a small way, as being quite comic at certain times.

There is nothing in history like the Western cinema dance-hall scenes. How unfortunate history was written before motion pictures were invented. They could have helped color it so. How they could have improved upon every chapter devoted to the growth of our glorious country between the Pacific and the Mississippi. How they could have livened up some of the duller pages, unillustrated, that we wade through in the sixth grade. The gold rush of '49 has never done so well as it has in the cinemas. Art has improved upon nature. If another gold rush could only be instituted, certainly half the citizens of the country could be relied upon to do the thing up handsomely this time, and be got ready for a drive across the states and life in the dance halls of the West that would show they had not been asleep at the cinemas or looked upon good advice in vain.

In many ways, the "Western" is a picturization of the country's suppressed desires. It is what the best of America would be if it lived up to its reputation. It is what many of us like to think it is. Being entirely concerned as a rule with the reckless doings of men, it appeals to women and small boys inordinately. It is what a brave life of freedom would be if we only had a good stage manager.

A healthy tradition will go out when the "Western" fails to appeal. A slice of our history out of which we have built a veritable culture will topple at our heels. Surely this will never take place though; at least not so long as the producers keep the tradition going. They have shown us our country as it never was and we can not get along without the vision now.

"Comments on the Screen," *Indianapolis Sunday Star*, July 21, 1918, 5.33.

A strong paternal feeling exists in the heart of the filmmaker for his children, the exhibitors. Almost tenderly he supplies them with their little needs. Each cinema goes to the exhibitor with an accompaniment of press sheets and music cue papers which tell the cinema displayer all he need ever know.[89] The press sheet informs him as to the plot so that he may be relieved of the necessity of seeing his own pictures; a brief perusal of this paper, his feet on the desk, and he is familiar with the most delicate of the play's situations. The music cues tell him how suitably to chaperone the cinema with dulcet and appropriate sounds.

While the screen drama is silent, we all know the theater in which it is given is not. Music fills the air as he or she, on the sheet, quarrel and make up, go out into the cold storm with their children or hunt for the papers in the safe. This last, especially if the hunter is in a hurry and is using an electric flash to see his way around the dining room, would require from the orchestra or lonely pianola player, the use of what it, in professional musical parlance, called an "agit." This is brief for agitate—music of a hasty and exciting caliber.

Besides "agits"—though they are the most popular and nearest capable, each time they are played, of making the shivers go down the spines of the paid spectators—other well-known varieties of music are mentioned on the orchestral sheet. In order that the exhibitor's way may be made as smooth for him as glass, these various types of music are employed and indicated by the filmmaker and tacked onto the sub-titles in a printed schedule of the play sent out regularly to the prospective displayer. This cue-sheet, as it is called, is a marvel of conventionality. It is also a potent indicator of the melodramatic merits of the play. If it has many "andante dramaticos" or "allegro appassionatas," the exhibitor can get ready to hang out the s.r.o. sign and look for a full house. The music follows the play as meekly as Mary was ever followed by her lamb; where the plot goes, it goes; its people are the plot's people and naught shall come between them.

Illustration makes everything clear. The cue-sheet given out with "Her One Mistake," a cinema where, one supposes by the title, though titles are misleading now-a-days, as we find out, the heroine comes supplied with a past, is a delightful case in point.[90] The naked plot of the play stands out to the reader after peeking at its cue-sheet as plainly as though he had written the scenario or helped direct the show. No imagination is needed to become fully acquainted with the meaning of the play. Like high-lights, the music cues with their associating subtitles, plucked from the film show up everything. To proceed:

Reel 1: At screening, advice is given to play an allegro vivace, 2-4. This cinema begins brightly; light stimulating music leads up to whatever may follow. "At Silver Beach," the second cue, demands and gets, let us hope, a lente, 6-8; the use of a flute here would be pretty; doubtless a moonlight scene, made at a California studio anytime between 10:00 a.m. and 4:00 p.m. before the actors go home from work, is utilized at this juncture and the first stage tradition for romance steps into the play. Then the heroine says: "I'm awfully tired, mother." Apparently, things are going badly for her; she's young; we suspect a villain. She gets an andantino con espressione, 4-8; a girl's best friend is her mother.[91]

Reel 2: "Enter Mr. Scully." Ah! He comes! The kingly male! He comes as he does it, accompanied by Andantino con espressione, but with 9-8, the highest fractional average any one has received so far. On this second appearance we become more intimate with him; the Mr. is dropped. "When Scully Enters Rooms," Andantino Appassionato 4-4 is played. Appassionato! We are thrilled! Is he villain or hero? Both become passionate at times. Just when we are all agog to sound his identity and grow intimate with his moral values, delay is introduced into the film to whet our appetite by suspense—another old trick. "Five Years Later"—Andante 2-4, we are informed. How quiet and introspective this music must be; what ravages time can make. Then "When Charlie Plays the Piano" we are to hear "Mother o' Mine." We are "on" to Charlies; the films are full of him. He is part of every play. He sits in a disreputable boarding house and idly strums the battered keys of an old Chickering cornered in a dirty living room. He sentimentally thinks of his gray-haired mother as he plays—the music tells you so—and the spectator weeps.

"The Bulls Have Found Us," the next title, puts us all off the scent. Is this a Mexican play or one of the underworld? We don't know where we stand. When young, we thought bulls were animals; familiarity with cinemas entitles us now to the knowledge that bulls may also be the O'Learies and Reillies called, during Robert Peel's unpopular administration, "peelers." "Won't You Let Me Say Good-by?" is answered by "I'm Coming Tonight." Both get Andantes. Then "When Miss Gordon Enters Charlie's Rooms"—we fear Charlie has forgotten his gray-haired mother at this crisis in his life—Andante Dramatico sets the pulses going. "At Struggle" Allegro 4-4. This is a fifty-fifty affair. We grip our chairs.

Allegro! How suitable that it should be followed by Il Penseroso. Life is sunshine and shadow. "And then—Half an Hour Later"—the dashes are not our own—we know the worst. "Adagio Cantabile, Segue Into Dramatico Andante." Cantabile means singingly. Perhaps, on second thought, it was not so bad as we feared when we first got excited. Maybe Charlie had honorable intentions, after all, with Miss Gordon, and has made the girl superlatively happy. Singingly—life is not so bad. We get hopeful; if the cantabile on the cue-sheet had been replaced by a patetico we might still have grounds for our opening suspicions, but this play has a happy ending; we can see it from here. Cantabile told the tale.

A valse triste, ¾ a dram. Tension, 9-8—this must be Mr. Scully again; that was his batting average—and a moderato, 4-4, finish reel 5. An even balance prevails at the last moment of the cinema, from which we infer a promise of marriage is received and carefully retained. A little excitement precedes its coming—dram. Tension—and a little sentimentality comes before that. A valse triste is a very moving strain of music. All get ready for the final embrace. Five hundred feet more and it comes twenty feet long.

What would we do without music? We would be bereft of one of our greatest sensory advisors. "Her One Mistake," melodically speaking, is a successful one. In her second and third she could do no better, we are assured. Miss Gordon must rest content. Once is often enough for any one—but a cinema star.

Genevieve Harris

Genevieve Harris was rather unique among these women writers. In early 1916 she became a film reviewer for *Motography* (published in Chicago), a position she held until July 1918, just before the trade journal merged with *Exhibitors Herald*.[92] Although several men also served as reviewers (e.g., Thomas C. Kennedy and George W. Graves), Harris was the most constant, regular writer. Her weekly reviews covered not only features but also serial episodes and short comedies, westerns, and others. She also conducted a few interviews with stars such as Fairbanks and Pickford, and her last columns were notable for unusual interviews with local theater managers.[93] This experience and her knowledge of the industry proved invaluable when in August 1918 she took over reviewing films in the *Chicago Post* from Oma Moody Lawrence and began editing the weekly "Photoplay News and Comment" page in early November. She likely was no more than twenty-five at the time, according to her obituary, which still described her as a "motion picture and dramatic critic for the old *Chicago Evening Post*."⁹⁴

In an early column, Harris reviewed Selig's *A Hoosier Romance*, based on the poem by James Whitcombe Riley, and wondered why the industry didn't produce more simple stories of farm life. She had particular praise for the director, Colin Campbell, who came up with his own poetic effects that caught the poem's spirit, and for Colleen Moore in one of her first starring roles. A month later, she warmly applauded the "intelligent patriotism" of the second CPI feature, *America's Answer*.⁹⁵ In a third column, Harris took readers on a surprising tour of the new Famous Players–Lasky rental exchange in the city, and the one department she highlighted was where many young women inspected and repaired film prints.⁹⁶ However, she said nothing about the intense efforts to unionize exchange workers, and particularly all those film inspectors.⁹⁷ Finally, she reported on a luncheon where Rothapfel and Goldfish jointly spoke to exhibitors and writers. Based on their speeches, Harris asked what moviegoers found most important: "the artistic presentation" of a theater's program (Rothapfel) or "the picture itself" (Goldfish). Implicitly siding with the latter, she urged movie fans to encourage more and more "good pictures."

"Riley Poem Is Basis for a Fine Picture," *Chicago Post*, August 22, 1918, n.p.

"A HOOSIER ROMANCE"   There are many of us who wonder occasionally why producers who complain of the dearth of good screen subjects do not turn their attention to farm life, not ranch or plantation dramas, but real farm stories. Surely, the background and the characters are picturesque enough. Why couldn't they be woven into attractive picture plays? "A Hoosier Romance" proves beyond a doubt that they are excellent material when a director with vision manipulates them.⁹⁸

Colin Campbell is a remarkable director in several respects, but his dominant characteristic seems to be a peculiar facility for catching an author's idea, for seeing thru the words to the spirit behind.⁹⁹ He showed this in the filming of the Rex Beach stories, "The Spoilers" and "The Ne'er Do Well," and in "The Crisis" and "The Garden of Allah."¹⁰⁰ The writer remembers seeing several years ago a three-reel version of the poem, "The Dream of Eugene Aram," which Mr. Campbell directed, and noting then his power of translating poetic effects into pictures.

Here again he has a poem as the basis of his picture. The subtitles are all taken from the poem and the story follows Riley's. But there must be something more than the externals. The atmosphere, the feeling must be true to the original, and in that the director has succeeded admirably. Here is a photoplay as real, as human as a Riley poem.

Among the players, Colleen Moore and Thomas Jefferson, as daughter and father, run away with the honors, although the entire cast is good. Edward Jobson and Eugenie Besserer as the kind-hearted squire and his wife are just as you would want them. Harry McCoy looks and acts the part of the real lover very well. Perhaps, if you wish to be very critical you will say that Frank Hayes as the widower overdraws the role, but he is surely funny. Then there is a sympathetic white pony which deserves mention. If Colleen Moore continues to do as good work in succeeding pictures, she will wake up some morning very soon to find herself in the first ranks of popularity.

The interior settings are well arranged and the exteriors are among the most beautiful ever filmed, especially those taken in the blossoming orchard. The costumes of the characters give a quaint touch to the picture. There isn't much plot in the picture, but there is a world of pathos, humor and truth.

The story can be told in a few words. It tells of the love between a farmer's daughter and the hired "hand." The girl is motherless and her father is surly and avaricious. He breaks up the romance as soon as he discovers it and insists that his daughter marry a rich widower more than twice her age. He crushes her spirit and she consents. But the young lover returns on the day of the wedding and, with the aid of the squire and his wife, kidnaps his sweetheart and marries her.

And the telling of this simple story makes so enjoyable a picture that we can only say to Mr. Campbell and Colonel Selig, "More, please."

"A Visit to a Film Exchange," *Chicago Post*, October 26, 1918, 4.

The average picture patron is keenly interested in the activities of the studios and has usually a fairly accurate knowledge of the work therein. He is interested in many phases of the management of his favorite theater. But of the link between studio and theater, that great circuit of film exchanges which employs an army of workers and which puts much of the "industry" in the "fifth American industry," as the motion picture world calls itself, he knows almost nothing.

And yet more of his enjoyment than he guesses is due to the faithful work of the film exchange. The fact that the exhibitor may announce weeks beforehand the date of a feature's showing, the advertisements and photographs he posts, the cleanliness of the film, its freedom from breaks and mis-frames, all these things depend on the work of the film exchange.

The local Famous Players–Lasky exchange illustrates well the importance of this connecting link.[101] It was recently moved into new quarters at Eighth Street and Virginia Avenue, so recently that the paint on the [?] walls isn't dry and all the departments haven't as yet arranged their belongings on their respective floors.

Thru this organization all Famous Player–Lasky pictures, from East or West coast studios, must pass before they are shown at any theaters in the Chicago territory. The booking offices arrange contracts and dates of the showings at many theaters in Chicago and the near-by towns which show Paramount-Artcraft features.[102] The studios ship to the exchange here as many prints of each picture as it needs to fulfill its contracts. The exchange must take care of these, see that each theater gets the right picture on the right date, and examine the prints as they come back to see that each is in good condition.

There are five-reel dramas, two or three a week besides the specials, the two-reel comedies of various series, the travelogs, the animated cartoons and the magazine-on-the-screen features, not to mention the reissued favorites. Not only must the pictures themselves be taken care of, but the advertising accessories which go with each, posters, photographs, slides, booklets, and so on.

The exchange occupies six floors and among its departments are those devoted to publicity, to the booking of the features and the renovating of the films. Many thousands of feet of film, wound in lengths usually of a thousand feet upon metal spools, are stored in its vaults. Film, as you know, is celluloid and highly inflammable. The vaults are therefore fireproof and equipped with automatic sprinklers.

An interesting department in which many girls are employed is that of the inspection and renovating of film. The celluloid strips are run from one spool to another and the keen-eyed inspectors note any defects in the tiny pictures which would be glaringly evident magnified on the screen.

After a certain number of showings, the film must be given a chemical bath to remove the grime and grease which it has accumulated in the projection machines.

The exchange has a comfortable little theater of its own where all Paramount-Artcraft pictures have their real premiere Chicago showing before the managers, salesmen and sometimes exhibitors and newspaper critics.

In short, the exchanges are an efficient branch of an important industry; their work made interesting not so much by the glamour which surrounds things theatrical to the average person, but by that uncertain quality—the public taste. A new star on their program is fascinating to them, not entirely because of her fetching eyes, tho there are real "uns" among the employees, but because they are curious to know how she will "get across," how she will appeal to you and to me, the great public which pays the bills.

"Two Views on Film Problems," *Chicago Post*, December 7, 1918, 9.

S. L. Rothapfel is known in the film industry as the most artistic exhibitor of picture plays. He was the first man to dignify pictures by surrounding their presentation with beauty of color and fitting music. He is at present the director of the Rialto and Rivoli theaters in New York city, and his methods are an inspiration to other exhibitors who wish to make the showing of motion pictures an art as well as a business.

Samuel Goldfish was a pioneer in the producing of the better class of motion pictures.[103] He began his connection with the industry in the foundation of the Lasky company, where he was associated with Jesse L. Lasky and Adolph Zukor. He is now the president of the Goldwyn Pictures corporation, of which he was one of the founders.[104]

Mr. Rothapfel and Mr. Goldfish are very good friends. They are traveling together to the Goldwyn studios on the West coast. On Thursday, while in Chicago, they were guests at a luncheon and on that occasion each addressed the group of exhibitors and writers there to greet them.

The views of these good friends are almost diametrically opposite on motion picture questions, and as each expressed himself frankly and forcefully, their speeches were most interesting. Both, however, are working toward the same goal, that of making the picture play a better, more worth-while entertainment than it now is. Each is tremendously sincere, but Mr. Rothapfel believes that the artistic presentation is the most important element, Mr. Goldfish, that the picture itself is the thing. So, you see, it is a friendly rivalry, which works out for the good of pictures, anyway.

But I wonder, dear picture patrons, what you would have thought could you have listened to these clever men set forth their ideals. They are giving their talents, and are investing their money in pictures with the aim of giving you something worth while. They are as sincere as any artists in any other line. The exhibitor told how he worked to please his public. The producer told of the missionary work in the early days in persuading famous artists to play in pictures and great writers to turn their attention to photoplays, of the developing of untrained players into real stars, of the fight to make clean pictures as profitable as sensational films.

Whether the exhibitor or the producer leads in the progress of the film industry does not much concern you and me. But we have our part to play, although Mr. Goldfish and Mr. Rothapfel placed no responsibility upon our shoulders. Let us place it there ourselves, and let it be the responsibility of encouraging good pictures, if a company goes out of its way to engage a great artist, to picturize a fine story, to photograph wonderful scenes, pay it the tribute of appreciation. Tell your friends about it and send them to see it, if the director of your theater provides beautiful music for the picture, selects clean photoplays, gives added attractions and courteous service, thank him for it. Tell him when you like a picture. Discourage the coarse and vulgar by appreciating the finer pictures.

There have been too many societies for the "uplift" of the screen as well as the stage. But if we would each individually take upon ourselves the simple, courteous little obligation of appreciating what producers and exhibitors may do for us, we would quickly reap our reward in having better, stronger stories presented in more artistic fashion. Try boosting the good instead of knocking the bad, and show Mr. Producer Goldfish and Mr. Exhibitor Rothapfel that we Mr. and Mrs. Picture Patron are doing our share to help the cause of good pictures.

Charlotte S. Kelly

Several unsigned columns of "Comments on the Screen" followed Janet Flanner's departure from the *Indianapolis Star* in early August 1918. A month later, Charlotte Kelly began signing the weekly Sunday column, and soon her column was appearing irregularly during the week.[105] Whether Kelly had a newspaper position prior to this is unclear.

Kelly's columns were not as flashy as Flanner's, but she exhibited a clear, sometimes rather formal, lightly ironic style. Initially, she rarely reviewed a specific film; instead, she revealed a range of interests. In one column, Kelly looked wide-eyed at all the different subjects she found in the cinema, from scientific microscopic images and war scenes to historical films and current political and social scandals. In a second column, however, she oddly contrasted the "old days" of a recent past (just three or four years earlier) with the current cacophony of advertising and confusing expectations of what roles a star might play. Another column (not included here) got more specific about how the "knockout type of advertising" had become such a source of laughter for moviegoers.[106] A third column, while highlighting how objects like cigars and cigarettes shown in close-up could serve to typify the initial sense of a character, implicitly revealed that moviegoers had grown quite familiar with such clichés.

"Comments on the Screen," *Indianapolis Sunday Star*, September 22, 1918, 13.

When the glowing tip of a lighted cigar appears on the blackness of the screen the experienced "movie fan" quickly assumes an attitude of watchful waiting. He feels quite sure that he is about to gain a view of a certain type of man whose manner of smoking or not smoking the cigar will give him an insight into the plot.

Perhaps it is the bulky outline of a politician that is revealed, seated in his swivel chair, his cigar tilted at an aggressive angle, while a crowd of cringing ward heelers hang upon the words he utters between puffs. We know instantly that some mischief is afoot. It may be that the hero is going to be "sent up" on a "framed" charge, or, more thrilling still, the rascal may be instructing his henchmen to abduct the heroine for purposes better not spelled out. The smoker is not always the master of the situation, however. Sometimes his cigar remains unlighted, and from the vicious way in which he chews it we are convinced that the hero is now victorious and the villain is foiled.

If the point of a light expands to show, not a cigar, but a cigarette, slanting jauntily from between the lips of a debonair youth, there is no doubt but that we see before us the hero. In the case of the cigar, we can gauge with some accuracy the state of mind of the player and the stage to which the plot has advanced. How much more difficult it is to judge of the hero's thoughts may be seen from the fact that he smokes almost constantly. For some unknown reason he is apt to be not so discriminating as the villain. On second thought, however, we must not blame him too much for this. Any one will surely admit that the villain has all the best of it, for the cigarette does not lend itself either to surly mouthing or animated chewing.

Then, too, no one shares the villain's prerogatives unless, perhaps, a burly detective finds it necessary to disguise himself, while the ubiquitous cigarette may be seen in the hands of almost any one, from a precocious infant to the luxuriously clad "vampire," seated in her sumptuous boudoir, calmly blowing rings while she waits for her next victim. Even the comedian finds it useful. He strikes the match on his face or hand to show how "rough" he is, lights his mustache or burns his nose before he manages to light his cigarette, and then concludes by putting the hot end in his mouth. The Westerner, too, uses it, but never in ready-made form. He always "rolls his own," and if he is sufficiently expert, he need not rope a cow or brand a horse to prove his genuineness. When we see him rolling a cigarette with one hand while the other is gently stroking some one's wavy locks—it may be the heroine or it may be his pony—we know him for a real, dyed-in-the-wool Western actor.[107]

We have heard that tobacco may be purchased in other forms, but the screen takes no cognizance of them. Who has ever seen the gay millionaire smoking a pipe? Perhaps occasionally we see him attired in slippers and bathrobe, lolling at ease in a chaise lounge. He is caressing a beautifully colored meerschaum. But that rich color was surely imparted by the smoke off screen, of his hard-working man. The cigar and cigarette have the field to themselves.

"Comments on the Screen," *Indianapolis Sunday Star*, November 3, 1918, 13.

Many and wonderful are the things brought to light by the cinema. A persistent picture goer can claim to have seen life in the diversified scenes thrown on the silver screen. What would our dainty, timid grandmothers have thought if they, as girls, had been permitted to witness in any shape the sometimes appalling sights mirrored in the moving picture theater for any eye to see, be they innocent or sophisticated, curious or indifferent? The cinema conscientiously searches out everything and impartially presents its finds for the inspection of a grateful world.

Nothing is too distant for it to bring across seas and continents to a crossroads village. Nothing is too sacred to picture in a scientific presentment of most intimate details. No historical event is too ancient for reproducing with much attention to facts. No divorcee has a reputation too shady to prevent her being starred.[108] The tiny and myriad life of submarine regions is picturized as accurately as the aerial maneuvers of a wide-winged plane, soaring above the battle fields in Europe. Everything from the home life of the Seminole Indians to the latest political or social scandal is utilized as material for the photoplay.

Conditions were not always thus. In the early days we could go to a moving picture theater with some assurance of seeing the sort of picture which the title implied. In those times of current event reels, which, in the space of fifteen minutes show us a regiment of American troops entraining for some sailing point, a Red Cross parade, the mayor at work in his war garden, a group of aeroplanes deploying for flight, the most up-to-date method of preserving fruits, and any number of other activities we can not prophesy with any degree of certainty what we may see.[109]

When the photoplay industry was younger—we admit it is still quite young—we saw advertised a picture with some such thrilling title as "The

Race of Death," and when we viewed the picture itself, we found it true to its name.[110] A real race, usually involving a train, was staged in order that the picture might not belie its title. Now, with advertising in its glory and regiments of adjectives attacking us in full force from every billboard and magazine, we are, as a rule, somewhat uncertain what kind of scenes will be presented for our edification.

In the old days the name of the star was associated with a type of picture. If Pearl White was the name blazing over the door of our favorite theater, we knew that a stirring tale of adventure was being depicted within. Nowadays a star who has built up a reputation in light society dramas is as likely as not shown in any role but the expected one. She may be a crook, a siren, a gun-woman, a school girl or a Belgian refugee. It has been reported with some authority that William S. Hart is to be seen in his next picture in evening clothes.[111] Although it strains the faculties to give credence to such rumors, we must make the effort, for an open mind and a facile imagination are acquired by practice, and to judge from the weird and incongruous concoctions shown recently, nothing less than the most flexible of imaginations will be capable of appreciating the newer attractions.

"Comments on the Screen," *Indianapolis Sunday Star*, November 24, 1918, 6.1, 3.

In an industry as big as the motion picture business, there are apt to be many phases, incidental to the main issue, that are nevertheless of considerable interest to the public. The photoplays themselves are presumably the most entertaining feature of the business, but a number of other factors incidental to making pictures are sometimes almost as interesting and often more amusing.

First of all, there is the star, whose clothes are a fascinating topic of conversation for all the ladies, from admiring grandmother down to wise school girl, who can tell you just what effect a certain gown is intended to give. The star's hair dressing is copied, her style of walking, talking, and dancing imitated, her taste in husbands discussed and all her private affairs, if they can be ascertained, talked over with a great deal of concern.

Men who act for the screen come in for a share of discussion, too, but on the whole one does not hear such a variety of comment on them. It is usually summed up in a sentence or two. "Isn't he the best looking thing!" or "Wouldn't you just love to be his leading woman?" seems, when accompanied by appropriate gestures, to convey worlds of meaning, and then the conversation turns to subjects that lend themselves better to articulate expression.

The energetic men who prepare the advertisements for the various producers and, in fact, all the men connected with the advertising of moving pictures, have for some time been providing the public with notices, that, in their power to amuse, surpass many of the cinemas to which they are supposed to call attention. This feature of the industry has recently developed to disproportionate dimensions, due, of course, to the tremendous competition between companies. An attempt has been made to curtail advertising since the government has taken its strong stand for conservation, but the absurdities that still persist are numerous.

One company has issued a novelty to be used for the exploitation of one of its madcap stars, who will soon appear in a new photoplay. It consists of a tape measure, one side of which is marked with the regulation indication of inches, halves, and so forth. The other side bears the query, "Are you a perfect 36?" referring to the title of the coming picture.[112] These tape measures are to be distributed by boys throughout the city and will probably give rise to as much laughter as the comedy to which they are related.

The general run of newspaper, magazine, and bill board advertising of motion pictures is so overburdened with superlatives that it is ridiculous instead of convincing. Sketching through the current numbers of two or three magazines concerned with the industry we find pictures characterized as stupendous, surpassing, as having ten times the grip of an average photoplay, as possessing the greatest publicity and exploitation possibilities of any picture ever produced, as being the greatest drawing card of the day. No doubt, there is some film that answers one of these descriptions, but they can not all be super de luxe productions. It is a physical impossibility.

People like to laugh, and many of the moving picture advertisements offer too good an incentive to mirth to resist. Government regulation has to some extent curtailed the knockout type of advertising, and we can only hope that the laughter provoking qualities of the advertisements can in some way be transferred to the comedies produced by the respective companies.

Notes

1. At this point, none of the fifteen names of women are searchable because their newspapers are not digitized.

2. For more information on Leffler, see Abel, *Menus for Movieland*, 102, 152–53, 190–91.

3. Those three women are Miss Sursa of the *Evansville (IN) Courier*, May Cameron of the *Evansville (IN) Press*, and Miss Kimble of the *Fort Worth (TX) Record*.

4. See Ishbel Ross, *Ladies of the Press: The Story of Women in Journalism by an Insider* (New York: Harper & Brothers, 1936), 412–13.

5. The other women are Mary Ley of the *Akron (OH) Times* and Grace Murphy of the *Lawrence (MA) Eagle-Tribune*.

6. "Film Co. a Success," *Chicago Defender*, February 3, 1917, 7. Even earlier, Charlotta Bass promoted the Lincoln Motion Picture Company in "Talk of the Town," *California Eagle*, July 1, 1916, and "Opening of the New Angelus a Notable Success," *California Eagle*, July 8, 1916, cited in Everett, *Returning the Gaze*, 117. For more information on the Lincoln Film Company, see Barbara Tepa Lupack, *Richard E. Norman and Race Filmmaking* (Bloomington: Indiana University Press, 2014), 18–22.

7. See also Mae Tinée, "Merle La Voy Shows 'Allies in Action,'" *Chicago Tribune*, March 20, 1917, 14.

8. At least one brief review in Washington, DC, was explicit: the film "is expected to prove a potent factor in the gaining of recruits" ("Crandall's," *Washington Star*, May 6, 1917, 2.2).

9. By contrast, see Percy Hammond's review of the film, "damning with faint praise," in "News and Comment of the Theater," *Chicago Sunday Tribune*, April 28, 1918, 7.1. Particularly unkind to Lillian Gish, he also mocked the response of many to Dorothy Gish: "Ain't she cute!"

10. On *Down to Earth*, see Mae Tinée, "O Boy, This Is Good for What Ails You," *Chicago Tribune*, August 20, 1918, 16.

11. Mae Tinée, "S.O.S., S.O.S., . . .—; . . .—S.O.S., S.O.S.," *Chicago Tribune*, June 6, 1917, 16.

12. Mae Tinée, "Gobs of Gloom: Mae Tinee and Percy Hammond," *Chicago Tribune*, October 17, 1918, 10.

13. Ring W. Lardner, "In the Wake of the News," *Chicago Tribune*, March 30, 1917, 16. Ringgold Wilmer "Ring" Lardner (1885–1933) became famous as a sports columnist for a number of newspapers, particularly the *Tribune*, and as a short story writer, but he also wrote plays, skits, and songs.

14. Sydney E. Abel, "Maybe Mae Tinee Doesn't Read the Ads," *Chicago Tribune*, April 26, 1917, 6.

15. "Latest News of Chicago," *Motography*, February 16, 1918, 328.

16. Mae Tinée, "Courtesy Lost Art in Some of Our Movie Theaters," *Chicago Tribune*, February 16, 1918, 10. This appeal for proper etiquette contrasts sharply with that of the Film Girl and Oma Moody Lawrence.

17. Mae Tinée, "It Wasn't Raised to Be a Comedy—but, Alas—it Is!," *Chicago Tribune*, October 14, 1918, 10. See also her gratitude that *Tarzan of the Apes* ended with *The Romance of Tarzan*, in "Being Final Chronicles of a Monkey Man," *Chicago Tribune*, October 3, 1918, 10.

18. *Joan, the Woman* is readily available for purchase online.

19. Raymond Hatton (1887–1971) played secondary roles in a hundred films in the 1910s and 1920s and continued to appear in films and television into the 1960s. A successful stage actor, Tully Marshall (1864–1943) entered the movies in 1914 and performed as a popular character actor in hundreds of films through the early 1940s. Lillian Leighton (1874–1956) was another successful character actor in hundreds of

films from the 1910s through the 1930s. Charles Clary (1873–1931) was a successful character actor from the 1910s through the 1920s.

20. Could this be innuendo suggesting a gay appreciation for Bushman, a former body builder and male model? See chapter 1, note 116.

21. Under the title *Mères françaises*, *Mothers of France* survives in a 35mm print at the Cinémathèque française (Paris).

22. Celebrated as "the queen of pose and the princess of gesture" by the 1870s, Sarah Bernhardt (1844–1923) made numerous world tours before starring in *Camille* and *Queen Elizabeth* (both 1912). Despite having one leg amputated in 1915, she performed for French soldiers during the war and appeared in this film and another in 1916. Indefatigable, she continued to act in the theater but collapsed and died of uremia in March 1923. For an excellent analysis of *Mothers of France* and its historical context, see Victoria Duckett, *Seeing Sarah Bernhardt: Performance and Silent Film* (Urbana: University of Illinois Press, 2015), 163–86.

23. The *New York Times* reviewer added: "She typifies to America the joy, the warmth, the strength, the capacity to drink to the full of life that is France" ("Sarah Bernhardt in Real War Film," in Amberg, *The New York Times Film Reviews*, 27). A year earlier, in his weekly theater column, drama critic Burns Mantle had written a snotty, elitist review of *Jeanne Doré*, in which Bernhardt had to perform in a way he found "pathetic" ("Another Bachelor Romance Presented on New York Stage," *Chicago Sunday Tribune*, January 16, 1916, 8.2).

24. The theater was the downtown Rose, and DeMille's *Joan the Woman*, starring Geraldine Farrar, was playing simultaneously at the nearby Colonial ("Motion Picture Directory," *Chicago Sunday Tribune*, April 8, 1917, 7.5).

25. After acting in short films for Vitagraph, beginning in 1914, Constance Talmadge (1898–1973) played the Mountain Girl in *Intolerance*. From *Scandal* on, she became increasingly popular as a comic actress and established her own studio in 1919. Initially a model for illustrated song slides, Norma Talmadge (1894-1957) began acting at Vitagraph and, by 1913, was a popular actress. Leaving Vitagraph, she eventually contracted with Triangle to star in features written by Anita Loos and directed by John Emerson. In 1916, she married the producer Joseph Schenck; a year later they formed the Norma Talmadge Film company. Appearing in dozens of films, including *The Branded Woman* (1921) and *Smilin' Through* (1922), she and her sister Constance were voted the most popular movie stars of the early 1920s. By the decade's end, her popularity was waning, and she retired in the early 1930s. Schenck, whom she had divorced in 1934, however, had helped her amass a huge fortune.

26. A British playwright, novelist, and short story writer, Cosmo Hamilton (1870–1942) probably was best known for his London and New York stage productions. But he also composed more than twenty film scenarios.

27. A skilled banjo player, Harry C. Browne (1878–1954) was more known for a 1916 phonograph recording of a racist coon song than for acting in a series of movies in the 1910s and 1920s.

28. A successful stage actor in Paris, Émile Chautard (1864–1934) became Éclair's head of film production in 1913, immigrated to New York in early 1915 and acted in

and directed features for World Film (1915-18) and Famous Players–Lasky (1919-24). He continued acting in such films as *Seventh Heaven* (1927), *Upstream* (1927), and *Blonde Venus* (1932).

29. After performing onstage with her parents, Clara Kimball Young (1890-1960) joined Vitagraph in 1909, becoming one of its most popular stars in nearly one hundred short films. From 1914 to 1916 she acted in Selznick and World Film features; in 1916 she formed her own studio in partnership with Harry Garson, but mismanagement caused her career to suffer by the early 1920s. One of her striking attributes was her lovely big eyes.

30. A Polish American playwright and short story writer, Max Marcin (1879-1948) composed nearly a dozen scenarios, beginning in 1919.

31. *Hearts of the World* is readily available for purchase online.

32. Another stage ingenue, Lillian Gish (1893-1993) joined Biograph in 1912 and quickly became one of Griffith's favorite players. Before *The Birth of a Nation*, she appeared in *The Musketeers of Pig Alley* (1912), *The Mothering Heart* (1913), and *Home, Sweet Home* (1914). After the Civil War blockbuster, she starred in major Griffith films, from *True Heart Susie* (1919) to *Orphans of the Storm* (1921). Her unusually long career included stage performances, sound films, and television and radio appearances.

33. Dorothy Gish (1898-1968) joined Biograph with her sister in 1912, came into her own as a comic actress in *Hearts of the World*, and starred in comedies such as *Peppy Polly* (1919). She too enjoyed a long, if less luminous, career onstage and in films and television. Initially a salesgirl in Los Angeles, Mae Marsh (1894-1968) began acting in small parts at Biograph. By 1912, Griffith was giving her major roles, which culminated in the innocent Southern sister who dies in *Birth of a Nation* (1915) and the wife whose baby is taken from her in *Intolerance* (1916). Although she continued playing fewer and few leading roles thereafter, she became an important character actor from the 1930s through the 1950s.

34. After a long stage career with his own stock company, George Fawcett (1860-1939) took on character roles in more than a hundred films from 1915 through the early 1930s.

35. A best-selling writer from Indianapolis, James Whitcomb Riley (1849-1916) often wrote in dialect, as in "Little Orphant Annie," and was known as the "Hoosier Poet" or "Children's Poet."

36. After first acting in Triangle films, Colleen Moore (1899-1988) found early fame in this film and *Little Orphant Annie* (1918). For several years she worked on features for Fox, Famous Players–Lasky, and Marshall Neilan and popularized the Dutchboy bobbed haircut.

37. Harry McCoy (1889-1937) performed in more than a hundred films between 1912 and 1935, often as a comic character actor.

38. A former stage actress, Eugenie Besserer (1868-1934) worked in the movies from the early 1910s through the early 1930s, often playing mother roles, as in *The Jazz Singer* (1927).

39. W. K. Hollander's review of the film only differs from Mae Tinée's by not being so unkind to Harry McCoy ("Motion Picture News," *Chicago News*, August 23, 1918, 12).

40. Samantha Barbas, *The First Lady of Hollywood: A Biography of Louella Parsons* (Berkeley: University of California Press, 2005), 57.

41. Louella O. Parsons, "Seen on the Screen," *Chicago Herald*, November 20, 1917, 6.

42. Barbas, *The First Lady*, 58–60.

43. The "theater and turf" *New York Morning Telegraph* had a Sunday section devoted to "motion pictures and photoplays" by January 1910. Expanding to four or five pages in 1912, that section soon was sold as a separate eight-page supplement. Its importance had lessened by 1918, but Parsons's extensive industry contacts led to lengthy reports on industry news, interviews with studio heads, and celebrity "personality sketches" (ibid., 63–65).

44. Founded in 1912, Keystone was the most popular and influential producer of comedies under Mack Sennett. From 1915 to 1917 it joined Triangle, after which Sennett used the New York studio to direct features, often starring Mabel Normand, while others produced short comedies.

45. Juanita Hansen (1895–1961) was a Sennett "Bathing Beauty" who performed in comic shorts. After leaving Keystone, she starred in serials from *The Brass Bullet* (1918) to *The Yellow Arm* (1921). Like Normand she suffered from a drug addiction and later established a foundation to raise awareness of the dangers of drugs.

46. Gloria Swanson (1899–1983) first found popularity paired with Bobby Vernon in Keystone comedies such as *Teddy at the Throttle* (1917). In 1919 she become a major Paramount star in Cecil B. DeMille's *Don't Change Your Husband* and *Male and Female*.

47. Canadian-born Mack Sennett (1880–1960) joined Biograph in 1908, eventually directing the company's comic shorts. He founded Keystone in 1912, directed many of its comic shorts, and from 1914 on became the studio's production manager in charge of a dozen or more major stars, from Arbuckle and Chaplin to Swanson.

48. Canadian-born Marie Prevost (1896–1937) also was a "Bathing Beauty," appearing in dozens of Keystone comic shorts and later starring in Lubitsch's *The Marriage Circle* (1924).

49. Born of Danish parents in Utah, Mary Thurman (1895–1925) was a teacher before joining Keystone as a "Bathing Beauty." She achieved some fame in Allan Dwan's *A Broken Doll* (1921) and died young of pneumonia.

50. After a successful vaudeville career, Polly Moran (1883–1952) joined Keystone as a "Bathing Beauty" and developed into a brash, knock-about comedienne.

51. Beginning in 1914, Peggy Pearce (1894–1975) acted in Keystone comic shorts and then a few features through 1920.

52. Beginning in 1915, Vera Stedman (1900–1966) acted in a series of Keystone comic shorts as a "Bathing Beauty." She had a long career in minor roles through the 1930s.

53. Beginning in 1914, Ethel Teare (1894–1959) appeared in many Keystone comic shorts and then worked at Kalem in the late 1910s.

54. A vaudeville comedienne, often performing as a male impersonator, Kathleen Clifford (1887–1962) turned to film in 1917 and played opposite Fairbanks in *When the Clouds Roll By* (1919).

55. This name-dropping list of important industry figures and their congratulatory letters is a good example of Parsons's practice of self-promotion.

56. James W. Gerard was the US ambassador to Germany from October 1913 to February 1917. His book *My Four Years in Germany* (1917) was the basis for a documentary feature film in 1918. J. Hamilton Lewis served as a US senator from Illinois (1913–19, 1931–39). An ally of President Wilson, he received knighthoods from Belgium and Greece for wartime activities. After being involved in President Wilson's reelection campaign, George Creel was appointed chairman of the new Committee on Public Information (CPI), a propaganda agency that produced and distributed scores of patriotic shorts and nonfiction feature films between 1917 and 1919. Many later influential figures in public relations trained under Creel. Edward N. Hurley was an Irish American businessman and friend of Thomas Edison, Henry Ford, and Harvey Firestone. Charles M. Schwab became the first president of U.S. Steel but soon left, in 1903, to head Bethlehem Shipbuilding and Steel, the world's largest steel-producing firm. In April 1918 he became responsible for all major shipbuilding in the United States. Here Parsons implies that she will be joining these high-level government officials and businessmen at this celebratory industry dinner.

57. "Dorothy Day Sees a Picture and Writes an Editorial," *Des Moines Tribune*, July 11, 1919, 4.

58. Aldura Haynes, a young staff writer for the *Des Moines Capital* (which is not digitized), is quoted as reviewing *Hearts of the World* in a Rialto ad that appeared in the *Des Moines Tribune*, September 18, 1918, 9. After graduating from the University of Iowa, she reportedly worked for the *Capital* from April 1918 until her marriage in June 1919.

59. Dorothy Day, "The Great Plays of 1918," *Des Moines Tribune*, January 2, 1918, 4. Only a year later did the *New York Times*, for instance, publish such a "best films" list ("The Year's Best," in Amberg, *The New York Times Film Reviews*, 65).

60. Dorothy Day, "News of the Movies," *Des Moines Tribune*, February 1, 1919, 2. Born in Canada, Mary Pickford (1892–1979) had a short acting career in touring stage productions. In 1909, Griffith hired her at Biograph and soon gave her leading roles. After a short period at IMP, she returned to Biograph and became a star in a series of shorts, including *The New York Hat* (1912). Following a successful brief return to Broadway, she joined Famous-Players to star in numerous feature films that soon made "the girl with the golden curls" the most popular actress in the world. An astute businesswoman, she became the first to sign a million-dollar contract and formed her own production company. In 1919, along with Griffith, Chaplin, and Fairbanks (whom she married in 1920), she established United Artists and continued to produce and perform as a popular star in movies throughout the 1920s. She retired in 1933, acted in several stage and radio plays, and kept producing films into the late 1940s.

61. Long a successful stage actor, William S. Hart (1864–1946) played leading roles in *The Virginian*, *The Barrier*, and *The Trail of the Lonesome Pine*. In 1914 he signed with Ince to bring his "westerner" figure to the screen, directing and starring in a

series of mostly two-reel westerns. So popular did Hart become in features such as *The Aryan* and *Hell's Hinges* (both 1916) that in 1917 Paramount-Artcraft offered him a lucrative contract for a series of westerns from *The Narrow Trail* (1917) to *The Toll Gate* (1920). In 1918 a popularity poll in *Motion Picture Magazine* put Hart among the top four movie stars in Hollywood. British-born Herbert Rawlinson (1885–1953) was a relatively important movie star by the late 1910s and acted steadily in films well into the 1940s. Most of his silent films are considered lost.

62. In 1914 the *Chicago Examiner* had 240,000 subscribers, the fourth highest in the city.

63. Recently I discovered that the University of Illinois Library holds microfilm of the *Chicago Herald and Examiner* from May 1918 into 1932, so some other researcher should read what Kelly wrote about the movies during the year(s) following May 1918. See Randolph Theatre ad, *Chicago Tribune*, January 1, 1919, 22; and Ascher's Chateau ad, *Chicago Tribune*, April 15, 1919, 18. In May the *Herald and Examiner* reviewer quoted was simply named the Observer (Illinois Theater ad, *Chicago Sunday Tribune*, May 11, 1919, 7.8).

64. "Chicago's Flag," *Chicago Tribune*, September 20, 1921, 3; Kitty Kelly, "Where It Hits the Spot," *Chicago Tribune*, December 25, 1924, 4; and "Kids Like Toys Best," *Chicago Tribune*, December 24, 1925, 4.

65. Audrie Alspaugh Chase, "In Memoryland," *Chicago Tribune*, March 16, 1961, 16.

66. "Audrie Chase, Once Tribune Writer, Dies," *Chicago Tribune*, November 21, 1965, 1B.16.

67. "Obituaries," *Pittsburgh Press*, November 22, 1965, 53.

68. For more information on early newspaper movie contests, see Jessica Leonora Whitehead, "Local Newspaper Movie Contests and the Creation of the First Movie Fans," *Transformative Works and Cultures* 22 (2016), https://journal.transformativeworks.org.

69. While praising Viola Dana, especially in the final scene, W. K. Hollander focuses on details of the melodramatic plot: the train wreck that brings together her rival with her fiancé and a misunderstanding about a pair of silk stockings ("You Just Can't Help Being Sorry for Her," *Chicago News*, February 18, 1918, n.p.).

70. John H. Collins (1889–1918) became a major director at Edison, beginning in 1914, and even more so at Metro until he died prematurely in the influenza epidemic. Recently, several of his surviving films were shown at the Giornate del cinema muto in Pordenone, Italy.

71. Myrtle Reed (1874–1911) was a popular novelist best known for *Lavender and Old Lace* (1902), adapted into a very successful play and later a Frank Capra film.

72. Viola Dana (1897–1987) first achieved success onstage playing the leading role in *Poor Little Rich Girl*. She joined Edison, married director Collins, and starred in films like *The Cossack Whip* (1916). Following Collins to Metro, she became a real star in *Blue Jeans* (1917). After Collins's death, Dana continued with Metro into the 1920s, but her popularity slowly waned.

73. This film is readily available for purchase online.

74. In 1893 E. Burton Holmes (1870–1958) became a professional travel lecturer who, much like Lyman H. Howe, performed for social and cultural elites in prestigious venues across the country. By 1916 Paramount had begun distributing his travelogues as a weekly program release, which continued well into the 1920s. Holmes himself kept touring as a travel lecturer.

75. In 1916 Paramount began distributing the Bray Studios' *Pictograph*, a screen magazine that included an animated cartoon. In August 1919 Goldwyn took over the *Pictograph*'s distribution.

76. The Belgian writer Maurice Maeterlinck (1862–1949) was best known for symbolist dramas from *Pelléas and Mélisande* (1892) to *The Blue Bird* (1908). In 1911 he was awarded the Nobel Prize in Literature. In 1919 Goldwyn hired him to write scenarios, but none were produced. A French illustrator and graphic designer, Maurice Tourneur (1876–1961) joined Éclair as a filmmaker in 1912 and then moved to the United States in 1914 to direct a series of critically praised feature films, from *The Wishing Ring* (1914), *Alias Jimmy Valentine* (1915), and *Trilby* (1915) to *A Poor Little Rich Girl* (1917) and *The Bluebird*. After his pictorialism went out of style in the mid-1920s, he resumed his filmmaking career in France in the 1930s and 1940s.

77. Unlike the *New York Times* reviewer, Kelly thinks that Tourneur's film has even more "poetic appeal" than Maeterlinck's play and that its magic works wonders for children ("'The Blue Bird' a Hit on the Screen," in Amberg, *The New York Times Film Reviews*, 33–34).

78. Several months later, Harold Hefferman introduced a similar film review contest in Detroit ("You Are to Decide Merit of Photoplay," *Detroit Sunday News*, September 22, 1918, 5.1).

79. One of several feature films promoting the US role in the Great War, *Over the Top* (1918) was based on Arthur Empey's book of the same title, which sold more than a quarter of a million copies, and Empey (1883–1963) played the hero. In 1917–18 he toured the country in support of the US entry into the Great War and then set up his own production company to write and direct feature films throughout the 1920s.

80. Scottish-born William Duncan (1879–1961) started as an actor for Selig and Vitagraph and was known for leading roles in serials like *A Fight for Millions* (1918), some of which he wrote and directed.

81. Harold Ross (1892–1951) was a young reporter before enlisting in the US Army, where he edited *Stars and Stripes*. With his wife, Jane Grant, in 1925 he cofounded the *New Yorker* and became an original member of the Algonquin Round Table.

82. Flanner also twice contributed a column on successful local artists, for example, "Impressions in the Field of Art," *Indianapolis Sunday Star*, June 9, 1918, 6.5.

83. Janet Flanner, "Comments on the Screen," *Indianapolis Sunday Star*, June 9, 1918, 6.1.

84. Born in Germany, Samuel Lionel "Roxy" Rothapfel (1882–1936) started his show business career in 1908 by managing the Family Theater in Forest City, Pennsylvania. Soon he took over movie theaters in Minneapolis and Milwaukee for the Saxe brothers. In 1913 he moved to New York City to manage the Regent and then the Strand, Rialto,

and Rivoli. By 1918 he had become famous for his lavish stage prologues introducing feature films, much imitated in palace cinemas across the country.

85. William Parsons was president of the National Film Corporation and starred as Smiling Billy in a series of Capitol Comedies released by Goldwyn.

86. Capital Film did advertise its "two reel specials" in *Motion Picture News* in January 1919.

87. Once he became known as a national riding and roping champion, from 1909 to 1917 Tom Mix (1880–1940) acted in, wrote, and directed many Selig westerns, initially two-reelers and then feature films, beginning with *In the Days of the Thundering Herd* (1914). In 1917 Mix contracted with Fox Film, and features like *Western Blood* (1918) and *Treat 'Em Rough* (1919) made him a rival to William S. Hart.

88. A successful stage actor, along with his brother Dustin, William Farnum (1876–1953) first starred in *The Spoilers* (1914). For half a dozen years he was a popular star in Fox Film features, from *A Soldier's Oath* (1915) to *Riders of the Purple Sage* (1918). He continued to act in the movies into the early 1950s.

89. Flanner's use of *cinema* to refer to a film or film print is unexpected but perhaps not unusual in such a satirical piece.

90. Fox Film's *Her One Mistake* (1918) was directed by Edward J. Le Saint and starred Gladys Brockwell in the double role of Harriet Gordon and Peggy Malone.

91. These numbers apparently refer to exaggerated or tongue-in-cheek time signatures.

92. In her second week of reviewing, she praised *The Foundling* (with Pickford) and *Jeanne Dore* (with Bernhardt) ("Current Releases Reviewed," *Motography*, January 22, 1916, 192–93, 196). One of her last pieces singled out the Alhambra in Milwaukee ("Theatre Has Its Audience Sing," *Motography*, July 13, 1918, 65).

93. For Fairbanks, see Genevieve Harris, "A Round-the-World Serial?," *Motography*, June 24, 1916, 1440; and for Pickford, see Harris, "The Sweetest Girl in the World," *Motography*, August 5, 1916, 305–6; two interviews with theater managers are Harris, "Proving That Ideals Pay: A Story of a Chicago Theatre. [Central Park]," *Motography*, April 20, 1918, 735; and Harris, "Woman Manager Packs Three Houses [Mrs. Flossie A. Jones]," *Motography*, June 1, 1918, 1043. She also interviewed Carl D. Elinore, who had been "arranging music for photoplays for the past eight years" in Los Angeles (Harris, "Setting 'Hearts of the World' to Music," *Motography*, May 11, 1918, 893, 911).

94. "Obituaries," *Chicago Sunday Tribune*, August 10, 1973, 3.14. Later Harris served as a woman's page editor of the *Eau Claire (WI) Leader* and then "worked in public relations for the National Livestock and Meat Board."

95. Genevieve Harris, "A War Picture All Should See," *Chicago Post*, September 14, 1918, n.p.

96. Research in both the trade press and newspapers reveals that young women staffed nearly all inspection and repair departments in rental exchanges.

97. See, for instance, Richard Abel, "The Middleman of the Movies: US Film Exchanges, 1915–1919," forthcoming in the *Historical Journal of Film, Radio, and Television*.

98. In a short review of *A Hoosier Romance* one movie fan "allowed plot and players to go unnoticed in his anxiety [about] what he believed was poor light and camera work" ("Detroit Critics Pick Flaws in New Films," *Detroit Sunday News*, October 13, 1918, Film sec., 1).

99. Scottish-born Colin Campbell (1859–1928) directed numerous films for Selig, and Harris lists those adapted from Rex Beach stories.

100. Rex Beach (1877–1949) became a famous novelist with *The Spoilers* (1906), which became a 1911 stage play and Selig's 1914 feature film. Beach himself produced and scripted other adaptations from *The Barrier* (1917) to *The Iron Trail* (1921).

101. Famous Players–Lasky had consolidated its eight subsidiaries into a single corporation in December 1917. Most of its production output was released through Paramount Pictures.

102. Founded in 1917, Paramount-Artcraft was a high-end division of Paramount Pictures known for its release of Pickford and Hart features.

103. A successful garment salesman, Polish-born Samuel Goldfish (1879–1974) in 1913 became a partner in the Lasky company. In 1916 he changed his name to Goldwyn and with the Selwyn brothers, who were Broadway producers, formed Goldwyn Pictures.

104. Founded in 1916, Goldwyn Pictures soon became a major Hollywood studio that Marcus Loew bought in 1924 and merged into Metro-Goldwyn-Mayer.

105. Charlotte S. Kelly, "Comments on the Screen," *Indianapolis Sunday Star*, September 8, 1918, 5.1.

106. Charlotte S. Kelly, "Comments on the Screen," *Indianapolis Sunday Star*, November 17, 1918, 6.1, 2.

107. Here Kelly likely is thinking of Hart, who was expert at rolling a cigarette and striking a match with his thumbnail. In a rare courting scene in *The Return of Draw Egan* (1916), he hugs his pinto pony before moving to embrace the heroine.

108. The divorcee referenced here could be a movie star or a prominent social figure.

109. A newsreel in late 1918 probably would not seem different from what Kelly describes here.

110. This likely is Kelly's own generic fictional title.

111. In one long scene in *Branding Broadway* (December 1918), Hart did appear in evening clothes, but he played a character more consistently in that attire in *Poppy Girl's Husband* (March 1919).

112. Goldwyn's *Are You a Perfect 36?* starred Mabel Normand. Several stunts like this promoted the film ("Goldwyn Suggests Stunt for 'A Perfect 36,'" *Motion Picture News*, November 16, 1918, 2941).

○ 3 ○

A Peak Period for Women Writers, 1919–1921

The three years following the end of the Great War saw another explosion of newspaper movie pages and review columns. Four newspaper women continued their editing and reviewing work from before: Mae Tinée, Charlotte S. Kelly, Genevieve Harris, and Dorothy Day. At least five new writers joined them: Marjorie Daw (*Cleveland Plain Dealer, Detroit Journal*), Virginia Tracy (*New York Tribune*), Harriette Underhill (*New York Tribune*), Virginia Dale (*Chicago Journal*), and Alberta Hartley (*Des Moines News*). Yet most likely there are others, whether "hidden" under first-name initials, like H. Underhill in the *Motion Picture News*' "First Annual Newspaper and Theater Directory," or quoted in theater ads, as was Hazel Bye (*Indianapolis Times*) in late 1919.[1]

The directory suggests that even more men had been assigned to editing movie pages and writing film reviews—that is, if those with first-name initials really are men. Some, like Carl Sandberg at the *Chicago News*, are missing because the directory gathered no information from Chicago.[2] Also missing are Tony Langston, who used a column in *The Competitor* to calm a black mother's fears about letting her children attend the movies, and Lester A. Walton, who, in his weekly *New York Age* column, found Oscar Michaux's *The Brute* (1920) "neither original nor any too pleasing."[3] Other reviewers appeared in newspapers yet to be digitized: from Guy Price (*Los Angeles Herald*), C. Miles (*Minneapolis Journal*), H. Wise (*Minneapolis Tribune*), W. Rowland (*Milwaukee Journal*), and W. Lanvorigt (*Washington [DC] Star*) to C. H. McKinley (*Flint [MI] Journal*), C. Saunders (*Grand Rapids [MI] Herald*), W. Muse (*Mason City [IA] Globe Gazette*), J. Plummer (*Wheeling [WV] Register*),

N. Skerritt (*Worcester [MA] Gazette*), and W. Rock (*Youngstown [OH] Vindicator*).[4] At least one man appeared in a digitized small-town newspaper: Clarence Lucas (*Moline [IA] Dispatch*), a copy writer who signed a column of short reviews, "Four Best Films of the Week," in late 1919.[5] Another returned to his column of industry news from before the United States entered the war: N. D. Tevis (*La Crosse [WI] Tribune*). In addition, sometimes a few others were quoted in theater ads or referenced in "Best Films of the Year" columns: Robert Sherwood (*Life*) and Quinn Martin (*New York World*).

Beginning in 1919, then, men may have been more numerous than women editing newspaper movie pages and writing reviews. As a consequence, whenever possible (within the limits of access), the pages that follow will note pertinent differences between a woman's and a man's review of the same film, their take on a particular star, or their choice of other subjects.

Marjorie Daw

Not to be confused with the movie actress of the same name, Marjorie Daw first wrote a column for the *Cleveland Plain Dealer* in 1918, profiling people in the movie industry.[6] Three months later she became the paper's photoplay editor, a position she held until September 1919, when the *Detroit Journal* hired her as its photoplay editor. There she edited the Saturday and daily pages devoted to the movies, with columns and articles that sometimes explicitly addressed women. Why she left the *Journal* in March 1920 and what became of her are unclear.

In the *Plain Dealer*, Daw often adopted a chatty, playful style, evidenced in her quip exploiting a quote from Kipling: to "those who cry down the cinema as an entertainment [and] exclaim, 'It's very pretty, but is it art?' The real movie fan doesn't worry about anything so banal."[7] But she also offered concise observations and commonsense advice to her readers in reviewing films like *Treat 'Em Rough*, with Tom Mix, and CPI's patriotic feature *Under Four Flags*.[8] She also could be ambivalent, as in her praise of Lillian Gish despite the "trite story" of Griffith's nostalgic "small town" film, *True Heart Susie*.

In the *Journal*, Daw could be no less playful, as in her fanciful, slang-filled story of Chaplin and Fairbanks, like little boys playing hooky one afternoon. "That's the nicest thing about these two fellows," she sighed. "They just don't seem to grow up." But she could be serious too, repeating the advice of several others before her: that motion pictures were an exciting new professional field for women, especially as scenario writers.

"Favorite Stars Listed in Suitable Film Roles," *Cleveland Sunday Plain Dealer*, June 15, 1919, Editorial/Dramatic, 4.

GRIFFITH'S "TRUE HEART SUSIE" PHOTO PLAY OF MERIT AT STILLMAN D. W. Griffith's "True Heart Susie," featuring Lillian Gish and Robert Harron, is the attraction this week at the Stillman theater.[9]

From time to time discussions have arisen and waxed warm over the "art" of D. W. Griffith. Considering the question as I viewed his newest Artcraft picture unfolding on the screen I decided that it was not art at all, but a direct application of common sense, or in other words the unusual ability to recognize the obvious, that makes Griffith's pictures so interesting.

Griffith's pictures appeal to the imagination, touch the heart, stir old memories, send us away pleased with ourselves and the world. And with Griffith, "True Heart Susie" is the best of his "small town" stories yet presented. It is filled with humor and pathos. Its characters live and breathe.

The story is trite and the plot as simple as to be hardly a plot at all. It purports to be built about incidents that actually happened. No one will doubt that after seeing the picture. It is delightfully human. Susie is the "plain and simple" country girl who loses her sweetheart to the wiles of the girl who uses rouge and puts her hair in curl papers.

"In the fell clutch of circumstance," Susie does not "wince or cry aloud." She goes about her business, a little sad, perhaps, but very sanely, and in the long run she gains her ends, and we suppose she lives happily ever after, because the last we see of her she is receiving the long desired kiss through the honeysuckle vines about the kitchen window.

Miss Gish's interpretation of Susie is a gem. Robert Harron is acceptable as always as the small town boy who becomes a country minister, and Clairine Seymour is good as the indiscreet wife.[10]

"Doug and Chas. at the Circus," *Detroit Journal*, November 11, 1919, Today Page, 1.

There's no particular reason why Charlie Chaplin and Doug Fairbanks shouldn't go to the circus if they want to.

Seems sorta odd, though, to think of the two funniest stars in the movies traipsing off to the side-show, doesn't it?

That's the nicest thing about these two fellows. They just can't seem to grow up. There's Charlie with a barrel or two of money and a wife and a lovely home and Douglas with a coupla kegs of money and a lovely home and everything, and the two of them play hookey one fine afternoon and go over to the circus lot and play hob with the animals and gobble up a lot of red lemonade and have a perfectly grand time.

All this happened the other day in Los Angeles.

"They's a circus over in that old vacant lot by the cheese factory," said Douglas, leaping listlessly over a few chairs.

"Less go," remarked Charlie, turning his toes out.

So they removed their make-up, got an advance on their next week's salary from the cashier (who was none too sweet about it, either) and sneaked out the back way and acrost the railroad tracks and up past the watering tank and through the tannery yard to the big tent.

"Looket them elephants," said Doug, hitching his pants up.

"Where's the snake charmer?" asked Charlie, hopping sideways on one foot.

All was excitement and balloons in their vicinity, with peanuts and monkeys and squawkers and kids amalgamating in one glorious aura of joy.

Doug watched the trapeze performers. Charlie hung about the monkeys' cage. Together they had their fortunes told in the side-show and stared, open-mouthed, at the living skeleton and the bearded lady.

They spent a dollar and forty cents for peanuts to feed the elephants, and only the strong arm of Doug saved Charlie, the inquisitive, from extinction under the hoofs of the horses in the chariot race.

"Can't yuh let me see nothin'," Charlie remonstrated.

"If yuh gotta see somethin'," replied Doug, "they's a bareback rider that'll knock your eye out." Whereupon Charlie tipped his hat over one eye, grasped his trusty cane, and away they went.

When the last side-show had been visited and the last balloon popped itself out, the two dirtiest and richest urchins in the picture game departed sadly for home.

Doug sighed. Charlie whistled woefully, if that can be done.

"Gee—don't yuh hate to grow up, Charlie?"

"Un-huh! I'll race yuh to the gate."

"Still Another Field for Girls," *Detroit Journal*, November 14, 1919, Today page, 1.

A new field for clever women is offered by the motion picture industry.

Stories suitable for the screen are required by all of the studios and high purchase prices are paid for acceptable matter.

In the writing of scenarios women excel, according to Perry Heath, script editor at Universal City.[11] Mr. Heath says that the feminine mind devises more brilliant plots than the male writer and that the work of a trained woman scenarist is usually better than that of a trained male writer.

With more than twenty producing outfits at work at Universal City the demand for suitable stories is unprecedented and many acceptable stories are found in each morning's mail.

The readers search the stories carefully, for sometimes obscure ideas make a detailed report to Mr. Heath and indicate whether or not the story has possibilities. Sometimes it is sent back to the writer for revision, more frequently it is "revamped" by a staff writer, but if it contains the germ of an idea the writer soon finds himself with a substantial check and the script is turned over to a continuity expert for the technical work of putting the events in proper order for the screen.

"The amateur writer," Mr. Heath says, "furnishes the studios with the best material—less stereotyped and frequently brilliant with an absolute new idea."

Mae Tinée

For a few years after the Great War, Mae Tinée remained an important and still controversial film reviewer not only in Chicago but also across the country. Whereas before she had called attention to a propagandistic French film, now she singled out several excellent "alien films" from Germany, notably those directed so well by Ernst Lubitsch.[12] An exception was *The Cabinet of Dr. Caligari*, whose diabolical tale and "queer, futuristic-cubic" set gave her "the willies." Again, she highlighted what she considered especially masterful American films: George Loane Tucker's *The Miracle Man* (1919), Rex Ingram's *The Four Horsemen of the Apocalypse* (1921), Cecil B. DeMille's *The Affairs of Anatol* (1921), even Lois Weber's *The Blot* (1921).[13] And she devoted high praise not only to Pola Negri in Lubitsch's *Passion / Madame Du Barry* but also to Alice Joyce for a career-reviving role in Mrs. Sidney Drew's *Cousin Kate* (1921) and to Harry Carey, her "idea of a real western hero," in *Hearts Up* (1921).[14] Several of these films topped her "ten best photoplays of 1921," but she excluded *The Three Musketeers* (1921) because Fairbanks was "not an especially well chosen D'Artagnan," for "Dumas' hero . . . was [not] much of a clown."

However, Tinée continued to be unkind to some stars. She could not refrain from lamenting Theda Bara, this time urging her to learn from how she sat quietly, as she does just once in *The Beautiful Dancer* (1919).[15] In an unusually frank pseudoletter to "America's Sweetheart," she even took Mary Pickford to task for accepting the leading role in Frances Marion's "mess" of a story, *The Love Light* (1921), and for being bossed around on "how to smile" and "how to hold your hands." In a rare break from film reviewing, she also pummeled the public by using the musicians' strike in September 1920 to argue that exhibitors were so wrong to believe their patrons' claim that "the picture's the thing" and mistakenly think they would enjoy a film in silence "without being annoyed."

"Great Cast; Great Director; Great Picture!," *Chicago Tribune*, September 15, 1919, 22.

"THE MIRACLE MAN"   You've been crying for something "different." Here you have it. "The Miracle Man" is an unusual picture. It is a great picture. And George Loane Tucker is its director.[16]

It has been proved in the past that Mr. Tucker's name on a film warranted the highest grade of excellence. Here is a director who works like a Trojan nor ever rests until he is satisfied with his output. He is his own severest critic and taskmaster. And how well he understands picking a cast!

Do you remember Betty Compson?[17] Little Betty of the comedies? Well, who except a George Loane Tucker would have seen in her a great emotional actress? In this instance you first meet her as a tawdry little "skirt," member of a gang of underworld fakers: the wanton, hot-lipped, heavy-eyed mistress of the leader of the gang. And through a strange cycle of events you follow her, marveling more each minute at the work she does.

Tom Meighan is leader of the gang.[18] His religion is "Money!" And he believes in allowing nothing to interfere with his religion. His are the brains of the crooks who blindly follow his lead. His is the remarkable idea that furnishes the motif for the story. Together they will go to the village where lives the white haired patriarch credited with powers to heal the sick and crippled. Together they will stage a miracle that shall bring believers flocking to Fairfield. And they will cash in on the profits.

Joseph J. Dowling as the deaf, dumb and blind prophet seems more a presence than a character.[19] He has invested the role with a remarkable quietness that holds you as no other interpretation could.

Then, Lon Chaney![20] Cast as one of those weird and horrible beggars who through contortions can make of themselves such objects of horror and pity that none could refuse them aid, he is hideous, convincing and immediately likable—when unfolded.

The other characters are all well taken. The story holds your interest from start to finish. When I heard it had been filmed I was quite excited for long ago I read it in a magazine and it made an indelible impression. George Cohen, you know, made a play of it which ran for about a year, on Broadway.[21] And in the course of human events George Loane Tucker laid a magic hand upon it.

And made of "The Miracle Man" a miracle picture.

"Right Off the Reel," *Chicago Sunday Tribune*, September 19, 1920, 8.2.

Do the picture fans know their own minds? The recent strike of the musicians has made this question a poignant one, for since the day of the "nickel shows" a large per cent of moviegoers have protested volubly against music with the films. The cry has been: "When we go to a motion picture theater we go to see the picture. We don't wish to be annoyed by a lot of jangle and din. We want to enjoy our picture in peace."

When the musicians struck there was loud rejoicing on the part of those who felt that at last they had secured their heart's desire. "The picture's the thing," they exulted. "Now we can enjoy ourselves without being annoyed."

However, the stubborn exhibitor insisted the picture should not remain unaccompanied. He introduced vaudeville acts—the best he could procure—to take the place of the music that was stilled.

Then the stage hands struck, and vaudeville was no more a feature on the bill. It would seem that the persnickety fan should be happy, but—for some strange reason the automobiles that had once crowded the streets near popular neighborhood theaters became conspicuous by their absence. No longer did long lines of patrons force the beautiful cashiers to work fast and use their hands. Long tiers of empty seats greeted the eye of the theater manager as he wandered disconsolately about trying to achieve a pleased smile and failing miserably.

"The picture's the thing," so many of his patrons had complained. "You should worry about the musicians' strike! We're glad they're gone."

Perhaps. But what the exhibitor wishes to know now is, if the motion picture fans do not like music, why, now that the music is back, is he swamped with business when, a brief week or so ago he was a lonely figure by a deserted box office.

The picture's the thing.

Is it?

"Alice as 'Kate' Comes Back into Her Own," *Chicago Tribune*, January 15, 1921, 14.

"COUSIN KATE"   One of the most bewitching love scenes beheld in pictures for many a day is staged in "Cousin Kate." It's the place where the beautiful lady authoress who thinks she doesn't believe in love meets in a woodland cottage the rangy hero who most emphatically does. In the glimmer of firelight to the accompaniment of a raging storm he tells her the story of "The Three Bears"—and captivates her hitherto errant heart.

The exquisite humanness of the episode; the atmosphere of intimacy, romance, and nursery lore charm, woo you into their circle of flickering shadow and warm glow and speak much for the artistry of Mrs. Sidney Drew, who for some time will direct the efforts of Miss Joyce who has needed just such help as Mrs. Drew is giving her.[22] In "Cousin Kate" she is again the Alice of old days. She is beautiful, womanly, gracious and displays the old whimsical humor which has been missing in late in her characterizations.

There are a number of new and clever people in the cast. Gilbert Emery is a "different" and attractive type of leading man.[23] Beth Martin as the prim maid who foregoes marriage with him because he insists on painting pictures on Sunday and she is "willing to suffer" for her principles, is smug, strait-laced and tepidly pretty, as she should be. Freddie Verdi as her small brother is another youngster to watch out for. Looks as if he might be somebody some day.

The film is finely staged. It is just long enough. The photography is excellent. Altogether a photoplay that should please the majority—mightily.

"O, Mary, Mary, and We Held Our Breath for This," *Chicago Tribune*, January 25, 1921, 14.

"THE LOVE LIGHT"[24]   Here's a picture that makes you burn to offer advice. You want to take "America's Sweetheart" by the shoulders, sit her down—hard—in a corner—and start out on her something like this:

"Look here, Mary, what's the idea, anyhow? Here we've been holding our breath until you should come out in a new picture, and you go and give us something like 'The Love Light.' Rather, you do give us 'The Love Light.'[25]

"What's the matter with it? To begin with, it's a war picture and that alone is enough to damn it. The war is over, Little Mary! We're trying to forget. And here you go and harbor a German spy and make him the father of your pictorial child and let him use you to sink a ship bearing wounded soldiers home! Mary, Mary, what was the matter with you when you read that scenario? Don't you know your public yet?

"Then, who picked the cast? It's not a bad cast, but it certainly could have been a better one. Though come to think of it, I reckon a good many folks would balk at playing in 'The Love Light,' even as support to your charming self.

"And as to that charming self—don't you let any director tell you how to smile or show you how to hold your hands! That is, not again. Somebody sort of bossed you this trip, I'm thinking, until you seem a medley of Constance Talmadge, Marguerite Clark, and Mary Pickford, and not much of any.

"Then, my dear, aside from the war twist to your photoplay, I think that story a mess. There was only one place it seemed funny—that where the farmyard fowls drink the wine—and much of that was trick photography—or that slow camera stuff—whatever you call it. I didn't feel sorry for you in your saddest moments—something all wrong there, you see—and I didn't give a hurrah how the thing came out. What I did like was some of the scenery. Those rockbound coasts and breaking waves are something to see.

"Just why 'The Love Light,' Little Mary, when there were so many good stories you might have had? Just why the unknowns in the cast when you might have surrounded yourself with splendid people? Just why—well—just why? An honest admirer of yours honestly wishes to know."

That's what you want to say to "Little Mary." Bless her heart—tough luck!

"Famous 'Best Seller' Makes a Fine Photoplay," *Chicago Tribune*, March 28, 1921, 18.

"THE FOUR HORSEMEN OF THE APOCALYPSE"[26] You will admit, when you have seen "The Four Horsemen of the Apocalypse" that Rex Ingram, a young man and little heard from, deserves to be bowed into the front rank of directors.[27] He has made a splendid picture.

It was no easy matter to boil down and assemble for screen purposes a big, powerful, colorful book such as is Ibanez's. The act of elimination could have been performed by many—and by many, how badly! This Mr. Ingram, however, kept his head in the clouds and his feet on the earth, and, with the assistance of June Mathias, who prepared the scenario, while telling the main story, simply managed to inject a soupcon of everything the book contained.[28] The picture then abounds in broad sweeps of the brush, delicate attention to detail, tender lights, and deep shadows. (I'm not the art editor. What do I talk like that for?)

Not too much can be said in commendation of the work of every member of the cast—those whose names are mentioned and a number whose names are not. There is never a moment when any one apparently strives for effect. Everything that is done is natural—"from de heart oudt."

The four sinister horsemen, Conquest, War, Pestilence, and Death, appear just often enough to thrill. Some directors would have rung them in world without end and spoiled a fine effect.

The Chicago censors, I am told, felt called upon to use their scissors on a dance and a kiss. Not Mr. Fitzmorris, I bet—and I'll wager there was nothing that needed cutting at that. But, heavens, we have to earn our money, I suppose!

The story hasn't been given here because nearly everybody has read it. Even if you're not familiar with the book, I believe you'll enjoy the picture more if I don't go more into detail.

Go and see "The Four Horsemen of the Apocalypse." It is worth your time and money.

"'Passion's' Players Do Not Act; They Live Their Parts," *Chicago Tribune*, May 10, 1921, 24.

"PASSION" FEATURING POLA NEGRI[29]   There can be no possible doubt about it. "Passion," sent to our screens as a flaming example of foreign efficiency, is a powerful photodrama. The seething events that had to do with France in the days when the gamin Du Barry ruled a dissolute king and a decadent court are presented to you with vividness, picturesqueness, and a virile demand on your sympathies and senses. The Lubitsch-Pola Negri description of the rise and fall of a courtesan holds you for a good two hours spellbound—but unoffended.[30]

Admitting the great dramatic force of the production, its finely intuitive and imaginative attention to detail, the splendor of its sets, and the beauty of the photography, that thing that impresses you most is its realness. The players do not act—they live their parts. Was there a camera about? Evidently they did not know it.

Pola Negri's Du Barry is a stirring characterization. Here is a great actress with a dynamic personality. Her courtesan, rather than brazenly immoral, is impishly un-moral. She is bad because she likes to be bad—and to be agreeable. You don't think Louis should—but you understand how—Louis could. Her tragic downfall causes you several moments of real pain.

Pola Negri is great. But so is every member of the supporting cast great. Looking back, I cannot remember finding one fault with any of the acting. Scene blends into scene—and you, the unseen spectator, flush and pale, witness riots and are afraid, suffer hunger with the citizens and with them shake your fist at the triumphant Du Barry and her doddering royal lover, but when the king dies, feel the cold wave of his fear, and with his mistress on the scaffold, know panic—and—pity!

Two hours, nine reels—Orchestra Hall! The picture is over. You start and look about you. Outside is the Boul' Mich' and you had thought you were in Paris in the days of Louis XV.

"Whoops, My Dear! Do Bring on the Strait Jacket," *Chicago Sunday Tribune*, May 15, 1921, 8.3.

"THE CABINET OF DR. CALIGARI"[31]   "The Cabinet of Dr. Caligari" is certainly like no film you have ever seen before. It is a weird, mad fantastic thing whose settings remind you of nothing so much as the [?] groupings of varicolored particles seen through the eye of a kaleidoscope.[32]

So far as I am concerned, pictures of the kind may play in their own backyard. I don't like them. They give me the willies. But then I don't like Poe either and look who Poe is. Come to think of it, the esteemed E.A. should never have died till he saw Dr. Caligari. With what lugubrious joy would he have witnessed this German study in insanity. Vurrily, Caligari is a Poe Charlie Chaplin!

The ravings of a madman furnish the motif for the picture. In a queer, futuristic-cubic sort of garden you meet a youth and a kindly old gentleman sitting on a bench. The youth points to the slowly advancing figure of a woman, clothed in white, and says:

"See? She has been like that since that terrible night. Since then no one has ever dared mention in her presence the name of Caligari."

And he plunges into one of the strangest tales the screen has ever unreeled of a diabolical old doctor who has a somnambulist to execute crimes that he conceives and does not dare carry out himself.

Nobody knows who is this KILLER. It is the youth telling the story who finally tracks him to his lair and finds him to be none other than the esteemed head of the insane asylum, who, you are told, has gone mad on the subject of somnambulism.

Not until the end of the picture is it revealed to your muddled wits that the supposed Dr. Caligari, really the esteemed Dr. Sonnow, is about the only sane person in the place.

The picture is nothing to be seen if you are imaginative or nervous. Taken late at night with a piece of mince pie, I should say it would prove fatal. And keep the children away from the thing!

Just the same, "The Cabinet of Dr. Caligari" is undeniably clever. It is most artistically acted. The lighting is a marvel of spookiness. And if you are looking for something different, well—it is certainly different with a vengeance.[33]

"Here's Where De Mille Out-De Milles Himself," *Chicago Tribune*, August 15, 1921, 14.

"THE AFFAIRS OF ANATOL"[34]   Look at the cast and after you've got through gasping over the array of famous names that greet your eye, let me tell you that everything about "The Affairs of Anatol" has just as much class. If ever there was a de luxe picture this is it. Where the money came from to produce it—ask me, ask me—and I can't tell you.

There isn't a moment's bad acting, unless, perhaps, you find as I do, that Agnes Ayres is unconvincing.[35] The staging is immense, the costuming—O, la, la—the scenery something to dream about, and the photography, the quintessence of photographic art.

The picture was suggested by the play by Artur Schnitzler.[36] The story is of a young married man who yearns to help others—pretty and of the other gender—and gets badly stung. His wife, Miss Gloria Swanson, sleek and gorgeous, understands him better than he thinks she does, and, far from reaching out a marital right and dragging him home, puts a muffler on her impatience and jealousy and is rewarded as she should be.

Those about whom his affairs revolve are Wanda Hawley as a jazz baby, whom he used to go to school with, but who has changed—ah! how she's changed; Agnes Ayres, as a farmer's wife, whom he rescues from drowning and who steals his pocket book to help her husband; and Bebe Daniels as the wickedest woman in New York—or supposedly the wickedest woman in New York—who borrows $3,000 from him, to pay the famous surgeon who operates on her husband—"My husband, my sweetheart—he's full of shrapnel and now the war's over nobody remembers him but me!"[37] Right there little Miss Daniels does some great acting.

With what is commonly known I believe as consummate art, the director keeps you on mental tiptoe for something scandalous that never happens. You just get your eye to the keyhole and the lights go out, as it were.

The subtitles are clever.

Rave on! I won't!

"Take Your Hankie for You May Weep over 'The Blot,'" *Chicago Sunday Tribune*, August 28, 1921, 8.3.

"THE BLOT"[38] A picture like "The Blot" makes us pause, in our hurried passage through the business of living, and think. The title has reference to the true but shocking fact that college professors and clergymen are not adequately salaried to support their families in a decent manner. Lois Weber takes up this problem and skillfully makes of it an extremely worthwhile film.[39]

Don't be alarmed. It is not a sermon, but a vivid portrayal of truth. It is the story of an impoverished college professor who is unable to provide his wife and daughter with even the necessities of life. And it shows how a rich man's son discovers a new outlook upon life which is far better than the old one.

The professor's daughter works in the public library. She is beautiful and sweet, and is loved by three men—the young minister, the son of a prosperous shoemaker next door, and the rich man's son.

I won't spoil the story for you recounting it here. It is, as advertised, a "heart tale," and if you have sensitive tear ducts you will need a handkerchief or two.

Yet it does not drip with sentimentalism. There is nothing exaggerated. It is a real chapter out of many lives, and as a piece of film work is remarkably well done.

The directing is good. Every one in the cast is fine. In fact, the three suitors of the professor's daughter are all so nice that we want each one to be the lucky man. You won't blame them for falling in love with her, because she is adorable.

Don't avoid "The Blot" for fear of having your afternoon and evening ruined by looking facts too squarely in the face. Outside of the definite problem which the film introduces, the underlying romance of it makes up for any harrowing which your soul may experience.

It's a good picture.

"The Ten Best Pictures of 1921—as Seen by Us," *Chicago Sunday Tribune*, January 29, 1922, 8.1.

THE TEN BEST PHOTOPLAYS OF 1921   "Life" gives us the idea. (Credit where credit is due.) The photoplay reviewer of "Life" has picked what he thinks the ten best pictures of the year. His choice consists of the following: "The Kid," "The Four Horsemen of the Apocalypse," "A Connecticut Yankee in King Arthur's Court," "One Week," "Scrap Iron," "Sentimental Tommy," "Disraeli," "The Three Musketeers," "Little Lord Fauntleroy," and "Woman's Place." "The Kid" he considers the best of the lot, and the others are ranged according to his idea regarding their merit.

I do not venture to say which of the ten photoplays named at the head of this column is the best. And please be reminded that there were many exceedingly good pictures that could not be mentioned among the ten—because ten's ten, and there you are. Here is why, however, it seems to this department the leaders were above par.[40]

Take "THE FOUR HORSEMEN OF THE APOCALYPSE." It was marvelous because the director was able to take a big, powerful, colorful novel, subject it to the operation of elimination, and bring it to the screen, powerful and colorful, though necessarily deprived of much detail which had made the Ibanez story the thing of worth and beauty that it is. The main story was there intact. All the high lights were there, yet the film was not too long. That was art.

"OVER THE HILL," adapted from the poem by Will Carleton, absorbed your interest and tugged at your sympathies from beginning to end without one moment of getting maudlin or sloppy.[41] THAT was art. To my way of thinking it is the greatest "Mother" picture ever made.

As to "THE KID." There can be no doubt that its main attraction lay in the kid himself, depicted by little Jackie Coogan, a dear and clever little fellow, who marched right into the hearts of old and young alike, and by his marvelous team work with Mr. Chaplin caused sighs and tears to blend with devastating effect on the emotions.[42] "The Kid," therefore, is a good picture because it warmed the heart and was withal a clever piece of work.

"PASSION." THERE was a picture! It was made in Germany by Ernst Lubitsch and—I quote myself—"was a flaming example of foreign efficiency." In it Pola Negri performed a most difficult feat. She portrayed the life of Du Barry in the days of decadent French court life vividly, but without giving offense. This was no small thing to do. The great thing about "Passion" was the manner in which the director made every facial expression, every flutter of drapery count.

"LITTLE LORD FAUNTLEROY" was such a winsome thing! Mary Pickford's work in the two roles, that of Dearest, the mother, and Cedric, the son, was almost unbelievably clever. The staging and sets in the film were remarkable, and the director marvelously blended old world charm with new world pep and humor.

"DECEPTION," like "Passion," was foreign made, and directed by Ernst Lubitsch. In it mass and detail were worked out perfectly, and the story of Henry VIII and Anne Boleyn was told simply, but with great power. As in "Passion," the director never permitted a wasted moment or a bit of padding.

"THE PASSION FLOWER," a story of strange loves and hates, featuring Norma Talmadge, was characterized by a beautiful reticence. It could easily have been offensive to the extreme but even its worst moments left one stirred, but far from indignant, at the mode of their treatment. An extraordinary and masterly production.

"THE DEVIL" had George Arliss, who never on the stage was a more polished, smooth, or brilliant actor than in this screen version of his famous play. 'Nuff ced.

"FOOTLIGHTS" was memorable because, after a series of pathetic failures, it brought the beautiful and capable Elsie Ferguson back to the screen in a picture that was absorbingly interesting and beautifully done. The fans had felt so sorry for Miss Ferguson for so long. In "Footlights" they buried their woe. The sun came out, and they beheld a rainbow in the sky. (And the rainbow proved indeed a bow of promise. See "Peter Ibbetson," if you don't believe it.)

"THE QUEEN OF SHEBA" was a great big, beautiful thing with an exquisitely beautiful woman in the leading role, who could display her beauty without rousing an evil thought. It could not be said that she wore clothes—and it could not be thought that she was without them. Aside from this characterization the picture was almost perfectly acted, and was a world beater from the standpoint of production.

I said before there are many other pictures deserving of comment. A lot of you will probably let out a howl because "The Three Musketeers" is not included in "The Ten Best Photoplays." There is a reason, however, for this omission. While the film was well done, Douglas Fairbanks, to one person's way of thinking, is not an especially well chosen D'Artagnan. Dumas' hero, I don't believe, was much of a clown. He didn't fight with his feet. He met his enemies squarely, face to face. Mr. Fairbanks—well, you saw the picture.

So, take 'em or leave 'em. I think the pictures listed above are the ten best of 1921. You go ahead and think differently if you want to; we've had our say. If you want yours—go to it!

Charlotte S. Kelly

Throughout 1919 Kelly's "Comments on the Screen" column was a fixture in the *Indianapolis Sunday Star* on pages devoted to photoplays. Again, rather than review individual films, she took up issues apparently being debated at the time. Of those selected here, one column claims that stars are what draw audiences to the cinema, but she hopes the public will agree more and more with Shakespeare that "the play's the thing." Another decries the flood of "ordinary five-reel" films and promotes the production and exhibition of good short reels such as *Pathé Review*. Another column, not included here, criticizes moviegoers who so freely share faulty opinions, despite their ignorance of the risks an actor takes or the plausibility of a story's plot.[43]

Although her column disappeared in late January 1920, there are several traces of her after that. Little more than a week later, she gave a talk titled "Making of Moving Pictures" at a meeting of the Alliance Française and turned out to be Mrs. Charlotte Kelly.[44] Quoted at length in an ad for the Circle theater in late February 1920, however, she seems to have continued reviewing films for the *Indianapolis News*.[45] That ad pairs her review with those of Wilbur Hickman (the *Times*) and Bertram Taylor (who likely replaced her at the *Star*). All three describe in detail the new stage setting, "Palace of Arts," at the theater. Taylor lavishly lauds "real man" Lewis Stone in *The River's End*, while Kelly gives equal attention to Marjorie Daw and Jane Novak. Yet what to make of this puzzle? For the Alliance française talk, she is named (mistakenly?) Mrs. Charlotte Kelly; six months later, according to a brief *Times* news item, a Miss

Charlotte Kelly marries a Randle C. Dean.[46] How long her reviewing may have lasted remains unclear, for her name does not appear when one searches the digitized *News*.

"Comments on the Screen," *Indianapolis Sunday Star*, January 26, 1919, 6.1.

Among the many bits of philosophy which the publicity men of the photoplay companies like to send us we regard as most illuminating the following obvious untruth from one to the well-known producers:

"The popularity of motion pictures is largely due to good stories."

What a different aspect the life of the motion picture reviewer would wear if only this piece of fiction were true! This little sentence has lighted up so many new views on motion pictures for us that we are almost blinded by the brilliance of the publicity man's imagination and the general shiningness of motion picture stars.

For we have always had the impression that it was the star, and not the story, that drew the crowds. It matters little in what romantic story Mary Pickford is featured; people flock to see her in any sweet little picture, the main thing being that there be a personable hero on whom she may fix her affections, becoming clothes and settings for the star, and plenty of close-ups.

If a Douglas Fairbanks film is announced, the exhibitor knows that his theater will be filled with admirers who want to see the active player kept in motion; whether the story is logical or new or cleverly constructed is not an inquiry to which the exhibitor must have a ready answer. "When will your Fairbanks picture be shown?" is the question, not "Has he a good scenario?"

The popularity of any given motion picture is due largely to the popularity of the star. Shakespeare said "the play's the thing," but this aphorism is sadly out of date. The play should be the thing, but under present conditions, the star's the thing and until the public demand changes, the play is obscure by comparison. Of course, there is a demand for good stories, but even the best story does not command the patronage which is drawn to a theater when a popular star is to be seen.

That there is a trend toward making the story of greater importance can not be denied. Productions like "The Squaw Man," "The Heart of Humanity," "Hearts of the World," all make the players subordinate to the play, and these photoplays have made money for their exhibitors.[47] But the fact that the pictures of this sort can be named so easily and so briefly indicates that progress in this direction is slow. For a half dozen pictures exemplifying

Shakespeare's pithy remark there are hundreds that demonstrate that the public wants to see its favorites, not a picturization of an excellent story.

The education of the public to a liking for pictured stories rather than for pictured people is gradually being accomplished, and when the day comes that finds our correspondent's delightful romancing true, the motion picture will be much farther advanced artistically than it is today. It is not possible to create an artistically perfect photoplay in which one player so outranks not only all the other players, but also the director, the plot of the cinema, the settings, and indeed everything about the film, from the photoplay to the captions, that the star shines out against a comparatively dull background. The whole thing is out of proportion; and besides, no star is big enough to hide the multitude of imperfections which creep in when most of the producer's attention is devoted to the featured player. One indication that stories are constantly becoming more important is the enormous prices paid for them. Instances where $10,000 has changed hands for an exceptional idea embodied in a story are not common, but there are a few, and $5,000 has been paid for many stories. Our optimistic publicity man could have been just as interesting and considerably more truthful if he had said, "The popularity of stories is largely due to the possibilities in them for making motion pictures."

"Comments on the Screen," *Indianapolis Sunday Star*, February 9, 1919, 6.1, 12.

Feature films have held first place in the affections of motion picture devotees for a long time, but it seems likely that short reels may take their place in the not so distant future if the long pictures continue to meet with critical comment and the one and two-reel productions improve as rapidly as they have been doing recently. People like short, clever comedies, educational films which present new and unknown facts, travel pictures which take one to strange and interesting places, in fact, they like anything better than the ordinary five-reel photoplay with which the market is flooded. The exceptional feature film, of course, meets with exceptional success, but many producers have felt the demand for good short reels, and are specializing in them.

One large company, which keeps a sensitive finger on the pulse of popular demand, is spending much money and attention on the improvement of its short reels, enriching them with color and hesitating not at all to experiment with the suggestions made by science for the general improvement of the photoplay, developing, printing, or, indeed, any phase of the making of the films. Mr. Paul Brunet, who is the manager of the company, is very enthusiastic about the work and has the following information to give out concerning it:

"We are doing a vast amount of work here in America at present, but the Review really had its inception eight years ago when Pathé established the first cinematic scientific library. An achievement, acclaimed by the scientific world was photographs showing the life and action of the spirochaetes pallida—the tiniest bacillus known to science—the study of which has been a large factor in preserving the health of the allied armies. This film has been shown all over the world and has attracted profound interest among scientists. A large number of them have been acquired by individual physicians and they have been used by the United States Army in clinical and hygienic lectures."[48]

A point on which this company specializes is the most powerful microscopic camera, of which the wonder is that it will explore the animal, the vegetable, and the mineral kingdoms—magic journeys to knowledge, fascinatingly conducted, which are both rare entertainment and valuable instruction.[49] Here, indeed, is a field infinitely rich in marvels and strange things—a region of enchantment, from which young and old, the eager seeker and the blasé, alike, will emerge refreshed and filled with wonder of infinite creation. For here is a library of wonders.

A triumph for American ingenuity is the specially designed camera which enables one to make an analysis of motion.[50] So quick is this specially designed American camera that makes these photographs that the observer may easily follow the course of a bullet fired from a revolver. The first picture under this class, shown in the Review, is an analysis of the plays in a baseball game. It was given a private showing recently to baseball writers and experts; they are most enthusiastic regarding it, and declared that, apart from its entertaining quality, it might prove of great value in training.

These pictures are taken by the special camera at the rate of 160 a second, or ten times the normal speed of a motion picture camera. They are projected at the normal rate of 16 per second. At this speed it takes ten seconds to project 160 pictures that were taken by the analysis of motion camera. The action, therefore, is slowed down to ten times less than normal.

Some of the interesting features will show the slowed down action of a nimble fingered stage magician; high jumping horsemanship; high diving, in which the body of the beautiful swimmer seems to float through the air; boxing, tennis playing and a variety of subjects which will cover nearly every familiar human motion.

After years of experimentation Pathé has completed rapid progress for hand-coloring film.[51] In registration, in toning, and in general chromatic harmony, this method has never been approached on the screen. Mr. Brunet says of this phase of work, "In the experiments made by experts, it was demonstrated that film might be printed by machinery almost as rapidly as color printing on art paper; but, as the object of all our years of experimental endeavor was to find the most perfect way, the conclusion pointed finally to the hand system. It gives smoother, more rounded results, and to the execution, I am told, is added, as in the painting of a picture, a measure of human expression. Which would account for much of what is styled 'feeling,' in many of our colored views of landscape."

Raymond L. Ditmars, one of the curators of the New York Zoological Society, will be a regular contributor to Pathé Review.[52]

His first contribution shows how music affects animals. To the expert who has given time to the study of the mystery of rhythm in sound and in motion—as well as to the person who regards these things as merely odd, these exhibits of Mr. Ditmars's will furnish great entertainment. Why should a bear dance to the tune, as though he enjoyed the melody as well as the thinking man, and knew and appreciated the rhythm of the composition? Why should the hyena howl a long wild note blending strangely with the strain?

It is evident that if other producers turn so much of their attention to the making of short films, five-reelers will lose in drawing power what the short film gains.

Genevieve Harris

Despite the *Chicago Post*'s smaller circulation, Harris was an influential columnist, probably rivaling Mae Tinée and W. K. Hollander. She was an astute reviewer, but, unlike Tinée, she rarely mocked a film or star. Griffith's *Broken Blossoms* (1919), for instance, particularly impressed her with the acting of Lillian Gish, Richard Barthelmess, and Donald Crisp and with the camerawork and sets of the Limehouse district in London. His next big feature, *Way Down East*, was equally impressive, again for Gish's performance, as well as for bits of business from minor players and for the now famous scenes of Gish being rescued on the ice-jammed river.[53] A second view of *The Four Horsemen of the Apocalypse* (which she recommended for any good picture) confirmed the film's success, especially in the amazing Argentine section and in the moving scene between Julio, now in the uniform of France, and his father.[54] Harris fell in line with most others in praising *Passion* and Pola Negri, but, unlike Mae

Tinée again, she looked forward to viewing the "weird mystery story" and so-called futurist backgrounds of *The Cabinet of Dr. Caligari*. Both films, along with *Deception* (with its many "big scenes" and fine acting by Emil Jannings and Henny Porten) and *The Golem*, she believed, countered exhibitors' fear that audiences were prejudiced against foreign-made pictures.[55]

Yet Harris's interests ranged far beyond film reviewing. She was an early advocate of Mrs. Sidney Drew not merely as a comedian but as a filmmaker in her own right. Harris's promotion of Rex Ingram and Mrs. Drew led Harris to urge fans to give credit to directors—as well as scenario writers and others behind the camera—equal to that bestowed, with reason, on stars.[56] She waded into the debate over censorship by supporting the Illinois branch of NAMPI in its campaign opposing a legislative bill to establish a state censorship board.[57] She devoted a column to describing the Stratford, a new theater on the Far South Side of Chicago, marked notably by its forty-member symphony orchestra, the musical settings that introduced each feature, and its "special 'jazz' orchestra."[58] Reciprocally, she led readers on a tour of the Fox Film studio in New York City. In another column, she assumed an implicit position of uplift: perhaps the most important function of musical programs in movie theaters was that they were educating the public to "the great music of the world."[59] Finally, she was fascinated by the surprising, supposed randomness of newsreels and took the unusual position of promoting the Society for Visual Education and its creation of "complete picture courses" as "a new and vital force" for teaching schoolchildren.[60]

"Mrs. Drew as Film Director," *Chicago Post*, February 1, 1919, 4.

Mrs. Sidney Drew has played many roles in the charming Drew screen comedies.[61] She has still another part to play in the stage play "Keep Her Smiling," in which she and her husband co-starred. But her most interesting role is one the public does not see. It is that of motion picture director.[62]

The Drew comedies have, from the first, been announced as written and directed by Mrs. Drew. But one must see this talented lady at work to realize how much they are her creation. Out at the Essanay studios, where the latest offering, "Squared," is now being filmed, Mrs. Drew is the dominating force. She supervises each set, gives instructions to property men, electricians and camera men. She rehearses each scene carefully, and is a stickler for detail.

"The lettering on a lawyer's office isn't arranged in that fashion. It will have to be changed. Let's see—there should be some pencils on that desk and the books should be placed this way. Does that gate swing open easily?"

With comments such as these she examines each feature of the newly erected set. When she was satisfied the action began. The scenes were carefully rehearsed and then photographed several times.

"I love the work," said Mrs. Drew, for a moment turning her attention away from the players, cameras and lights. Her enjoyment was very evident. "But without my husband to carry out my ideas I wouldn't get very far, I fear. No director can make a good picture without good actors.

"I don't like to act myself. It doesn't interest me at all. The thing I love best is to work out my ideas before my typewriter. That's where my real work is. Here, on the floor, I simply follow the ideas I have written into my scenario." She showed her working script of the comedy. In it were written out in detail not only the stage business for each scene but the emotions and thoughts each player was to enact.

"The serious business of being funny," sighed Mrs. Drew. "It surely is a business, but it's great fun, too. Mr. Drew and I give our best to our work, and we are glad the people like our pictures. We are tremendously interested in them. I, in fact, have only three interests in life—my husband, my home and my work."

"Griffith Play Returns," *Chicago Post*, October 18, 1919, 8.

D. W. Griffith's latest feature, "Broken Blossoms," a picture which has, without a doubt, been given the highest praise ever awarded a motion picture, both by critics and the general public, returns to Chicago for an engagement, beginning today, at the Randolph theater.[63]

"Broken Blossoms" was introduced to Chicago last summer at the Illinois theater, at regular theater prices. It will be shown at the Randolph at popular prices, and shown continually from 8:30 in the morning until 11 at night. This will give many who did not see the picture at its first presentation an opportunity to witness the production, which has been hailed as the most artistic the screen ever presented, and it will also allow those who have seen it to re-view it, to enjoy again its beauty and charm.

There are a number of remarkable features about "Broken Blossoms." In the first place, it shows us a new phase of D. W. Griffith's art. Abandoning for a time the spectacular effects of his "Birth of a Nation," "Intolerance" and "Hearts of the World," he presents a simple but very intense drama chiefly concerning only three persons, a prize fighter, his abused little daughter and a young Chinaman. The plot of the picture is taken from one of the stories in Thomas Burke's volume of London sketches, "Limehouse Nights," the one entitled "The Chink and the Child."[64] In sordid settings, Mr. Griffith has presented a drama of rare beauty and poetic appeal.

One of the finest features of the drama is its acting. It is difficult to say which of the three artists in the leading roles does the best work. There is Lillian Gish, whose work as the little waif of London streets surpasses anything her fondest admirers ever imagined she could do and astonished those who hadn't believed her very much of an actress. There is Richard Barthelmess, formerly an actor of conventional juvenile roles, who plays the idealistic Chinaman so well that he at once took a place among the screen's great actors.[65] And there is Donald Crisp, for several years a director himself, who became an actor again at Griffith's request, and who gives an unforgettable, tho a very terrifying, portrayal of the brutal prize fighter.[66]

Another phase of the picture which has been widely commented upon is the excellence of the photography. The scenes of the London fog have been most realistically pictured. The settings representing many of the scenes in the Limehouse district were made from sketches and photographs taken while Griffith and his company were in England after filming the battle scenes for "Hearts of the World."

"Broken Blossoms" is a picture not to be missed by anyone who loves photoplays. It is also a picture which appeals as much to those who ordinarily do not enjoy pictures as to the most ardent "fan."

"Motion Pictures in Education," *Chicago Post*, May 22, 1920, 8.

The Society for Visual Education, a most enterprising organization which has been busily engaged in making the sort of pictures its members, all prominent educators, believe best suited for use in schoolrooms, gave a showing of its first production this week before a group of teachers and clubwomen. The use of films in schools has been favorite subjects for discussion and experimentation since the cinema came into existence. But little progress was made along this line until very recently, when a number of educational experts, under the leadership of Prof. Ray Moulton of the University of Chicago, combined efforts and decided to go about the matter in a new way.[67]

The pictures shown were designed for use in teaching civics, history, astronomy and geography. They are the forerunners of complete picture courses on a wide variety of subjects, but it was impossible to view even a portion of these films without realizing that a new and vital force has come into the school curriculum. In the first place, the films bear the same relation to theatrical pictures that textbooks bear to fiction. They are scientifically planned to give instruction, not to amuse. But they instruct clearly and vividly. It is no more to be expected that a child should learn the subject from one viewing of the picture than that he should comprehend it from one reading of a textbook. Both are to be studied. But the impression which remains after the pictures have been studied is more lasting, it is believed, than that which the printed word alone leaves. The films are to be studied in connection with textbooks, in many cases.

Especially interesting is the manner of teaching history by pictures. One film dealing with the English and French settlements in America and the conflict that arose, was shown as an example and was an interesting combination of animated maps, scenics from different parts of the country under discussion and historical scenes specially staged.

Founded on sound principles and managed by men and women who are leaders in their field, this latest attempt to make pictures for school children is meeting with response from educators thruout the entire United States. The society publishes a monthly magazine, "Visual Education," devoted to this subject, and thru it is endeavoring to prepare the schools for the use of this new medium of imparting knowledge. But the films themselves are the important consideration, judging by the fact that there are many schools equipped for showing pictures and unable to get the material they wish. And for the making of the right kind of school films the Society for Visual Education apparently has both the equipment and the ideas.

"Photoplays as Topics for Talk," *Chicago Post*, August 20, 1921, 2.10.

I sometimes wonder how much of the popularity of motion pictures is due to the fact that they furnish such good food for conversation. Toss the subject of photoplays or photoplay stars among almost any group of persons and you have solved the problem of what to talk about. Everyone sees pictures nowadays and each person seems to have a different idea about them. Favorite stars? Isn't there a peculiar bond between you and anyone who can "rave" about the player you like best? And if you agree upon certain photoplays, don't you feel that the understanding between you is strengthened?

Even if some of the group care nothing for pictures, that in itself starts an exciting discussion. Are pictures as bad as their detractors claim? You cite instances of artistic productions to prove that they are not. You mention actors and actresses who have achieved great characterizations thru the pantomime of the screen. Your opponent learns enough about recent productions to arouse his curiosity, and as a result probably makes a point of seeing the picture you have mentioned. If he is displeased with them, he loses no time in seeking you out to tell you of the imperfections. But the point is that he goes to see them, and possibly something in the program, the music, the news weekly, the travelog, interests him enough to lure him back.

And among dyed-in-the-wool devotees there is a chance for wide differences of opinion. The picture one grows enthusiastic over has bored someone else to extinction. A keen battle of wits may result as the one defends the story and acting the other ridicules.

It isn't so long ago that an intelligent discussion of motion pictures was made difficult or impossible by the fact that there were a vast number of cheap pictures, two or three reels in length, which were shown for one day only at each picture house. Now there are the big features which run for a week, or even a season, at the picture theaters. You are given every opportunity to see the films you hear discussed.

Differences of opinion on the merits of productions are as yet chiefly the result of the variations in taste. But with the growth of artistic ideals in the making of films, it is becoming necessary to have some understanding of art, of drama, of literature, even of history, in order to discuss motion pictures. Does it seem possible? And perhaps these fine pictures which stimulate artistic appreciation will educate the public gradually to a love of more beautiful things.

You may argue pro and con regarding the educational benefits of the "movies" themselves. But there is little room for argument in the statement that they are stimulating a certain critical judgment in those who take them seriously or joyously enough to get into lively discussions of them.

"Photoplays," *Chicago Post*, August 24, 1921, 12.

"THE BLOT" "The Blot" contains some of the very best work of Lois Weber, the only prominent woman director in pictures. Miss Weber, who undoubtedly has talent of a high order, frequently mars her productions by sensational scenes and by oversentimentality. Somehow in this picture she lays aside her mannerisms and gives us a story told sincerely, simply, in a series of beautifully directed scenes.

Poverty, especially when it brings hunger, is ever a favorite subject with this director. (She must have been nearly famished sometime in her youth and have been deeply influenced by the experience.) Usually her heroine is some poor working girl starving on the street. Tears, too, usually bedew a large proportion of each of her pictures.

Well, in this story the heroine and her family suffer from lack of nourishment, for the father is an underpaid teacher. But the tears are not many. Claire Windsor, the most intelligent actress Miss Weber has chosen to direct, gets her effects across without the aid of close-up pictures of streaming tears.[68] Margaret McWade as the worried mother gives a perfect performance of repressed grief.[69]

As the foregoing might tell you, the tone of the picture is pathetic. It is a serious presentation of the trials of members of the underpaid professions during the recent epoch of high cost of living and big wages for manual labor. The families of teachers, ministers and librarians, people of culture and refinement, suffered because the salaries did not keep pace with the rapidly mounting expenses.

The picture depends for its interest upon the vividness with which the various characters are drawn and upon contrast. There is the contrast between the professor's family, sensitive, proud and poor, and their next-door neighbors, the shoemaker's brood, noisy, prosperous, suspicious, but kind at heart. Then there is a glimpse of the extravagant lives of the very rich.

The various types are all excellently played. The settings are realistic. The story is interesting thruout, its humanness preventing it from becoming too somber or "preachy." In it Lois Weber achieves that which she has tried to do and failed in many preceding pictures: she depicts various phases of real life in a way which illustrates her theme without making a sermon of the picture.

"Photoplays," *Chicago Post*, September 5, 1921, 12.

"OVER THE HILL"   From the Fox studios, where the "vampire" plays originated, and the most sensational historical spectacles were made, there comes this picture, the greatest imaginable contrast to those scarlet productions. "Over the Hill" is the story of a mother's love for her children and a boy's love of his mother. It is based on Will Carleton's "Farm Ballads," taking its title from "Over the Hill to the Poorhouse," and it is packed with "heart throbs."

A story of home and mother is always "sure fire" with an American audience, and when it is presented with such realism, such fine acting and clever direction, as we have it here, it is one of the most effective themes in the world. In "Over the Hill," your emotions are skillfully played upon in irresistible fashion, not thru theatrical "hokum" but thru reality.

It is the sincerity and the patient attention to detail that lifts this production out of the class of the ordinary sentimental dramas and gives it its real power. It is the work of Mrs. Carr, who in the role of the "mother" proves herself a great emotional actress, and of William Welsh as "dad," and of the youngsters in the cast and the players who appear as the grown-up children that make it a great play.[70] The story is so poignantly real that it must move even the most cynical.

The opening scenes, the prologue, showing the mother's busy day with her half-dozen youngsters and dad, who can't find congenial employment, are as exquisite in their blend of humor and pathos as anything the screen ever showed. The children who appear in this part are really remarkable for their entire lack of self-consciousness and for their dramatic ability. Three of them are Mrs. Carr's own children, and they, doubtless, inherited their ability.

The plot begins after the children have grown up and gone to homes of their own. Mother and dad and one of the boys, the "wild Indian," Johnny, keep the old home. Then Johnny is sent to prison for a crime his father committed, and mother's sorrow begins. Dad dies, a victim of remorse, and mother is left alone. After John is freed, he goes west, sending home money for her each month, but a hypocritical brother keeps the checks.

A tragic time follows, when mother is an unwelcome guest in the home, first of one and then of the other of her children. At last she is determined to be a burden no longer, and makes her way "over the hill to the poorhouse." Of course, Johnny returns to rescue her from her hard lot, and the blow he delivers to the brother who had kept the money from her is, to the audience, one of the most satisfactory things in pictures.

There is a good deal of heart-break in the story, made almost unbearable at times by the reality with which it is played. You forget that you are witnessing a great piece of acting, as Mrs. Carr ages before your eyes, as her smiling face grows tragic. It is art so fine that it conceals art.

First honors, of course, go to this lady. Next to her in prominence is Johnny Walker in the role of the "black sheep" son, who turns out to be the only one devoted to his mother, after all. He has a most sympathetic role and plays it well. But I might go thru the entire list of players and praise each one, did space permit. Mrs. Carr's work, tho, overshadows them all.

"Over the Hill" is an achievement in photoplays. It is certain to repeat here the great success it has had in the east, and which it so thoroly deserves.

"Second Thots on 'Four Horsemen,'" *Chicago Post*, September 10, 1921, 2.4.

Is "The Four Horsemen" as good a picture as it seemed on first viewing?

This question has arisen in my mind so many times since the opening of Rex Ingram's film version of Ibanez's novel when the splendor of the production and the sweep of the emotion it aroused had almost made impossible a calmly critical estimate of the play that I determined to see it over again.

Sometimes this is a dangerous experiment, this re-viewing of a picture which has made a deep impression. And yet, if the production is really great, it is as well worth seeing again as a great book merits re-reading.[71]

Well, "The Four Horsemen" stands triumphantly the test of a second view. In fact, I'm inclined to believe one's appreciation of it is deepened when the picture is considered critically and in detail. It is a production which will set a standard for many years to come.

Aside from the fact that Rex Ingram had as photoplay material a strong story set against a marvelous background, there are a number of remarkable features about this picture. One of its outstanding characteristics is its vividness. The director's attention to detail is not alone responsible for this. An imagination and an eye for the picturesque were needed. It is realism with something added. It is that sort of realism, plus something more, which marks Kipling's work. And it doesn't need a war background to bring it out. In fact, on a second viewing, it is the Argentine portion of the picture which makes the deepest impression.

The picture is also remarkable for the acting it contains. There isn't a moment when any player steps out of his part. Whether he is going about the ordinary business of life, or meeting a great emotional crisis, each person is consistently true to character from first to last.

The finest scene in the picture, in my opinion, is that between Julio and his father, after the latter has returned, heart-broken, from his ruined "castle on the Marne," to find his son in uniform. With anything less than the most sincere, most assured and artistic acting, this scene would have been maudlin. As it is, it is worth seeing the whole picture again, just for that scene in which Julio, formerly almost arrogant, now diffident, stands before his father in the uniform of France. And the father never believing the gay Julio, exempt because of his Argentine birth, would go voluntarily to the aid of France, exclaims: "My son, fighting for my country, when it isn't his!"

It's an unforgettable picture, "The Four Horsemen." If you haven't seen it, let me urge you not to let the opportunity go by, for the production is nearing the close of its engagement.

And even if you have seen it, you will find it can be viewed again with pleasure.

"Romance Factory," *Chicago Post*, December 17, 1921, 2.13.

New York, Dec. 16.—A trip to Santa Claus' workshop may be taken only in childhood's dreams. But I have come from an even more enchanting place, the factory where romance is made.

"Won't you let us show you 'how the wheels go round,'" the invitation was sent from one of these modern magic shops, the Fox Film studio in New York city, an invitation which needed no urging for its acceptance.[72] You, too, I'm sure, would like to have come with us, but since that wasn't quite a possibility—with your Christmas shopping and all—perhaps you'd like to hear all about it, anyway.

The place where romance is made, but you would never pick out that great, somber, factorylike building at 55th street and 10th avenue as the home of the modern Merlins who do their work of enchantment. It suggests business efficiency and speed, none of the delightful temperamental, whimsical qualities the word studio implies. However, I was to learn that the studio part, tho the heart of the whole affair, was, after all, only a part.

Let us visit the studio section first then. What's this? The clock whirrs back a hundred years or more and you've stepped into the past. You are in a quaint, old-fashioned English room, and you seat yourself before a great fireplace. There are old-fashioned pictures on the walls, old books in the bookcase, real books they are and really old. One lies open, face down on the mantel. You pick it up and find it a volume of "Romeo and Juliet." There is no chance that the camera would reveal what that book was, or that the miniatures on the wall were actually of the period of the rest of the room, but all these details aid the players in keeping the illusion as they go thru their parts.

It is the room of Edmund Keane, the great English actor. They are filming a story of his life, a story based on Dumas' drama. He will walk in presently. Ah, here he comes!

But it isn't Edmund Keane; it is William Farnum. We are introduced, and he talks of his recent trip to Europe. And here's a ragged boy—but his manners are courtly. Here's a pretty child who has the poise of a great lady. It's "real" life still.

Then the lights go on—strange lights that turn our faces green and our lips purple. The camera man is at his post. The director, Herbert Brenon, who just now was chatting with us, stands near the camera. Mr. Farnum has become Edmund Keane; Peggy Shaw ("Follies" girl) has become a demure little maid of 1815. On the side lines, waiting are other characters of the story—the little boy and girl, a stately ambassador, a lovely Italian lady. The action begins. Again and again they go thru their parts, usually to piano music, with the accompaniment of the hammer blows of carpenters who, in an adjoining set, are rebuilding old Drury Lane theater.

So, thru the lens of the camera, onto the ribbon of celluloid, goes the little, old-fashioned room, the romantic, charming personages, the appealing story. The players will exchange their costumes for modern garb. The carpenters will tear down the room. But the picture has been caught and will be seen by tens of thousands of people all over the world. And how is it to get from that camera to all those waiting screens?

Tomorrow we come back to the Fox plant; this time not to the studio but to the laboratories. There, on millions of little squares not much more than an inch in length, we find our scene of yesterday.

Into darkrooms, developing baths, "fixing" vats, drying-rooms go the strips of celluloid negative—all the little scenes and big scenes, in varying lengths of film. Most fascinating of all is the department where the positive prints, the film which goes to all the theaters, is washed and dried by intricate machinery which looks like a great loom and which finishes its work by winding the ribbons of celluloid onto their bobbins of tin—the completed reels. These great laboratories form in themselves a fascinating world.

The romance created in the studio has been captured and immortalized. It now becomes a commercial commodity and there is a great selling force organized to take care of it. It is an international department, for the activities of the Fox Film company are worldwide.

A visit to a huge plant like that of the Fox Film company is at once a bewildering and an inspiring experience. It gives one a sense of the magnitude of this business of providing motion pictures to the world. It isn't entertainment alone that this army of artists, technicians and business folk are manufacturing. They are preparing the food for the hearts and minds of millions of people. We talk of the romance of business. This is the business of romance.

More of the various departments of a great studio we shall tell you later, and of all the intricate details which go to make a photoplay.

Virginia Tracy

A well-known reporter and writer, Virginia Tracy (1874–1946) spent nearly a year reviewing films for the *New York Tribune* in 1919. She was an unusually knowledgeable and astute reviewer in her lengthy weekly columns, and it is unclear why she stopped reviewing in late 1919. She did, however, write scenarios for *The Queen of Sheba* (1922), *Nero* (1922), and *The Shepherd King* (1923), as well as several novels from the late 1920s through the 1930s.

Like Genevieve Harris, Tracy devoted a full column to making an argument (quite rare at the time) that, in some fifty short films produced for Vitagraph and then Metro, the team of Mr. and Mrs. Sidney Drew created a series demonstrating that "human and simple comedy" could be as popular as it was sustained and significant. As "Every-woman's Husband," Sidney's

Henry Minor bumbled into follies and slight mishaps, but it was his wife, Polly, who usually had "the last word, the wise gesture, the gracious little triumph" in any one of their films. The Drews' films offered a refreshing contrast to all the mayhem in other comedies. Tracy also reviewed the reissue of Cecil B. DeMille's *The Cheat* (1915), ostensibly to debate the value of realism versus romanticism in films with friends but also to double down on her distaste for the cheating heroine (Fannie Ward), a "dilapidated little rat of a very human being," and her admiring fascination for the Japanese collector (Sessue Hayakawa), a "Lucifer of malign magnificence."

Tracy also could write in high praise of stars like Fairbanks and directors like Griffith and Tucker, but not without reservations. In a column on Fairbanks, she returned to his first film, *The Lamb* (1916), to recover the astonishment she shared with others at his "adorably diverting stunts" and "friendly grin." In *Manhattan Madness* (1918), however, all the stunts, tricks, and smiles left "him no time to act"; and his starring role as a conventional hero in *Arizona* (1918) was even worse: "The seriousness he plays as solemnly as he would Othello; he does the lighter scenes as if he were a mechanical toy." Tracy was enthralled by Griffith's "exquisitely simple and exquisitely pure" *Broken Blossoms* (1919), and her review praised not only the quietly expressive acting of Gish and Barthelmess but also the unusually poetic use of color in tinting and toning. When it came to *True Heart Susie* several months later, unlike Marjorie Daw, Tracy found the film too studied and insistent: Griffith seemed to be overdirecting Gish, as if "squeezing simplicity out of [her] face," and there were far too many explanatory intertitles. Although Tracy agreed that *The Miracle Man* was a solid, good picture, she hedged: "There were too many close-ups of too many people with large tears rolling down their faces," and the film's "homestretch was a little too long and even too limp." But she was quite aware of how out of step with the audience she felt at the theater's last show she attended.[73]

"The Dazzling Sameness of Douglas Fairbanks," *New York Sunday Tribune*, January 26, 1919, 46.

During the latter day of the year of our Lord 1918 something happened. We saw something. We saw a printed likeness of Douglas Fairbanks and it wasn't smiling.

It not only wasn't smiling, but it was frowning. Not for the sake of cuteness, either, but to look angry. And our heart behaved like Hiawatha's, "for the heart of Hiawatha throbbed and shouted and exulted." All because we said to ourselves "He's going to play a real part again. For if he were only going to jump he would jump smiling."

Past as the young movie makes another history there must be other Rip Van Winkles still alive who remember "The Lamb," produced three years ago last fall, as Fairbanks's first picture and a smashing success.[74] Those are invited to consider with us of what this success was composed.

"The Lamb" starts out as a comedy of character—the character of a young millionaire, whose lady love is obliged to dismiss him as a coward. Now, the lamb is no lion, because he has never studied the lion's part; he has never in his life done anything but lap cream, and facing danger is as impracticable for him as raw meat. So the poor little lamb starts a regular course in courage, and the scenario goes sliding along a very delicately graduated incline from comedy to farce, from farce to fantasy, so that it may then turn from the fantastic to the heroic with no strain. We need not say that when the heroic reenters so does the heroine, who trembles to find herself alone among infuriated savages with nobody for her defense but the lamb she left behind her. There comes a time when she knows better: when he and she lie in a little hollow of the plain with their last shot gone and the savages creeping in upon them in an ever-tightening circle, and she kisses his sleeve, pressing her face close against his shoulder, so that she may keep it there until she dies. His face you can still see, and if you deny a gulp of sympathy then, just because melodrama and last shots and savages are "old stuff," away with you to your little theatres, for you will never know one picture from another. In any case, you will hardly be smitten with the lockjaw of astonishment to hear that all the while a regiment has been riding to their rescue, but we can't help hoping you feel at least an amused indulgence for the heroine when she is with some difficulty detached from her hero and driven to the fort a little nervous about there being nobody but the army to protect her, that you smile with the lamb when, reviewing this result of his busy day in which he fought a war, he says to himself, "Sherman was wrong."

Well, in "The Lamb" Fairbanks astonished us with some adorably diverting stunts; our glee roared out at sight of them, and when they continued to grow more and more numerous in each picture they continued also to astonish and to charm. They still were used only as snap to the fun's eventual whip-up of smilingly thrilling romance, never interfering with the hero's reactions to all the delights and dilemmas which a young American-very-human being is liable to on his way through the world. No comedy amounts to much unless it has wisdom, and the friendly grin of these comedies—most of them, as we remember, by Anita Loos—was very wise: they and Fairbanks played together so perfectly that, like the gentleman in the poem, "we laughed with joy as we looked at them," and to know we were on our way to see them was like knowing, last winter, that there was sugar in the pantry and the coal had come. Indeed, there fell a quiet moment, at the table on the balcony of a pictured country club, when we thought: "Yes, Fairbanks is so knowing a comedian that he can act perfectly without a scrap of action to act on." And from that time to this, we have never seen him do—speaking in exceedingly round numbers—any acting at all. For that last quiet moment occurred in "Manhattan Madness" just before the tricks began; tricks madly delectable not to Manhattan only but the whole continent—oh, the wild they made! All the world wondered! So since then Fairbanks has become a prestidigitateur, pure and simple, and his tricks leave him no time to act.

For while in "Manhattan Madness" they were essential to the idea's happy nonsense, now there has to be so many of them that there isn't room for any idea.[75] As first ornaments in the design, they became its centre; then they ate up the design altogether and left nothing whatever but themselves swinging irrelevantly in midair like trapezes.

And this seemed actually admitted when they began to be advertised by a wide smile, just such a smile exactly as a trapeze artist favors his audience with when he trips in, ready for his act. It is a smile of announcement, not of expression: If you wish stunts, prepare to see them now!

Indeed, it was easy to gauge their popularity and the tremendous pressure put upon their perpetrator to perpetrate nothing else, simply by observing how that smile spread over the composite likeness of the movie male. Every firm possessing an athletic star set him smiling till the movie magazines looked like pamphlets advertising tooth powder, even the Olympian Farnums showing their teeth from every page. George Walsh ceased to be a hero, a lover and an actor, and took to hopping over things, and when the face of Wallace Reid appeared cleft in twain by the same smile we felt that our trust must never stray again beyond Hart, Keenan and the vamps, who can be relied upon occasionally to shut their mouths.[76] Not that we have a prejudice against smiles; we should be sorry to see even a comedian always sad. It is the "always" in any kind that affronts us, the cut-and-dried, the inescapable, the smile that won't come off. From any flexibility become hard and fast, good Lord deliver us!

But then came the frown, the rainbow!

It was in an advance advertisement of Fairbanks as Lieutenant Denton in "Arizona." For ourselves we should never have selected Denton as a Fairbanks vehicle, because Denton is a purely conventional hero in a purely conventional situation; still, we did not doubt that he could limber up such a part, that he would fill it full of simplicity and freshness and nature no matter how he tripped up the romantic gait of a "straight lead" to do it. We thought, "He has rebelled. And he is using the name and fame of 'Arizona' as the opening wedge to get back into acting again." We even had hopes that the public had shown signs of rebelling with him against himself and that that was why he had undertaken such imposing troubles as Denton's. Alas, the frown was no true rainbow, but a mirage!

The truth about "Arizona" is so bad that we have to stop and say our prayers before we utter it. For though we went twice to see what a Fairbanks' performance of Lieutenant Denton would be like we never did see. It wasn't there. In its place was just a sort of smear across the film, as if an automobile had shot past and vanished.

Remember the heavenly repose of him, there at the table in "Manhattan Madness," and now observe him unable even to get seated at the table in "Arizona" without giving three backward kicks at the bench behind him! Time was when he achieved with little conspicuous movement a great variety of expression; now he achieves every movement all the time with no expression at all. Finally, to the mania for doing something every moment he has added the mania for doing it so fast that nobody can see what he does do.

Yet in the occasional seconds—all funeral—when his head is still enough for us to see his face, that face is crossed by none but the most obvious changes and few enough of them. The comic and serious elements of his Denton form not a blend but a sandwich. The seriousness he plays as solemnly as he would Othello; he does the lighter scenes as if he were a mechanical toy. And not only do the mechanical toy and Othello never blend into one, but no communication ever takes place between them; they live in absolutely separate air-tight boxes out of which each is let to do its turn at a given cue, but no identity or motive of mutual life exists between them. Now, as a poor little lamb trying to be a lion you may be as funny and as sad as you like in a single breath and then your next breath may be as profound as any lion ever drew and every pulse in the audience will stand still until you draw it, but you cannot be a mechanical toy standing on your head in one scene and then somersault through the window and land into the next scene as Othello with any sort of convincing effect.

We clutch to ourselves the hope that this lack of convincingness is due partly to the wretchedly old-fashioned stiltedness of both titling and directing in the serious scenes; still more to the extreme choppiness of the scenario's construction which makes impossible any emotional continuity whatever. By emotional we mean merry as well as serious emotion, any kind of freely flowing feeling, for this is the lifeblood of any picture, without which it is merely a kaleidoscope. There is no surer way of destroying all interest than to have no developed scenes but only a pell-mell of whisking flashes that react on the audience much like the springing on and off of the lights when a trolley car is going over an intricate junction of switches.

But then we scarcely think of Fairbanks as helplessly obedient in the hands of his scenarioist and, moreover, in the scenes of young love, often easily and gayly titled, the scenarioist has made a distinct attempt to provide the star with opportunities for exactly his own gifts. Fresh and natural little scenes they smilingly await the spontaneous, engaging drollery, the quaintness and perceptiveness, the funny, tender, human charm which would once have led us through them, happy captives. His way of treating them now is to whoop past them on the run and the only thing that ever arrests his flight is some opportunity to jump over something. Every significant moment is deliberately shirked. One title tells us, as if we were reading a story, that "all through the night conflicting emotions surged within him, but nothing could break his indomitable spirit." After this do we see the conflicting emotions or the indomitable spirit refusing to break? Fear not, tender-hearted—we see a bugler blowing the warning that it is time to get up. [. . .]

"ON THE TRAIL OF THE MOTION PICTURE," NEW YORK SUNDAY TRIBUNE, FEBRUARY 2, 1919, 46.   "I have just read your article on Fairbanks, and I can't get down to my own dull job until I send you my whoop of joy," writes Harvey O'Higgins to Miss Virginia Tracy, whose articles are one of the features of the Sunday moving picture page. "It is a pippin," continues Mr. O'Higgins.[77]

"A Truce between Romance and Realism," *New York Sunday Tribune*, February 9, 1919, 54.

The acquaintances who were wandering around the neighborhood with us looking for a congenial movie kept arguing bitterly as to whether romance or realism would eventually succeed on the screen. The wife acquaintance declared that the time had passed for hairbreadth escapes or million-dollar pageants, which seemed to be what she meant by romance, but the husband acquaintance insisted that that time could never pass, since what people went to the movies for was to forget their troubles—not to watch farmers feeding pigs, nor shopgirls trimming Christmas trees in Harlem flats, this appearing to be what he meant by realism. The battle as to which must soon drive the other from the screen was interrupted by the lights of a movie sign advertising a reissue: Fannie Ward and Sessue Hayakawa in "The Cheat."[78]

We gathered in the combatants to see "The Cheat" because here was, at least, success. And success of a singularly determining kind, we ourselves having seen it for three years in one return engagement after another, till now, in the midst of competing overnight popularities, came the reissue—a movie Methuselah still up to date as the new map of Europe!

Now, to our mind the perfections of "The Cheat" are perfections which we should not altogether care to see grow upon pictures. Doubtless in uninspired hands the picture form does lend itself to weak, dreary, lagging, struggling shapelessness, and certainly "The Cheat" achieves at a bound the economy and unity of the play form: but some of us no more want plays when we go to see pictures than pictures when we go to plays. We can't help scenting a danger in this complete competency of stagecraft, so compact, so firm, so balanced, moving so evenly and yet suspensively toward a climax which has not a loose thread, every incident constructive and yet naturally stressed, each scene developed just to its fullest expressiveness, neither more nor less, and each colloquially phrased little title carrying the story as far as where the action can pick it up again and no further, toward a punch which might very well land square in the jaw of the Grand Guignol.[79] All plot and punch and sex warfare and suspense and nature a la Sardou, theatrical as the display lightning makes of itself on a summer night, but its foundations laid by the most naturalistic treatment while our credence is being caught and colored by every known firework only after the sex interest is well started. "The Cheat" is the very model of that "well made play" which the stage has so recently sloughed off.

The heroine is she about whom centres that naturalistic treatment which in the beginning snares our credence for "The Cheat." She is simply a mean, lively, pretty, greedy, natural little animal, equally familiar to our recognition as our neighbor's clawing kitten and as the fellow creature whom we have all got to reckon with. For whether or not we like to admit that there is no room for such a person in well made society drama, there she is; conceived with no more extenuation or blame, set before us with as little arrangement and as entirely on her own feet as if life itself had set her there. Incredible that neither the actress nor the author nor the producers have failed each other, that nobody has played her for sympathy, but so it is! However gaudy the incidents of her story, the Cheat herself shows us her shallow little nature in its shabbiest moments—nagging her husband, leaving her servants without the wages which she has spent for new clothes, speculating away the Red Cross fund intrusted to her, and when detection approaches, making an adventuress's bargain with the villain for his check. Then when the villain becomes too much for her and, having taken horrible advantage of her one honest impulse, tries to send her husband to prison on a false charge, we at last offer our—what? Our sympathy, no less!

For this dilapidated little rat of a very human being when asked to suffer too much even for her faults puts up a magnificent game fight against cruel odds, and a human being putting up a game fight against odds always gets the sympathy, always will and always must—we heard our romantic acquaintance when he capitulated with a nudging whisper: "Oh, well, I'm for realism, too, when it's really interesting!" But the unmollified stare of the realistic wife was just then following the villain, and we feared her wrath, for there is no concealing the fact that the villain is a romantic figure.

To start with, he is—for no particular reason but that he may have sliding paper doors to his study—not only a villain, but a Japanese. He has therefore the advantage over common villains in morning coats that he may go swathed in a kimono as in some gorgeous crime and is thus indeed first shown to us, amid the most beautiful of somber lighting, doing something cryptically wicked in that study with the sliding paper doors. Why it should show a more deceitful nature to concoct villainy behind transparent doors than opaque ones we do not know, but we accept the suggestion with hypnotized greed; even when his worst habit turns out to be collecting curios and we discover that the wickedness he is perpetuating is merely the stamping of some new acquisition with a branding iron, the design of which he has tossed off as lesser men do book plates, we are not misled. We know that in the drama collecting curios has ever been a habit leading to strange crimes, and we have only to look at him, with the smoke from the branding iron rising as from the Pit about his head like the halo of a lost angel to recognize him as belonging to the great old race of demon-heroes now almost vanished from the stage as from Harlem or Chicago; Lucifer of malign magnificence rising here on the screen again to prove themselves one of the eternal pipe dreams of the human heart. It is true that when we see our Lucifer later away from home in American clothes and quite simply a young gentleman among other young gentlemen we have a blank moment. But no, he isn't trailing those clouds of glory and emblazoned kimonos even around the house unless there is going to be trouble. And there is.

We must be greedy indeed if we are not satisfied by the fuss Lucifer makes when the little Cheat refuses to pay up by the scorn with which he offers her his revolver when she threatens to kill herself and by the glance of righteous, of awful indignation which he gives her when she tries to kill him instead, after he has branded her on the shoulder with that smoking iron of his. This terrible and frozen scorn continues to rebuke us till, after the picture, we begin to ask ourselves what, after all, he has to be so scornful about?

Surely something besides the possession of a pair of paper doors and the not necessarily graceful tendency to brand ladies with hot irons is necessary for a gentleman may assume the attitude of a god among wild beasts! Yet what else does he do? He triumphs over no one, he accomplishes nothing, he doesn't even take advantage of his wound and die harrowingly, and yet he makes his case a Lucifer and a demon-hero; he simply leaves it to Mr. Hayakawa to make him appear an extremely superior person and thus, indeed, he does appear. In fact, we never see "The Cheat" without feeling socially, not to say racially, snubbed. We have even vowed to follow the next Japanese we meet out walking till we see him miss a trolley or pit on the street or otherwise fall to the level of our inelegance—where, alas, we should still cut no particularly luciferesque figure working a branding iron. We are afraid it takes superiority after all, especially when our realistic acquaintance comes down to earth and speaks, "Of course, you have to let yourself go a little when they're romantic—like that!"

"What Screen Comedy Owes the Drews," *New York Sunday Tribune*, April 20, 1919, 4.4.

We wish we could remember the comic movie from which perhaps two years and a half ago we emerged into the welcome decency of the Tenderloin at midnight and breathed an air of hot asphalt, gasoline, dust and cosmetics that came to us like incarnate ozone after the crumbling squalor of mummy-smut which for two reels had closed our lungs. But perhaps the essence of this attempt at amusement was its unremarkableness, its being a specimen so true to the cipher type, a perfect thirty-six of antediluvian futility. What we do remember was the ultimatum of the actress in whose company we had been seeing many "comics" in search of the usually admirable acting of some comedian friends of ours, acting which had, however, got washed out to sea and lost in the vast, senseless tide of bromide and bustle, of mothers-in-law and jealous wives and siren typists and night-shirts and oglings and old maids and fathers kicking suitors and babies held upside down—real babies, mind you, really held upside down, really screaming themselves into convulsions, but not with the screams of joy that convulsed their audiences—the whole howling, wallowing mass of vulgarity mixed with insipidity, in the faces of which rose that ultimatum. "Well, I've come to the conclusion that you simply can't put over comedy on the screen. There must be some reason why it actually won't register there."

We roared like the Carolina rattler and drew back with a hiss. Not indeed that we suspected her of attacking the cosmic farces of the great Charles, for about him we had already exchanged confidences ecstatic enough to permit of our even admitting that, after all, the further his adventures were kept away from food the better, we knew that she referred to the naturalistic comedy which, either in acting or scenario, we had long sought in vain. What we couldn't hear was the essentialness of her accusation and we made haste to wither it at the root by inquiring whether she had ever seen Douglas Fairbanks. What did she think, for instance, about "The Half Breed" or "Double Trouble" or "His Picture in the Papers" or "Passin' Through" or—[80]

"Yes," she retorted, "but what's happening even in his scenarios lately? He's beginning to act as if he had to work his way through a gymnasium."

"Have the goodness to remember," our picture-loyalty replied, "that he has, nevertheless, put over perfect comedies on the screen. You're not at liberty to say comedy won't register on the screen simply because we've got to say that the public won't support what it registers."

But three years dead! Nay, not so much, not three! Out of what limbo do we amazedly fish the collapsed ghost of such a heresy? Which of a dozen no less than perfect comedies of this year alone can we look in the eye—we, who never foresaw them, who never guessed in the public disposition that readiness, that cordial understanding which gave them a foothold when we offered them nothing but our groans? For if this year, in pictures of emotional appeal, we have been fed mainly on much watered gruel of a temperature suggesting that it had been standing a long time on the steam-table, in comedy the screen has opened to us whole orchards and dairies of fresh delight, haven after haven of charm and sympathy, of laughter and observation and kindness.

But between these two phases had occurred, of course, that beginning which brought all the rest to pass; that phase when we began scolding, "Well, they see what the Drews are putting over, don't they? And they see how the public simply eats it up! Can't any of the rest of them take a hint from the Drews?" And soon every one was doing it! Not in stupid imitation, but in a happy release to truths and jokes they had perhaps long been longing to show us but hadn't dared; the whole world of experiment in human stumbles and grins and bright, easy tears and comfortings had suddenly taken heart. This was what little more than two years of Henry Minor and his wife, Polly, of the standard implicit in the trademark "Mr. and Mrs. Sidney Drew" had brought about.[81]

In the beginning it wasn't, as we remember, the dear Minors; it was just the usual fussing husband and wife—there were even lingering traces of the typist and mother-in-law. It would be extremely interesting to know whether from the start the authors were looking forward to a chance at Henry and Polly, and these staler beginnings were only feelers of the public pulse, or whether by more fortunate accident an embryo Henry and Polly appeared in some sketch and were so well received that the Drews were encouraged to go on with them. At any rate, it is now one of the securest strands of screen history that they did go on, and that the public followed as if they had been pied pipers, as if it could never get enough of the charmed life which, after all, was so exactly its own life, only seen over for it, shown to it with the sweetest, funniest charm and truest knowledge of the deep affectionateness and kindly conscience which, in its scramble to get somewhere and back in time for something else, it often so drearily and blindingly forgets it has.

The Drews, in showing commonplace life to commonplace eyes, justified it to itself, and, at the same time, mocked at and enlightened it as to its failures and its faults by making them funny enough and homelike enough for their recognition to be at once endurable and unavoidable. The Drew scenarios were content to take the slightest occurrence, the lightest emotion, which could bring no matter how tiny a discord into the life of Henry and Polly, develop the discord and resolve it—that was all. Only the light emotion must be genuine, the slight occurrence representative, so that the discord should resolve not itself alone but the memories of a hundred others in every audience. At first these things used to happen between Henry and Polly in isolation, as if they had only just moved into the neighborhood, but presently there began to grow up about them a whole suburban life, so human in general and so American in particular that it is, for the great majority of us, the neighborhood we were brought up in, and probably for all of us it has at least long seemed as if we had only to take the trolley or the local to arrive in the accustomed midst and know at once its pleasant levels and the small, sharp indentations of its familiar miseries.

It is the pleasant levels which by her own prettiness and common sense and astutely feminine charm that Polly usually walks; it is almost always she who is left with the last word, the wise gesture, the gracious little triumph. And what a boomerang this masculine chivalry is! For, of course, it is to Henry, so apt to be stumbling among the sharp familiar miseries, to Henry's capacity for winding himself up in difficulties and twisting himself up in perturbations, in follies more sensitive though less graceful than his wife's, that our sympathy flies back with a poignancy that Polly never has need of; we feel the safety in which she lives and which is so largely contributive to her delightfulness as being, after all, not wholly disconnected with a certain amount of capacity in Henry, at least, during office hours; we come to a full belief in an underlying responsibleness in him. There returns to us the plaint of one married lady to another in the days of their early middle age: "When I was a girl, of course, I liked to see the heroes young and terribly good looking and all dressed up, with exciting things happening to them. But now I feel so left out of things like that, I feel as if they would just snub everything I was interested in and anyhow I want to say to them, 'Well, you don't interest me, either!' Don't you think it's silly of them" (appealing to her friend) "never to have men that are really interesting, like our husbands?" Henry Minor is the triumphant response to that appeal. There is a sense in which he is Everywoman's Husband, or, at any rate, every American husband, however much nicer he may be than that one of Clara's, in whom we cannot imagine what she ever saw, or however much less dazzling than that one of Mary's, so terribly good looking and all dressed up, like a young hero to whom exciting things might happen, that we cannot imagine how she ever caught him; yet there will be something of Henry Minor in him if he is really a husband for all.

We are told that when Sidney Drew died nearly fifty unreleased pictures were completed, and not only these, but all in existence, can, of course, be long reissued. But even when Polly's pretty dresses have come old-fashioned and the Ford and flivver manners of our day are left far behind the interest of days when everybody hitches his aeroplane to his front steps, even if a fire should explode every scrap of celluloid that holds the record of our Minors, the most important thing about them will persist—the fact that they called upon something honorable in public taste and that the public honorably responded. That is what has put faith into the effort all about us. We shall never have on the screen a human and simple comedy which is not in this sense stamped with the legend "Mr. and Mrs. Sidney Drew present"—

"Best of Griffith in 'Broken Blossoms,'"
New York Sunday Tribune, May 25, 1919, 37.

At last! This fervent exclamation has risen during the ages to quite some several lips, we admit, but never from a fuller throat. Lately we have been hearing of apprehensive Senators asking themselves: "In saving the world have we lost our republic?" For some long while now ardent volunteers in the motion picture ranks have been quaking: "In achieving Broadway theatres and orchestras de luxe and sterilized air and settings à la Ballin and lingerie up to date, in gaining the world have we lost our Griffith?" And, if so, mightn't we indeed "weep, weep, and tear our hair" over the monstrous bargain? Earnest picturites have run to his every new offering, their hands clutching their palpitating hearts—those of us earnest picturites, anyway, who have excitable dispositions!—longing for the opportunity not to criticize, appraise or withhold, but once more simply to salute the captain of the host. That opportunity has come. We, quite as well as Candida's poet, know the hour when it strikes. We had not followed Griffith's new adventure three minutes before we knew that what we were adventuring into was a new epoch in pictures. For the day after "Broken Blossoms" was exhibited the screen was at least five years ahead of where it had been the day before.

This was so from the technical standpoint of course, since it was true at all, but also from the standpoint of dramatic intention. The technical innovations are but a means to this end; the end of putting over a picture without regard to any stereotyped regulations in subject or construction; above all, in length. The programme picture—detestable phrase!—must be just five reels. If the subject is too long, cut off its head; if too short, pad it with footage! No other single condition so accounts for the poverty and monotony of our scenarios. To be sure, "special features" of ten reels or so may be specially produced if bolstered by immense battles or propaganda or by being historical or taken from the Bible or because they give exhibitions of swimming. But no special feature has dared to produce a mere intimate story about human beings which continues so long as it has something to say and ceases when it has said it. This has long been the prayer of our heart, and in "Broken Blossoms"—adapted from "The Chink and the Child" in Burke's "Limehouse Nights"—this is exactly what Griffith has done.

With a cast of six characters, only three of whom are more than sketches, and without as much as a rope or a ball dress to sustain it, it runs, perhaps, seven and a half reels, so that it is neither a programme feature nor a special feature; nor can whole families say they attend in order to show Georgia how Lincoln was assassinated, or how Salome danced. The picture's beauty is in and of itself. It is a tragedy pure and simple—exquisitely simple and exquisitely pure. Its maker has taken his own time to saturate his mind with the story, and then to saturate the story with his own vision of it. Conceived and projected in a mood jealously honorable, it has made no concession whatever. It has the serene accomplishment of an artist who has exacted from himself nothing but perfection.

The first novelty made us start wildly. The huge expanse of screen, which Griffith does not break by any device of picture frame or slate, dawned upon us in deep rose. Theoretically, we loathe definite colors in pictures, and, indeed, the eye quails before the chromo blows and bashes that may now assail it in injudicious hands; but there was no resisting this field of rosy palpitating light, which seemed to be drawing us through it into the dawn. And so, indeed, it was; it "faded us in" to China, China of pale bronze, against a background of dim, dense blue, irradiated whenever the sun struck it, with washes of hot gold. These shades of rose and blue and orange and bronze are the only colors used, but there is more of the Orient in them than in a hundred solidly built Chinese streets, swarming with wild animals and foreigners, to show how much they cost. The shadings never wobble and hop nor show an outline of strange prismatic zigzags, occasionally spitting red and green in your face, as the professedly colored pictures do, and the scenes change with a melting smoothness, in which "flashes" have at last wholly disappeared, the dim blue, or later, the rich brown, simply deepens up like mist from the far borders of the screen, blotting out what we are not now meant to see, or enhancing by its massing cloudbanks the close-up, which has stolen upon us unawares.

But when the Chinese priest has struck the sacred bell and his nephew, a young poet and philosopher who must seek his fortune in the new world, but hopes also to carry to its young barbarians the ancient message of peaceful contemplation—has made his pious farewells, all the splendor of color dies away; his ship sails down a river of as misty spiritual suggestion as the River of Souls itself, until, going west and passing other ghost ships going east, it disappears into the ocean to our own world of brown and gray within the London slums.

Here lives Battling Burrows, a Cockney prizefighter who vents all his strength on beating his little daughter, a fair and delicate drudge worshipped at a distance like something holy by the young Chinese, how poor, lonely and despised. When she has fainted from the vilest of her father's beatings it is across the door of his little Oriental shop—heaven has come to the Chinaman. He hides his little goddess in his loft, which he transforms into a temple with all the best his stock affords; feeds her, nurses her, bathes her wounds, wraps her in embroidered silk, decks her with Chinese headdresses of flowers and, careful to treat her always as a little girl, teaches her what it is to smile—heaven has come to the child. So, in the temple loft these two humble and gentle souls, without harm in them, escape a while to a meek happiness. Then the father's discovery of what he can understand only as a "daughter of his taking up with a dirty Chink" requires him to avenge his family and racial honor, and this costs all three lives. It is in that temple which the father has smashed to bits that the Chinaman arranges in seemliness the broken body of his little goddess and once more makes her fair in silks and flowers. After due prayer he seeks his own death at the foot of her couch, before the police can make good their claim to this Chinese murderer and abductor, now safe and far as the girl is out of our civilized life. But we see, once more in China, that the priest still strikes the sacred bell, and going east and going west along the misty River of Souls, the ships still pass each other in the night. Hereafter, in a better world than this—

Now, is it not a singular thing that a story of torture, murder and suicide, enlivened only by a prizefight and—a prizefight, mind you, where the wrong man wins!—should have the effect of some flower softly unfolding its slow sweetness and as softly fading into nothingness when its time comes? Why does this heavyweight of deadly explosives strike us as something frail and fine, of no more bulk than a wreath of wood smoke? Innumerable pictures have hauled us through every known orgy of pain, yet this one remains with us like a sacrament.

Perhaps this is because everything may be thus transmuted by poetry and here, with no sordidness or squalor shirked, is certainly the mood of the poetic. Griffith and his Bitzer have seen to it that the haunted and haunting magic of the old river side shall snare our senses with its brown smoke-stained mystery in a setting and a photography so creative that it lets loose on us at once the whole charm of London's mellowness.[82] We have never seen such a capture of atmosphere as this, calling up in its few sets the whole quaint, rich, grim, story soaked suggestiveness by which the lower Thames holds our imagination in an immemorial net. In this beauty, from which we never escape, every element of interpretive beauty is combined by an unflagging artistic vigilance, so that where visual beauty must not be forced it is the more reinforced by beauty of execution. The acting by Lillian Gish and Richard Barthelmess of the two most exacting parts is so woven into the picture, repeating in its apparent monotone its myriad reflections of variety and suggestion, that it seems murderous to tear it out and praise it; even the girl's fearfully realized passion of terror somehow does not break the web. And see how large a part of all this exquisite expressiveness comes from the rigidity, the scant and meagre movements, of those subdued, propitiating souls! Compare their inhibited, mouselike motions with the beautiful free sweep of the boy's arm with which, when all is lost, he strikes his own death blow, and see what a story of release that tells! See the effect of using for the Oriental temple in the loft the same radiance of color which we had in China, thus setting it off from the brown slums like fairyland, and then, by the poignant loveliness of the scenes there in, making the slums unreal and fairyland the reality. So that when, even in death, these children come home to their real fairyland again, we feel all must be well. From end to end this is the only alleviation Griffith uses.

The picture offers, however, another and deeper consolation: the deep humanity in which it has been conceived. Its horrors are not shown for their own sake, but for the sweetness enduring in their midst; the tender and lowly virtue that is ridden down by the black brute beasts of prejudice and cruelty remains unsullied and uncorrupted by them; in this picture, which might be called in Maeterlinck's phrase, "The Treasure of the Humble," we feel for its living persistence, and there arises in us an immense desire to behave, while yet we may, as well as possible; to kill in ourselves the least inflection of Battling Burrows and to bring ourselves as near as may be to the high decency of the Chink and the Child. There is a line in "Roderick Hudson" which has always seemed to us the truest salutation to fine and human art, and it best expresses the mood in which "Broken Blossoms" leaves us: "We ugly mortals, what beautiful creatures we are!"

"Griffith's Hand Too Heavy on 'True Heart Susie,'" *New York Sunday Tribune*, August 3, 1919, 4.6.

If we lived in a nice, quiet desert where we couldn't hear the wicked people who persist in contradicting us we doubt if we should attempt to hang any sermons round the neck of "True Heart Susie," justly celebrated long before reaching our neighborhood. The picture is very finely made of very fine materials but there is something wrong with it. To preach about this something wrong would be irresistible if we were at all certain that we knew what it was. In the absence of this certainty we were hesitating even to put forward our few hints.[83]

But to hear that it suffers from padding is too much! Particularly after our frequent inward exclamations as we watched it that there wasn't even a superfluous bit of business, a stray flash. We have seen Griffith far more inspired, but never more controlled, more scrupulous, more exactly selective. If you don't believe us, look at the story.

A TALE OF DEVOTION   Two schoolchildren begin to "go together." At least William allows Susie to tag after him, to become his adorer and helper and confidante. As he grows up his penniless ambition is to study for the ministry. Susie has a little money; she defies her guardian aunt and sends it to William, making it appear to come from a benevolent old gentleman. By the sale of her pet cow, by the marketing of eggs and by all sorts of extra farm-turned pennies she makes enough to keep William going. Though he does not know where the money comes from, he knows well where to turn for counsel and for sympathy; the two young people become identified in the mind of the whole village, and by their united strength the boy makes good; he comes home in all the smug and yet funereal young pomp of his own idea of himself as a minister; he overawes the village, and when Susie walks through it with him, the observed of all observers, and is treated to ice cream soda by him on his first day in town she has her little hour of perfect triumphs. Her very little hour! For at that soda fountain William sets eyes on Betty, the flyaway little milliner who has failed financially in the larger neighboring town and is looking for a husband. Susie is a plain, dowdy little prude, but she tries to fight for William; then when Betty has captured William she tries to bolster up the miserable failure of their married life. But after a few years, when one of Betty's indiscretions results in a cold that kills her, it is a very disillusioned William who comes again to dump his bewilderment and exhaustion and his shattered self-sufficiency into the arms that have always been ready to receive them.

WHAT THE AVERAGE PLOT CONTAINS   This is the plot of "True Heart Susie: the Story of a Plain Girl." When it has been got into five reels can there be much room for padding? Think about how much an ordinary five-reel picture contains. The heroine and her family are shown to be in reduced circumstances. After an insult or so while looking for work she gets a position as companion to a spoiled heiress with a pearl necklace. The pearl necklace disappears. The heroine is suspected. The hero—he may be the brother of the spoiled heiress or her restive fiancé, or, which takes longer, a humble Westerner imported to guard the jewels, even a millionaire's son who has cured himself of drunkenness by hiring himself out as a chauffeur—the hero proves the heroine's innocence. They are betrothed and fade out in one long kiss.

If this is the quantity, to say nothing of the quality, generally presentable in five reels, can "True Heart Susie" be anything less than a miracle of economy, of proportion? Is it any less a miracle because it preserves Griffith's essential air of wandering easily at large, through life?

A TOO-STUDIED SIMPLICITY   Yet we have our own sufficiently vague complaint against "True Heart Susie." For all it satisfied in us was our intelligence, our artistic conscience. Somehow that more vital motion picture target, our heart—rather an impressionable, not to say sentimental heart, at that!—was never really struck. We kept waiting to hear the bell ring, but we never felt its pulsation. And sometimes we felt that perhaps this was because the director was aiming at it so deliberately, so candidly, that he gave us too much warning. We were too conscious of him standing a little between us and the picture and pointing out, a trifle too emphatically, its funniness, its pathos, its simplicity, as though a hand were occasionally laid upon the continuity and we became aware of a voice saying: "Just a minute! Hold that till they notice how true this is and how lovely is its homeliness." And we reply: "Its fun, its simplicity and its pathos are all there, it is true, and its homeliness is lovely." But we never gulp inarticulately and begin to snivel. Something moving and spontaneous is not there; something studied and insistent challenges rather than releases our emotion.

If we were asked to lay our own hand on any element contributive to this over-premeditation we think we could touch two—the number and explanatory insistence of the sub-titles, prone to repeat the gist of the scenes as though we could not see for ourselves who was behaving badly and whose heart was breaking, and the length of time for which many of the close-ups are held. We have before now offered prayer and sacrifice for longer close-ups. Certainly there ought to be some middle way between those which affect us as if something or other had just swung past the window and those in which Griffith appears to be squeezing simplicity out of Lillian Gish's face, so as to be sure that we have grasped how exquisite and how simple it is. Certainly the expression is held before us too long, or else it is not really significant and compelling enough for the time it is held. Isn't it possible, then, that another reason for the picture's lack of spontaneity may be due to his Belasconian over-direction of his star?

DIRECTORS WILL OVERRIDES ACTRESS   Everything you insist upon an actress's doing may be admirable and yet the mere insistence may give her an air of being stage-managed to death. Miss Gish never suggests this is straight work, but of late Griffith seems to have determined that she shall be a character comedienne. And always the same character! It is as though he had decided that the sisters should be at least as near alike as possible; as if, while experimenting in molds, he had produced one which did not quite fit Dorothy but which he liked so much that he determined anyhow to cram on Lillian.[84] The result is a performance, a series of performances, admirably intelligent and exactly accomplished—oh, how far too exactly! For in the end the effect is merely that of obedience. The life that moves it is visibly not that of the actress's will, but the director's, and consequently that movement is only galvanized; the quaint, queer, funny little figure of Griffith's contrivance is only an automaton, after all.

There is no doubt that in the beginning it made a hit; it was so novel, so unexpected, we were glad—in a world of lazy specialists—to see an evasive and poetic personality get down to the hard labor of characterization, freshening itself away from any danger of sentiment's cloying sweetness and boldly seeking variety. But as repetition follows repetition the thing ceases to be variety or even novelty. We see more and more clearly how little it is revelation and how much it is stunt; mechanical stunt, obedient to that vision in Griffith's mind which is only "the triumph of memory over experience."

CHARACTER CREATED FROM IMAGINATION   For quaint, queer, funny and pathetic as the little figure is it is not a reality of to-day, any more in rural than in urban communities; it is something which Griffith remembers out of his childhood and even more, perhaps, out of that world of Dickens which was once the real childhood world of all of us. Done just once in just such an atmosphere she might have remained a sort of classic, but to surround her with our own day is to make a contrast not in type but in era. The spirit of Susie is as real as ever, but her exterior—clothes, make-up, manners—no longer exists, and to pretend that it does is to turn that beautiful reality, "the story of a plain girl," into the story of an eccentricity; a single and not a representative case.

It has been our hard fate to celebrate here the faults of "True Heart Susie" instead of all its wise and lovely virtues; these can still easily be seen for themselves and are so much worth seeing as to return upon the memory with even a more seizing charm than the first glance made one aware of.

Dorothy Day

In early March 1919, on the front page no less, the *Des Moines Tribune* again promoted Day as someone who "knows more about pictures than anybody else in Iowa." "Thousands of movie fans," the paper claimed, "turn to her columns every day."[85] Her film reviews continued to appear within the *Tribune*'s "News of the Movies" column until the midsummer of 1920, but with a few exceptions during the final year, they became shorter and less trenchant, perhaps because, from April through November 1919, she also penned a column in the *Des Moines Sunday News* that drew on publicity material to summarize the new feature film releases of the coming week.[86] She already may have been transitioning to a new position, for Dorothy Day disappeared around the time that Dorothy Gottlieb became head of the public relations department for A. H. Blank's circuit of cinemas and eventually for the Central States Theater Corporation, aligned with Paramount, from 1933 to 1950.[87]

Were her reviews, in the *Tribune*'s punchy lingo, "intimate, personal and full of pep"? Sometimes, yes. The pep was there in her review of DeMille's *Don't Change Your Husband*: neither she nor the "girls" in an afternoon audience could resist the "he vamping" of Lew Cody, and they "giggled and laughed [...] at the typically 'husbandish' details." Movie stars more and more caught her eye, whether "regular chap" Harry Carey and the young boys who flocked to see him in person; the "glorious treat" of Mabel Normand and her stunts in *Mickey*; or the "vivid personality" of Nazimova in a double role in *The Red Lantern*, whose Orientalism was perfectly acceptable at the time.[88] Also catching her gaze were the theater lobby decorations for the latter film, as well as the atmosphere of A. H. Blank's new Des Moines theater on its opening night, featuring DeMille's *For Better, for Worse*.[89] While fans "stormed the Rialto" to see *Salomé* one Sunday, she seemed unsure if what appealed was the horror of the story, Theda Bara as "a creature of evil," or her costumes—more than she had worn earlier in *Cleopatra*.[90] One telling detail was Day's description of John the Baptist, whose skin was made to look "so white," which set him off as a "beautiful man" against the other characters. Finally, near the end of her tenure at the *Tribune*, Day printed Anita Stewart's tongue-in-cheek "ten commandments," which should "be pasted up over every girl's dressing table." Was she excluding her own fans when she wrote, "All of us can think of someone who ought to read them"?

"News of the Movies," *Des Moines Tribune*, February 18, 1919, 10.

"Don't Change Your Husband" "Old Wives for New" left you with perplexing thinking material to keep your mind busy for several days and its sequel "Don't Change Your Husband" gives you a few more sidelights on this ultra modern and ultra puzzling problem—married life.[91] There isn't a man or woman, young or old, who is not more or less interested in the simple little game of remaining happy though married. It's such a ticklish business, this idea of binding two people together morning, noon and night. One likes one thing that makes the other sick, and the other just can't live without something that his marital partner detests. Oh, it's a great idea and it takes real tact to become a nice quiet little partner!

But—I'm not here to discuss marital problems. So let's talk about Gloria Swanson's beauty, her lovely, easily managed hair, her too gorgeous gowns and her ability to make Leila Porter a very human, spoiled little wife. Let's rave about Lewis J. Cody's art at "he vamping."[92] Honestly, girls, do you believe that you could resist that or'nery devil? Elliott Dexter can't possibly be a male vamp, can he?[93] But when he reforms, loses his soft fat and dolls up—then—oh then is when he shines.

The Garden was packed with feminine persons yesterday afternoon. I'd give a whole lot to know just what they all thought of "Don't Change Your Husband." I know they giggled and laughed and nodded and whispered at the typically "husbandish" details. I know I enjoyed it immensely.

I would like to put this question before the house, however, why is it that in "Old Wives for New" the husband found happiness after he changed wives but when the wife changed husbands in this picture she got terrifically stung and was only too glad to change back?

Getting down to brass tacks, "Don't Change Your Husband" is a remarkably good picture. The settings are superb, the cast is magnificent to the most unimportant extra, and the action runs with a velvet smoothness. Whether you are married or not, take the male light of your eyes to see "Don't Change Your Husband," it will give him ideas, maybe, and won't do any harm.

"News of the Movies," *Des Moines Tribune*, April 1, 1919, 9.

"Mickey"   Well, I've seen Mickey.[94] Honest to goodness, I had been waiting for that picture for so long that I felt as if I were going to one grand and glorious treat when I strode up to the ticket window yesterday. And it was a treat, too, for "Mickey" is surely a joy.

In spite of the fifteen months spent in making, the long weeks spent in titling and editing, one can pick out several points to "critic," but who wants to "critic" a picture that keeps you in delicious chuckles from beginning to end and one that leaves you in an uncommonly good humor and apt to break out in smiles any time when you think of some of the stunts that Mickey pulled off.

"Mickey" is the story of a delightful little girl who lived way out west somewhere in a log cabin with Joe Meadows, an old prospector, and the only mother she ever knew, Minnie, an Indian squaw. Mickey wore overalls and great boys' shoes. Her hair hung in tangled curls and she was the epitome of youth—a regular tomboy girl who rode like a trooper, snapped when people stepped on her dignity, took baths a la whatever you call it when you don't wear a bathing suit right out of doors, and—in short, you'll rave about Mickey.

But—her foster father, Joe, sent her back to an aunt in the city, where in due time she became the maid of all work, abused and everything. Finally her mine that was thought to be a flivver turned out to be a winner and things changed—and there was a horse race, a slide on a roof, a "des-prit" battle in a deserted house, and—and, anyway it's corking good entertainment, and to tell much more would only deprive you of having a real good time for nearly two hours.

"Mickey" is a different photoplay. There is not one conventional happening in the whole eight reels and that very unconventionality is the big charm of the picture—that is the big charm part next to Mabel Normand.[95] For instance, there is a horse race: the villain has plotted to put the hero in bad and Mabel rides the former's horse to win for the latter. She is just about to win—and you are sitting back confident that she will win and save the day—when she doesn't, but I am not going to tell you what she does do.

Wheeler Oakman, Lewis J. Cody, Minnie, George Nichols and Minta Durfee score in the cast.[96]

"News of the Movies," *Des Moines Tribune*, May 27, 1920, 12.

Anita Stewart, than whom there is no prettier, has compiled a set of ten commandments to be pasted up over every girl's dressing table.[97] Here they are. All of us can think of someone who ought to read them.

1. Happiness of the right kind doth not come in bottles. So beware the incense of the perfume bottle. Water, most beloved fluid of man, doth not smell. So why should a girl saturate herself like a worm dipped in fish lure.
2. Honor the powder puff and use it sparingly. A shiny nose is rather to be chosen than a walking flour advertisement.
3. Lift not thine lip stick. Though it may prevent irritating chaps, it also prevents loving ones.
4. Bead not thine eyes for those smeared are known for misbehavior. Teach not your eyes to "string" like beads.
5. Many's 30-cent collar has gone to laundry through the wicked rouge pot. A natural blush is worth a bucket of rouge.
6. A pen can be pushed, but an eye-pencil must be led, so do not be deceived.
7. Try not thy hair to dye in accordance with the latest in kid gloves. A brunette is a brunette, but a bleached blonde is a drug on the market.
8. Vex not thy manicurist with fingers stained with nicotine. Besides thy lungs are meant for other things else than holding up thy lavaliere.

9. It's an ill wind that blows someone no good; but don't let it blow you any hair wavers for loblollying with such is a free ticket to the bald-headed row.
10. The price of style is high heels and both are too high.

Miss Stewart is at the Des Moines in "The Yellow Typhoon" this week, a Harold MacGrath story in which she takes a double role.[98]

Rae McRae

McRae was a feature writer for the *Des Moines Register* and the *Des Moines Tribune*, promoted as one of "Thirteen Big Reasons Why You Should Read the Evening Tribune Every Day."[99] Throughout 1919 she contributed local stories aimed "straight at the heart." Examples included the strenuous daily activity of sixty-two-year-old Mrs. John Frederick, the first French war bride to come to live in the city, and the closing of the general hospital at Fort Des Moines, whose educational department had retrained thousands of returning soldiers.[100]

"Breaking into the Movies" is not only a clever little self-deprecating story but also a tongue-in-cheek exposé of a fake actor-training "school" scamming naive young men and women desperately hoping to get into the movies.

"Breaking into the Movies," *Des Moines Register*, July 13, 1919, 2.

Dorothy Day and I took a plunge into the movie whirl the other day, and we're telling the world that the water's cold and you have to break the ice if you want to be in the swim.

Dorothy, who knows more about movies than the men who make 'em, felt it her duty to investigate a little advertisement running in the papers, calling for "five young men and women for moving picture work."

And I, who go only when it's Dorothy Gish or Charlie Chaplin, felt the lure of the "pitchers," and went along, too.

Each bolstering up the courage of the other, we put the best face possible and much Djer-Kiss powder on what beauty we possess and ventured forth.

A room in a downtown office building, lined with "stills" of Mary Pickford, Bill Hart, et al., we found to be the studio. A Victrola at one end of the room was surrounded by a circle of chairs.

A small office was partitioned off in one corner, and there a timid young applicant for stellar honors was reading over a training contract which was being explained to her by a young man with a pompadour and an air of boredom.

A blond woman of heroic size in a bright jersey dress thrust her head out the door and called, "Sit down!"

We sat.

TAKING THE PLUNGE. Then, slowly coming to and realizing our right to free and unhampered movement by authority of the constitution of these United States, we got up again and began looking at the pictures on the walls.

The little applicant came out presently, and hurried past us to the door, blushing furiously.

Dorothy and I held a hurried consultation and decided to tell them who we were and that we simply wanted to know the what and why and wherefore of things.

"Come in!" called the lady, and we did.

The Bushman-like young chap cast an appraising eye over us and said in a frigid tone: "Had any experience?"

Awed by his manner, I hesitated to speak of the burning hot afternoon long, long ago, when as the unfortunate mother-in-law in "The Wild Rose of Iowa," I clutched two weeping children borrowed for the occasion and permitted a horde of high school boy Indians to scalp me with a breadknife for the sake of art.

So I said, "No."

Francis X., then, with the air of a busy man intent on going straight to the point and wasting no time, clipped out: "Interested enough in your own future to spend several weeks training?"

"You're no earthly use to us unless you're trained, you know," interrupted the blond lady, who said she was Mrs. J. Drew and that she had been assistant director for Harold Lockwood for years. "You're no use to us while you're training, of course, so we ask you $3 a week, for three lessons a week; if you can qualify, we give you a part in a picture we will produce here soon. There is plenty of room at the top for trained players, for all the stage stars who have gone into movies are going back again, you know—they miss the applause and everything."

"Interested for yourselves?"

THEY ARE DISCOVERED! I shook my head, but Dorothy nodded, and then each of us in an effort to agree, switched and Dorothy shook her head just as I nodded.

The faux pas caused young Francis X. to look upon us with suspicion and disfavor, immediately.

He turned coldly away from us and fingered a pen.

"Then," he said, "as I have only a few minutes to spare, if there is some other time you could come back and discuss the matter? I—don't believe we could use you anyway, do you?"

Dorothy blushed at this slight upon our personal pulchritude, but I did not, having caught the young man glancing at my hand which held a bright yellow pencil—sign and symbol of the newspaper writer!

And then—such is fame!—he gazed searchingly at Dorothy and mused, "Haven't I seen you before? Aren't you Dorothy Day?"

It was out.

Madame was terribly hurt.

A Picture Theda Bara "You," she said to me, "seem to take a suspicious attitude."

"But then, of course, I can see you are new to newspaper work—you will not feel so when you have had more experience!"

Dorothy snickered.

"Now, you," she turned to Dorothy, "can realize the importance of our proposition, I can readily see."

And because our little deception—which would not have taken place if we'd been given time to announce ourselves—they wouldn't have us in their old picture, so there!

"Of course, we use professionals for principals," said the blond lady, "but each of the local people has a good part. We made a similar picture in Florida recently, and sold it—in Miami—wasn't it?"

But Harold did not reply. He coldly turned his back on us, and at this unkindest cut of all, we left, just as an embryo Theda Bara of the future, in summer furs and silk stockings, entered.

Virginia Dale

Little is known about Virginia Dale before she began reviewing films for the *Chicago Journal*. One complication is that no copies of the *Journal* seem to survive before 1921. She did begin writing at least by early 1919, according to a Wisima Film ad for *The Eyes of the World* in *Exhibitors Herald and Motography*.[101] In October the *Fort Wayne Sunday News* also reprinted her review of *Broken Blossoms* in full.[102] The *Journal* considered Dale important enough for its readers by 1921 to post a series of small ads repeatedly promoting her reviews.

While Dale was no less engaged than Harris or Tracy by *Broken Blossoms*, she seemed most impressed by the "blood red tragedy" of the ending, in which Griffith dared to leave the audience "without the sedative of a happy finale."[103] In another column not included here, she also liked "the vitality" of *Dream Street* (1921) but found it lacked "the art of subtlety"—the "agony is a bit too agonized."[104] Like Kitty Kelly three years earlier, Dale interviewed an "independent" exhibitor, Andrew Karzas, and profiled his career in the city as a kind of model.[105] Karzas began with a small theater farther south on Halsted and moved to another small one in Hyde Park; as the best sign of his success, he built and managed "the famous Woodlawn," a picture palace located on the West Side of Chicago. Like Parsons earlier, Dale visited the Fox studio (nearly the same time as Harris) in Fort Lee, New Jersey, where Herbert Brenon and William Farnum were at work. What particularly struck her was not only the music performed for the actors to "work in rhythm" in a scene but also all the actors walking around in costumes from every age of history in a kind of "Alice's wonderland." And she was one of the few newspaper columnists to notice the yellow makeup on actors' faces; when recorded on orthochromatic filmstock, that makeup ensured that audiences would perceive characters not as ethnic but as "properly" white.[106]

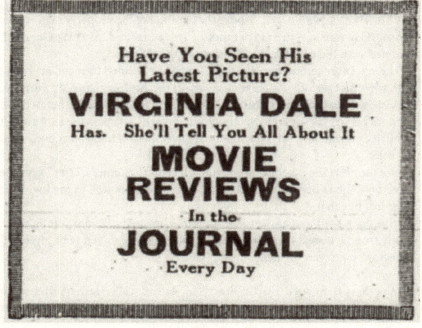

Figure 4. Virginia Dale advertisement, *Chicago Journal*, July 30, 1921.

"Fox Studios Hive of Industry," *Chicago Journal*, December 17, 1921, 7.

New York, Dec. 17—a motion picture studio—where make-believe is the big, important business. 7,000 people oft times working simultaneously throughout a six-story building a solid block square, a million dollars worth of three sheets quartered in the basement and a yearly pay roll many times that, that's a Fox dedicated to the mushroom of commercialism, the movies.

The studios are places that would make Alice's wonderland seem dull by comparison. The people walking about are the cream of the decades—gentlemen in silver buckles of colonial times, Oliver Twist's mother in frills and a mobcap, an American person in rolled stockings and a strictly eastern tremor of shoulder blades, and a far-eastern sheik in a very bored state and a radiant turban.

Set! To the initiated it means the replica of places or things made to order beneath the studio roof. They are surrounded by blinding lights that give even the yellow make-ups a greenish tint.

The camera with its way of recording so unfailingly stands in shadow. By it is the director's chair—and Heaven help the unwary who may sink into it!

MUSIC PLAYS ITS PART   Above the hammer of the property man comes the sound of music. A myriad of tunes—"Trovatore" and "Ain't We Got Fun?" mingled with the soulfulness of "Asleep in the Deep."

The actors are temperamental folk. They have decided they can act better with the aid of melody. "It makes us work in rhythm," explains Mr. Farnum.

A messenger came from that vague place, the front office. He handed Mr. Farnum his weekly stipend. "Six thousand dollars," whispers the $40-a-week publicity person, and Bill flips open the envelope and hands its contents to his valet.

Not far off is the ingenue. She stands close to the camera. "Cry," says the director—Theda Bara's husband by the way. And tears well in the ingenue's eyes; just like that.

"She does it without any trouble," says the director, and adds, a little sadly, "Only trouble is, real tears don't film as well as those mixed with glycerin." Directors are never satisfied.

PLAYS EACH SCENE FOUR TIMES   "Again," calls Herbert Brenon to $5000-a-week Mr. Farnum, and Bill performs again and yet again, but rather because four negatives are made of every picture.[107]

In the vaults above this negative is stored in different steel compartments. This is a precaution against destruction; one is shipped abroad, the other three remain here.

After the picture is completed and film-cutters and directors have done their best, the result is handed over to a gray-haired little woman known as the film editor. She has been kept in total ignorance of the story, its intentions and idea. She looks at the finished production and makes changes and additions as needed. Hers is one of the most important chores there.

At the conclusion of each day the previous day's "take" is thrown on the screen of one of the company's four projection rooms. When everything is satisfactory orders are given to wreck the set.

Nowadays practically all the "props," furniture, drapes, etc. are rented from interior decorators, many of whom specialize in renting to producing companies. They base their weekly rentals on a 10 per cent appraisement of the articles' value.

Every theater contract made throughout the world passes the personal O.K. of President William Fox; every print seen comes from the home offices in New York; they are then sent to branch exchanges and there distributed.[108]

FILMS GO ALL OVER WORLD   The colossal sums to be realized from film rentals may be seen after a look at the booking department, where a great corps of clerks is kept busy on thousands of daily contracts from all parts of the world. Weekly contracts bring anywhere from $1.50 for short-reel subjects to several thousand dollars for special productions.

Special departments, each entirely on its own, are severally responsible for features, regular programme photoplays, straight comedies, slap-stick, cartoons, news reels and a magazine section.

The motion picture industry has probably more ramifications than any other single commercial enterprise. It includes art as well as the most technical of mechanical knowledge, factory efficiency and the best trained export and general transportation skill. It must buy all sorts of brains and power, and the proof that it buys wisely lies in the fact of its importance as a world industry and its unprecedented success.

Harriette Underhill

After touring with several theater companies, Underhill returned to New York after her father's death in 1908 and took over his sports column at the *New York Tribune*. "A rare beauty" with "flaming orange" hair often framed by "a large black picture hat," in the words of Ishbel Ross, Underhill "was cynical to the core, scorned sentiment, had a sophisticated wit, [and] was generous and courageous."[109] In 1916, for a weekly column in the *Tribune*, she began interviewing stage actors who had turned to the movies in New York studios. A fluid, articulate writer, she let her interviewees speak as they wished, rarely calling attention to herself. In late 1919 she was hit by a car and severely crippled, but she continued to write, taking over Virginia Tracy's film review column for several years.

In one of seven columns included here, Underhill was as dazzled by Fairbanks as was Tracy (initially), especially in *When the Clouds Roll By* (1919), "a monumental achievement in nonsense," and even in *The Mark of Zorro* (1920), although he was much less the character than the movie star who took an audience "into his confidence." She also had high praise for Norma Talmadge, despite a very conventional plot, in *The Branded Woman* (1920); the "wonderfully looking creature" Nazimova in another double role in *Madame Peacock* (1920); and Pola Negri in *Passion*, so "spontaneous and gay and totally without affectation."[110] In her review of *Madame Peacock*, Underhill was so taken with the dialogue, adapted from the play, that she reproduced some of the telling exchanges that the theater star in the film has with an author, producer, and adoring audience.[111]

Two of Underhill's reviews contrast sharply with those of Mae Tinée. She appreciated the hair-raising scenes, accentuated by ingenious set decors, in *The Cabinet of Dr. Caligari* and called attention to the creators (director, scriptwriter, set designers) rather than the actors. She found *The Love Light* "a fascinating story beautifully produced and marvelously well acted," with a "gorgeous performance" by Pickford in Frances Marion's unusually sustained war story. Yet, like Mae Tinée, Underhill also thought highly of Weber's next film after *The Blot*, *What Do Men Want?* (1921), slightly editing the heroine's final line: "Men want only what they [are not quite sure they] possess." And she made an observant remark on Weber's style: "She never has any 'big moments' in her pictures, and her people act as they do in real life. It is delightfully restful to watch one of her pictures."[112] Is this one reason why Weber fell out of favor in the early 1920s?

Like Day, Underhill was attentive to the theater experience in at least four columns. After briefly noting the program framing *Madame Peacock* and the Spanish-themed program for *The Mark of Zorro*, she described more specifically Rothapfel's prologue and epilogue of three candles being snuffed out onstage at the end of *Passion*—to symbolize Madame Du Barry's death— and his "elaborate program surrounding" *The Cabinet of Dr. Caligari*, which amplified yet also softened an audience's response to the puzzling German feature. She even wished that, rather than flash those unconvincing zigzag letters onscreen, a member of the Capitol chorus would simply have shouted "Caligari" several times at the end. Like Charlotte Kelly, Underhill was offended by moviegoers who read intertitles out loud and, specifically during *The Branded Woman*, the two women seated behind her who kept up a running commentary on the stars—not always gracious.

"On the Screen," *New York Tribune*, December 29, 1919, 9.

Douglas Fairbanks's new picture at the Rivoli is a monumental achievement in nonsense. It refuses to be classified. It has something to offer to every one. Those who like slapstick, those who like farce, those who love tragedy, those who insist on plot and even those who insist on romance will like "When the Clouds Roll By."[113] Oh yes, we must not forget to include those who think you won't be married this year if you fall upstairs and break your neck, or that it is bad luck to have a motor-hearse run over you, for the new picture is founded on the art of superstition.

The story is by Douglas himself, in person, and perhaps that is why it really is entirely different from any other story that ever has been done on the screen. At least the cause is different, even if the effect is the same. The motive matters not so much if it makes Douglas smile and smile and be an athlete.

There is a Doctor Metz in the story. In fact he opens the thing by appearing at a lecture and stating that for many years guinea pigs and rabbits have been used for experimental purposes and that he has decided to sacrifice a human for the sake of science. He will prove, he says, that a man may be persuaded by the power of suggestion to believe anything and that he may even be induced to kill himself.

The man he has selected is Daniel Boone Brown, in other words Douglas Fairbanks. The hero is introduced at a midnight repast, at which his valet feeds him raw onions, broiled lobster, Welsh rarebit, mince pie and coffee. Strange to say his dreams are perturbed ones and yet the stuff his dreams are made of is familiar stuff. There is the one about floating in the air and the one about walking on the ceiling, and of course the one about attending a party and then discovering that you have forgotten to put on your clothes.

Doug Fairbanks can do most anything, but he can't walk on the ceiling, and we should like to know how this one is done. Perhaps it is possible to turn the picture upside down or something.

All of this is a part of the plot of the villainous Dr. Metz to weaken the resistance of his victim. He has a chart with Daniel Boone Brown's brain marked off into little sections, and he puts a cross on the chart as he introduces new elements in the plot to drive his victim mad.

The author himself seems to have taken this part of it seriously, although no one believed it was going to be anything more than a chance to do some more stunts. But he really does go mad when the doctor finally introduces jealousy. And this brings us to the girl. She is Lucette Bancroft, attractively played by Kathleen Clifford. Humor at last rushes in and puts Reason back on her throne, and then Daniel pursues the villain and the girl and finally marries her on the roof of a house floating around in a flood. The minister has taken refuge on the roof of his church.

The couple have a wedding supper on a captured watermelon and say they'll be happy when the clouds roll by.

The picture is the best that Fairbanks has done since the early days when he used to have "his picture in the paper" and get "in again out again." You feel like exclaiming, "You have come back to me, Douglas, Douglas!"

There is a Mack Sennett comedy, "The Speakeasy," the Rivoli Pictorial, and a lovely Paramount-Post picture, "Memory Lane."[114] There are also some fascinating pictures of the coral garden taken undersea.

Emanual List sang "Down Deep Within the Cellar." The music is reminiscent of "Long, Long Ago," and as the scene showed the singer within the cellar, seated in front of a keg and holding a large stein, the moment was a tense one. When, at the end of the song, he raised the stein and drank deeply, and with evident relish, there wasn't a dry eye in the theater.

The overture is "Il Guarnay," and there is a most effective dance called "Snowflurry."

"On the Screen," *New York Tribune*, September 6, 1920, 4.

How fortunate it was that "The Branded Woman," which is the feature at the Strand this week, fell into the hands of Joseph Schenck and that he set Norma Talmadge and Percy Marmont the task of redeeming her.[115] A share of the credit should go to Anita Loos, also, for her very facile titles. Titles are so prone to step out of the picture and sort of slap one in the face. But, as we were saying, Miss Talmadge, gracefully assisted by Mr. Marmont, saved the day for "The Branded Woman" is of the brand well known to all theatergoers, and the story never once wandered off the beaten path.

If the first reel had been shown and a prize offered for the best written solution, it is probable the first prize would have to be divided into 1,000 parts. For after the first few hundred feet of film there could not be a movie fan who would not have guessed the rest.

Beautiful and innocent girl at a fashionable boarding school; mother who runs a gambling house; grandfather who keeps beautiful and innocent girl ignorant of her maternal ancestor's transgressions; mother also kidnaps daughter; daughter who marries fine, upstanding man without telling him of her mother's peccadillos; blackmailing gambler; pearl necklace pawned to supply his demand; substitution of fake pearls discovered; dénouements; denouncing of wife by husband; renouncing of husband by wife; explanations; clasp; fadeaway.

But if you enjoy good acting without the suspense of watching a tale unfold then assuredly you will enjoy "The Branded Woman." Miss Talmadge is such an artist, she does things so completely, that you feel no lack in the story. Her work as the very young girl who receives her first beau in the drawing room at the boarding school is particularly effective, perhaps because she appears in such parts less often than in stronger roles.

And Percy Marmont has a way of winning sympathy for stupid, worthy young husbands who are always ready to believe the worst of their wives. For absolute intolerance and pig-headedness show us a very good young man, preferably an Englishman. That was Douglas Courtenay, the man whom Ruth married. But whether you like Douglas Courtenay or not, you've got to like Percy Marmont.

George Fawcett departs a little from tradition in his portrayal of the grandfather, Judge Whitlock. He was more rough and ready than one would expect, and very refreshing. Vincent Serrano does not carry the charm which is his to the screen; but then no one expects "Velvet" Croft to be anything but disagreeable.[116] Gaston Glass hasn't much to do as the youthful admirer whose hopes are nipped in the bud, but he does it well.[117] Grace Studdiford and Jean Armour are the two mothers.

If we ever own a motion picture theater we shall conduct to the door all persons who read titles aloud. Behind us were two rank offenders, women, who not only read all the titles, but informed every one that Miss Talmadge was getting stouter, that Mr. Marmont had a profile like a cameo, that the star gave all her clothes to extra girls, etc., all the time the picture was running. It was terrible. And we thought when we got back to New York it was going to be perfect.

On the bill besides the feature was the Strand Topical Review, a comedy called "The Kick in High Life," which really had little kick, a song tableau, "Moonbeams," from "The Red Mill," sung by Betty Gray and the overture "I Pagliacci."

"On the Screen," *New York Tribune*, November 29, 1920, 8.

For once every one must agree that a title has been changed with good effect. "The Mark of Zorro" at the Capitol used to be "The Curse of the Capistrano" when it was in book form, but Zorro is so much less apt to be mispronounced and it is also much more euphonious.[118]

This is Douglas Fairbanks's latest picture, and all the time we were watching it we couldn't help wondering what the original story was like. It couldn't have been anything like the screen version, for there couldn't be another hero like Fairbanks. For instance, if an author had narrated that Zorro climbed the side of the church, slid in the window, changed clothes with a monk, walked out again, broke open jails, jumped from the floor to the first balcony and escaped on foot carrying a señorita in his arms with fifty armed soldiers after him no one would bother to read any further. He would say there ain't no such hero. But seeing is believing, as Dulcinea sagely remarked, and on the screen Zorro does do it, or at least Douglas Fairbanks does, for never once do you think he is Zorro.

PICTURE IS ENTERTAINING   The picture is entertaining and amusing but not in the least convincing. When Zorro is backed up against a wall with 100 men waiting to shoot at him the only surprise lies in wondering which one of them he is going to pick up by the heels and hurl at the others. Douglas Fairbanks has never yet come to grief nor is there a suggestion of it. So all one has to control are his risibilities.

The picture is directed by Fred Niblo and it is very well done and the background is all that one could ask in picturesqueness.[119] The story is of California 100 years ago and Zorro is the handsome masked avenger who goes about putting a "Z" on the cheek of the oppressors. Any one who speaks sharply to his native servant or kicks the cat feels a cold breeze on the back of his neck, and there is the window open and Zorro ready to brand the offender.

TAKES AUDIENCE INTO CONFIDENCE   We knew all the time that Zorro was only Don Diego Vega with a mask and a false mustache, and indeed it requires no great amount of movie sense to know this, for the only ones who are kept in the dark are the people about him. The audience he takes into his confidence, but as they are all with him from the first he has nothing to fear from that quarter.

And Oh, what a good time Fairbanks had making the picture! The costumes are extremely becoming and the tight white trousers and folded red sash reveal the fact that the popular athletic, smiling hero hasn't taken on an ounce of flesh where it would spoil his profile.

The picture is going to make you sigh for the good old days of chivalry when men like Zorro gave up their seats in the subway and tempestuously wooed the ladies of their choice and carried them away to their castles to have breakfast with them every morning.

Some excellent work is done by Noah Beery as Pedro and Robert McKim as Captain Ramm.[120] The girl is Lolita, played by Marguerite de la Motte.[121] "The Mask of Zorro" is well worth seeing.

The program is more or less Spanish and "España" is the ruling motive in the music. We had the advantage over the other people in the theater. A Spanish family sat directly behind us, and the father read all the titles out loud and translated them into English for the wife and kids. But we can't promise this for every day, although he did say something about mañana.

"On the Screen," *New York Tribune*, January 10, 1921, 8.

"The Love Light" is a fascinating story beautifully produced and marvelously well acted. After so long an absence Mary Pickford has returned to the screen in something that is very much worth while, for the picture, which is the feature at the Capitol this week, is one of the very best we ever saw. To begin at the beginning, Frances Marion has given Miss Pickford a story in which the interest is sustained to the very end.[122] It is a war story, though it would hardly have done to have shown it during or immediately after the war, for one of the heroes is German. Of course, he turns out to be a spy, but he is a noble spy. In selecting two men who were not especially well known on the screen to play two lovers the plot is not revealed till the end. Where you have a well-known hero to play the lead you always know that he is going to be the good one and marry the heroine.

Miss Pickford shows herself to be a supreme artist in this latest picture. Her charm certainly has not lessened and she gives a gorgeous performance as the little Italian girl who loves, all unwittingly, a German spy. We do not know the name of the man who played this spy, but he was very good. Unusually fine performances were also given by Raymond Bloomer as Giovanni, who simulates blindness as well as ever we have seen it done; and Evelyn Dumo as Mana and Albert Frisco as Pietro.[123]

Miss Pickford is Angela, the watcher in the tower of a lighthouse somewhere in Italy, and one day a marvelously perfect male creature is washed up on the rocks from the ocean. Angela brings him back to life and he tells her that he is an American, inadvertently a deserter from one of the battleships. She hides him in her hut and then marries him secretly, only to learn later that he is a German spy and that it is his submarine which has sent her brother, Mario, to his death.

The lighting, the photography and the settings are things of great beauty. The titles are so good that they pretty nearly stand alone out of all the pictures we have seen this season, and the direction leaves nothing to be desired. If "The Love Light" has any faults they were not apparent to us for the entire eight reels. Frances Marion wrote and directed this picture.

A very elaborate program has been arranged around the feature. The overture is "Queen of Sheba." Then comes the Butterfly Ballet, with Mlle. Gambarelli; then the prologue, which is called "Italian Fantasy," with Eric Bye, assisted by the ensemble and the ballet corps. Mlle. Gambarelli and Alexander Oumansky are seen in this also.

"On the Screen," *New York Tribune*, April 4, 1921, 6.

For those who may fancy as we did, that "The Cabinet of Dr. Caligari" is a political story of Austria or points east, let us say at once that it is nothing of the sort. Dr. Caligari is a weird looking person who travels with a circus, a fair or carnival it is rather, and with him he carries a cabinet. In this cabinet is another weird looking person who seems to be afflicted with sleeping sickness. The only time he awakes is when Dr. Caligari, his master, bids him.

The picture is at the Capitol this week and it is advertised as the first futuristic picture. But do not let that discourage you. The settings are designed in a most ingenious way and they do look like perfectly good specimens of futuristic art; but really they are designed merely to interpret the words of the narrator and the artist has succeeded marvelously in so doing.

As soon as we learned the secret of the thing, which you do not do until the epilogue, we wanted to stay and see the picture all over again and fit on our new found clues. Fortunately at the theater they do not chase you out when you arrive at the end of the journey as they do on the Staten Island ferry, for instance, so you may see the picture over again on its return trip.

The picture was made abroad by Karl Mayer and Hans Janowitz.[124] The art settings are by Hermann Warm, Walter Reimann and Walter Rohrig so it's not difficult to guess the land of its birth.[125] However, we do not see how anyone can possibly come forward and claim that it is propaganda, though perhaps we do not know a propaganda when we see one.

The picture sets itself the task of raising your hair from your head, and it succeeds from the moment the actors appear in the prologue. The apex is reached when Cesare's long, ghostly fingers close about the sleeping Jane's throat. Here, unless your hair is pretty solid, it will be tugged loose from its moorings. We should love to tell the plot and the nature of the dénouement, but we are going to keep the secret.

However, it isn't revealing any secret to say that some of the ghostly figures are strung on wires, so when they appear to be walking in a strange, unearthly fashion they are really never touching the earth. It is ingenious, indeed. We think the scene when the doctor goes mad would be improved by having some member of the chorus, without which no Capitol production is ever complete, shout "Caligari" from the scenes instead of having it flashed all over the screen. Those silent messages that zigzag in the background are never convincing.

Mr. Rothapfel doesn't believe that one picture makes a program, and an elaborate program surrounds the feature. The overture is Tchaikowsky's "1812." Then comes Fritz Kreisler's "Capris Viennois" with ballet and chorus, another dance done to Russian folk melodies. Drigo's Valse done by Mlle. Gambarelli and Delibes's Mazurka. Laurence Hope's love lyrics are elaborately staged and sung by Erik Bye. On the picture program is "Prizma," "A Day with John Burroughs" and Capitol News.

"On the Screen," *New York Tribune*, November 15, 1921, 8.

Lois Weber has called her latest picture "What Do Men Want?" and Wid Gunning is presenting it at the Lyric Theater.[126] Now, many people who go to see the picture fancy that the title should read "What Men Want," and that is not the idea at all. Miss Weber simply asks the question, but does not answer it any more than George Bernard Shaw did in "Heartbreak House." As a matter of fact men want a lot of things, just as women do, only for some strange reason a woman is more likely to go on being contented with her lot even after she ceases to regard her husband as her hero.

In "Heartbreak House" Mr. Shaw also says that when your heart is broken it is the end of happiness and the beginning of peace, but he might well have said when you cease to be in love it is the end of happiness and the beginning of peace. Now, unfortunately, all attractive men must have imaginations and if they have they are bound to use them at times in picturing themselves as heroes in thrilling if indiscreet love affairs; they love to wonder if they are as attractive to women as they used to be before they were married and then, unless they are too lazy, they go to find out. Every woman ought to know this and not mind. If she cares enough about him to wait for his return, why he's sure to come back after he has found that he can still break a heart or two on the outside. As another director remarked last season, it is foolish to change your husband, for the next one will be just the same, unless he has no imagination, which is worse.

At the end of the picture the hero says "What do men want? They want the brains to appreciate the fact that the only lasting happiness is found beside the domestic hearthstone." The heroine says "Men want only what they do not possess," which we think should be modified to "Men want only what they are not quite sure they possess."

Miss Weber has put the picture on with her usual veracity. She never has any "big moments" in her pictures, and her people act as they do in real life. It is delightfully restful to watch one of her pictures, and whether she selects people who do not care to rave or rant or whether she instantly squelches all hifalutin tendencies when she takes them in hand, the result is the same. Miss Weber's pictures are filled with sane actors and actresses![127]

Claire Windsor, the girl, is, to my mind, as beautiful as any actress on the screen, and there is a Lady Clara Vere de Vere look about her that is charming. Frank Glendon is attractive as the restless hero, but we especially liked the work of George Hackathorne, as the quiet brother, and of Edith Kessler, as the unfortunate Bertha.[128]

Halam Cooley is the young man who had a system which he believed made all women love him.[129] It is not an especially attractive role, but Mr. Cooley plays it well. Miss Weber wrote the story and directed the picture.

There are some rather interesting pages from "Life" and an elaborate prologue called "The Dance of Life." Billy Halbrook is seen as the man, and Dorothy Lane, Lola Foster, Cecile Rivlin, Barbara Kitson, Margaret Roberts and Gail Beverly represent Youth, Love, Wealth, Ambition, Truth and Passion.

Alberta Hartley

Little is known about Alberta Hartley, who, likely as a staff writer, served as the *Des Moines News*' film reviewer from January 1920 through February 1922. She also may have edited the *News*' unsigned weekend movie page.[130] What she did afterward is unclear.

Hartley's short reviews tended to be chatty, directly addressed readers, and sometimes were quite pointed in their criticism. Although she described the new Strand theater's opening night in no less detail than Day did earlier for the Des Moines theater, she was pleased to confess how naughtily surreptitious she had to be to enter the theater late. She shared the scoop of an inside story about how Adolph Zukor believed that *Humoresque* would appeal far beyond "the large Jewish population of New York City" and had it released as a special, not an ordinary, feature.[131] She agreed with Underhill in praising Weber's *What Do Men Want?* but took note of this "pioneer woman motion picture director" and her attention to the "little details of small town life." She found the story of William DeMille's *Midsummer Madness* (1920) too "hackneyed and worn [. . .] to keep an audience 'enthralled,'" but she also got a little snooty in disapproving of the heroine's indiscretion. Hartley reserved her real scorn, however, for the male scenario writer of Fox's *Why Trust Your Husband* (1921).[132] "Who, but a man," would make a male character so clever at being fickle and then "dare to make blockheads" of the women? So much for the recent passage of the Nineteenth Amendment giving women (not all of them, of course) the right to vote.

"At the Movies," *Des Moines News*, January 3, 1921, 3.

"Midsummer Madness" may be a technically perfect picture, it may be artistically constructed, and all that. But the theme, although it has been given a different angle than has been shown on the screen for some time, is hackneyed and worn, and much too commonplace to keep an audience as "enthralled" as has been exploited.[133]

The story is based on Cosmo Hamilton's novel, "His Friend and His Wife," and is the tale of a wife, who piqued at her husband's neglect and absorption in business affairs, finds herself on the verge of an entanglement with her husband's best friend.

Even tho your sympathy goes out to the lovely little woman who has been neglected, still you feel just a wee bit disappointed in her when she displays her weakness by permitting her husband's best friend to make love to her. She lacks the discretion that a matron of the right type should have, and it is hard to approve of something on the screen that you would not approve of your next door neighbor doing.

[William C.] DeMille has succeeded in bringing the four leading characters so close to you that you feel they are really friends of yours. His mistake was in picking a story that should lose for them your respect.

The cast is one that would be hard to surpass. There is Lois Wilson, winsome and lovely, who takes the part of the neglected wife; Conrad Nagel, who has certainly proven himself worthy of distinction, in the role of "her husband's friend"; Lila Lee as "her best friend," also wife of "her husband's friend"; and Jack Holt as "her husband."[134]

It is at the Rialto this week.

"At the Movies," *Des Moines News*, January 28, 1921, 10.

Of one thing I am sure after seeing "Why Trust Your Husband," which is at the Majestic for the rest of the week. A man wrote the scenario.

Who, but a man, could make such satirical thrusts at the holy state of matrimony?

Who, but a man, would credit a man with being as fickle, and as clever about it, as the leading male characters of our story?

Who, but a man, would dare to make the blockheads of women the writer of "Why Trust Your Husband" does?

But then, some things must be overlooked by my sex I suppose, for the sake of humor.

Pretty Eileen Percy is seen as the bride of one year, whose husband is always "swinging some big deal."[135]

Her sister also possesses one of "them there things," but his failing is the Camel Club of Home "Hooch" makers.

A note concerning masked balls, pretty girls, dates, etc., is accidentally dropped and immediately the plot thickens, and keeps on thickening until we find our two heroines in a sad plight in their endeavor to discover which husband was the unfaithful one.

Of course, it is both, and, proof that a man wrote the story, it winds up by the guilty parties escaping and the dear wifies caught in a raid.

The plot reaches its climax when with earnest pleadings to be forgiven each wife seeks the protective arms of her beyond-reproach husband.

"Movie News," *Des Moines News*, February 2, 1921, 2.

Were you there last night? I mean at the opening of our new Strand Theater.

I was, fortunately, for owing to a miscalculation of my time I ordered one French pastry too many and arrived there just in time to be told "the house is full." If I hadn't had so much previous experience with bargain counter rushes I would have missed it all.

But, as it was, I dodged under the ropes into a profusion of flowers and ferns, untangled myself there and proceeded up the stairs, finally settling myself on the bottom step. It was lovely, wasn't it? The proscenium opening is hung with deep festoons of turquoise blue velvets with applique at the top of burnt orange, trimmed across the bottom with deep bullion fringe of the same coloring.

DRAPERIES EFFECTIVE   This combination has as a background taupe velvet, the stage curtain, the bottom of which is blocks of taupe and black. Special lighting devices have been arranged to show these colors effectively, and, much to my surprise, the taupe colored curtain produced real chamelionistic qualities and slowly changed color from blue to rose and then back to the original taupe.

The wall and ceilings are pleasantly colored in blue, gold, coral; black and old ivory over the Oriental plastering, accentuated in the true English tradition.

Four murals gave each side wall in sand and black colors, and around these a frame of antique gold is effected.

Miss Ethel Tamminga's vocal offerings, "Your Eyes Have Told Me So" and "Some Little Bird," were greatly appreciated by the initial audience.

"FORBIDDEN FRUIT"   A word for the picture, which is truly exceptionally good. It is "Forbidden Fruit" a Cecil de Mille production.[136]

"Forbidden Fruit" is a melodrama, and in less artistic hands than the great De Mille could have been made a painful joke. But he has brought out with characteristic deftness every value put in the play by Jeannie MacPherson, and the result is a well told, smooth-running and skillfully developed romance.

While the story is strong and far above the average it is dwarfed by the production itself. The settings are undeniably the real thing. Elaborateness and magnificence is always in prominence, and particularly is this true in the gowns worn by Kathlyn Williams and Agnes Ayres, who play in the leading feminine roles.[137]

The cast is most capable. Theodore Roberts gives his usual inimitable portrayal, and Forrest Stanley and Clarence Burton also do their bits, quite big bits, well.[138]

Notes

1. Isis ads, *Indianapolis Star*, November 6, 1919, 9, and December 9, 1919, 9. A Press Bureau committee member of the Indiana Federation of Clubs, Bye moved to Chicago after marrying in early 1920 ("Announces List of Committees for Federation," *Indianapolis Star*, December 29, 1919, 7; and "Announcement of Marriage," *Indianapolis News*, February 16, 1920, 4).

2. See note 18 in the introduction.

3. Tony Langston, "Theatricals: Morals and Movies," *The Competitor*, January 1920, 73–74, quoted in Everett, *Returning the Gaze*, 153–54. Langston was the *Chicago Defender*'s drama critic. Lester A. Walton, "Sam Langford's Wallop Makes 'The Brute' a Screen Success," *New York Age*, September 16, 1920, quoted in Everett, *Returning the Gaze*, 161. Michaux himself wrote "The Negro and the Photo-Play" for *Half-Century*, May 1919, 9. See also Delsarte Film's adaptation of Birdie Gilmore's *Jungle God* in "Our Growth and Importance in the Amusement World," *The Competitor*, June 1921, 38, referenced in Kyna Morgan and Aimee Dixon, "African-American Women in the Silent Film Industry," Women Film Pioneers Project.

4. One or more of these photoplay editors named in the directory could, of course, be women.

5. See the "Dispatch staff" ad, *Moline Dispatch*, November 27, 1917, 11; and "Clarence Lucas' Four Best Films of the Week," *Moline Dispatch*, November 1, 1919, 10. This column also included brief comments on half a dozen "other good pictures."

6. Ads extolling the *Cleveland Plain Dealer*'s promotion of the movies were reproduced in "From 100% to Zero," *Motion Picture News*, July 12, 1919, 505; and "Selling the Picture to the Public," *Moving Picture World*, December 11, 1920, 738.

7. Marjorie Daw, "Every Cinema Has Its Day during the Sultry Months," *Cleveland Sunday Plain Dealer*, June 1, 1919, Editorial/Dramatic, 4. Born in India and educated in Great Britain, Rudyard Kipling (1865–1936) began to publish short stories in the 1880s. After lengthy travels he settled in London, writing poems such as "The White Man's Burden" (1899) and more stories and poems in *Just So Stories for Little Children* (1902), *Puck of Pook's Hill* (1906), and *Rewards and Fairies* (1910). Although awarded the Nobel Prize for Literature in 1907, Kipling has remained a controversial "Poet of the Empire" ever since.

8. Marjorie Daw, "Old Favorites Return, New Stars Scintillate," *Cleveland Sunday Plain Dealer*, January 12, 1919, Editorial/Dramatic, 4.

9. This film is available for purchase online.

10. After playing supporting roles for Pathé and in *Toto the Clown* serials, Clairine Seymour (1898–1920) worked for Griffith as a light comic actress and finally landed a leading role in *The Idol Dancer* (1920). That year she fell ill from an intestinal disorder and died of pneumonia.

11. Perry Heath (1884–1933) wrote fifty produced scripts; the first was *Burnt Wings* (1920).

12. See also Mae Tinée, "Alien Films Come from Abroad to Ripple Our Cinema Waters," *Chicago Sunday Tribune*, May 22, 1921, 8.3.

13. Earlier she did describe Weber's *Forbidden* as "an awful lot of mush" (Mae Tinée, "Are Husbands Funny? Well, See 'Forbidden,'" *Chicago Tribune*, September 17, 1919, 18).

14. Mae Tinée, "Mr. Carey's Our Idea of a Real Western Hero," *Chicago Sunday Tribune*, January 16, 1921, 7.2.

15. Mae Tinée, "Of Lords, Ladies, and Pins—and a Demon Twin Sister," *Chicago Tribune*, September 24, 1919, 18.

16. Initially a stage actor, George Loane Tucker (1872–1921) turned to writing scenarios and directing films and first gained success with *Traffic in Souls* (1913). After directing several films for the London Film Company, he returned to the United States in 1916 to direct films for Goldwyn, with *The Miracle Man* his most successful and profitable. He died in 1921 after a long illness.

17. After a short career in vaudeville, Betty Compson (1897–1974) was hired in 1915 by Al Christie to star in short films and then features. After *The Miracle Man*, she signed a contract with Paramount, briefly established her own production company in 1921, and then moved to London to star in four films directed by Graham Cutts.

18. After a successful Broadway stage career, Thomas Meighan (1879–1936) contracted with Famous Players–Lasky to star in a series of films that included *M'Liss* (1918), with Mary Pickford. A very popular star after *The Miracle Man*, he appeared opposite Gloria Swanson in DeMille's *Male and Female* (1919) and *Why Change Your Wife?* (1920).

19. Joseph J. Dowling (1850–1928) had a long career onstage before turning to the movies in 1913. He worked with William S. Hart and Charles Ray before *The Miracle Man* and later with Pickford in *Little Lord Fauntleroy* (1921).

20. Initially a stage actor and then a character actor for Universal, Lon Chaney (1883–1930) became a star with *The Miracle Man* and a master of makeup, playing grotesque or tortured characters in *The Penalty* (1920), *The Hunchback of Notre Dame* (1923), and *The Phantom of the Opera* (1925).

21. A famous producer, composer, and star of Broadway musicals, George M. Cohen (1878–1942) wrote and produced the play that was adapted into *The Miracle Man*.

22. For information on Mrs. Sidney Drew, see note 61. Sidney Olcott discovered Alice Joyce (1890–1955) as a photographer's model and "Gibson Girl" and hired her in 1910 to appear in scores of films for Kalem, where she quickly became a major star. From 1915 to 1921 she worked for Vitagraph, but her stardom waned until it briefly revived in *Cousin Kate*. During the rest of the 1920s, she usually appeared in supporting roles.

23. Gilbert Emery (1875–1945) was a short story writer, teacher, reporter, and member of the American Expeditionary Forces' Liaison Service with several French balloon companies. *Cousin Kate* was the first of many films in which he appeared, mostly in the 1930s and 1940s.

24. This film is available for purchase online.

25. This scathing attack is so unlike Harriette Underhill's praise for the film or that of the *New York Times* reviewer ("The Screen," in Amberg, *The New York Times Film Reviews*, 87).

26. This film is available for purchase online.

27. Irish-born Rex Ingram (1892–1950) began acting in films in 1913 and then became a writer-director, principally at Metro. After *The Four Horsemen of the Apocalypse*, he married Alice Terry and established a small studio in Nice, on the French Riviera. An important Spanish writer, Vincente Blasco Ibañez (1867–1928), published several novels that were adapted into hugely successful films. They in-

cluded *The Four Horsemen of the Apocalypse* (1921) and *Blood and Sand* (1922), which made Valentino a star, as well as a spy film, *Mare Nostrum* (1926).

28. Initially a stage performer, June Mathias (1887–1927) was selling scripts for successful feature films by 1915 and won a contract with Metro in 1918. Within a year she became the head of Metro's scenario department and one of the most powerful screen writers in Hollywood.

29. A well-known Polish stage actress, Pola Negri (1897–1987) went to Germany in 1917 to act in films for UFA. She worked with Lubitsch on a series of very successful films, such as *Carmen / Gypsy Blood* (1918) and *Madame Du Barry / Passion* (1919). The latter was based on Max Reinhardt's Berlin production of *Sumerun*, in which Negri had appeared in 1917. Paramount invited her to Hollywood in 1922, and Negri became one of the most popular stars of the 1920s. *Madame Du Barry / Passion* is available for purchase online.

30. Ernst Lubitsch (1892–1947) was a very successful German director and actor, especially in comedies and historical dramas between 1913 and 1921. *Madame Du Barry / Passion* (1919) and *Anne Boleyn / Deception* (1920) made him famous internationally, and he eventually immigrated to the United States in 1922, directing *Rosita* (1923), with Pickford, and *The Marriage Circle* (1924).

31. *The Cabinet of Dr. Caligari* is readily available on DVD.

32. Again, Mae Tinée's take on *Caligari* is quite opposite that of Underhill and the *New York Times* reviewer. In one of two columns, the latter can't decide whether its highly original style is "cubistic" (analogous to Marcel Duchamp's painting *Nude Descending a Staircase, No. 2*) or "expressionistic" ("A Cubistic Shocker" and "The Screen," in Amberg, *The New York Times Film Reviews*, 91, 92–93).

33. In two *Chicago News* reviews, Carl Sandberg described the extremes of audience responses: some called it the year's most original, innovative film; others found it "the craziest wildest shivery movie that has come wriggling across the silversheet." Although Sandberg sided with the former, he did write tongue-in-cheek: "It looks like a collaboration of Rube Goldberg Ben Hecht Charlie Chaplin and Edgar Alan Poe" (Fetherling and Fetherling, *Carl Sandberg at the Movies*, 38–41).

34. This film is available for purchase online.

35. Agnes Ayres (1898–1940) gained stardom opposite Valentino in *The Sheik* (1921) and then took major roles in several DeMille films.

36. Born in Vienna and trained as a doctor, Arthur Schnitzler (1862–1931) became a major and controversial playwright with *Anatol* (1893) and *Reigen* (1897).

37. Wanda Hawley (1895–1963) acted for Fox Film and Famous Players–Lasky in the late 1910s and chiefly played character roles until she left the movies in the late 1920s. A child actor onstage and on-screen, Bebe Daniels (1901–71) starred in two-reel comedies with Harold Lloyd before contracting with DeMille to play character roles in *Male and Female* (1919), *Why Change Your Wife?* (1920), and *The Affairs of Anatol*. She had a successful career through the 1920s and became a popular singer-actress in musicals in the 1930s.

38. This film is available for purchase online.

39. The *New York Times* did not deign to even review *The Blot*.

40. Among these titles are the following lost films: *Over the Hill*, *The Passion Flower*, *The Devil*, *Footlights*, and *The Queen of Sheba*.

41. Will Carleton (1845–1912) was well-known as a rural Michigan poet whose "Over the Hill to the Poor House" (1872) became the basis for this film. In 1919 the Michigan legislature named October 21 Will Carleton Day.

42. A child actor in vaudeville and film, Jackie Coogan (1914–84) became a major star playing opposite Chaplin in *The Kid*, which led to more starring roles throughout the 1920s. By the mid-1930s, his mother and stepfather had squandered much of his earnings, which resulted in the California Child Actor's Bill in 1939.

43. Charlotte S. Kelly, "Comments on the Screen," *Indianapolis Sunday Star*, February 16, 1919, 6.1, 11.

44. "Clubs and Sororities," *Indianapolis Sunday Star*, February 1, 1920, 4.1.

45. The Circle ad, *Indianapolis Star*, February 25, 1920, 10.

46. "Society," *Indianapolis Times*, July 15, 1920, 6.

47. Kelly likely means DeMille's remake of *The Squaw Man* (December 1918) and Allen Holubar's *The Heart of Humanity*, with Dorothy Phillips (early 1919).

48. At the time Paul Brunet was vice president and general manager of Pathé Exchange. *Pathé Review* was the company's "screen magazine," which gathered short nonfiction films, from color travel pictures to "slow motion films," in a weekly that complemented *Pathé News*. For another column on nonfiction films, see Kelly, "Comments on the Screen," *Indianapolis Sunday Star*, June 15, 1919, 5.1, 12.

49. The pioneering expert on microscopic filmmaking, Jean Comandon (1877–1970) headed Pathé's department of scientific popularization in Paris.

50. Brunet's reference to an American camera is unclear. Lucien Bull (1876–1972) pioneered innovative "stop motion" cameras for Pathé in Paris and achieved a rate of fifteen thousand images per second in *Décharge d'un revolver / Firing a Gun* (1914).

51. Coloring films by hand was long outdated, superseded by Pathé's automated stencil-coloring system, along with high-quality tinting and toning, often combined in travel films.

52. A famous herpetologist, Raymond L. Ditmars (1876–1942) began producing *The Living Book of Nature* in 1914. By 1919 it included fifty-three short subjects taken by slow-motion, time-lapse, and macroscopic cameras.

53. Genevieve Harris, "Reflections on 'Way Down East,'" *Chicago Post*, March 19, 1921, 12.

54. Harris's first columns about *Four Horsemen of the Apocalypse* focused on production details and then a profile of its little-known director, Rex Ingram ("A Few Facts about 'Four Horsemen,'" *Chicago Post*, March 19, 1921, 12; and "A Famous Novel Filmed," *Chicago Post*, March 26, 1921, 4).

55. On *Deception*, see Genevieve Harris, "Another Imported Film Merits Praise," *Chicago Post*, August 9, 1921, 12; on *The Golem*, see Harris, "Photoplays," *Chicago Post*, August 18, 1921, 12.

56. Genevieve Harris, "The Stars Still Rule," *Chicago Post*, November 29, 1919, 4.

57. Genevieve Harris, "For Freedom of Screen," *Chicago Post*, May 3, 1919, 6. Founded in 1916, the National Association of the Motion Picture Industry (NAMPI) had a governing board in which producers and distributors outnumbered exhibitors. Concerned with censorship, taxation, and exhibitor relations, NAMPI soon became the industry's central trade organization.

58. Genevieve Harris, "The Stratford Pleases Public," *Chicago Post*, September 18, 1920, 6.

59. Genevieve Harris, "Music and the Pictures," *Chicago Post*, March 12, 1921, 8.

60. Founded in 1920, the Society for Visual Education was one of a half dozen organizations devoted to the Visual Education Movement as an important part of the country's modernization. The society published a monthly journal simply titled *Visual Education*.

61. The second Mrs. Sidney Drew, Lucille McVey, acted as Polly to her husband's Henry in a series of very popular middle-class domestic comedies, first at Vitagraph (1914–16) and Metro (1916–17), then independently through Paramount until Sidney's death in 1919. Mrs. Drew wrote the comedies' scripts and later produced and directed several short comedies for Pathé Exchange and Vitagraph's *Cousin Kate* (1921)—see the selected review by Mae Tinée. For further information, see Casiana Ionita, "Mrs. Sidney Drew," Women Film Pioneers Project.

62. Mae Tinée had interviewed the Drews a week or so earlier, and Mrs. Drew seemed to control the interview ("Right Off the Reel," *Chicago Sunday Tribune*, January 19, 1919, 7.4).

63. This film is readily available for purchase online.

64. London-born Thomas Burke (1886–1945) gained fame with *Limehouse Nights* (1916), a collection of short stories set in a lower-class district of London full of Chinese immigrants. Griffith would adapt two more of the collection's stories into *Dream Street* (1922).

65. A stock company actor, Richard Barthelmess (1895–1963) owed his entry in the industry to Alla Nazimova. After playing opposite her in *War Brides* (1916), he appeared in several dozen films before becoming a major star in *Broken Blossoms*.

66. Born in London, Donald Crisp (1882–1974) traveled to New York in 1906 and by 1910 was a stage manager for George M. Cohan. From 1912 on he played bit parts and character roles in scores of films before joining British army intelligence during the war. An assistant to Griffith, he became an important director in his own right in the 1920s.

67. An astronomy professor at the University of Chicago, Forest Ray Moulton (1872–1952) served several times as secretary of the American Association for the Advancement of Science.

68. After playing bit parts, Claire Windsor (1892–1972) starred in several Weber films, including *What Do Men Want?* A major star throughout the 1920s, she was known for her fashion sense.

69. A successful vaudeville performer, Margaret McWade (1871–1956) at one point teamed with Margaret Seddon in a stage act called the Pixilated Sisters, reprised in

Mr. Deeds Goes to Town (1936). In 1914 she entered the film industry and played supporting character roles while continuing to tour onstage.

70. Mary Carr (1874–1973) appeared in more than a hundred films between 1915 and 1956, often as an acclaimed mother or grandmother figure. Beginning with *Traffic in Souls*, William Welsh (1870–1946) also appeared in more than a hundred films between 1913 and 1936.

71. See also a discussion of seeing the rerelease of DeMille's *The Cheat* in Virginia Tracy, "A Truce between Romance and Realism," *New York Sunday Tribune*, February 9, 1919, 54.

72. Founded in 1915, Fox Film merged Greater New York Film Rental and Box Office Attractions into a single company. While the initial Fox studios were in Fort Lee, New Jersey, the company opened its Hollywood studios in 1917.

73. Virginia Tracy, "The Miracle Man Renews a Hope," *New York Sunday Tribune*, September 7, 1919, 4.8. A rare instance of Mae Tinée being more in step with audiences than was Tracy.

74. *The Lamb* is one of three early Fairbanks films available in a DVD for purchase online.

75. *Manhattan Madness* is one of four Fairbanks films available in a DVD for purchase online.

76. Raoul Walsh's younger brother, George Walsh (1889–1981), was a skillful athlete who entered the movies in 1914, often playing character roles that involved stunts and fights. He starred in several films, including opposite Pickford in *Rosita* (1923). A well-known Shakespeare stage actor, Frank Keenan (1858–1929) came late to the movies in 1914 and acted in dozens of films, including *The Coward* (1915) and *The Thoroughbred* (1916), through the 1920s.

77. This brief note from a moviegoer follows Virginia Tracy's column.

78. A successful stage actress, Fannie Ward (1872–1952) agreed to perform in DeMille's *The Cheat* (1915), which made her and Hayakawa major movie stars. With an unusually youthful face, she appeared in two dozen films over the next four years, went to France to star in several early Raymond Bernard features, retired, and opened a beauty shop in Paris. *The Cheat* is readily available for purchase online.

79. Grand Guignol was a popular Paris theater founded in 1897, and its principal playwright was André de Lorde, whose many plays of horror and terror (often only one act) led to a generic use of the term for creative works of spectacular brutal horror.

80. *The Half Breed* and *His Picture in the Papers* are available for purchase online.

81. Sidney Drew (1863–1919) acted with his first wife, Gladys Rankin, in light comedies onstage and then briefly in Kalem and Vitagraph films before Rankin died in 1914. Partnered with Lucille McVey, the new team produced fifty very popular one- and two-reel situation comedies of domestic life for Vitagraph and Metro through 1919. For information on Mrs. Sidney Drew, see note 61.

82. A famous pioneering cameraman, Gottfried Wilhelm "Billy" Bitzer (1872–1944) first shot both nonfiction and fiction films for American Mutoscope & Biograph.

When AM&B reorganized as Biograph in 1908, Bitzer became the regular cameraman for D. W. Griffith. Using a Pathé camera, he developed and/or standardized such techniques as closeups, fades, dissolves, irises, backlighting, and mattes. After Griffith left Biograph in 1913, Bitzer continued to serve as the primary cinematographer for nearly all of his films, from *The Birth of a Nation* (1915), *Intolerance* (1916), *Hearts of the World* (1918), *Broken Blossoms* (1919), and *Way Down East* (1920) to *Lady of the Pavements* (1929).

83. More in line with Marjorie Daw, the *New York Times* reviewer believed that in this film's simple story, Griffith "has brought [more] meaningful humanity to the screen [. . .] than it has ever been in a motion picture play" ("The Screen," in Amberg, *The New York Times Film Reviews*, 55).

84. For information on Dorothy Gish, see chapter 2, note 33.

85. "People Who Make the Tribune," *Des Moines Tribune*, March 4, 1919, 1.

86. Magdaline (a pseudonym) began signing the "News of the Movies" in late June 1920, but the content was similar to Day's in the *Des Moines Sunday Register*. In early July Leah Durand took over the column, focusing on short star profiles and advance film publicity. Another woman, Fannie Fillmore, had been writing this column in the *Des Moines Sunday Register* from November 1918 through March 1919.

87. However, a later theater ad printed Day's review (or was it a bit of publicity?) of *Nomads of the North* without giving a source (Rialto ad, *Des Moines News*, February 2, 1922, 11). *Variety Obituaries*, vol. 6, 1964–1968 (New York: Garland, 1988), n.p.

88. Dorothy Day, "News of the Movies," *Des Moines Tribune*, March 11, 1919, 5; Day, "News of the Movies," *Des Moines Tribune*, May 13, 1919, 5. See also her delight with "Connie, the irrepressible" in *Romance and Arabella* and the "ever delightful" Pickford in *Pollyanna* (Day, "News of the Movies," *Des Moines Tribune*, April 4, 1919, 14, and, January 31, 1920, 2).

89. Dorothy Day, "News of the Movies," *Des Moines Tribune*, July 12, 1919, 3.

90. Dorothy Day, "News of the Movies," *Des Moines Tribune*, March 4, 1919, 7.

91. Both of these films are available for purchase online.

92. An experienced stage actor, Lewis J. Cody or Lew Cody (1884–1934) entered the movies in 1914 and became an important player with Mabel Normand (whom he married in 1926) in *Mickey* (1918) and in several DeMille features. He continued in character roles into the early 1930s.

93. A successful Broadway actor, Elliott Dexter (1870–1941) came late to the movies in 1915 and usually performed character roles in more than half a dozen films for DeMille until retiring in 1925.

94. This film is available for purchase online.

95. A New York artist's model, Mabel Normand (1892–1930) began acting for Biograph in 1909 and became a popular star in Sennett's Keystone comedies, sometimes with Chaplin. In 1916 she and Sennett formed a production company but lost it when Triangle collapsed in 1918; Normand returned to stardom with several Goldwyn features in the late 1910s and early 1920s. Her career was tarnished by a cocaine addiction

and the scandal of William Desmond Taylor's killing in 1922. After she contracted tuberculosis in 1923 her health declined, and she died in 1930.

96. A stock company stage actor, Wheeler Oakman (1890–1949) began acting in the movies in 1912. His career of usually playing character roles lasted into the 1940s. George Nichols (1864–1927) acted in secondary roles in the movies from 1908 to 1928, often playing the father to Normand's character. He also directed many short films in the early 1910s. Minta Durfee (1889–1975) acted in many Keystone films, often with Fatty Arbuckle, whom she had married in 1908. After *Mickey* she left the movies and separated from Arbuckle just before the 1921 scandal that destroyed his career. She was a close friend of Normand. Minnie Ha Ha apparently was an older Native American actress named after the tragic lover of Hiawatha in Henry Wadsworth Longfellow's long poem, *The Song of Hiawatha* (1855).

97. Anita Stewart (1895–1961) began acting for Vitagraph, notably in *A Tale of Two Cities* (1911), and became a popular movie star in the 1910s, aided by her brother-in-law Ralph Ince. In 1918 Louis B. Mayer let her produce her own films, and her stardom lasted into the early 1920s. Born in Poland and raised in Canada, Louis B. Mayer (1884–1957) became a movie exhibitor in Haverhill (MA), eventually organized a distribution agency in Boston, formed Metro Pictures in New York City in 1916, and founded Louis B. Mayer Pictures in Los Angeles in 1918. When Marcus Loew created Metro-Goldwyn-Mayer in 1924, Mayer headed the West Coast studio that produced unusually popular, profitable films through the 1940s.

98. Initially a reporter and columnist, Harold MacGrath (1871–1932) became a best-selling writer during the early twentieth century. He wrote the scenarios for the extremely popular serials *The Adventures of Kathlyn* (1914) and *The Million Dollar Mystery* (1915) and for a number of features in the late 1910s and early 1920s.

99. "Introducing to You Some Stars of the *Evening Tribune*," *Des Moines Sunday Register*, January 26, 1919, 22. Dorothy Day also was one of these "stars."

100. Rae McRae, "Sixty-Two Years Young," *Des Moines Sunday Register*, June 22, 1919, 13; McRae, "American Women Extravagant to Wear Such Long Skirts, Says French Bride," *Des Moines Sunday Register*, July 27, 1919, 12; and McRae, "Few Men Return to Prewar Vocations," *Des Moines Sunday Register*, October 12, 1919, 7.

101. Wisima Film Company ad, *Exhibitors Herald and Motography*, March 20, 1919, 12.

102. See also the brief quotes from her review in the Illinois ad, *Chicago Tribune*, June 10, 1919, 19; and the Wick ad, *Simpsons Leader* (Kittanning, PA), October 5, 1919, 4.

103. Virginia Dale, "New Picture Adds to Fame of Griffith," *Fort Wayne Sunday News and Sentinel*, October 18, 1919, 3.12.

104. Virginia Dale, "'Dream Street' Shows Griffith Master Director," *Chicago Journal*, June 25, 1921, 8

105. Virginia Dale, "Andrew Karzas Wins Success in Movie Uplift," *Chicago Journal*, June 11, 1921, 8.

106. For a brief analysis of this filmmaking practice to ensure whiteness, see Richard Abel, "The Skin Color of Identity in Early American Cinema," paper presented at the Society for Cinema and Media Studies conference, Toronto, March 17, 2018.

107. Brenon and Farnum were a major director and actor, respectively, at the Fox Fort Lee studio.

108. A fur and garment entrepreneur, Hungarian-born William Fox (1879–1952) acquired nickelodeons and then larger movie theaters in New York City, formed the Greater New York Film Rental Company in 1907, and founded Box Office Attractions to produce features in 1914. One year later, his Fox Film became one of the first vertically integrated companies in the industry.

109. Ishbel Ross, *Ladies of the Press: The Story of Women in Journalism by an Insider* (New York: Harper & Brothers, 1936), 412–13.

110. Harriette Underhill, "On the Screen," *New York Tribune*, December 13, 1920, 8.

111. Harriette Underhill, "On the Screen," *New York Tribune*, October 26, 1920, 8.

112. Referencing a *New York Times* ad, Shelley Stamp contrasts the "disparaging comments" of the *Times*' male reviewer with those of women reviewers, including Underhill (*Lois Weber in Early Hollywood* [Oakland: University of California Press, 2015], 182).

113. *When the Clouds Roll By* is available for purchase online.

114. *Paramount-Post Nature Pictures* were released weekly or biweekly by Famous Players–Lasky.

115. Percy Marmont (1883–1977) appeared in eighty films between 1916 and 1968, sometimes as a leading man but usually as a supporting character actor.

116. A successful stage actor, Vincent Serrano (1866–1935) appeared as a character actor in a dozen films from 1915 to 1927.

117. French-born Gaston Glass (1899–1965) appeared as a character actor in dozens of films from the late 1910s through the 1930s.

118. *The Mark of Zorro* is available for purchase online.

119. Initially a stage monologist, Fred Niblo (1874–1948) turned to film acting and directing in 1916. He found great success with *The Mark of Zorro*, *The Three Musketeers* (1921), *Blood and Sand* (1922), and *Ben-Hur* (1925).

120. A successful stage actor in New York, Noah Beery (1882–1946) and his brother Wallace turned to movie acting in 1915. The villainous role in this film made him a highly rated character actor throughout the decade, and his rich basso voice led to even greater success in the 1930s. Robert McKim (1886–1927) appeared in a hundred films between 1915 and 1927, often as a villain, from William S. Hart's *Hell's Hinges* (1916) to *Wagon Tracks* (1919).

121. Trained as a dancer, Marguerite de la Motte (1902–50) also starred opposite Fairbanks in *The Three Musketeers*. She appeared frequently in feature films throughout the 1920s.

122. Trained as an artist, Frances Marion (1888–1973) became a writing assistant to Weber in 1914 and two years later was writing scenarios for Famous Players–Lasky.

After serving as head of World Film's writing department, she became Pickford's official scenario writer and one of the top Hollywood scriptwriters in the 1920s.

123. Raymond Bloomer (1886–1948) was a character actor in a score of films from 1913 to 1927.

124. Carl Mayer (1894–1944) wrote the script for *The Cabinet of Dr. Caligari* and then *Der letzte Mann* (1924) and *Sunrise* (1927) for F. W. Murnau. In 1933 he left Germany and served as an advisor to the British film industry. After serving in the war, Hans Janowitz (1890–1954) wrote the script, with Mayer, for Robert Wiene's *Caligari*. After working on two Murnau films, he entered the oil business.

125. Hermann Warm (1892–?) was a major art director not only for *Caligari* and Fritz Lang's *Destiny* (1921) but also Carl Dreyer's *Passion de Jeanne d'Arc* (1927) and *Vampyr* (1931). A member of the group of artists known as Der Sturm, Walter Reimann (1887–1936) was an important set designer for German films in the 1920s and early 1930s. Walter Röhrig (1897–1945) also was an important German art director in the 1920s and 1930s.

126. 35mm prints of *What Do Men Want* survive at the US Library of Congress and UCLA Film Archive. In December 1914 "Wid" Gunning began editing the influential "Films and Film Folk" page for the *New York Evening Mail*. After leaving the newspaper, he launched *Wid's Daily* in 1917, which turned into *Film Daily*. Gunning also exhibited films as a sideline.

127. The *New York Times* reviewer asks his own unkind question: "Why does Miss Weber devote the really worthwhile time of herself and her staff to those simplified sermons on the screen which make a transparent bluff of dealing wisely with problems of human nature but get nowhere at all?" ("The Screen," in Amberg, *The New York Times Film Reviews*, 106–7).

128. Frank Glendon (1886–1937) was a character actor in dozens of films well into the 1930s. George Hackathorne (1896–1940) was a character actor in scores of films through the 1930s. "Lady Clara Vere de Vere" (1842), a Tennyson poem.

129. Halam Cooley (1895–1971) also was a character actor in a hundred films through the 1930s.

130. See, for instance, Alberta Hartley, "Des Moines Theaters Have Real Thrillers Booked for the Week," *Des Moines Saturday News*, January 8, 1921, M.1; "Anita Loos Tells Secrets of Scenarios," *Des Moines Saturday News*, February 26, 1921, 1.2.

131. Alberta Hartley, "Zukor Judged," *Des Moines News*, January 8, 1921, Movies, 1.

132. The story was by Paul Cazeneuve; the scenario, by William M. Conselman.

133. The *New York Times* reviewer focused on Lila Lee and her much improved acting skill ("The Screen," in Amberg, *The New York Times Film Reviews*, 83).

134. Trained as a schoolteacher, Lois Wilson (1894–1988) won a beauty contest in 1915 and turned to film acting. Mentored by Weber, she became a Paramount star from 1919 to 1927. Born in Iowa, Conrad Nagel (1897–1970) quickly became a movie star as a tall, unspoiled midwestern figure, working steadily through the 1920s. His baritone voice allowed him to transition to sound films in character roles and later

to host radio and television shows. A young vaudeville performer, Lila Lee (1901–73) contracted with Famous Players–Lasky in 1918 and soon became a popular movie star throughout the 1920s. After a series of jobs, some in Alaska, Jack Holt (1888–1951) became a stunt man and actor for Universal and then a tough guy character actor from the 1920s through the 1940s.

135. Initially an artist's model, Irish-born Eileen Percy (1900–1973) entered the movies in 1917 and appeared as either a star or a character actor in more than fifty films through the early 1930s.

136. This film is readily available for purchase online.

137. Initially a touring stage performer, Kathlyn Williams (1879–1960) joined Selig in 1908 and acted in dozens of short films. Her most famous role was in *The Adventures of Kathlyn* serial (1913–14). From the late 1910s through the early 1930s, she was a popular character actor.

138. Forrest Stanley (1889–1969) played supporting character roles in dozens of films through the 1930s. A touring stage actor, Clarence Burton (1882–1933) appeared in more than a hundred films between 1912 and 1932.

○ 4 ○

Women Writers Carry On, 1922–1923

One source for identifying newspaper columnists writing about the movies during this period is the 1925 *Film Daily Yearbook*, which compiled a list of the ten best pictures of 1924 as selected by "critics of some of the best known daily newspapers in this country."[1] The New York newspapers named twelve columnists, five of whom were women, but none of those seem to have reviewed films. The columns of both Louella Parsons (*New York American*) and Rose Pelswick (*New York Journal*) instead were full of star profiles, industry information, and gossip.[2] F. W. Mordaunt Hall (*New York Times*) would become the best known of the city's film reviewers, but he did not sign "The Screen" column until October 6, 1924.[3] The rest of the country's newspapers named forty-four columnists, fifteen of whom were women. Not among those columnists, of course, was D. Ireland Thomas, who contributed an irregular gossipy column in the *Chicago Defender*.[4] Of the women, Elizabeth Kern (*Omaha World-Herald*) and Polly Wood (*Chicago Herald and Examiner*) definitely wrote film reviews, and their newspapers are accessible either on the web or on microfilm. Three others, Prunella Hall (*Boston Post*), Leah Durand (*Des Moines Register* and *Tribune*), and Prudence Nicholas (*Des Moines Capital*), also chiefly wrote gossip columns and edited movie pages.[5] Whether or not the remaining eleven women reviewed films is unclear, because their newspapers have not yet been digitized. However, as with the 1919 *Motion Picture News* directory, there is a crucial caveat to the *Film Daily Yearbook* compilation. No newspapers are listed from major cities such as Cleveland, Cincinnati, Kansas City, Philadelphia, San Francisco, and St. Louis. Moreover, the *Chicago Journal*, *Chicago Post*, and *Chicago Tribune* are missing, as is the *Chicago News*, still offering Carl Sandberg's reviews.

Despite Ishbel Ross's claim, men rather than women overall seemed to dominate the motion picture field of the newspapers. Yet that was not true of Chicago, where Virginia Dale, Genevieve Harris, Mae Tinée, and Polly Wood reigned as the city's movie mavens. Except for Kern's columns in Omaha, Harriette Underhill's in New York, and Grace Kingsley's in Los Angeles, consequently, the columns by the Chicago reviewers nearly fill this last chapter.

Grace Kingsley

By the 1920s Kingsley had become an influential columnist for the *Los Angeles Times*, primarily sharing industry information and interviewing movie people but also writing reviews. Her column soon was syndicated and continued to appear well into the 1950s.[6]

The two columns selected here offer quite different takes on Hollywood films in the early 1920s. Her review of Richard Barthelmess's acting and Henry King's direction in *Tol'able David* offers evidence of why the film so quickly became "canonical." Her criticism of movie comedies, notably those of Chaplin, Arbuckle, and Lloyd, however, makes a revealing contrast with earlier tributes by her colleagues to the Drews, Fairbanks, and Normand.

"Flashes," *Los Angeles Times*, January 23, 1922, 3.4.

"TOL'ABLE DAVID"   They didn't know you were looking at them, those folks in "Tol'able David"—so they went ahead and made a drama big with the real tragedies and comedies of everyday life.[7] They didn't know you were looking at them—so it is not forced on you, neither the tragedy nor the comedy.

Nobody posed nor strutted, nor was sorry for himself.

But it's all there for you to take or leave, one of the greatest pictures of the year, or that has ever been made, because of its poignant sincerity, its thrilling suspense growing naturally out of its situations and its characters, its homely, but startling, reality.

No matter where you chance to be sitting in the Kinema Theater, you won't be sitting there long. You'll be right up among those homely folks of the mountains—Joseph Hergesheimer's characters.[8] Henry King, who directed, has managed to preserve most skillfully the atmosphere, the sinister suspense, the characterizations, the soul drama, which is, after all, the only real drama of Hergesheimer.[9]

Richard Barthelmess' playing of David, the lad who dreamed his dreams, but who was held in leash by his own humble nature and petty circumstances, and whom everybody called "Tol'able David," is a many faceted gem, a character which it will take long to erase from our memory.

Poor Tol'able David! Longing to avenge his brother's injury, by which he was made an invalid for life, but held in check by his mother's clinging to his feet, crying "David, David, you're the only man we got now!"

Poor Tol'able David, drudge in the grocery store, when his soul longs to be the Jehu of the mountains, driving the United States mail hack as his brother did before him. Poor Tol'able David, face to face with the big tragedy of his young life when he loses that mail on his very first trip. A small thing that, but that vivid in Barthelmess' hands, even as our own everyday tragedies are vivid in our lives.

I defy anyone not to thrill and weep when David finally arrives, bruised and blood-stained from his battle with the sinister Hathburn.

Doubtless there's nobody on the screen who could give this role not only the poignant appeal, but also the vivid force which Barthelmess does.

All the characters are astonishingly real and convincing, like the people you have known, no matter how those people have been dressed or what their manners. Lack of space alone prevents me from singing a separate paeon of praise for Gladys Hulette as Esther Hathburn, to Marion Abbott as David's mother, to Walter P. Lewis, Ernest Torrence, Ralph Yearsley, Forrest Robinson, Laurence Eddinger, Edmund Gurney, Warner Richmond, Harry Hallam and Patterson Diall.[10] They all live and breathe and are your neighbors.

Oh, for the day when we shall see more "Tol'able Davids" in pictureland.

"Day by Day Our Comedies Grow Sadder," *Los Angeles Times*, January 14, 1923, 3.29.

Day by day, in every way, our comedians are getting gentler and gentler! Charlie Chaplin and Harold Lloyd indeed are becoming regular tear chasers.[11] We tremble now even for Larry Semon and Buster Keaton—when are they going to turn refined on us?[12] I hear that Larry, indeed, has a sneaking desire to play "Deburau" and that Buster is going to turn Beau Brummel.

Mack Sennett's bathing girls are now bathing in tears! Phyllis Haver, Marie Prevost, Mary Thurman, all the lovely, joyous throng, have dry-cleaned their bathing suits and offered them to the poor.[13]

Even Louise Fazenda, hardy perennial in the laugh garden, is going to die in her next picture—"Main Street."[14]

"Oh, I've got to diet so I can die!" Louise told me gleefully the other day.

And Mabel Normand in a costume play. She of the negligee in "Fatty and Mabel Adrift," when the villain pushed the house into the ocean.

They all seem to be longing for tragedy relief in their comedy lives.

But I'll tell you right now—when Ham Hamilton plays "Hamlet," I'm going to quit.[15]

Alas for the furtive few of us who still like to laugh without also paging the tear, who love to see the fat man topple and the villain hit on the head with the resin beer bottle!

How times are changed, indeed! The custard pies have retired from the garbage pail of art, one might say, to their rightful, dignified place in the pantry, and the last siphon bottle I heard was taken to the museum along with the slap stick.

GAG OR "PAG"—WHICH?   One morning in the dim long ago of 1918 I went out to the Chaplin studio to find Charlie raging up and down the stage, teeth clenched and tears in his eyes, as he wrinsled over a new gag that was just a-borning. Nowadays he smiles as he tells you how, pretty soon, he is going to play the tragic Pagliacci!

How careful Charlie used to be about those gags! I remember one hot day when he was making "A Day's Pleasure," and the tar in which he was supposed to stick, in the Ford scene, just wouldn't jell. Out romped Charlie to mix the near-tar himself. And when he got through it stuck, too!

We suspect now that Charlie is going to park his pants and his cane permanently, and comes out in his next picture wearing trousers and a Fedora. Probably he won't fall down once. We may as well face it. No more will Charlie stoop to pick up an imaginary fluid dollar; no more will his nether integuments cause him comic worry; no more will the suspense of his comedy depend partly on his suspenders.

"The Kid" was the best picture that Charlie ever made, and it was full of whimsicalities, as well as of ordinary gags. Who will ever forget heaven and the feathers flying when the angels scrapped? That's the sort of thing we remember rather than the near-sad stuff about the child.

AND "GRANDMA'S BOY"   So, too, "Grandma's Boy" was a work of genius.[16] But Lloyd did not top it with the more psychological "Dr. Jack." It isn't the psychological twist or autosuggestion that we remember so well in "Grandma's Boy" as it is those kittens licking the grease off the young swain's boots. Grandma was a wise old dear, but we shall have forgotten her long after we remember the young lovers tumbling into the stream when the big pig arose beneath their feet.

When Fatty Arbuckle dropped his two-reelers and went in for the five-reel comedy dramas he let me in on the reason for making the change.[17]

"It's just about a hundred times easier," he confided, "to make a comedy drama than a two-reeler, and you get more for it. Also you get more fame. People go in and laugh when they see you in a jazz comedy, but all the same they think to themselves, 'Pooh, that's nothing! He's just a boob.' Yet you have worked yourself sick and your brain is fagged thinking up new gags for that comedy."

Then there's another reason. The war is over now, and nobody has anything national to feel sad about, so they are making the comedies sad. Sad, and so "ruffined," as Trixie Friganza says.

There's nothing left for Arbuckle, it seems, but the funny stuff. Nothing, that is, smiled Chaplin the other night, except the nursewife in "East Lynne" or "Juliet"!

Even as this story goes to press we find that Fatty is to play "Handy Andy." No doubt he will be awfully peeved because there isn't a single tear in the whole thing.

Harriette Underhill

In 1923 Underhill contracted tuberculosis but kept writing for the *New York Tribune*.[18] Although invited to Hollywood and feted with parties, she hated the place and returned to New York. According to ads in *Film Daily*, she was still reviewing films for the *New York Herald* and *Herald-Tribune* from late 1924 through late 1925.[19] She finally died of TB in 1928.

Many of Underhill's columns drew on her chatty interviews with stars or with filmmakers such as Reginald Barker, who agreed with her on the singular importance of the director to the worth of a motion picture.[20] But she often wrote trenchant film reviews. Her review of *Smilin' Through*, for instance, offers a glimpse, rather different from Virginia Dale's, of why Norma Talmadge was a popular, accomplished star in the early 1920s. Her second viewing of Erich von Stroheim's *Foolish Wives*, which she loved, reveals intriguing differences between the original fourteen-reel release and its ten-reel rerelease.

"On the Screen," *New York Tribune*, January 27, 1922, 8.

Like the well known bus man who took his vacation on a bus, we went to the Central Theater yesterday for a second view of Erich von Stroheim's "Foolish Wives" because it was our birthday and a local holiday.[21] Also because we had promised to drop in and see it in ten reels instead of in fourteen, as it was the opening night. Now, if any one expects us to say that we like the picture better in its pocket edition, we shall have to disappoint him, merely because, having found what we consider the perfect picture, we are loath to part with any of it. If Mr. Laemmle wishes to give us a birthday present it can be a print of the original picture as it was in 320 reels; but of course we realize that it was necessary to have the end come before the midnight hour had struck. People in the theater like to call it a day along about 11 o'clock, and, as a matter of fact, all of the part that comes after the death of the villainous count failed to interest us to any great extent.

That part is now in the discard, which is a decided improvement, but we should like the duel scenes in as they were. Our attitude is much the same as that of the little girl who cried bitterly when she viewed the picture of the Christian martyrs because, she said, the littlest hen wasn't getting [?], and we are afraid that our [?] interest in the prolonged waiting on the part of the hero for the villain to come and shoot him through the heart in the cold, gray dawn was because we knew that said villain could do it so easily. For some reason we do not always espouse the cause of [?] on the screen as we should.

The picture originally possessed a sensuous quality which we found delightful. It still has this to a certain extent, but we couldn't help feeling yesterday as we once did when we got hold of a school edition of Shakespeare. Some of the scenes which some people considered objectionable have been cut, though it is probable that this happened merely in the pruning for brevity, as many others to which even the most pure-minded could not object also have been discarded, and Mr. Laemmle, who financed the picture to the extent of $1,000,000, surely had the courage of Mr. Von Stroheim's convictions. On the opening night he had the best picture we had ever seen. He still has it.

"On the Screen," *New York Tribune*, April 17, 1922, 6.

This is a fitting time to show Norma Talmadge's beautiful picture, "Smilin' Through," with Sir Arthur Conan Doyle here teaching us that it is not only a short journey into the next world but also a pleasant one. In the final scene of the picture, which is at the Strand, the lovers are united, their etheric bodies meeting in the old garden. The young John Carteret turns and sees himself, an old man with his head bowed on the table, and he knows that it is what mortals call death. "But if this is death," he says to Moonyeen, "why are they so afraid to die?" "Some of them are, poor dears," answers Moonyeen, "because they do not know how beautiful the end of the journey is. If they did they would go smilin' through life."

As far as direction goes, we should say that "Smilin' Through" is the perfect picture. It is so beautifully done and with such a light touch that all of it seems very real, and that is the most important of all. Miss Talmadge plays with a gentle whimsicality that robs her scenes of any hint of the melodramatic.

She does not portray heartbreak by pounding her chest, nor by heaving her shoulders nor bulging her eyes. She does not seem a screen actress, but a girl who loves her uncle, even though he will not permit her to marry the man she loves. She tells him what she thinks about it and then goes smiling through until John Carteret can see things her way.

Miss Talmadge is seen in two roles. She is Moonyeen, who was killed on her wedding day by a jealous lover, Jeremiah Wayne, and she is Kathleen, a niece, who forty years later loves Kenneth Wayne, a nephew of Jeremiah. Miss Talmadge gives a gorgeous performance throughout the picture, but we couldn't help preferring her in her 1876 costumes. Those styles certainly were becoming. Wyndham Standing we liked much better as the young lover of Moonyeen.[22] He did not suggest old age to us, perhaps because he looked too old. Harrison Ford was better in the 1876 episode, too, we thought. There was a clever characterization, while as a plain lover he has no particular distinction.

Glenn Hunter is very good as Willie Ainsley, a young man who was always trying to propose but who never received any encouragement.[23] Alec B. Francis adds to the enjoyment of the occasion by his portrayal of Doctor Owen.[24] The titles are excellent and are probably the work of James Ashmore Creelman, who did the scenario from the play by Allen Langdon Martin.[25] Sydney Franklin directed the picture, and it would be an afternoon well spent if other directors would go to see the picture.[26] Most of them could learn something from it, but would they? There is a prologue to "Smilin' Through" with Frank Mellor and the Strand quartet.

The overture is "Cavalleria Rusticana," with Eldora Stanford and a chorus.

Mae Tinée

Mae Tinée continued to rank among the best film reviewers, although still quite controversial, not only in Chicago but also across the country. In early 1922 she introduced a weekly column titled "Kick Korner," asking readers to write to her with complaints or "kicks" about producers, exhibitors, or specific films in order to improve the movies.[27] Those "kicks" came in droves and occasionally called the critic herself to task. Two were especially vehement: "You seem to have a pretty good opinion of yourself and your column and I think that is all rot" and "when I saw your picture in the W.G.N. some months ago, I never could have believed that so cruel a nature could hide behind such a kindly face."[28] As a sign of her influence, however, in early 1924 one column closed with this: "Reprints of any review by Mae Tinée printed in the last thirty days may be obtained by mailing a stamped, addressed, return envelope to (or by calling at) The Tribune's Public Service Bureau, 11 South Dearborn street."[29]

Mae Tinée was no less chatty than before, but sometimes in praising a film she punched up a column with more slang. Take the pseudo-Spanish title of her *Blood and Sand* review: "Valentino Lova da Lady, Keela da Bull! Caramba!" Labeling a fan of Valentino a "Pollyanna," she has her say, "bubbling with enthusiasm": "How we girls would brave heat and thunderstorms and strikes, coal AND rail, to get to see that picture—and it wouldn't be our JOB, either." Or, just ten days later, her review of *Nanook of the North*: "Pity the poor Eskimo? O, I don't know. He's much too busy with one problem—that of merely living—to be bothered with any others [...] [and] living, it seems, isn't easy in Eskimo land." And she kept it up months later in reviewing *Robin Hood*: "Everybody in town who hadn't anything to do—and some who had—parked themselves in front of the theater to see Douglas and Mary arrive. [...] It is a great picture. Sets that will turn Griffith green with envy! The biggest things you ever saw in your lives! Scenery—well—!"[30] Moreover, she was as uninhibited as ever in dumping on that "little sop" of a film, *Pay Day*: "Mr. Chaplin [seems] a little bit tired of his job and a trifle bored."[31] With exaggerated shock, she also "lauded" *Night Life in Hollywood*: "The producers show you a Hollywood that makes by contrast Little Eva a shrieking Salome, yearning for the gore of Uncle Tom [...] a Hollywood that would have been firmly recommended in the Elsie books."[32] "Watch the expressions on the countenances of your fellows as they ENTER the theater. Then, again, as they go OUT! O, BOY!"[33]

By late 1923, however, Tinée seemed to be toning down her language. Could that have been in response to some of her readers' kicks? Beginning with an unexpected rave for *Merry-Go-Round*, she started opening her columns with a "Good morning!"—sounding like a friend or neighbor sitting at a reader's breakfast table—and left with a cheery "See you tomorrow." Still, her respect for the dictatorial Stroheim was not unalloyed: "If a certain kind of lemon was to be plucked and it grew in Bakersville—why giddyap, to Bakersfield for the lemon. No studio lemon would do." Despite the "slim and padded" story in *Flaming Youth*, she marveled at the film's star: "If the vamps, professional and otherwise, already in the field don't watch out, young Miss Colleen Moore will walk away with all the bacon—for O' how that child has learned to use her eyes and vibrate!" Yet her praise of *Anna Christie* and the remarkable Blanche Sweet was unalloyed with irony: "'Anna Christie' is LIFE. Not the Maytime of life. The other side. The kind of life people—some people—don't know about perhaps—but a kind that crime annals show exist. The kind of life that a lone, mongrel, unfed, unclean, frightened puppy suggests."[34]

Although another woman would take over as the *Tribune*'s film critic under that name, according to Ishbel Ross, Frances Peck was still writing as Mae Tinée into the mid-1930s.[35]

"Valentino Lova da Lady, Keela da Bull! Caramba!," *Chicago Tribune*, August 23, 1922, 18.

"BLOOD AND SAND"[36]

> Home again, home again from a foreign shore.
> And if it only WOULD be cool
> We'd like our job much more.

"However," Pollyanna would remark, "there's always something to be thankful for. And," she would probably contend, just bubbling over with enthusiasm, "how perfectly WONDERFUL to come home to a brand new Rodolf Valentino picture! Just THINK," she would say, "how we girls would brave heat and thunderstorms and strikes, coal AND rail, to get to see that picture—and it wouldn't be our JOB, either."

Quite right, Pollyanna—and if you want a little advice before you go to see the picture, why—Go see it—providing your mother is willing.

You will find it a taunting, throbbing tragedy shadowed romance of the bull ring; its hero a toreador who worships his wife with a clean, white devotion, but becomes the victim of a mad infatuation for another woman.

Say what you please, for or against Valentino—give him something to act IN and he can act. This story by Ibáñez has kept him on his tiptoes. As the toreador he is a dashing gamin, bold hearted, passionate, superstitious child of sunny Spain, idol of the Spanish people, for whom he debonairly provides thrill after thrill in the arena. Lithe and unafraid he is until his eyes meet the flaming ones of the siren who is to be his bad genius.

Like Kipling's immortal "rag, bone, and hank of hair," she doesn't care—but she DOES like to experiment. Juan Gallardo suffers and doesn't understand, and, trying to understand, loses his cunning. In a moment of recklessness that is not daring he comes to the end which, sooner or later, the author believes is dealt to those who live by pandering to cruelty.[37]

Valentino as Juan, the idol, fills the role with lilting romance. When the Americans in the café ask, "Who is that man?" he permits to the hero several moments of crude and boyish braggadocio. His Juan in the siren's drawing room is gauche and uncomfortable. These touches are the sure trademarks of the artist.

Lila Lee as the wife passes pathetically and lightly through the story. Nita Naldi—sensation huntress—is a sensation in herself.[38] Gloria Swanson as Gloria would like to be, perhaps, and Alla Nazimova as she thinks she is.

There are many "bonny bits" of work on the part of the supporting cast—Juan's mother, for instance—and the tale as told pictorially is full of action and color, excellently staged, set and directed. As in "The Four Horsemen" there was the Dreamer, in "Blood and Sand" there is the Philosopher. I found him unnecessary—but that's no sign that you will.

Pollyanna would say, "That IS no sign that you will."

"Real Life Reeled in Eskimo Land," *Chicago Tribune*, September 2, 1922, 12.

"NANOOK OF THE NORTH"[39]   Pity the poor Eskimo? O, I don't know. He's much too busy with one problem—that of merely living—to be bothered with any others. Railroad and coal strikes mean nothing in his life. He should worry only were a fish, speared through the ice, to slip away, or a walrus family, stalked with infinite patience for miles through breath-taking cold, to spy him in time and make their escape.[40]

"Nanook of the North" is one of the most comprehensive and interesting educational pictures ever filmed.[41] It was actually photographed in the frozen north and the actors are actors only in so much as they permitted a photographer to travel along with them and "take" them as they worked, slept, and played.

Living, it seems, isn't easy in Eskimo land. What one eats, what one wears, and what covers one when one sleeps must be trapped. Mother's seal coat doesn't come in a box. It is peeled off a seal, just killed. After mother's coat has been attended to, why it is time for dinner. With sharp knives Mother and Father cut into the raw flesh and they and the children got to it. One can imagine the impatience they would show were somebody to come along with a frying pan and a bunch of fire and insist on cooking the banquet for them. I don't know the Eskimo word for "why," but Nanook and his family would certainly want to know under such circumstances.

The only thing the building trades and the labor unions could possibly have in common with Nanook and family, is when it comes to the question of constructing an igloo. Then—Nanook would show 'em. What's all the fuss about when in an hour a perfectly comfortable dwelling can be constructed out of lumps of ice, with Father placing the blocks and Mother filling in the chinks. When the house is finished—it's finished. Furniture? Bah! Where's the little old bearskin? We'll all lie down on that. Then we'll cover ourselves with our clothes. Then because we're tired, we'll go to sleep, and when we wake up, well—that will be another day.

Another day that may bring blizzards, but Nanook, "The Bear," and Nyla, his wife, "The Smiling One," are used to blizzards. It will probably bring hunger, but God is good and there are fish, and walrus, and seals, and white foxes if one only has patience and exercises a little ingenuity.

The picture might be succinctly termed a real life drama of Eskimo family life. But how different from ours. What, for instance, would an Eskimo family do with a divorce court?

"Nanook of the North" reopens Orchestra hall today. It is an interesting picture for anybody to see, and is certainly one that no school child should miss.

"'The Merry Go Round' Worth All It Cost," *Chicago Tribune*, September 25, 1923, 2.1.

"THE MERRY GO ROUND"[42]   Good morning!

This is the picture that nearly gave Universal heart failure. Mr. Eric Von Stroheim, I understand, was accorded the direction in the first place. It seems, however, that he demanded too much "atmosphere"—which in turn took too much money from the company's coffers. Mr. Von Stroheim was, it appears, fond of issuing orders that the entire company move from one part of California to another. No "lot" scenes for him. If a certain kind of a lemon was to be plucked and it grew in Bakersville—why, giddyap, to Bakersfield for the lemon. No studio lemon would do.

For a long time this eminent director is said to have proceeded with appalling magnificence on his atmospheric way, until, in about the middle of the picture, with a great gasp the company got over the dizziness with which "The Merry Go Round" had afflicted them—and Mr. Rupert Julian took the megaphone.[43]

Between the two directors, though, a splendid job has been accomplished. They have certainly established Mary Philbin and Norman Kerry as actors of the first water.[44] It will be a long time after you see the picture before you will be able to forget the scenes between these two. Just one thrill after another. Just one bit of magnificent pantomime after another.

In fact, the entire film may be said to be that.

The story is of a careless count who unexpectedly falls in love with a girl who grinds the organ for the merry go round of a German Coney Island known as the Prater. She returns his passion madly, knowing nothing of their difference in station—for the count has told her he is a necktie salesman and has omitted to mention the fact that the emperor expects him to wed a proud and haughty countess who smokes big, black cigars.

Intertwined in this romance are the lives of the girl's father, a clown; various persons who run the concession; a hunchback who loves Agnes; an orangoutang that loves the hunchback; the giant who owns the whole show; and, of course, various personages of the court.

The world war comes into the picture just long enough to make the ending the sort of ending it is.

Most certainly "The Merry Go Round" is romantic, fascinating, striking, human, and marvelously well done from all points of view. And DON'T forget to write in and tell me what you think of the work of Mary Philbin and Norman Kerry.

See you tomorrow!

"Introducing a Candidate for Vamp Honors," *Chicago Tribune*, October 31, 1923, 2.1.

Colleen Moore Best Part of "Flaming Youth."[45]

"FLAMING YOUTH"   Good morning!

This picture, taken from the book by Warner Fabian, is a long tale of woe predestined to teach the world at large what may happen to a flapper with a penchant for petting parties, and no mother to guide her.[46]

Human nature, having been as it is since the world began, the moral of the picture, as presented, resolves itself more or less into an appeal to the senses. There is plenty of incident that suggests the idea that the publisher, at the last moment, demanded several thousand more words from the author, that the author wrote them and insisted the additions and inserts were so GOOD they must be used in the picture.

As in "The Thundering Dawn," there is plenty of good acting and photography but the story is slim and padded (get me, Stephen?) and the best thing the photoplay does is to establish the fact that if the vamps, professional and otherwise, already in the field don't watch out, young Miss Colleen Moore will walk away with all the bacon—for O' how that child has learned to use her eyes and vibrate!

Ladies throughout the country will be thrilled by the presence of Elliott Dexter and Milton Sills in the cast.[47] There are several wild parties where the only water visible spurts from fountains. There's a long, sad death scene with the principal in the interesting event being most unbelievably beautiful and philosophical in a most De Millian boudoir. This for those who would see how the other half lives—and dies.

But the story? La la! You could write a better!

See you tomorrow!

Elizabeth Kern

In September 1922, as E.M.K., Kern replaced a columnist with the initials A.H.M. to write "This Week at the Movies," printed on the Women's page of Monday's *Omaha World-Herald*.[48] Nearly one year later she signed herself Elizabeth Kern, and the paper implicitly promoted her with this "editor's note—The World-Herald aims to give a fair and impartial criticism of motion pictures shown in Omaha."[49] She continued writing the column at least into 1925, and an ad for *The Thief of Bagdad* reprinted a telegram in which Fairbanks thanked her for "a most wonderful review."[50] According to her Omaha obituary, Kern was identified as working "for this newspaper's Women's News Department for 44 years when she retired in 1953."[51]

Kern's columns tended to be short but pithy. In her reviews of feature films such as *Flaming Youth*, *Anna Christie*, and *Little Old New York*, she often credited not only the actors and director but also the studio, scenario writer, author of an adapted work, and sometimes the distributor. She was relatively unique in congratulating Bradley King for her scenario adaptation of *Anna Christie*, "Eugene O'Neill's prize-winning play." But, like Kitty Kelly earlier, she also urged movie fans to see nonfiction films, from Mr. and Mrs. Martin Johnson's *Trailing African Animals* to the International News' footage of the devastating earthquake in Japan. Early on, Kern reported on the specialized tasks in producing a film, singling out Alvin Wyckoff's "atmospheric lighting," for instance, in *Blood and Sand* and the deft editing of location and studio shots in *The Impossible Mrs. Bellew*, starring Gloria Swanson.[52] In the latter column, as well as another describing three kinds of moviegoers, she asked her readers directly if they could spot the difference in a film between location and studio shots and if they really imagined they counted as a "mythical [. . .] ideal fan."[53]

"This Week at the Movies," *Omaha World-Herald*, October 23, 1922, 7.

Atmospheric lighting is the term applied by Alvin Wyckoff, head of the department of photography at the Lasky studio in Hollywood, to his practice of emphasizing each scene in a photoplay, according to the need and tempo of its dramatic action.[54] Explaining his practice, Wyckoff says: "Photography is the vehicle that carries the story of a motion picture. Therefore, the photography must always be in sympathy with the theme of the scene. Atmospheric lighting was primarily designed to heighten the dramatic effect. It may be overdone. The moment it assumes the preponderance all its value is lost and irreparable damage is done. The story is the important thing; photography is only a means of conveying that story first to the screen and thence to the spectator.

"For [an] example of atmospheric lighting—take Valentino in 'Blood and Sand.' He has a slight scar on one cheek. By throwing a shadow from his hat brim that parallels this scar and bringing out the scar by light and shadow, we succeeded in producing an interesting character quality. Remember Theodore Kosloff in 'Fool's Paradise'?[55] In a majority of his scenes he wore a sombrero. Whenever the action showed him in a sinister mood I lighted his face in such a way as to throw a heavy shadow from his hat brim across his eye. Small as this may seem, it gave a tremendous effect on the screen. These are just two incidents that especially stand out as examples of the art of proper lighting."

"This Week at the Movies," *Omaha World-Herald*, August 13, 1923, 5.

"Trailing African Wild Animals" There is at the Moon an unusually fine camera record of a fascinating expedition, which is well worth seeing. In fact, we think every person should see this Metro picture, "Trailing African Wild Animals," which is the record of two years spent by Mr. and Mrs. Martin Johnson away from civilization.[56] During that time they explored Abyssinia and photographed, mostly "close-ups," a wide variety of very interesting beasts. Now and then there is a thrilling view of Mr. and Mrs. Johnson shooting a savage rhino, lion, or other inhabitant of the jungle. This record was obtained through the use of blinds erected in Never Never Land. The pictures were photographed through a long-focus lens, which gives a series of remarkably vivid scenes. A striking feature is not only the wide variety but the immense numbers of the animals photographed.[57] For instance, there is a tree literally black with monkeys, big herds of giraffes, great gatherings of zebras of different species, many scenes of lions, antelopes, elephants, rhinos and other animals too numerous to mention.

"This Week at the Movies," *Omaha World-Herald*, November 26, 1923, 3.

"Flaming Youth" Lots of pep, moments that border on the gasping point, jazz, a snappy story, pretty women, dashing heroes, gorgeous settings and a thrill ever and anon—that's "Flaming Youth," the First National picture, based on Warner Fabian's novel of the same name, at the Rialto. The man who wrote the story, we have been told, is a New York doctor who didn't dare sign his name. The novel is one of those risqué things that couldn't be translated to the silver screen. But the scenario writer, Harry O. Hoyt, and John Francis Dillon, the director, have done well in pantomiming certain situations they could not present otherwise.[58] Risqué episodes are filmed up to a certain point and then the director lets you use your imagination. But don't go to the theater with the expectation of seeing sensational scenes similar to those described in the book, for you'll be disappointed. Clever idea that, isn't it?

Colleen Moore as the 1923 flapper supreme eclipses all her former characterizations. We think that her portrayal of a modern flapper has no parallel on the screen and we are sure you'll agree with us. Elliott Dexter is perfect as Dr. Bob and Milton Sills does fine in the role of the lover. Excellent support is given by Myrtle Stedman as the mother and Phillips Smalley as the father.[59] Gene Corrado in a small role is very convincing.[60] It is an entertaining, high class picture, with a moral that is not paraded but is there just the same. See it by all means.

"This Week at the Movies," *Omaha World-Herald*, December 3, 1923, 3.

"ANNA CHRISTIE"[61]   Thomas H. Ince has produced Eugene O'Neill's prize-winning play, "Anna Christie," the First National picture at the Rialto this week, with a total disregard of censors.[62] For anyone who is not afraid to face life this picture can not fail to hold powerful appeal. Mr. Ince has kept faith with the playwright—down to the most unimportant detail. The lines of the play have been used as titles and where the lines could not be used, pantomime most effectively conveys the thought. It relates to the love story of a social outcast and an Irish stoker and makes you feel O'Neill's psychology of distressed souls. Bradley King, who wrote the scenario, and John Griffith Wray, who directed the picture, both must be congratulated.[63]

As for the players, they seem to be inspired. Never has Blanche Sweet, who is seen in the title role, done better work. She has presented a characterization that is marvelously real. William Russell, a leading man, has made a place for himself with the big ones by his vigorous portrayal of the Irish stoker.[64] It is easily his best performance. George Marion's study of the old skipper, the role he played on the stage both in this country and England, is a perfect characterization.[65] The only other woman of the story, "Marthy," is capably presented by Eugenie Besserer.

You'll find no expensive sets or handsome costumes or mobs in this production. Nothing here but stark realism—a wharf saloon, a coal barge and the sea.

"This Week at the Movies," *Omaha World-Herald*, December 10, 1923, 4.

"Little Old New York"[66] You will like "Little Old New York" which opened yesterday at the Rialto. A very sweet love story is told by an excellent cast in a setting of the early nineteenth century in this Cosmopolitan picture which stars Marion Davies.[67] Are you numbered among those people who think that Miss Davies can't act? If so, by all means, go to the Rialto this week. You will change your opinion, I am sure. Miss Davies who made such a hit in "When Knighthood Was in Flower," is called upon to act a role entirely different from anything in which she previously has appeared. Her characterization is the best thing she has ever done on the screen. She has discovered the art of simplicity. Harrison Ford is excellent as the lover. He would make any girl's heart go "pitty pat." Fine characterizations are given by Mahlon Hamilton, Harry Winston and Louis Wolheim.[68] The settings by the famous artist, Joseph Urban, recreate the charm of old New York and add materially to the effectiveness and the enjoyment of the production.[69] The costumes are perfect and the interiors and interior decorations will make antique dealers sick with envy. Sidney Olcott is responsible for the excellent direction of Luther Reed's adaptation of the play by Rida Johnson Young upon which the picture is based.[70]

Mr. Olcott has directed with great skill the prize fight and mob episodes. The story moves smoothly and without confusion, despite the numerous characters. This picture is worthy the attention of every person who loves good acting and pathos mingled with humor, and especially those who are curious about life in by-gone days in little old New York.[71]

Virginia Dale

Through the 1920s, Virginia Dale served as both the motion picture and drama editor of the *Chicago Journal*. Theater ads often used quotes from her reviews to promote individual films, and not only in Chicago.[72] By the late 1920s, she was known as a magazine writer of short stories and author of an entry summarizing the Chicago season for Burns Mantle's annual theater volume.[73] Whatever career she had after the *Journal* ceased publication in 1930 is unclear.

Most of Dale's columns reviewed individual feature films, and the one title she praised unequivocally, unlike Polly Wood, was *Robin Hood*.[74] She had quibbles with other films. She found *Smilin' Through*, with Norma Talmadge, disappointing because the "stageshine" she was hoping to see was missing. She liked *Flaming Youth*, but she warned Colleen Moore to avoid becoming "too cute."[75] Although expertly crafted, *Foolish Wives* flaunted two disgusting male leads.[76] She attributed *Merry Go Round* solely to Rupert Julian and lauded its alluring backgrounds, which compensated for the lack of a coherent story.[77] Moreover, she praised Lubitsch's import, *The Loves of Pharaoh*, for its lighting effects, attributed to an "American cinematic technique."[78] Her frustration with Cecil B. DeMille's upper-class melodramas was more than a quibble: in *Saturday Night* the director seemed once again dazzled by money and could not help concocting the opulent display of an infamous bathroom scene. While Dale believed that female fans and their changing tastes were responsible for the rising and falling fortunes of male stars, she worried that sudden stardom could overwhelm an unprepared young actor like Olive Thomas, leading to her untimely death.[79] But Dale also devoted columns to less expected subjects, from the career of June Mathis, a model scenario writer, to a description of the Rothacker company, Chicago's major manufacturer of industrial and advertising films as well as the release prints of First National features. Fulfilling her readers' demand for gossip, she created the foil of a "Chatty Caller" who, as if sitting beside her, kept serving up tasty tidbits in column after column.

"At the Theaters," *Chicago Journal*, January 21, 1922, 9.

"SATURDAY NIGHT" De Mille, that showman of matrimonial modes, has etched for us a complicated design of woe and weal. The greatest press agent for marriage in the world, this producer always manages to subjugate his intention to an ideal, and we who are not idealists suffer by the transfer. Tis as if De Mille himself stood ready with upraised finger to admonish "Naughty, naughty" when our expectations leap ahead.

"Saturday Night"—which they tell us is not a bathing picture—is class distinction swung upon a railroad trestle; the hoi polloi in a drawing room and silken train and both representatives of the four hundred million choked almost to death in a tenement fire.

BOTH PRICELESS AND CHEAP A master of situation and a believer in that whatever glitters is gold, De Mille purchases your interest with cheap symbolism and your admiration with a rare touch or two somehow sandwiched in.

The lady who so delicately broke a cookie made in the shape of a heart as a subtle indication that her own was hardly as severed is an unworthy resort for a man to drop to who can contrive a situation so marvelously dramatic as a man's rescue of another's wife because kind calls kind in a final summary.

The puppet-players who here work for—and by—De Mille are chiefly Leatrice Joy, Edith Roberts and Conrad Nagel.[80] The little Roberts is the daughter of a washwoman—not even a laundress—whom Nagel marries in a spirit of pique when his fiancée (Miss Joy) elopes with her chauffeur.

MONEY DAZZLES PRODUCER   Here then is your lovely situation. A shuffling of the commonest garden variety of dandelion and the most exotic of hot house blooms. The inevitable finish must be that each will gravitate naturally to its own again in the course of time.

The fault one must find with our producer's remedy is his assumption that the only sensitized humans are those with money. The affluent two who find themselves mismarried (if the words may stand) are the two whose loyalty to an illusion is strongest. It is probably as possible for one who chews gum to remain steadfast as it is for the lady who smokes an expensive Russian cigarette.

OLD JOKE REAPPEARS   Of course, it is a bit of jovial comedy to see others astonished at the suggestion of a bath in midweek—a De Mille bath would astonish Aphrodite herself!—and a low trick to play to have the bromide "but it isn't Saturday" thrust into the story. I should hardly care to leap into the fountain spray in the picture myself in a prosaic search for cleanliness; one's passion for the thing next to godliness is not rightly governed by the particular society set of which one is a member.

There perhaps lies the fault of the picture: C. B. De Mille has gone by class instead of standards.

But—there is a gloss to "Saturday Night," a sophistication, a carefully wrought gift-book edition sort of thing. Beautifully contrived, no one cares particularly what is written inside.

"Moving Pictures," *Chicago Journal*,
February 10, 1922, 13.

CHATTY CALLER BRINGS NEWS OF FILMDOM   The Chatty Person leaned confidentially over the desk.

"Had you heard," began the Chatty Person, "that Mrs. Fred Niblo is to be leading lady for Fairbanks in his next picture?"

"Mrs. Fred Niblo?" came the question, a bit doubtfully. "who—?"

"Why Enid Bennett, of course. Don't you keep up with the times? She's the director's wife; you knew that. But since she has become a real mamma she hasn't done a thing before the camera. Niblo is miles older than Enid. He was once the husband of George Cohen's sister, Josephine. Remember? And he has a son almost as old as Enid himself. They're one of the most adoring couples in California, I guess.

"Speaking of love and that sort of thing. They're saying now that Marjorie Daw and Johnny Harron are seriously 'keeping company.'[81] Johnny is poor, dead Bobby Harron's brother. He hasn't done much in the films yet, but everyone expects great things of him. Griffith never did get over Bob's tragic death.

"Did you hear about Max Linder?[82] He's that French comedian who has tried longer to make people laugh in America than anyone in the world. Every time he gets a good start in the right direction he has a nervous breakdown or something. He's back again now, bent once more upon making comedies.

"He owned a movie theater in Paris and sold it a few weeks ago. They say he wanted the money. Well, he gave a party the other night with the loveliest favors for every one. There was a two-carat diamond ring there, in a grab bag or something. Ruth Wrightman, a scenario writer for Goldwyn, was the lucky grabber.[83]

"And while we're on the subject of comedy, there's at least one person who doesn't think Larry Semon is a bit funny. She's his ex-landlady. She has brought suit against him for something like $500 and for more which she alleges is due her for damages to her property.

"Lupino Lane is hard at work over at the Fox plant.[84] He's the Englishman, you know."

"Yes," said I. "He played with Delysia here not so long ago."

"Um hum," the Chatty Person went on, "that's the one. He comes of one of the old theatrical families of Britain. He's doing slapstick.

"Henry Kitchell Webster's 'The Real Adventure' is almost done.[85] Florence Vidor has the leading part and her husband, King, is directing her.[86] Jackie Coogan is having a lovely time working these days. His picture is called 'Lost and Found,' and there are about twenty-five youngsters Jackie's age in the thing. Wouldn't you hate to be the director on that job?

"And, oh, my dear!" the Chatty Person waxed enthusiastic, "had you heard that Ed Wynn was listening wistfully to the call of the silent drama?[87] They tell me that this summer he will take a flyer with the camera."

"Well, I've got to go. I don't know another thing anyhow except that Gloria Swanson is getting some gorgeous clothes for a picture called 'The Gilded Cage' and that David Powell is going to play opposite her in it."[88]

"Moving Pictures," *Chicago Journal*, March 29, 1922, 9.

"SMILIN' THROUGH"   To the screen has come "Smilin' Through" with some of the stageshine strangely missing. A glorious creature, Miss Talmadge, whose spirited playing seldom fails to bring enthusiasm from her audiences. But something about the ghost visitations and fleshly alternates in the present piece make small allure.

Why?

Wyndham Standing gives himself to perhaps the best character part he has played before the camera. As the aged and crotchety individual who for many years nursed hate for the man who shot his bride, he is appealing and strong. That immobile face of his gains by the impersonation of age a shield for itself against its own immobility.

Harrison Ford, the lover in the modern part of the story, as well as the desperado in the velvet breeches of the past, shows surprisingly that he can be dramatic as occasion requires, as well as an excellent comedian.

Norma Talmadge herself is a lovely thing to gaze upon, and surely the most thoughtful person the cinema has raised for itself. The lack of grip in the photoplay is by no means because of her lack of power.

The moments were poorly handled and small suspense created. The fact that the means outstripped the result in the plot is something, of course, which we here may not quarrel with. But perhaps to a greater degree here than in its first incarnation did the play become unsympathetic by this race.

The photography of the picture is good, though one feels, with the opportunity at the photographer's hand, more might have been accomplished.

But all this does not mean "Smilin' Through" will not be what the producers call a successful picture. By all means, it is destined to be a box office attraction.

"Moving Pictures," *Chicago Journal*, May 5, 1922, 14.

CHICAGO MOVIE MAKERS CELEBRATE ANNIVERSARY   In the days when the motion picture was a mongrel, wailing for attention, a few optimists thought Chicago might be the permanent home of the new and smashing thing. They argued that as a location it couldn't be beat—that is the way they expressed it. They would tell you there was the sand for snow scenes and the lake for ocean and that down at Starved Rock one could achieve all the mountain scenery ever needed for picture making.

In the light of the present coast-to-coast hegiras for anything over ten feet of film, with ocean voyages and excursions to the Andes or Alaska as calmly assayed as a week-end to Ravenswood, one pulls down one's sleeve for the purpose of laughing in it.

Charles Chaplin, the Talmadges, the Beerys, Henry Walthall, Gloria Swanson, Agnes Ayres, Bryant Washburn, Kathlyn Williams and a host of others posed for a camera first within the boundaries of this settlement by the lake.[89]

Gradually Manhattan absorbed our film activities. Presently the optimists found themselves in New York or nowhere. In time Los Angeles sunshine gave the east a taste of its own medicine, but that is another story. What is

Figure 5. Assembling Department, *Moving Pictures* (Chicago: Rothacker Film Manufacturing, 1919).

important now is that of all the producers and manufacturers who started out with blithe and hopeful spirit here actually one survived. He is Watterson Rothacker.[90]

The Rothacker plant celebrates here this week its twelfth anniversary. It is Chicago's chief claim now to distinction as a film manufacturing point. Did you ever know that Mary Pickford's negatives, Fairbanks', Chaplin's, Jackie Coogan's, Ray's, Neilan's, the Talmadge sisters' and others all sent for developing in Chicago?

There is no larger industrial film producing plant in the world than Rothacker's. It not only develops millions of feet of pictures taken in the west and the east, but it is busily engaged in making commercial pictures. These deal with all subjects. The Rothacker plant employs an army of workers.[91]

"Spendthrift Youth Owns Filmdom," *Chicago Journal*, February 17, 1923, 11.

The movies have a lot to answer for. Nobody, leastwise no sensible person, can discount their influence nor tabulate their effect. And if they seem to catapult modernity back into a Babylonian vortex of misdeeds and sins not venial, that is not their fault. It is their misfortune, perhaps, made even more unfortunate, because a panacea is not possible.

Motion pictures put too many thousands of dollars into youthful hands. And there is no remedy, because in the nature of things it is really just that those who earn the thousands should be the ones to have it.

Such tragedies as the still mysterious Taylor murder, dozens of divorces, Wallace Reid's so recent death, Olive Thomas' death in Paris—all easily traceable to that coveted root, money.[92] Money is not necessarily evil, of course; it is the unwisdom of those who have it that makes the evil. But youth must always be unwise. And the filmeux is only youth.

It is not reasonable to expect a 17-year-old, who yesterday was living in a hall bedroom, to spend wisely $3,000 or $4,000 a week. For fifty-two weeks! To live with head unturned when every newspaper in the country, when almost everyone in the civilized world, pays large tribute and admiration to him.

Olive Thomas was a cash girl. Within a few months she leaped into the prominence of being the sister-in-law of the best-known woman in the world, with a salary of four figures weekly, with a husband who had money without end to spend on her, and did; press-agented everywhere as one of the earth's beauties, the little Thomas had no foundation upon which to stand. She had no education; she had learned nothing of the beauties which dollars in her pocket might buy. She was a child. And she ran riotously to her death.

Reid had never known home life. His schooling was of the scantiest. Fine things had passed him by. In his early twenties he was one of the best-known men in the world. His name over a theater was the assurance of the greatest box-office receipts in the business. And he was given many thousands of dollars every week.

His work necessitated a twelve months' residence in California, a golden state of a surety, but a state where entertainment must be made up solely of gatherings. There is no time between pictures, except occasionally, for traveling. There are no theaters, exceedingly few places of amusement. Parties are the only way for the Hollywooders to find amusement. And Wally had many thousands of dollars a week to spend.[93]

There is no tragedy, no scandal connected with those who have worked long, who have found success after years of climbing up the ladder. The Farnums, Hart, Chaplin (who worked for years in his English music halls), Frank Keenan and countless others earn well and spend well and probably save in the same way.[94]

But the youngsters own the movies. It is their oyster. And every once in a while one of them is going to break. Bound to! There are too many dollars pouring into youthful hands, inexperienced hands. And there is no remedy. For, of course, those who earn the money have the right to have it.

"News of the Motion Picture World," *Chicago Journal*, October 25, 1923, 11.

Woman's place in the field of scenario writing has become ever more important, and in the success of June Mathis has reached its richest reward.

June Mathis has for several years now stood at the head of the scenario and continuity writers in the picture industry. The fact that she will accompany Charles Brabin, director of "Ben Hur" to Europe where the entire film will be made, to advise with him throughout the producing of the picture, is but another evidence that she has climbed further than any other woman in the business of making motion pictures.[95]

She was born in Leadville, Colo., and was educated in Salt Lake City and in San Francisco. While still very young she began her acting career by dancing and giving imitations in vaudeville. Later she acted a regular part with Ezra Kendall in "The Vinegar Buyer," then became a player in Lieber & Co. productions with James K. Hackett and with Pauline Frederick.[96] For two years she played the lead in "Brewster's Millions," then in "Going Some" and with Julian Eltinge in "The Fascinating Widow."

While appearing in the latter play in Los Angeles, she became seriously interested in motion pictures which she had hitherto regarded rather scornfully.

She had written verses and sketches for her own amusement and decided that upon the close of the play in Toledo she would go to New York and prepare herself to become a scenario writer. Screen adaptations of famous novels and plays had irritated her because they so often missed the big dramatic climaxes. She decided that her stage experience had taught her what audiences wanted in their film entertainment. She was not a trained writer, but had read widely.

She set herself to the task of learning how to write. She studied for two years under the guidance of an experienced magazine editor, working with the same enthusiasm and unremitting toil that she devotes to her work now that she is at the height of her career. This training included ten weeks of acting with a motion picture company, and always the study of the daily life of the people about her.

She then made her first adaptation—that of a play by a friend of hers. Edwin Carewe, Metro director, disliked the morbidness of the theme but liked the young scenarist's work.[97] He sent for her and she went to work for Metro. Within a year she was placed in charge of the scenario department and remained there for seven years. Among the originals which she wrote and sold to Metro during this period are "To Hell With the Kaiser," "Draft 258," "The Millionaire's Double" and "The Successful Adventure." She wrote a number of originals for Bushman-Bayne, as she wanted to get away from the department and make her own productions.

It was later that she was assigned to adapt Blasco Ibáñez's novel, "The Four Horsemen of the Apocalypse" to the screen. The result was a success of the first rank. She worked in association with Rex Ingram on the picture and was instrumental in getting Valentino, whom she had not then met, to play the leading role. She next adapted Blasco Ibáñez's "Blood and Sand" for Valentino's first starring vehicle with Famous Players–Lasky.

Goldwyn Pictures corporation then offered her the post of editorial director at one of the biggest salaries ever paid to a woman worker.

She was given the assignment of preparing the continuity for "Ben Hur," but before completing that made the screen adaptation of Crawford's "In the Palace of the King." Her position with Goldwyn gives her supervisory responsibility for the expenditure of millions of dollars a year.

Genevieve Harris

Harris remained an influential movie page editor and reviewer for the *Chicago Post* throughout the 1920s and was often quoted in theater ads even beyond the city.[98] In late 1923 a story syndicated by NEA Services described her as a short story writer and "author of a course on scenario writing," as well as a movie reviewer.[99] It also claimed that she was "the only American woman who wrote her criticisms of American films in French for publication in the Parisian movie magazine, 'Le Courier.'"[100] At the time she was sailing for Paris to report on "French methods of film production and presentation."[101] Her obituary described her not only as the "motion picture and drama critic for the old Chicago Evening Post" but also later as "a woman's page editor of the *Eau Claire* [Wisconsin] *Leader*" and a publicist "for the National Livestock and Meat Board."[102]

Harris tended to write relatively lengthy, serious columns. She favored a variety of stars, from the "sparkling, ingenuous Constance Talmadge" in *Polly of the Follies* (1922) and Norma Talmadge, who never "appeared to better advantage" than in *Ashes of Vengeance* (1923), to Valentino, who proved he could really act in *Blood and Sand* (1922), and even Tom Mix, who was upstaged by his horse in *Just Tony* (1922).[103] And she capped that in an interview (too long to include here) with Pola Negri, who was "graceful, slim, cordial [and] prettier than she appears in her pictures" and who spoke Polish, Russian, German, French, Italian, and English.[104] In her reviews Harris often called attention to the director: the "queer, perverted mind" of Stroheim and his "horrible, contemptible" villain in *Foolish Wives* (1922); the explorer Robert J. Flaherty, whose excellent photography marked *Nanook of the North* (1922); and Rupert Julian, who alone was credited with *Merry Go Round* (1923), partly because "a unified impression in spite of its dual direction [. . .] seems to be presented from one point of view."[105] In raising the question of "what makes a great picture," Harris's answer was the perfect melding of story and star, that is, "one in which the story provides a consistent, vivid characterization which the right player not only plays but rather brings to life" so that the picture gets "under your skin."[106] And she returned to the question, arguing that "a second viewing is really the test of a great picture," for it "displays new beauties overlooked at first viewing."[107]

Moreover, Harris continued to take up a wide range of sometimes unexpected subjects. She devoted a whole column to the career of Jeanie MacPherson, DeMille's chief scenario writer, and to Hetty Gray Baker, Fox's managing editor responsible for the final print of a film. She had public librarians counter the argument that moviegoing was replacing book reading: "Whenever a motion picture version of a book is shown, the demand at the library for that story noticeably increased."[108] Harris did her own reporting on the success of the Chicago and Alton Railroad in fitting out a train car for passengers to view a full film program. Likewise, in May 1923 she toured the "Palace of Progress, a motion picture exposition" in Chicago, describing the exhibits that sketched the "entire history of motion pictures." At this early date, certain films already were being canonized, from *The Great Train Robbery, Quo Vadis*, and Chaplin's first Keystone comedy to not one but four Griffith titles. And she supported the many trade press stories that "American motion pictures are Americanizing the world" with observations from a globe-trotting Los Angeles clubwoman.[109]

Given all the hoopla over imported German films, as well as Lubitsch's and Negri's welcome into the American film industry, Harris's fascination with French films was unique. In late 1922 she devoted an entire column to the current state of French film art. It included a summary of the second annual Salon du cinéma (organized by Friends of the Seventh Art), during which fragments of twelve of the year's best films were screened, half of them American.[110] Most interesting, however, is a lengthy quote from a *Mercure de France* article by critic Léon Moussinac, in which he argued that the motion picture has to free itself from the "pernicious influence [of] the old rules of the theater" because it "is an independent art which must discover its own laws."[111] A year later, reporting from Paris, she quickly dispelled the myth that American films dominated the city's screens and described how the French were different. One way was the relative lack of publicity for French movie stars vis-à-vis American stars. Another was the French "taste for historical subjects," especially in lengthy serials, released weekly in "eight chapters of about four reels each," with their emphasis on "picturesque backgrounds [. . .] human interest and emotional appeal." Her current example was *L'enfant roi*, whose story dealt "with events at the beginning of the French revolution" and was "published in installments" in the Paris daily *Le Matin*.[112] At the time, these *films à épisodes* ensured that moviegoers could always find a high number of French films playing in their motion picture theaters.[113]

"Screen Writing Distinct Craft," *Chicago Post*, February 11, 1922, 2.10.

If there is one person competent to give an answer to that perennial question, "How can I learn to write for the screen?" Jeanie MacPherson is certainly "it."[114] And the desire to write stories for photoplay is second only to the desire to be a screen player. (Sometimes I doubt it is secondary.)

Jeanie MacPherson is an expert photo dramatist. She is a veteran in the profession, one of those youthful veterans of the film world. She writes for Cecil DeMille, who is not only a screen director but a dramatist in his own right, and an exacting "boss." To create or arrange a story which will satisfy the requirements of Cecil DeMille requires both ability and long training.

Back of the line, "Story by Jeanie MacPherson," which has been seen on the majority of Cecil DeMille's pictures from "Joan the Woman" to "Saturday Night," lies a story of unusually wide dramatic experience.

Miss MacPherson, an American girl of Scotch and French parentage and French education, began her professional career as an actress. When she entered the picture field, back in the days of two and three reel features, she wrote and directed her own stories, as well as playing the star part. The experience she gained at that time formed, she says, the foundation of her present success.

For there came a time when she had to choose between writing and acting. She liked acting better, but writing promised a longer and more profitable future, especially when the opportunity came to work under the supervision of Cecil DeMille, who had just turned his attention from the stage to the screen. For three hard years, her work was a sort of apprenticeship under this director. Then her ability and thoro knowledge began to bring her substantial success.

The advice of those prominent screen writers to all "would-bes" is this: "Get into a studio, if possible. Work in all departments. Then you will have a first-hand knowledge of the requirements and limitations of the screen."

Photoplay writing is so different from other forms of writing that Miss MacPherson believes those who aspire to do it should study it directly and not spend their time writing short stories or plays. The short-story writer uses too much description and not enough action. The playwright relies too much upon dialog. The screen story must be set forth in situations, action.

The trend of photoplay is toward the romantic, Miss MacPherson believes, and there is a revived interest in historical material. The costume play, so long feared by producer and exhibitor, has apparently found favor with the public.

Another tendency is toward comedy. "The public wants to laugh. Even a serious story must be lightened by humor if it is to succeed today," she says.

But above all, and at all times, there is need for "heart interest," the little touches which arouse sympathy, the big scene which stirs the emotions. A picture which does not arouse a feeling of sympathy, of liking for its characters, can never succeed, no matter how clever its plot, or brilliant its direction.

"Photoplays," *Chicago Post*, February 13, 1922, 16.

"POLLY OF THE FOLLIES"[115]   This is as gay a bit of film fun as we have seen recently. John Emerson and Anita Loos, who know how to be very amusing in the titles they write and the situations they think up, have supplied Constance Talmadge with the story.[116] Connie herself is a clever entertainer, when given half a chance. Here she has plenty of opportunity.

As Polly, a village girl, as the heroine and the "vamp" of her own home talent show, as Cleopatra in a vision scene, and finally as a member of the Follies chorus, Constance has a varied role and is very much in evidence thruout the picture. And in none of the phases of her role is she the oversophisticated, "flip" young person she has played in so many other productions and of whom many of us have grown weary. She is the sparkling, ingenuous Constance of her earlier successes in this.

The most novel and amusing part of this picture is the show which Polly and her chums give in her father's store to a wide-eyed audience of children. This show is a real "silent drama," and the actors speak no words. The explanations, or "subtitles," are supplied by advertising placards which the store contains. Well-known slogans such as "Eventually, why not now?" "They satisfy" and the like are pressed into service to carry on the plot. These, appropriately chosen, and the comments of the youthful audience are as funny as anything in the picture.

"Polly of the Follies" is light and frivolous, which is all that it pretends to be. You'll find many things to laugh at during its course. It is worth seeing if only because of that new version of the Cleopatra legend it contains. Constance as Cleo and John Daly Murphy as Caesar provide something novel in historical romance, I assure you![117]

"Photoplays," *Chicago Post*, February 14, 1922, 14.

"FOOLISH WIVES" Universal has made extravagant claims for this "million-dollar picture." But many of the published reports of those who saw the film at its first showing in New York gave quite a different impression. So many contradictory statements resulted in my approaching the subject in quite a neutral way frame of mind, prepared either to find it a masterpiece or a "chamber of horrors."

And this is what I found. A curious photoplay, which might be called a study in evil. Where other stories revolve about a hero, this one is centered upon a villain. And at all times it is his viciousness which is emphasized. Or, rather, it is the worst of his evil characteristics, for he has no good ones. In just the way that the usual story plays on the sympathies and the admiration of the audience, this one works upon our sense of the horrible, the contemptible. A queer, perverted mind this Von Stroheim seems to have!

It is evident that the story has been cut since its first showing in the east and that the scenes which aroused most criticism have been eliminated. This was wise, for enough has been left to give you plenty of thrill! It is a "creepy" sort of thrill, this sense of evil, of danger, of gruesome happenings which form the atmosphere of the story.

For his story, Von Stroheim built upon the coast of California a replica of Monte Carlo which those who know declare amazingly accurate. It certainly looks like all the pictures of this famous spot which we ever saw and the illusion of a European background is kept thruout the picture. The interior scenes, not only of the gambling salons and the villas, but of the mountain inn, for instance, are most carefully and interestingly staged.

The picture is really a series of episodes rather than a dramatically constructed play. The episodes concern the adventures of a Russian count and his two women confederates. This count is the most contemptible character imaginable. He is a moral degenerate, in fact, who has not even the virtue of bravery.

An American who comes on a diplomatic mission to Monaco is accompanied by his pretty wife. The count marks the wife as his prey. He does not make much progress in his exploit because fate steps in at every turn to save the young woman. It is another adventure which results in his final disaster.

The foreign atmosphere of the production and the skillful direction which makes the various episodes stand out with unusual vividness are the picture's best qualities. Its weakness lies in the fact that there is very slight sympathetic interest. The decent characters are rather vague, compared with the sharply drawn figure of the evildoers, the count and his aids. Rudolph Christian and Miss Dupont as the American wife play their parts creditably, but are overshadowed by the sinister figure of the count, as Von Stroheim depicts him, and the princess, as Maude George plays her.[118]

Dale Fuller as the maid who has been one of the count's victims, Cesare Gravina as the deformed counterfeiter and Malvina Polo (daughter of Eddie Polo) as his afflicted ward also have important roles.[119]

One might point out much that is unusual and very effective in the direction of this picture, if space allowed. The production is full of clever touches and dramatic episodes. Its direction has imagination and ability. There's no doubt of that. In the way it is handled, "Foolish Wives" is an artistic production. Whether or not its subject material will please is another question, one which depends upon individual taste.

"Woman Editor of Film Plays," *Chicago Post*, March 18, 1922, 2.8.

There are many types of editors doing various kinds of editing, but probably none among them is more interesting or has a more unusual job than a certain dignified, gray-haired New England lady whose big task is to edit all the photoplays put out by one of the biggest film production companies.

She is Miss Hetty Gray Baker, who originated the position she still holds, that of film editor for the William Fox company.[120] And in editing a photoplay, she works just as any other editor, changing and rearranging material, now discarding, now elaborating, in order to gain a harmonious, effective final result.

But since the material is film rather than "copy" or "proof," the technique of Miss Baker's work is somewhat different from that of an ordinary editor. The picture play is sent to her after the director has completed his work. The picture has been cut, the scenes assembled and the subtitles inserted. When Miss Baker sees it for the first time, in a projection room, she views it as a disinterested spectator might. She makes a point of having no advance knowledge regarding its production.

"If I had read the synopsis, listened to the director's comments or been told about it by the players, my mind might be influenced by that information. I do not even watch any of the scenes when they are taken in the studio. I want to know absolutely no more about that picture than the scenes on the screen can tell me. Then if there are gaps in the plot, inconsistencies, places which are not quite clear, I can see them more clearly than the director or scenario writer, who may be too close to the story to see its weak points."

When the picture has been viewed, Miss Baker decides upon the changes necessary. Scenes are transposed, some cut entirely, and subtitles are perhaps reworded. Miss Baker is given a free hand to make any changes she thinks best. Sometimes she even orders the retaking of scenes or the making of new ones to make the story clear.

Miss Baker, a college trained woman, came into her unusual profession after a number of years spent in library work. As a librarian, she became interested in literary work and the field of scenario writing, altho truly in its "infancy" then, appealed to her. She was one of the earliest and most successful of scenario writers, supplying old Biograph, Essanay, Selig and other pioneer picture companies with stories.[121] From a free-lance writer she became a member of a scenario staff, eventually entering the scenario department of the Fox company.

From this position she graduated into her extremely important and responsible post, where her unique "editing" puts her O.K. on the many productions of the Fox Film corporation.

"Photoplays," *Chicago Post*, August 22, 1922, 12.

"BLOOD AND SAND"   Here it is at last, the long heralded production of "Blood and Sand," the picture which, according to prophesy, was to prove to the world that Rudolph Valentino's fine acting in "Four Horsemen" was not a flash of genius which had died away; that he could repeat his performance if given a worthy role.

Does the picture do that? I think you will say that it does. I think you will agree that it gives Valentino's ardent admirers a chance to say to those whose admiration was not ardent, "I told you so. I told you the boy could act, that he was not just a matinee idol."

"Blood and Sand" is a colorful story, romantic, tragic and very thrilling. And its thrills are new. We have gasped over horse races, automobile wrecks, airplane exploits, until these subjects have lost much of their power to excite us, but we haven't enjoyed in films (nor in real life probably) the sensations of the bull fight. They certainly are exciting, especially since it is evident that the bulls weren't just playing a part. They meant business. They, at least, didn't know a camera was grinding. And in ferocity, these horned beasts make lions look kittenlike. I can imagine myself patting a lion's head (if he were real tame and in pleasant humor) but I'd hate to meet one of these wicked looking animals.

But the outstanding feature of "Blood and Sand" is the star's interpretation of the hero's role. As Juan Gallardo, Valentino successfully dispels all doubts one may have about his ability. He is an artist, nothing less. It is evident that his intention is to play Gallardo as Blasco Ibáñez created him, and Gallardo was a simple youth, awkward, conceited, and both brave and timid. He was never the gallant, never the grand signor. And Valentino is a fine enough artist to play him that way, and not as the dashing cavalier.

However, the star brings to the role a suggestion of subtlety and depth of feeling which adds to the fascination of the character without detracting from its realism. Perhaps it is this restraint, this sense of hidden feeling which accounts for much of Valentino's charm.

Nita Naldi as Doña Sol, the temptress, will probably have a vogue similar to Valentino's, after this picture. The character is an unusual one and Miss Naldi is an exotic type. She looks very foreign and she is beautiful with a sense of mystery and of evil in her beauty which makes her ideal for this part. Her acting lacks spontaneity and naturalness, but even this artificiality is in keeping with Doña Sol's practiced coquetry.

The rest of the cast is composed of admirable characters. Walter Long does some great acting as Plumitas, the bandit.[122] Lila Lee is charming as the wife. Rosa Rosanova as Gallardo's mother, George Field as his friend and a number of other players look and act convincingly Spanish.[123]

The book has been closely followed in the screen translation, which isn't surprising when we learn that June Mathis made the adaptation. Miss Mathis has a respect for authors all too unusual among scenario writers. And of course the book was filled with picturesque incidents which couldn't have made better film scenes if they had been created for the purpose. The breakfast scene at Gallardo's ranch, with Doña Sol and Plumitas as guests is one example.

In one way the story has been Americanized a bit and that is giving Gallardo a conscience. In the picture, the hero's fight is against his lawless love for Doña Sol. In the book, the ethics of this troubled Ibanez's hero very little. The break came only when Dona Sol tired of him. Gallardo's fight was with fear and it was this growing timidity which cost him his popularity, undermined his confidence and finally caused his downfall.

Judging by the first day's attendance at the Roosevelt, everyone intends to see this picture. Well, they will be treated to a splendid drama, one which they will not soon forget.

"Photoplays," *Chicago Post*, September 11, 1922, 14.

"NANOOK OF THE NORTH"   "Nanook of the North" is a real life story. It is a camera record of the activities of an Eskimo family. The father, Nanook, his wife, Nula, their children, one an infant, their team of dogs, the puppies who are too young to be put into harness, these are the characters in the story. So naturally do they go about their business, so industriously do they set to work, that it is difficult to realize that the camera was somewhere in the neighborhood, photographing them. They show no signs of self-consciousness and never reveal any desire to look at the camera. In this they are quite unlike the dwellers in the tropics who have been photographed by explorers.

The picture is both an interesting entertainment and a remarkable achievement. It is fascinating to see. The building of the snow huts is an intriguing process. Then there is the thrilling combat between Nanook and the seal he has speared. The seal is beneath the ice. Only Nanook's part of the fight is shown, a desperate struggle to keep the wounded creature from pulling the line thru the hole in the ice and making its escape. The life of the family depends upon the capture of the seal, which provides their food.

Another exciting episode in the film is the killing of a walrus, an exploit in which Nanook is aided by other hunters.

The man who took these pictures, Robert J. Flaherty, an explorer, has shown much cleverness, not only in filming difficult scenes, but in selecting the most interesting Eskimo activities to photograph.[124] He has picked out just the things one might want to ask about the existence up near the Arctic Circle.

The picture is also very beautiful. Snow and ice fields form the background of most of the scenes. The photography is excellent. The storm scenes will make the producers of melodrama green with envy. The snow, blowing like smoke across the white landscape, the little group of wanderers, struggling against the storm, the dogs trying to drag the sled across the drifts, these scenes are as vivid as any thrilling climax the most skillful director could stage.

I suppose "Nanook" may be listed under the head of educational pictures, for it contains accurate information about a little-known sphere of human life. But "Nanook" is much more entertaining than the usual production of this class. You may take the children along, knowing that the picture will add to their education, but you'll find that both you and they are entertained first, instructed incidentally.

"A French View of Film Art," *Chicago Post*, December 16, 1922, 2.9.

Having given you last week a glimpse into the mind of an English critic who concedes that there may be art in motion pictures, we might as well cross the channel and find out how the French feel about the cinema.

The admirers of motion pictures in France have formed a society the title of which makes clear their attitude for they call themselves "Friends of the Seventh Art." In the latter part of November this association held its second annual "Salon du Cinéma," at which the year's progress in the film world was as seriously considered from the artistic standpoint as are the innovations of the art of painting or music.

An interesting feature of this "Salon," as reported in "Le Courier Cinématographique" of Paris, was the showing of classified fragments of the best films of the year, grouped according to subject and style.

Of the twelve pictures selected for special consideration, six were American. (The productions were chosen from those shown in France during the year, of course.) Of these six, three were Griffith productions, "Way Down East," "Dream Street" and "The Two Orphans." The others were "The Storm," the Universal production starring House Peters (called "Torment" in France), Chaplin's "The Kid" and Fairbanks' "The Mask of Zorro."

Among the significant statements regarding the "seventh art" made in connection with this showing was an interesting appreciation of the cinema by Léon Moussinac, critic of the "Mercure de France," who stated that as preceding civilizations expressed their common aspirations, fixed their ideal in an art—the Greeks in tragedy, the medieval age in its cathedrals, so today the motion picture expresses the spirit of the age.

"The cinema has been hampered by the old rules of the theater," he says, "and it has not completely freed itself from this pernicious influence. But the photoplay should not be classed with the theater any more than with literature, sculpture, architecture or music. In truth, it proceeds from all the arts. It seems to be their expression enlarged, and it is that which gives us faith in its great future. It has drawn to itself all the essential truth of modern life to form a new beauty. It is an independent art which must discover its own laws. Its value will show itself little by little thru the slow efforts of its fine workers, who are still few.

"One must admit that the discovery of its riches has led to grave mistakes. Such blunders were inevitable. In music the symphony was not achieved at once. That required the fervent and sincere genius of several centuries. Why should the photoplay, whose possibilities are even greater, escape the period of struggle? And it must be said that those who could have helped it most have despised and ridiculed it.

"At the present stage of development of the photoplay, even the best films are only indications of what may be achieved. And even a poor film may, in a brilliant gesture, an expression of feeling, a flashing suggestion, reveal to us truths no less essential."

"Films Add to Joy of Travel," *Chicago Post*, February 17, 1923, 2.5.

Some day, when Baby Peggy is an old lady and looks back over what will have been, doubtless, a very eventful career, one of the things she will be most proud of will be that her picture had the honor of being shown in the first real motion picture show on a railroad train.[125] But Baby Peggy's grandchildren, who listen to the story, will say, scornfully: "Gracious, who ever heard of a train without its motion picture coach! Do you mean to say that 'way back in those days people had to travel all day long without a movie to amuse them on the way?" And they will shudder over the hardships of those voyagers in the same way that we pity our ancestors who came across the plains in a covered wagon.

For "the world do move," and the novelties of today become part of the ordinary life of tomorrow. And we who accept sleeping coaches and dining cars as necessary equipment in civilised traveling are soon to accept as equally commonplace a "movietorium" on a railroad train.

To the Chicago and Alton railroad belongs the credit of first successfully presenting motion picture entertainment to its passengers.[126] Working with the Chicago representative of the Universal Film corporation, Herman Stern, I. Lesserman and W. L. Hill, the passenger agent of the Chicago and Alton, C. R. Davidson and his assistants, a steel day coach on an express between Chicago and St. Louis, with a silver screen and two Acme portable projection machines, arranged a program consisting of a news weekly, a Baby Peggy comedy and the new Priscilla Dean feature, "The Flame of Life."[127]

The result was highly satisfactory. One of the surprising features was the clarity and steadiness of the picture on the screen. The finest theater could not boast better projection. The vibration and swaying of the coach had no apparent effect on the picture on the screen. There was not the eye-strain in watching the film that one feels in reading on the train.

A small screen was used, so that one could view the picture with comfort even from a seat very close to the screen. It was hung high enough so that it did not interfere with passengers walking thru the coach and they, in turn, did not interfere with the view of the picture.

Having shown that the plan of showing motion pictures on a train was entirely possible from a technical standpoint, the next point which the experiment settled was that the innovation was appreciated by the public. Almost every person on the train, in day coaches or parlor cars, accepted with delight the invitation to see the program. And their verdict was that the entertainment was a very welcome relief from the tedium of an all-day trip.

Instead, it gave one something of a thrill to watch views of Switzerland, scenes from troubled Constantinople, glimpses of that storm center, the Ruhr valley, as one sped swiftly over the placid Illinois prairies. It gave one a sense of the strange unity of the past and present to view an English mining story of 1870, as one traveled thru the coal mining districts.

"Film History to Be Shown," *Chicago Post*, May 10, 1923, 6.

The Palace of Progress, a motion picture exposition setting forth the short but interesting past of the films and the astonishing present which holds as much promise for the future, opens its doors tonight at the Coliseum. This exposition is being held at the same time as the convention of the Motion Picture Theater Owners of America, which has its first session here Monday morning and continues thru next week.[128]

While the theater owners are considering important problems, the amusement tax, censorship, royalties on music, contracts with producers, matters pertaining to the management of theaters, the public will be brought more closely into touch with the technical features of film production at the Palace of Progress.

Film stars have promised to be on hand, among them Elaine Hammerstein, May McAvoy, Charles Ray and Hope Hampton.[129] Special programs have been arranged for each day, and many of the leading jazz bands of the city will provide the music.

A whole series of exhibits will describe the entire progress of the motion picture from the invention of the kinetoscope by Thomas Edison in 1889 to the appearance of the teleview.[130] Visitors will also see, and hear, the marvelous talking motion pictures and the safety-first picture produced under the auspices of Mayor Dever's safety-first committee and the Motion Picture Theater Owners of America by the Atlas Educational Film company.

Every step in the making of a picture will be shown, including the making of submarine, X-ray and colored films.

The entire history of motion pictures during thirty years will be shown by means of a feature film.

The high points in the history, as brought out by the film, are:

> 1895—Latham Armat and Lumière put moving pictures on the screen.[131]
> 1897—"Inauguration of William McKinley." (International News.)[132]
> 1903—"The Great Train Robbery." (Edison.)
> 1905—"License No. 13," or "The Hoodoo Auto." (Vitagraph.)
> 1909—"The Lonely Villa" (Griffith.)
> 1910—"Quo Vadis" (Italian Cines) (Kleine F.B.O.)[133]
> 1911—"The Master and the Man" (Imp.) (Universal.)
> 1912—"Home Sweet Home" ("The Marriage of Roses and Lilies") Reliance Mutual (D. W. Griffith.)[134]
> 1913—Charlie Chaplin's first picture (Keystone) (Oscar Price, H. E. Aitken.)[135]
> 1915—"The Birth of a Nation" (D. W. Griffith.)
> 1918—"Broken Blossoms" (D. W. Griffith.)
> 1923—Teleview gives two eyes to one-eyed motion pictures camera.

"Photoplays," *Chicago Post*, August 28, 1923, 12.

"ASHES OF VENGEANCE"[136]   "Ashes of Vengeance" is the most elaborate production Norma Talmadge has appeared in. It is a romantic drama of the sixteenth century in France and is staged with all the magnificence necessary to reproduce the life in aristocratic circles of that time. Huge settings, beautifully staged and well photographed filled with players in the picturesque costumes of the period, form a gorgeous background for a love story which is unusual in itself.

The spectacular features of the production are not allowed to overshadow the emotional value of the story or the acting of the leading players, and that is a big point in the picture's favor. Norma Talmadge has never, in my opinion, appeared to better advantage than she does in this offering. As Yolande de Breux, eldest daughter of a noble family, she plays the "great lady" with a blend of simplicity and poise which is charming. She carries the role as easily and gracefully as she wears the elaborate and very becoming costumes of the time. She is beautiful and very appealing. Her work in this justifies her ambition to play "Juliet" and gives a promise of a very good performance of that spirited Italian beauty.

The basis of the story is the struggle between the Huguenots and the Catholic faction in France under Charles IX. During the persecution of the former group, Rupert de Vrieac saves the life of his fiancée by pledging himself to be a servant to the Count de Breux of the Catholic party and his hereditary enemy. De Vrieac is assigned to the bodyguard of the count's sister, the beautiful Yolande (Miss Talmadge).

Yolande, faithful to her family feuds, takes delight in humiliating de Vrieac, altho secretly she is moved by his romantic story. When she goes to visit her cousin, Denise, she encounters danger and adventure, due to the infatuation of the wicked Duc de Tours, betrothed to Denise, but preferring Yolande.

The gallant de Vrieac is there to save her. The fiancée for whom he had sacrificed himself has married another and during the exciting episodes which follow he and Yolande discover and confess their love for each other.

Thru a misunderstanding, Yolande believes that the other woman is still first in de Vrieac's affections and her pride forces her to change her attitude. De Vrieac doesn't know the reason and therefore cannot explain. This obstacle to their happiness is removed when Yolande learns that the lock of hair her lover is cherishing, which she thinks is that of his former fiancée, is only the "favor" given him by her own romantic little sister.

Conway Tearle is excellent as Rupert de Vrieac, stately in his humility, courteous and gallant under all conditions. His popularity, great already, will be increased by this picture. The role might have been created especially for him, or he for it.

Wallace Beery plays the villainous Duc de Tours. His acting is good, as it always is, but the part seems overdrawn in the story.

The balance of the cast is well chosen and contains the names of many film favorites.

"French Films Show Artistry," *Chicago Post*, December 29, 1923, 2.8.

Paris. France. Dec. 15—Without a lavish expenditure of money which marks motion picture production in America, but with a courage and determination which is admirable, the French photoplay producers have set about recovering the ground lost during the years of the war in the ever-changing, ever-advancing art and business of photoplay-making.

While it is true that there is nothing in France—or in any other country, for that matter—to compare with the astonishing magnitude of the film industry in the United States, it is not true, as often reported, that the preponderance of photoplays in Paris are of American origin or that French productions are negligible. At the present time there are at least as many French productions in the cinema theaters here as there are American pictures.

Of course, it is not surprising, in view of the strong organization and the wealth of the film industry in the United States, that American pictures should be so prominent all over the world. But photoplays are, or should be, something more than a commercial commodity, and therefore it will be better for the whole world when each industry contributes its own particular genius to the art of the screen. And there is an international exchange of ideas in this new field of expression. While patriotic consideration might influence us to favor American film monopoly, a broader spirit makes us interested in the contribution of other nations.

Judging by the French productions current in the capital at the present time, the artistic feeling for which this nation is noted has not failed to express itself in its picture plays. Good photography and a feeling for picturesque backgrounds, which go far in offsetting the American advantage of expensive settings, characterize French photoplays. Add to this good acting, not too theatrical, and a regard for drama and the logic of a story, and you have the basis of very worth-while picture plays.

A taste for historical subjects is another characteristic of French producers. Unlike American producers, who see in such themes chiefly an opportunity for spectacular display, the French emphasize the human interest and emotional appeal in these dramas. A production which illustrates this and which is the most distinctively French of the pictures I have seen here is a serial, "L'Enfant Roi" (The Child King), a production quite unlike any American offering.[137] In the first place, it has little in common with the sort of serial picture we have in America. It is rather to be compared with a continued story in a magazine. Its chapters are longer than the installments in our serials, but fewer in number. There are eight chapters of about four reels each.

The subject, which deals with events at the beginning of the French revolution, and has as its leading figures Marie Antoinette, a Swedish courtier devoted to her, and the unfortunate little prince, Louis XVI, is treated as sincerely and as artistically as it should be in one of our best feature plays. There is nothing of the trashy, sensational serial story as we know it about the production.

"The Child King" is one of a number of these chapter plays, tho not all are of so dignified a type or so artistically produced. The newspapers of Paris collaborate with the producers of the pictures and the story of each serial is published in installments in some newspaper. "Le Matin" is sponsoring "L'Enfant Roi."

The French newspapers are generous in giving space to motion picture criticisms and news of the film world. Each paper has its photoplay department and, considering the much smaller size of the Parisian newspapers compared to ours, the relative amount of space is greater. The cinema has its share of attention along with music, the theater, literature and art.

Nevertheless, the French players do not receive anything like the publicity devoted to our stars of the screen. Sometimes the names of the players are not even given on the screen, an omission probably due to the custom in French theaters of charging for the printed program. In no case are the players featured in advertising and theater announcements, as with us.

As a result of this lack of publicity for the French stars, American players are better known here than native players. A Parisian "fan" will discuss his likes and dislikes among American film personages, but when you ask about his preference among the French players, he will speak with admiration of certain productions, but be unable to name any of the players who took part.

The motion picture producers are realizing the value of this publicity, however, as proved in the case of the American players, and there is a movement on foot to give more prominence to the French actors and actresses. The photoplay departments in the newspapers and the numerous magazines devoted to film affairs offer an opportunity for making better known the players on the screen, of which the French producers might wisely take advantage.

Polly Wood

Polly Wood probably was a young staff writer or reporter when she began writing film reviews for the *Chicago Herald and Examiner* in July 1923.[138] She certainly was subordinate to Aston Stevens, the paper's chief drama critic, who reserved certain films for his own columns, especially those with female stars: Pola Negri in *The Cheat* and *The Spanish Dancer*, Constance Talmadge in *Dulcy*, Norma Talmadge in *Ashes of Vengeance*, Marion Davies in *Little Old New York*, and Colleen Moore in *Flaming Youth*.[139] Within less than a year, however, an Orpheum theater ad described Wood as the "seasoned critic of the Herald-Examiner."[140] The Chicago paper carried her review columns at least into early 1926, but whatever career she had later is unclear.[141]

Like several of her predecessors, Wood could be chatty and colloquial. See her review of *Hollywood*—"OH, BOY, if that disease called 'movietis' doesn't assume its most virulent form after you have seen 'Hollywood' you'll never enter another picture house as long as you live!"—or of the "mystery melodrama" *Red Lights*—"The plot gets me so completely bewildered that I'm mad when everything's over, because I can't remember who's who, and why."[142] She agreed with the city's theater owners that *Enemies of Women* was the year's best picture, better than previous adaptations of Vicente Blasco Ibáñez's novels, *The Four Horsemen of the Apocalypse* and *Blood and Sand*. Despite the replacement of directors in *Merry Go Round*, Wood marveled that the film turned out to be "an ideal combination—the fire of Von Stroheim controlled by Mr. Julian's steady hand."[143] While she could not forgive Fairbanks for losing his sense of comedy after *The Mark of Zorro*, in which his black shirt reminded her of "our Italian friend, Mussolini," she found Lillian Gish perfectly cast in *The White Sister*, giving "the most gorgeous performance of her career."[144] Wood's most novel column, however, revealed that the double that cameraman Charles Rosher used to light Pickford in rehearsals for *Rosita* was not an understudy actor but rather "an ideal woman," Wood slyly purred, that is, a life-size, "mild as milk" dummy named Maria.

"'Hollywood' Will Make Fans for Film Land," *Chicago Herald and Examiner*, July 23, 1923, 9.

"HOLLYWOOD"   OH, BOY, if that disease called "movietis" doesn't assume its most virulent form after you have seen "Hollywood" you'll never enter another picture house as long as you live! Never have I seen as many stars in one picture.

"What?" say you, consulting the above cast. "Who are those people? Never heard of 'em before." Well, nor have I, but they're only the actors. Wait until you see Pola Negri, Charles Spencer Chaplin, Doug and Mary, Tom Meighan, Nita Naldi, Cecil de Mille and the rest of Hollywood. Why, if I'd print all their names there would be no room to tell you about the picture.

The plan of "Hollywood" is clever. Here's one time when the director and his staff get abundant praise instead of blame. They have done nobly by our Nell, our Nell being, I guess, the film industry and us. There is nothing deep or soul-searching about the picture. It is a delicious confection, rather gratefully consumed and as easily forgotten.

I've almost forgotten the story already. It's about a country lass who wants to go into the films. She and her grandfather set out for Hollywood, but it is grandpop who gets the job and the pretty young thing goes without. In due time Grandma and Maw and lovesick Lem arrive in Hollywood to participate.

Into this frame James Cruze has set the actual activities of Hollywood, viz. the routine of the Studio, the stars in their native haunts—everything the fan wants to see for himself. The railroads are going to be awfully mad at Paramount's "Hollywood," because to see the picture saves you the fare to California.

"Hollywood" is the best example of showmanship I have yet to witness in the motion picture. It is intelligent entertainment. Don't miss it.

"'Zorro' Differs from Doug's Later Films," *Chicago Herald and Examiner*, August 10, 1923, 7.

Three years ago or more Douglas Fairbanks made "The Mark of Zorro." He was then his own master, but not quite the pretentious star he is today. It is interesting to note the differences between "The Mark of Zorro" and one of his more recent efforts, say "Robin Hood."

When Fairbanks made "The Mark of Zorro" he was building for himself the widespread popularity that is now his. I'll wager the first thing you notice about the picture is that the athletic Douglas was a romantic comedian.

LOST—A COMEDIAN   Douglas Fairbanks still depends upon romance, but he has forgotten, I fear, that he was once a comedian. Far be it from me to discourage a man and his art, but as a dispenser of entertainment I think the Fairbanks of "The Mark of Zorro" was far more proficient than the Fairbanks of "The Three Musketeers."

"Zorro," as you doubtless recall, was about a jumping-jack American Robin Hood. Like our Italian friend, Mussolini, he wore a black shirt and also a black mask.[145] He dashed through California—time, one hundred years ago—helping the oppressed and leaving a Z-like wound on the oppressors.

His Laughing Originality   All of which sounds like the 1923 model of Mister Douglas Fairbanks. But when it is added that Zorro, to throw his pursuers off the track, posed as a neurotic and languid young cake-eater you will recall the comic side of the picture. The element made "The Mark of Zorro" a laughing originality for which Fairbanks became known.

You'll find that "The Mark of Zorro" is still an entertaining affair, with a cast including Marguerite de la Motte, Noah Beery, Snitz Edwards, Claire McDowell and Robert McKim.[146] And perhaps you'll hope with me that Douglas, for old time's sake, will look at one of his former successes and realize that he is, among other things, an excellent comedian—when he so desires.

"Another Look at Year's Best Picture," *Chicago Herald and Examiner*, August 22, 1923, 7.

"ENEMIES OF WOMEN."[147]   As I told you several weeks ago "Enemies of Women" has been rated by theater owners as the best picture produced this year. In the "check up" department of an important film trade journal it received the highest percentage of the 1923 output.[148]

Its excellence is easily understood, and it is not surprising that all of you like it so well that you recommend it to your friends—and go to watch it for a second time. No wonder "Enemies of Women" broke the box office record of the Roosevelt during the loop showing, and no wonder that it is "packing 'em in" at the neighborhood houses now.

The novels of Vicente Blasco Ibáñez were made, it seems, to film. His dramatic, sweeping and colorful stories are gold mines of material for the expert director. Look at "The Four Horsemen" and "Blood and Sand." What fine bits of storytelling they were as they flashed upon the screen. And "Enemies of Women" is equally good—better from my viewpoint than the previous Ibáñez picture successes.

There is something about the character of Prince Lubimoff, especially as Lionel Barrymore portrays him, that seems to include the verities of human conduct. What a cynical, lustful, cruel, fearless and compassionate manner of man he is! It took courage to present him in the pictures. We have no "little theater" or "drama league" to boost the fine things of the films. Yet that courage has been rewarded a hundredfold—the much maligned film fan surrenders joyfully to "Enemies of Women."

I think it is because "Enemies of Women" is not alone an artistic achievement. It is, first, a good story. And none of us can resist a good story; that's why we go to the pictures and to the theater. And then, it has been done in a gloriously spendthrift manner—an expedition to Monte Carlo and Paris for the exterior scenes, a stellar cast which betrays not the fine work of Barrymore.

And back of the good story is the glamorous excitement of unfamiliar places and people—places we want to see, people we want to meet; the romance of Paris, Petrograd and Monte Carlo, the luxury and reckless living of princes and kings!

A fine piece of work, this "Enemies of Women."

"Maria Is Buffer for Mary in 'Rosita,'" *Chicago Herald and Examiner*, November 26, 1923, 9.

AND SHE'S THE ONLY "SUB" ON RECORD WHO WISHES STAR NO ILL-LUCK. Many of the [actors and actresses] have their doubles and understudies, but probably the most famous in the Hollywood colony is Maria. Maria is employed by Mary Pickford, and so satisfactory is she that she has a life-long contract with Doug's wife.

Understudies are, you know, nervous, nervy creatures. They may start out with the kindliest feelings in the world, but before the end of a picture they are wishing illness, death and worse upon the stars they represent. Calamity means good fortune to them.

But Maria is as mild as milk. She never offers gabby, useless suggestions. Nor does she sit around the "lot" like a spectre at a feast. In fact, she's a strange creature in many ways, because she doesn't eat, she doesn't sleep, and she is deaf and dumb. An ideal woman, in other words.

(Now your Aunt Polly will let the cat and the kittens right out of the bag—just like that. Poof!)

Maria is a dummy, whose waxen face, store hair and glass eyes are just exactly like Mary Pickford's. The contours of her cheeks, nose and chin are twin to those of Mary. She exists because Charles Rosher, cameraman de luxe at the Pickford studio, is so particular about his photography.[149] Which is a virtue, you'll admit, after you've seen "Rosita" at the Orpheum.

In order to save Mary endless hours of posing Maria was created. Mr. Rosher has to focus, experiment with lights, take sample "shots" and do a hundred and one things calculated to weary the steadfast nerves—and tempt "Klieg eyes." So, while Maria understudies, Miss Pickford can rehearse or rest or go watch Doug working on "The Thief of Bagdad."

Notes

1. "The Ten Best Pictures of 1924," *Film Daily Yearbook*, 1925, 623–28. The trade annual does not reveal how these selections were compiled.

2. Rose Pelswick's column was titled "At the Screen Door" in the *New York Journal* (with a circulation of 725,000). She wrote in a snappy, ironically solicitous style about interviewing stars, evidenced in her three-part article for *Photoplay* in early 1926: "Confessions of a Movie Critic," *Photoplay*, February 1926, 37, 141–42, March 1926, 70, 119–20, and April 1926, 68, 129–30. Thanks to Ben Strassfeld for scanning columns by Pelswick and Mildred Spain (*New York News*) during research on microfilm copies at the New York Public Library.

3. Mordaunt Hall, "The Screen," in Amberg, *The New York Times Film Reviews*, 213. British-born Mordaunt Hall (1878–1973) reported for several New York newspapers, served in the Royal Naval Volunteer Reserves during the war, and returned to New York in 1922. He probably was not one of the anonymous *Times* film reviewers before October 1924.

4. See, for instance, D. Ireland Thomas, "Motion Picture News," *Chicago Defender*, August 5, 1922, 6.

5. Prunella Hall's first column was "Screen Gossip," *Boston Post*, November 29, 1920, 19. The *Des Moines Register* and *Tribune* are digitized, but the *Des Moines Capital* is available only on microfilm. Leah Durand is described as "the Tribune's movie editor," in Priscilla Wayne, "A Woman's Views of the News," *Des Moines Tribune*, February 3, 1928, 18.

6. Grace Kingsley, "Hollywood in Review," *New Orleans Times-Picayune*, August 6, 1934, 14.

7. This film is available for purchase online.

8. Joseph Hergesheimer (1880–1954) was a popular fiction writer in the 1910s and 1920s. A *Literary Digest* poll of critics voted him the "most important American writer" in 1922.

9. Initially a theater performer, Henry King (1886–1982) turned to acting in the movies in 1913 and two years later was directing short films and then features. *Tol'able David* was his first really successful film, and he became a major director from the 1920s through the 1950s.

10. Walter P. Lewis (1866–1932) appeared as a character actor in more than fifty films between 1912 and 1931. A Scottish opera singer, Ernest Torrence (1878–1933) turned to theater acting after developing voice problems and then, in the movies, became a popular character actor through the 1920s. London-born Ralph Yearsley (1896–1928) was a character actor from 1921 until committing suicide in 1928. Warner Richmond (1886–1948) appeared as a character actor in more than one hundred films between 1912 and 1946. Patterson Dial (1902–45) appeared in more than a dozen films, mostly between 1921 and 1924. She married the author Rupert Hughes in 1925 but was herself a well-known writer.

11. Harold Lloyd (1893–1971) teamed with Hal Roach in 1914 to perform in short comedies as Lonesome Luke. In 1917 he created his Glass character for more short

comedies. In 1921 he and Roach turned to feature-length comedies, beginning with *A Sailor-Made Man* and *Grandma's Boy* (1922), and they produced twenty very popular films through the 1920s.

12. Initially a graphic artist and vaudeville performer, Larry Semon (1889–1928) began work in 1915 on Vitagraph comedies starring Hughie Mack. Later producing and acting in his own slapstick comedies, Semon became known for his elaborate gags. Beginning in 1899, Buster Keaton (1895–1966) performed in vaudeville comedy sketches with his parents as the Three Keatons. From 1917 on he costarred with Arbuckle in fourteen short comedies before getting his own production unit in 1920 for a series of two-reel comedies and then a dozen of the best feature-length comedies of the 1920s.

13. Phyllis Haver (1899–1960) was an original Sennett Bathing Beauty. In 1917 she starred in several two-reel comedies and continued to act in features throughout the 1920s.

14. Beginning with Sennett in 1913, Louise Fazenda (1895–1962) was a very popular comic actress who appeared in nearly three hundred films through the 1930s.

15. Lloyd "Ham" Hamilton (1891–1935) teamed with Bud Duncan in 1914 for Kalem's popular *Ham and Bud* series. In 1917 he joined Fox and starred in short comedies by the early 1920s.

16. *Grandma's Boy* and *Dr. Jack* are readily available for purchase online.

17. A popular vaudeville singer, Roscoe "Fatty" Arbuckle (1887–1933) joined Sennett to appear in Keystone comedies. Agile and acrobatic for his size (three hundred pounds), he starred with Normand in several dozen popular comedies for Paramount until he formed his own production unit in 1917 for an even more popular series of two-reel comedies. In 1921 he turned to feature-length comedies until his career was destroyed by a scandal and trials involving the death of actress Virginia Rappe (he was acquitted); thereafter, Arbuckle worked briefly with his friend Keaton and directed a number of films under the pseudonym William Goodrich.

18. See, for instance, the Paramount ad, *Film Daily*, August 5, 1923, 2. Chronicling America's digitized issues of the *New York Tribune* run through the end of 1922.

19. Paramount ad, *Film Daily*, October 10, 1924, 6; Associated Exhibitors ad, *Film Daily*, March 15, 1925, 5; and Universal ad, *Film Daily*, November 5, 1925, 3.

20. For examples of her interviews with stars, see Harriette Underhill, "Europe's Most Beautiful Star Here at Last [Pola Negri]," *New York Sunday Tribune*, September 17, 1922, 5.2; Underhill, "Valentino Tells the Universe All about It," *New York Sunday Tribune*, September 24, 1922, 5.2; and Underhill, "Close-Up of Betty Blythe with the New Teleview," *New York Sunday Tribune*, October 29, 1922, 5.2. For an example of an interview with a filmmaker, see Harriette Underhill, "The Most Important Thing in Pictures Is the Director," *New York Sunday Tribune*, November 12, 1922, 5.2.

21. Born in Vienna, Erich von Stroheim (1885–1957) immigrated to the United States in 1909 and entered the movies as a stunt man, bit player, and assistant director on *Intolerance* (1916). During the war he specialized in German villains and then turned to writing and directing *Blind Husbands* (1919), *Foolish Wives* (1922),

and *Greed* (1924). Thereafter, he returned to acting in France and the United States, most famously in Jean Renoir's *La grande illusion* (1937).

22. Born in London, Wyndham Standing (1880–1963) appeared in more than one hundred films between 1915 and 1948, sometimes as a star or costar and often as a popular character actor. A successful stage actor, Harrison Ford (1884–1957) became a leading man opposite Norma Talmadge, Marion Davies, and others in dozens of films from 1915 through the 1920s. Retiring from the movies in the early 1930s, he returned to the theater as an actor and director.

23. A Broadway stage actor, Glenn Hunter (1894–1945) turned to the movies and starred or costarred in more than a dozen films during the 1920s.

24. Born in London, Alec B. Francis (1867–1934) appeared in more than two hundred films between 1911 and 1934, primarily as an older character actor.

25. Initially a journalist, James Ashmore Creelman (1894–1941) was an important scriptwriter in the 1920s; later he worked on *The Most Dangerous Game* (1932) and *King Kong* (1933).

26. Sydney Franklin (1893–1972) began directing films in 1916, most notably *The Hoodlum,* with Pickford (1919).

27. Mae Tinée, "Closeups," *Chicago Sunday Tribune*, February 5, 1922, 8.1; "Kick Korner," *Chicago Sunday Tribune*, February 26, 1922, 7.9, 11.

28. "Movie Fans' Kick Korner," *Chicago Sunday Tribune*, September 10, 1922, 7.12; and "Movie Fans' Letter Box," *Chicago Sunday Tribune*, November 12, 1922, 7.19.

29. Mae Tinée, "Fiddlers Get Their Pay in 'After the Ball,'" *Chicago Tribune*, February 16, 1924, 15.

30. Mae Tinée, "Brave, Merry Outlaw Is a Cohan Grand," *Chicago Tribune*, October 16, 1922, 2.1.

31. Mae Tinée, "'Pay Day' Is Only a Sop to Eager Fans," *Chicago Tribune*, April 4, 1922, 22.

32. Little Eva was the central character, an innocent white child, in the many versions of *Uncle Tom's Cabin*. The "Elsie books" could refer to the Abbey series of thirty-eight popular girls' stories written by Elsie Jeannette Dunkerley (1880–1960) under the pseudonym of Oxenham.

33. Mae Tinée, "O Hollywood, Sinless, but So Maligned!," *Chicago Tribune*, January 5, 1923, 2.1.

34. Mae Tinée, "Anna Christie Is Life as You Don't Know It," *Chicago Tribune*, December 3, 1923, 2.1.

35. Ishbel Ross, *Ladies of the Press* (New York: Harper & Brothers, 1936), 411–12. Ross says Peck was married to David C. Kurner, with one grown-up daughter. The language of a negative review of *Citizen Kane,* signed by Mae Tinee and recently cited by Rotten Tomatoes, suggests that Frances Peck was still writing for the *Chicago Tribune* in 1941.

36. This film is available for purchase online.

37. Perhaps no fan of Valentino, the *New York Times* reviewer describes the Spanish bullfighter as a "Puritan-born hero" and not "a bit of fun"; moreover, the film "is

loaded with platitudinous subtitles" ("The Screen," in Amberg, *The New York Times Film Reviews*, 126).

38. Initially an artist's model and Ziegfeld Follies performer, Nita Naldi (1894-1961) first appeared in *Dr. Jekyll and Mr. Hyde* (1920). For several years, her "vamp" role in *Blood and Sand* made her a star before she left to act in a few British, French, and Italian films and retired in 1928.

39. This film is available for purchase online.

40. A Detroit film reviewer was more flippant: "It is a slice right off the flanks of life"; after seeing it, don't "rave if your steak is a trifle rare or your custard a bit too sweet" (Ed Harrison, "'Nanook' Rare and Novel Film Entertainment," *Detroit Times*, September 18, 1922, 9).

41. Carl Sandberg took two columns to laud *Nanook of the North*: its story surpassed anything by Jack London or Rudyard Kipling and compared favorably with that of Robinson Crusoe.

42. This film is available for purchase online.

43. A successful stage actor in New Zealand and Australia, Rupert Julian (1879-1943) immigrated to the United States in 1911, soon turned to acting in the movies, and started directing in 1915. He completed *Merry-Go-Round* after Stroheim was fired (apparently only ten minutes of the latter's footage was in the final print) and filmed most of *The Phantom of the Opera* (1925).

44. Discovered by Stroheim, Mary Philbin (1902-93) starred in *Foolish Wives*, *Merry-Go-Round*, and *The Phantom of the Opera*, appearing in twenty other films in the 1920s. Norman Kerry (1894-1956) entered the movies in 1916, appeared with Pickford in *A Little Princess* (1917), and soon became a popular leading man for Universal through the 1920s.

45. A reel of key moments from *Flaming Youth* survives in *Fragments: Surviving Pieces of Lost Films* (2011).

46. Warner Fabian was a pen name for writer Samuel Hopkins Adams.

47. Milton Sills (1882-1930) appeared in a dozen Broadway shows between 1908 and 1914. Debuting in *The Pit* (1914), he soon was a popular leading man in *Patria* (1917), *The Claw* (1918), and *The Woman Thou Gavest Me* (1919).

48. A.H.M., "This Week at the Movies," *Omaha World-Herald*, September 11, 1922, 6; and E.M.K., "This Week at the Movies," *Omaha World-Herald*, September 18, 1922, 6.

49. Elizabeth Kern, "This Week at the Movies," *Omaha World-Herald*, August 6, 1923, 3, and, October 1, 1923, 3.

50. Sun Theater ad, *Omaha World-Herald*, April 26, 1925, 8.

51. "Elizabeth Kern," *Omaha World-Herald*, November 5, 1963, 22.

52. E.M.K., "This Week at the Movies," *Omaha World-Herald*, October 30, 1922, 7.

53. Elizabeth Kern, "This Week at the Movies," *Omaha World-Herald*, November 6, 1922, 3.

54. Alvin Wyckoff (1877-1957) joined Cecil B. DeMille to shoot *The Spoilers* (1914) and worked with him through the early 1920s. He developed the selective lighting

technique marking *The Cheat* (1915) and shot several films using the Handschiegl color process.

55. A Russian-born ballet dancer, Theodore Kosloff (1882–1956) toured with the Diaghilev Ballet Company and then choreographed ballets, operas, and musicals in New York between 1912 and 1916. DeMille hired him as an actor to play "exotic" roles in films such as *Why Change Your Wife* (1920) and *The Affairs of Anatol* (1922).

56. In 1917 Martin (1884–1937) and Osa (1894–1953) Johnson went on a filming expedition to the New Hebrides and Solomon Islands, resulting in *Among the Cannibal Isles of the South Seas* (1918). Later expeditions led to *Jungle Adventures* (1921), *Headhunters of the South Seas* (1922), *Trailing Wild African Animals* (1923), and *Simba: King of the Beasts* (1928). After Martin's death, Osa continued doing lecture tours and produced the first wildlife series on television, *Osa Johnson's the Big Game Hunt* in 1952.

57. In his much more thorough praise, the *New York Times* reviewer also wrote that the film was endorsed by the American Museum of Natural History, and Mrs. Johnson addressed the Capitol theater audience ("The Screen," in Amberg, *The New York Times Film Reviews*, 149).

58. Harry O. Hoyt (1885–1961) was best known as a scenario writer from the 1910s through the 1930s, but he also directed a few films such as *The Lost World* (1925). John Francis Dillon (1884–1934) directed more than a hundred films, largely in the 1920s and early 1930s.

59. A successful stage actress in light opera and musical comedy, Myrtle Stedman (1883–1938) began acting in the movies in the early 1910s and played both leads and character roles largely in the 1920s. After a long career as vaudeville actor and theater stage manager, Phillips Smalley (1865–1939) entered the movie industry in 1910 with his wife, Lois Weber. His marriage and collaboration with Weber ended in 1922, after which he played supporting character roles throughout the 1920s and into the 1930s.

60. Italian-born Gene/Gino Corrado (1893–1982) played supporting character roles in hundreds of films from 1917 to 1954.

61. A 35mm print of this film survives at the Museum of Modern Art in New York. Founded by independent theater owners in 1917, First National Exhibitors' Circuit amassed a large circuit of movie theaters, especially first-run palace cinemas. Competing on a par with Paramount, it began producing films as First National Pictures in 1924 and eventually built a large studio in Burbank (CA), before coming under the control of Warner Bros. in 1928.

62. After serving as a marine transport worker and recovering from tuberculosis, Eugene O'Neill (1888–1953) joined the Provincetown Players as a playwright in 1916. By 1920 *Beyond the Horizon* and *The Emperor Jones* were being performed on Broadway, and *Anna Christie* won the 1922 Pulitzer Prize.

63. Initially a short story writer, Bradley King (1894–1977) began working for Thomas Ince as a continuity writer in 1915 and became an important scenarist by the early 1920s.

64. William Russell (1884–1929) appeared in more than two hundred films between 1910 and 1929, chiefly as a character actor.

65. A successful stage actor, George Marion (1860–1945) appeared in more than thirty films between 1915 and 1935, most notably as the father in *Anna Christie*, on-stage and on-screen.

66. Undercrank Productions has a DVD of this restored film for purchase online.

67. A prominent publisher of "yellow journalism" newspapers and quality magazines, William Randolph Hearst (1863–1951) formed the International News Service in 1909, which began releasing a weekly newsreel in 1916. His interest soon expanded to found Cosmopolitan Film, a production company, aligned with Paramount and largely devoted to Marion Davies's films. An early Ziegfeld Follies star, Marion Davies (1897–1961) became Hearst's mistress and a major movie star in Cosmopolitan features, notably in *When Knighthood Was in Flower* (1922). She had a genuine talent for comedy, later evidenced in *The Patsy* and *Show People* (both 1928).

68. A successful stage performer, Mahlon Hamilton (1880–1960) acted in nearly a hundred films between 1915 and 1950, mainly as a supporting character actor. After a varied career, Louis Wolheim (1880–1931) worked as a character actor in dozens of films from 1914 to 1931. Onstage, he starred as Yank in Eugene O'Neill's *The Hairy Ape* (1922).

69. A well-known architect, theater set designer, and children's book illustrator, Joseph Urban (1872–1933) became a Cosmopolitan set designer, working on several dozen films in the 1920s.

70. Initially a theater actor, Canadian-born Sidney Olcott (1872–1949) became Kalem's chief film director, with hundreds of films to his credit. After *Poor Little Peppina* (1916), with Pickford, his career slowed, but he later directed Swanson in *The Hummingbird* and Valentino in *Monsieur Beaucaire* (both 1924). Initially a journalist, Luther Reed (1888–1961) directed nearly twenty films from 1918 to 1930. Rida Johnson Young (1875–1926) was a popular playwright and songwriter best known for the book and lyrics to the operetta *Naughty Marietta* (1910).

71. The *New York Times* reviewer found *Little Old New York* a most exquisite production but thought the cross-dressed "Marion Davies far too feminine to be mistaken for a boy" ("The Screen," in Amberg, *The New York Times Film Reviews*, 158).

72. See, for instance, "Mightiest of All Movies," *Arlington Heights Cook County Herald*, February 29, 1924, 4; and "Largest of All Screen Canvases," *Lima (OH) News*, September 11, 1924, 10.

73. State-Lake Theater ad, *Chicago Tribune*, March 7, 1927, 18; and Mae Tinée, "Mr. Pepys' Review of Play Will Go for This Movie," *Chicago Tribune*, March 9, 1927, 31; Frederick Donaghey, "Mr. Mantle's Volume Dated 1928–'28," *Chicago Sunday Tribune*, December 16, 1928, 7.1.

74. Virginia Dale, "Time Can Not Tarnish This Film," *Chicago Journal*, January 27, 1923, 8.

75. Virginia Dale, "News of the Motion Picture World," *Chicago Journal*, October 30, 1923, 17.

76. Virginia Dale, "Moving Pictures," *Chicago Journal*, February 13, 1922, 9.

77. Virginia Dale, "News of the Motion Picture World," *Chicago Journal*, September 25, 1923, 10.

78. Virginia Dale, "Foreign Films Show American Influences," *Chicago Journal*, April 29, 1922, 7.

79. Virginia Dale, "Feminine Fans Make and Break Long Line of Heroes of Films," *Chicago Journal*, September 23, 1922, 7.

80. A young vaudeville performer, Edith Roberts (1899–1935) entered the movie industry in 1915 and played supporting character roles in more than a hundred films through 1929.

81. Marjorie Daw (1902–1979) entered the movies in 1914, became a minor star opposite Fairbanks in *His Majesty, the American* (1919), and played supporting character roles through the 1920s. John Harron (1903–39) was a supporting character actor in more than a hundred films through the 1920s and 1930s.

82. A successful French stage actor, Max Linder (1883–1925) joined Pathé Frères in 1905 and appeared in many short comic films. From 1909 to 1914 he starred in a series of "Max" comedies, which gained him worldwide popularity. In 1915 Essanay hired Linder to replace Chaplin and make a series of American comedies, without much success. Returning to France, he opened the Ciné Max Linder in Paris and starred in Raymond Bernard's *Le petit café* (1919). Returning to Hollywood in 1921, he made three more films, none successful. Despite chronic depression, he finished *Le roi du cirque* (1925) before he and his young wife committed suicide.

83. An early airplane pilot and race car driver, Ruth Wrightman (1897–1939) worked in the scenario department for Goldwyn Pictures.

84. A British stage performer, Lupino Lane (1892–1959) took up acting in short British films in 1915 and then made forty short films in the United States. Ida Lupino was one of his cousins.

85. Henry Kitchell Webster (1875–1932) was a popular writer. *The Real Adventure* was adapted, filmed, and released in 1922.

86. Florence Vidor (1895–1977) began acting in the movies after marrying King Vidor in 1915. *Hail the Woman* (1921) made her a star, and she had leading lady roles through the 1920s.

87. A Ziegfeld Follies star, Ed Wynn (1886–1966) acted on Broadway in the 1920s and hosted a popular radio show in the 1930s.

88. A Scottish-born stage performer, David Powell (1883–1925) appeared in dozens of American feature films between 1915 and 1925, often as a supporting character actor.

89. Gloria Swanson, Agnes Ayres, Bryant Washburn, and Wallace Beery all first performed for Essanay; Kathlyn Williams, for Selig Polyscope. After debuting at Keystone, Chaplin starred in the famous Essanay comic series. Harris may be exaggerating about the debuts of the Talmadges, Walthall, and Noah Beery.

90. A former journalist and editor of *Billboard* and several advertising publications, Watterson Rothacker (1885–1960) in early 1910 founded the Industrial Moving Picture Company in Chicago, perhaps the first to specialize in producing advertising and industrial films. By the late 1910s, the firm had become not only the Rothacker

Film Manufacturing Company but also the major laboratory for developing and printing Hollywood feature films for release.

91. Among those workers, as in many film exchanges, were scores of young women.

92. A socialite who abandoned his wife and daughter in 1908, British-born William Desmond Taylor (1872–1922) began directing films in 1914. After serving in the Canadian Expeditionary Force from 1918 to 1919, he returned to direct half a dozen films before being murdered (by his valet), which provoked a scandal implicating a number of popular women in Hollywood. A department store clerk in Pittsburgh, Olive Thomas (1894–1920) became an illustrator's model and Ziegfeld girl, leading to a short career as a movie star, notably in *The Flapper* (1920). Vacationing in Paris with Jack Pickford, her husband, and tired from a night of partying, she mistakenly drank a mercury bichloride solution prescribed for him and died five days later.

93. Mrs. Wallace Reid (Dorothy Davenport) sought to recuperate Reid's image in such films as *Human Wreckage* (1922).

94. Yet William Hart and Chaplin, for instance, were involved in marriage scandals.

95. Initially a successful stage performer, June Mathis (1887–1927) contracted with Metro as a scenario writer in 1918 and one year later headed its scenario department. Adapting *Four Horsemen of the Apocalypse* for the screen helped her cast Valentino in a starring role, and she worked closely with him thereafter. By the mid-1920s Mathis was one of the top three Hollywood scenario writers; a year after Valentino's death, she suffered a fatal heart attack. British-born Charles Brabin (1882–1957) played supporting character roles in the 1910s and 1920s. He married Theda Bara in 1921.

96. Discovered by Harrison Fisher, Pauline Frederick (1883–1938) had leading stage roles in *The Girl in White* (1906) and *Joseph and His Brethren* (1910). First acting in films such as *Zaza* (1915), she starred in *Sapho* (1917), *Madame Jealousy* (1918), and *Madame X* (1920).

97. A member of the Chickasaw Nation, Edwin Carewe (1883–1940) first joined the Lubin company as an actor. Soon he turned to directing for half a dozen studios and produced more than fifty films, including the recently rediscovered *Ramona* (1928), with Dolores del Rio.

98. See, for instance, "'Fabiola' at the Temple Sunday," *Alton (IL) Telegraph*, April 28, 1923, 6; and "Amusements," *Escanada (MI) Press*, September 23, 1923, n.p.

99. "Short Story Writer Studies to Review Pictures in French," *Abilene Reporter*, November 4, 1923, 5.

100. *Le courrier cinématographique* was one of several important early French trade journals, first published in July 1911 and edited by Charles Le Fraper. Harris's column was announced in "Sur l'écran," *Le courrier cinématographique*, September 23, 1922, 42. Her signature first came in an untitled column in *Le courrier cinématographique*, October 28, 1922, 22.

101. Harris contributed no review column to the *Post* between late December 1923 and May 1924, perhaps because she was still in Paris during those months.

102. "Obituaries, Genevieve Harris," *Chicago Sunday Tribune*, August 10, 1973, 3.14.

103. Genevieve Harris, "Photoplays," *Chicago Post*, September 1, 1922, 16.

104. Genevieve Harris, "The Charm of Pola Negri," *Chicago Post*, September 23, 1922, 2.11.

105. Genevieve Harris, "Photoplays," *Chicago Post*, September 25, 1923, 14.

106. Genevieve Harris, "What Makes a Great Picture," *Chicago Post*, September 2, 1922, 2.5.

107. Genevieve Harris, "Seeing Films a Second Time," *Chicago Post*, October 7, 1922, 2.7.

108. Genevieve Harris, "The Screen an Ally of Books," *Chicago Post*, November 11, 1922, 2.8.

109. Genevieve Harris, "Films Spread American Ideas," *Chicago Post*, March 10, 1923, 2.3.

110. The reference is to the first ciné-club in Paris, the Club des amis du septième art (CASA), led by Ricciotto Canudo (1879–1923), an Italian expatriate writer.

111. Léon Moussinac (1890–1964) was a book and magazine editor, a member of the French Communist Party, and an important film and theater critic. A prestigious intellectual journal, *Mercure de France*, turned leftist in 1920 and published his film reviews until 1926. In 1928 he and others founded Amis de Spartacus, a popular ciné-club that the Paris police shut down for screening Soviet films.

112. A major production company, Société des cinéromans, financed *L'enfant roi* (1923). Jean Kemm (1874–1939) directed *L'enfant roi*, as well as *Vidocq* (1923) and *Le bossu* (1925).

113. For more information on these Cinéromans *films à épisodes*, see Richard Abel, *French Cinema: The First Wave, 1915–1929* (Princeton, NJ: Princeton University Press, 1984), 23, 82–83.

114. Initially a stage performer, Jeanie MacPherson (1886–1946) began acting at Biograph and then Universal until Cecil B. DeMille hired her as a scenario writer in 1914. For more than a decade, she penned nearly all of DeMille's most popular films and ranked as one of the top three scenario writers in Hollywood.

115. A fragment of this film is included in *Fragments: Surviving Pieces of Lost Films* (2011).

116. After a career in stock theater companies, John Emerson (1874–1956) began writing and directing films, particularly the early comedies of Fairbanks. With Anita Loos, he continued writing (or lightly editing) scenarios, notably those starring Constance Talmadge. A child stage actor, Anita Loos (1889–1981) published a few short stories before submitting scripts to Biograph, including one for *The New York Hat* (1912). In 1916 with Emerson (her future husband) she wrote scenarios and clever intertitles for the first Fairbanks films and then for half a dozen features starring Constance Talmadge. *Photoplay* dubbed her "The Soubrette of Satire." What really made her name was the novel *Gentleman Prefer Blondes* (1925).

117. John Daly Murphy was a supporting character actor during the 1910s and 1920s.

118. Miss Dupont (1894–1973) acted in supporting character roles from 1919 to 1927. Beginning in 1915, Maude George (1888–1963) acted in supporting character roles through the 1920s, appearing in four of Stroheim's films.

119. A successful stage actress, Dale Fuller (1885–1948) joined Keystone in 1915, left to appear in Chester comedies, then played supporting character roles through the mid-1930s. The daughter of the popular serial actor Eddie Polo (1875–1961), Malvina Polo (1903–2000) appeared in just five films in the early 1920s.

120. "Another example of women who have succeeded in the industry," Hetty Gray Baker was known for editing "all the film that goes into the Fox News Weekly" (photo captions, *Moving Picture World*, February 28, 1920, 1481; and *Exhibitors Herald*, March 6, 1920, 89). She also was cited as one of many authors for Educational Film's two-reel dramas ("Begin Third Educational Drama; More Famous Stories Acquired," *Moving Picture World*, July 2, 1921, 99).

121. American Mutoscope & Biograph, founded in 1895, became Biograph in 1908. Griffith made it into perhaps the most important production company through the early 1910s. After he left in 1913, it quickly declined, released only reissues after 1916, and leased out its Bronx studio.

122. Beginning in 1910, Walter Long (1879–1952) worked with Griffith, most controversially in blackface as Gus in *The Birth of a Nation*. He had a long career as a supporting character actor through the early 1940s.

123. A successful stage actor in San Francisco, George Field (1877–1925) appeared in supporting character roles in two hundred films from 1912 to 1924.

124. A well-known still photographer, Robert J. Flaherty (1884–1951) first filmed the Inuit people on a prospecting trip in 1913, but fire destroyed the negative. In 1920 he spent a year filming what would become *Nanook of the North*, in which he cast local people for the major characters, refused to let rifles be used in hunting (common by then), and staged some scenes as in a fiction film. The film's unusual success led to others, including *Moana* (1926) and *Man of Aran* (1934).

125. Baby Peggy or Peggy-Jean Montgomery (1918–2020) was a major child film star, appearing in 150 short films between 1921 and 1924. After a brief stint in Universal features, she acted in vaudeville shows until 1929. After squandering the money she earned, her parents took the family to Wyoming, but she left in the mid-1930s to do stage work and write about Hollywood. In the 2010s she was a regular guest at the Giornate del cinema muto in Pordenone, Italy.

126. The Chicago and Alton also operated the first sleeping cars and dining cars.

127. A child stage actor, Priscilla Dean (1896–1987) first appeared in short films for Biograph and Universal and became a relatively important star from 1917 through 1927.

128. Founded in 1921, the Motion Picture Theater Owners Association merged with the independent Allied States Association of Motion Picture Exhibitors to form the National Association of Theatre Owners.

CHAPTER 4

129. After a short career on Broadway, Elaine Hammerstein (1897–1948) starred in several dozen films between 1915 and 1926, particularly for Selznick Pictures. May McAvoy (1899–1984) was a character actor in dozens of films from 1917 to 1929. A beauty contest winner, Hope Hampton (1897–1982) was "discovered" by Jules Brulatour (whom she later married). In the 1920s she starred in a dozen features, often as a siren or flapper.

130. William Kennedy Laurie Dickson (1860–1935) developed the Kinetoscope as a motion picture exhibition machine for Thomas Edison (1847–1931) between 1889 and 1892. It allowed a single viewer to watch a very short film for the cost of a vaudeville ticket. The device was popular until Dickson, the Lumières, and others developed film projecting machines for paying audiences. Invented by Laurens Hammond (1895–1973), Teleview was a system for projecting stereoscopic motion pictures, first exhibited in New York City in late December 1922. The cost of installation kept it from commercial development.

131. With Charles Francis Jenkins (1867–1934), Thomas Armat (1866–1948) invented the Phantoscope projector in 1895 using the Latham loop, pioneered by Woodville Latham (1837–1911). Edison bought Armat's patent and sold the machine as the Vitascope, and Armat refined the device into the Edison Projecting Kinetoscope. The Lumière brothers, Auguste (1862–1954) and Louis (1864–1948), invented the ingenious Cinématographe (it could record, develop, and project motion pictures), which had its first public exhibition in Paris in late 1895. The Lumière company hired many cameramen to shoot and exhibit short motion pictures around the world but left the film business by 1905.

132. With the exception of *License No. 13* and *The Master and the Man*, all of these films survive in one form or another.

133. Founded in 1906, the Italian film company Cines was best known for historical spectacles such as *Quo Vadis* (1913), *Antony and Cleopatra* (1913), and *Julius Caesar* (1914). Kleine F.B.O. refers to the Film Booking Office, the distribution company set up by George Kleine (1864–1931) in 1913 to import Italian spectacle films. Kleine later became a distributor of educational films. Later F.B.O. would become part of RKO.

134. After leaving Biograph, Griffith and Harry E. Aitken formed the Reliance-Majestic Studios, later renamed Fine Arts Studio, which became part of Triangle. Founded in 1912 by Aiken, Mutual Film distributed the films of Keystone, Kay Bee, Chaplin, and others until 1918, but its fortunes declined after the departure of Chaplin and the formation of Triangle.

135. Owner of Western Film Exchange, H. E. or Harry Aitken took over the Reliance and Majestic companies in 1911 and formed Mutual the following year. Forced out of Mutual in 1915, he founded Triangle, which, despite the success of Fairbanks and Hart films, was badly managed and collapsed in 1917.

136. This film is available for purchase online.

137. A 35mm print of this film survives at the Cinémathèque française (Paris).

138. Polly Wood, "How Prosperity Periled Home Told in Film," *Chicago Herald and Examiner*, July 6, 1923, 5.

139. Aston Stevens, "Stevens Is Happily Surprised; Finds 'Dulcy' Live and Amusing," *Chicago Herald and Examiner*, August 9, 1923, 11; "Negri Is Herself Again in 'Cheat,' Says Stevens," *Chicago Herald and Examiner*, August 29, 1923, 9; "Stevens Prefers Norma 1923 to Norma 1572," *Chicago Herald and Examiner*, August 30, 1923, 7; "Marion Davies in Little Old New York," *Chicago Herald and Examiner*, October 11, 1923, 11; "Pola Is Foreign as Ever, Says Stevens," *Chicago Herald and Examiner*, October 25, 1923, 7; and "Proving Colleen Starship Is Not Paste: Stevens," *Chicago Herald and Examiner*, November 2, 1923, 9.

140. Orpheum ad, *Chicago Tribune*, March 12, 1924, 22. Included in that review of *The Marriage Circle* was this sarcastic line: "Cecil DeMille tried it with his 'Don't Change Your Wife' series, but compared to Lubitsch, DeMille was a bungler."

141. Her last review may have been of *The Big Parade* (Shubert Garrick ad, *Chicago Sunday Tribune*, January 17, 1926, 8.2). John Joseph then took over from her for about a year. Theater ads in the *Chicago Tribune* sometimes quoted only her blurbs; at other times, she was paired with Mae Tinée, Genevieve Harris, Carl Sandberg, and Rob Reel.

142. Polly Wood, "'Red Lights' One of Pop-Eyed 'Mysteries,'" *Chicago Herald and Examiner*, September 19, 1923, 9. What would she have thought of Ivan Mosjoukine's fantastical *Le brasier ardent* (1923) had it been released in the United States?

143. Polly Wood, "Glamour and Life in 'Merry Go Round,'" *Chicago Herald and Examiner*, September 24, 1923, 7.

144. Polly Wood, "Lillian Gish in a Fine Piece of Acting," *Chicago Herald and Examiner*, November 12, 1923, 9.

145. This is early praise for Benito Mussolini (1883–1945), who became Italy's prime minister in October 1922 and soon its dictator. Fairbanks (and Pickford) were strong supporters of Mussolini. See Giorgio Bertellini, *The Divo and the Duce: Promoting Film Stardom and Political Leadership in 1920s America* (Oakland: University of California Press, 2019).

146. A successful Broadway performer, Hungarian-born Snitz Edwards (1868–1937) was a talented character actor during the 1920s. Claire McDowell (1877–1966) appeared in several hundred films between 1908 and 1945, usually playing supporting character roles and often mothers.

147. An incomplete 35mm print of this film in poor condition survives at the US Library of Congress.

148. Despite describing this film as "a long story beautifully directed," the *New York Times* reviewer thought its ten reels "would benefit a great deal by being cut still further" ("The Screen," in Amberg, *The New York Times Film Reviews*, 144).

149. A newsreel cameraman, Charles Rosher (1885–1974) became a Hollywood cinematographer in the 1910s, worked on several Pickford films, and, with Karl Struss, won an Academy Award for *Sunrise* (1927).

Afterword

What's next? Well, let's see what threads we might tease out of the columns by these movie mavens and what patterns we might perceive that could provoke further thinking and reflection. Overall, their expertise confirms the important role that journalism played in shaping the initial development of cinema as an entertainment and art form, as well as the emergence of American popular film culture. That role included not only promoting the industry as a new field of employment for professional women (especially, yet not exclusively, in all areas of production) but also opening up newspaper careers for smart, skillful women writers and targeting women readers with movie reviews and gossip in the Women's or Society section. These reviewers often wrote from an implicitly or even explicitly gendered perspective, in contrast to the columns of their male counterparts. That perspective is evident in their efforts to come to terms with a range of issues: the principles of aesthetic pleasure, the singular effects of the new medium, the bodily impact of stars, the observations of audience behavior, and a dawning sense of spectatorship. While they could offer different takes on a single film such as *The Birth of a Nation*, *Where Are My Children?*, *The Love Light*, or *The Cabinet of Doctor Caligari* and on directors such as D. W. Griffith, Cecil B. DeMille, and Lois Weber, they also could surprise. They paid little attention to Charlie Chaplin, for instance, seemed ambivalent about Mary Pickford, and celebrated Mrs. Sidney Drew as a neglected filmmaker. Directors and stars were hardly their exclusive subjects, however, for they highlighted the work of studio production personnel, scenario writers (specifically women), film editors, and exhibitors and the unfamiliar operation of a rental exchange, where many young women inspected and repaired film prints. Kitty Kelly's columns even revealed a treasure trove of detailed notes on the Chicago censors and the cuts they ordered each week to sometimes a dozen film titles. Finally, we can scarcely ignore the real pleasure of reading such witty, insightful, sometimes acerbic and parodic pieces of writing.

Now it is the turn of others to find more newspaperwomen than are selected here. And whatever writers turn up, researchers will have to address a range of questions. What differences may be uncovered among those doing film reviews, editing movie pages, and writing gossip columns? In terms of approaches, attitudes, and stylistics, what is characteristic or unique about each writer, and do those characteristics change or develop noticeably over time? Other questions to pursue could address not only newly discovered writers but also those in this volume. What further information might be relevant about the circulation and political affiliation of their newspapers, about the demographics and cultural scenes of the cities in which they lived and worked, and about particular historical events—from the Great War, the influenza pandemic, and immigration fears to woman suffrage, Prohibition, and racial violence such as "race riots" and lynchings—that may have impacted them? To what degree were these newspaper women engaged with the movie industry, and in what specific ways? What might be relevant about their married or single status, their economic and social status, their sexual orientation (if only implicit)? Did they have careers once they stopped writing about the movies in the newspapers, and what kinds of careers?

Researchers also may want to cast their inquiries farther afield. Some could do further research on newspaper men writing about the movies and explore notable similarities with and differences between female newspaper editors and writers. How many of these men besides those cited in this volume—for example, W. K. Hollander and Carl Sandberg in the *Chicago News*, the anonymous writers in the *New York Times*, Harold Hefferman and others in the Detroit papers—might be located and examined on websites or on microfilm? Others could do further research on newspaper women writing about the movies in countries besides the United States. In France alone during this period, research could focus attention on Colette, Germaine Dulac, and Lucie Derain. And what of Great Britain, Germany, Italy, Spain, Russia, or even Czechoslovakia?[1]

What discursive traces of long-forgotten voices will surface when we access and assess newspaper materials, whether as digital or microfilm documents, perhaps even pushing (to recontextualize Carlo Ginzburg) against the intentions of whoever produced such textual remains?[2] All of this ongoing research, in other words, has to inform the task before us—that is (to adopt an aptly domestic analogy), from the *fait divers* remains of these and other newspaper columns, collected and spun as if onto spindles, we weave such new threads of material into the historical tapestry of early American popular film culture, their colors, weights, and textures enhancing and perhaps transforming our vision of the patterns worked into the palimpsestic design of that tapestry.

Notes

1. Milena Jesenká, for instance, wrote at least one article on the cinema in *Tribuna*, January 15, 1920, reprinted in *The Promise of Cinema: German Film Theory and Criticism, 1907–1933*, ed. Anton Kaes, Nicholas Baer, and Michael Cowan (Oakland: University of California Press, 2015), 164–66.
2. Carlo Ginzburg, introduction to *Threads and Traces: True False Fictive*, trans. Anne C. Tedeschi and John Tedeschi (Berkeley: University of California Press, 2012),
3. See also Lisa Gitelman, *Paper Knowledge: Toward a Media History of Documents* (Durham, NC: Duke University Press, 2014), 17.

Appendix

Newspaper References

Newspaper circulation figures, *Ayer & Sons Annual and Directory*, 1920
*Digitized

Chicago population: 2,393,325

Chicago Day Book	daily	20,000–30,000

Source: newspapers.com or Chronicling America

Chicago Examiner, independent   daily   240,000
    Ayer & Sons Annual, 1914   Sunday   530,000
   Source: Chicago Historical Museum Research Center microfilm

Chicago Herald & Examiner, independent   daily   289,094
    (owned by Hearst)   Sunday   596.851
   Source: Chicago Historical Museum Research Center microfilm

Chicago Journal, Democratic   daily   115,932
   Source: Chicago Historical Museum Research Center microfilm

Chicago News, independent   daily   386,498
   Source: Chicago Historical Museum Research Center microfilm

Chicago Post, independent   daily   51,327
   Source: Chicago Historical Museum Research Center microfilm

**Chicago Record-Herald*, independent   daily   156,000
    Ayer & Sons Annual, 1914
   Source: newspapers.com

**Chicago Tribune*, Republican   daily   424,588
    Sunday   666,496

   Source: newsapapers.com or ProQuest

Cleveland population: 639,431
**Cleveland Plain Dealer*, Democratic   daily   167,720
    Sunday   206,861

   Source: newspaperarchive.com

Des Moines population: 105,652

Des Moines News, independent	daily	47,476
Source: Iowa State Historical Society Library microfilm		
Des Moines Register	Sunday	70,745
Source: newspapers.com		
Des Moines Register & Tribune, Republican	daily	111,517
Source: newspapers.com		
Des Moines Tribune	daily	29,000
Ayer & Sons Annual, 1914	Sunday	39,000
Source: newspapers.com		

Detroit population: 900,000

Detroit Journal, Republican	daily	109,889
Source: Detroit Public Library microfilm		

Indianapolis population: 280,000

Indianapolis Star, Republican	daily	84,859
	Sunday	96,051
Source: newspapers.com or ProQuest		

Los Angeles population: 500,000

Los Angeles Times, Republican	daily	82,181
	Sunday	123,438
Source: newspapers.com or ProQuest		

New York city population: 5,047,221

New York Morning Telegraph, Democratic	daily	51,610
Source: personal collection of microfilm		
New York Times, Democratic	daily	367,587
	Sunday	546,728
Source: newspapers.com or ProQuest		
New York Tribune, Republican	daily	118,386
Sunday		108,999
Source: newspapers.com or ProQuest		

Omaha population: 200,000

Omaha World-Herald, independent	daily	77,822
	Sunday	70,391
Source: newspapers.com		

Syracuse population: 140,000

Syracuse Herald, independent	daily	35,055
Ayer & Sons Annual, 1914	Sunday	51,620
Source: newspaperarchive.com		

Index

Abel, Sydney E., 70, 107n14
Absentee, The (1915), 26
Acme portable projectors, 229
Adams, Maude, 18, 57n17
Adams, Minnie, 56
Addams, Jane, 38, 63n77
Adventures of Kathlyn, The (1914), 57n15, 191n98, 194n137
advertising, 5, 106, 211, 244–245n90
Affairs of Anatol, The (1921), 120, 126–127, 186n37, 242n55
Aitken, H. E., 58n19, 230, 248nn134–135
Alhambra theater (Los Angeles), 21
Alhambra theater (Milwaukee), 114n92
Alias Jimmy Valentine (1915), 113
Alliance Française, 130
Allison, May, 67n119
America's Answer (1918), 98
Anderson, G. M., 63n68
Anna Christie (1923), 202, 207, 209–210
Antony and Cleopatra (1913), 248n133
Apfel, Oscar, 59n33
Are You a Perfect 36? (1918), 106, 115n112
Arizona (1918), 145, 147–148
Arliss, George, 129
Aryan, The (1916), 111–112n61
Ashes of Vengeance (1923), 219, 231–232, 234
Atlanta Constitution, 12
Atlas Educational Film, 230
Auditorium (Chicago), 89
Avenging Conscience, The (1914), 18, 19, 64n79

Ayres, Agnes, 126, 127, 183, 186n35, 215

Baby Peggy/Peggy-Jean Montgomery, 228, 229, 247n125
Bacon, Francis, 67n118
Balboa Film, 20, 58n26
Bara, Theda, 4, 39, 43, 52, 54, 64n82, 67n122, 70, 72, 120, 163, 168, 245n95
Barker, Adella, 54
Barrie, J. M., 57–58n17
Barrier, The (1917), 111–112n61, 115n100
Barrymore, Lionel, 236–237
Barthelmess, Richard, 134, 137, 145, 158, 188n65, 196–197
Bass, Charlotta, 12, 35–36, 62n62, 107
Bass, Joseph B., 35
Battle of Gettysburg, The (1913), 58n23
Bayne, Beverly, 52, 54, 66n116, 67nn119–120, 218
Beach, Rex, 98, 115n99, 115n100
Beautiful Dancer, The (1919), 120
Beery, Noah, 177, 192n120, 236
Beery, Wallace, 192n120, 230
Belasco, David, 18
Bell, Archie, 12
Ben Hur (1925), 192n119, 217
Bennett, Enid, 213
Bernhardt, Sarah, 57n17, 69, 72–73, 108nn22–23, 114n92
Bernstein, Isodore, 14, 15, 16, 57n13
Besserer, Eugenie, 77, 99, 109n38, 209
Birmingham Age-Herald, 12

258   INDEX

Birth of a Nation, The (1915), 4, 6, 22, 28–29, 35, 37–38, 49–50, 57n16, 58n20, 64n79, 66n114, 70, 75, 109n32, 136, 190n82, 230, 247n122, 251
Blaché, Alice Guy, 11
Blackwell, Carlyle, 20, 58n25
Blank, A. H., 44, 65n97, 162, 163
Blonde Venus (1932), 108–109n28
Blood and Sand (1922), 192n119, 202, 203–204, 207, 208, 218, 219, 225–226, 234, 236, 241n38
Bloomer, Raymond, 177, 193n123
Blot, The (1921), 120, 127–128, 139–140, 172, 187n39
Bluebird, The (1918), 86, 87–88, 113n76
Blue Jeans (1917), 112n72
Boggs, Anita Maris, 13, 57n10
Boston Post, 195
Bosworth Film, 13, 58n22
Bowen, Mrs. Louise de Koven, 37–38, 63n76, 64n78
Branded Woman, The (1920), 172, 173, 174–175
Branding Broadway (1918), 115n111
Brandt, Joseph, 81
Brat, The (1919), 67n123
Bray Studio, 113n75
Brenon, Herbert, 66n115, 143, 169, 170, 192n107
Brewster's Millions, 217
Brockwell, Gladys, 114n90
Broken Blossoms (1919), 134, 136–137, 145, 155–159, 168, 188n65, 190n82, 230
Broken Doll, A (1921), 110n49
Browne, Harry C., 74, 108n27
Brunet, Paul, 132, 134, 187n48, 187n50
Brute, The (1920), 116, 184n3
Bunny, John, 61n52
Bushman, Francis X., 4, 52, 54, 66n116, 67n119, 67n121, 72, 108, 167, 218
Bye, Hazel, 116

Cabinet of Dr. Caligari, The (1921), 5, 6, 120, 125–126, 135, 172–173, 178–179, 186n32, 193nn124–125, 251
Cabiria (1914), 28, 61n48
California Eagle, 12, 35, 59n35, 63n63, 63n67, 66n114
cameramen: Bitzer, Gottfried Wilhelm "Billy," 158, 189n82; Rosher, Charles, 21, 234, 237, 249n149; Wyckoff, Alvin, 207, 241–242n54
Camille (1912), 108n22
Campbell, Colin, 98, 99, 115n99
Capitol theater (New York), 173, 176, 177, 178, 179, 242n57
Carewe, Edwin, 218, 245n97
Carey, Harry, 120, 163
Carleton, Will, 128, 140, 187n41
Carman, 30, 39, 40, 61n50, 64n84
Carmen (1915), 23, 29–31, 37, 39–40, 60n41, 61n49, 61–62nn52–54
Carpet of Bagdad, The (1914), 18
Carr, Mary, 140, 141, 189n70
Carter, Mrs. Lelie, 18, 57n17
Central Press Association, 12
Central States Theater Corporation, 163
Chaney, Lon, 121, 186n20
Chaplin, Charlie, 4, 6, 42, 58n19, 63n68, 65n94, 72, 110n47, 117, 118–119, 126, 129, 166, 186n33, 187n42, 190n95, 196, 197, 198, 199, 202, 215, 217, 235, 244n82, 245n94, 248n134, 251
Chase, Al, 22, 85
Chautard, Emile, 74, 108–109n28
Cheat, The (1915), 145, 149–152, 189n78
Cheat, The (1923), 234
Chicago and Alton railroad, 219, 229, 247n126
Chicago censors, 6, 22, 38, 124, 252
Chicago Defender, 12, 59n35, 69, 195
Chicago Examiner, 12, 22, 85, 112n62
Chicago Herald, 12, 77
Chicago Herald and Examiner, 112n63, 195, 234
Chicago Journal, 37, 116, 168, 195, 210
Chicago News, 5, 12, 69, 116, 186n33, 195, 252
Chicago Palace of Progress, 6, 219, 229, 230
Chicago Post, 4, 13, 47, 48–49, 65n101, 68, 97, 195, 218
Chicago Record-Herald, 1, 13, 36–37
Chicago Tribune, 2, 4, 12, 13, 21, 47, 52, 85, 195, 249n141
Cines film company (Italy), 230, 248n133
Circle theater (Indianapolis), 130
Civilization (1916), 58n23
Clark, Marguerite, 18, 58, 17, 123
Clary, Charles, 71, 107–108n19
Cleopatra (1917), 163
Cleveland Plain Dealer, 12, 116, 117, 184n6

Cleveland Sunday Leader, 56n1
Clifford, Kathleen, 80, 110n54, 174
Clue, The (1915), 22
Cody, Lewis, 163, 165, 190n92
Cohen, George M., 121, 185n21
Coliseum (Chicago), 229
Collins, John H., 85, 86, 112n70, 112n72
Colonial (Chicago), 108n24
Come Through (1918), 83
Committee on Public Information (CPI), 111n56
composers, musicians, and songwriters: Beethoven, Ludwig, 33; Belibri, 49; Bizet, Georges, 30, 61n50; Breil, Joseph Carl, 6, 50, 66n111; Browne, Harry C., 74, 108n27; Duncan, Arthur, 87; Elinore, Carl D., 114n93; Fitzpatrick, Mildred, 88; Sousa, John Philip, 33; Work, Henry C., 49, 66n109
Compson, Betty, 121, 185n17
Conan Doyle, Arthur, 200
Connecticut Yankee in King Arthur's Court (1921), 128
Coogan, Jackie, 128, 187n42, 213, 216
Cordner, E. Q., 30, 39
Cordoba, Pedro de, 30, 40, 61n52
Corrado, Gene, 209, 242n60
Cossack Whip, The (1916), 112n72
Costello, Maurice, 61
Courrier cinématographique, Le, 245n100
Courtenay, Douglas, 175
Cousin Kate (1921), 120, 122–123, 185n22–23, 188n61
Craig, Britt, 12
Creel, George, 81, 111n56
Creelman, James Ashmore, 201, 240n25
Crescent theater (Syracuse), 42
Crisis, The (1916), 98
Crisp, Donald, 134, 137, 188n66
Cruz, Juan de la, 47
Cruze, James, 235
Currie, James Warren, 12

Dale, Virginia, 2, 6, 7, 69, 116, 168–169, 196, 210–211
Damon and Pythias (1914), 18
Dana, Viola, 85, 86 112n69, 112n72
Daniels, Bebe, 127, 186n37
Davies, Marion, 210, 234, 243n67
Davis, Richard Harding, 20, 58n25

Daw, Marjorie, 2, 3, 6, 116, 117, 130, 145, 190n83, 213, 244n81
Day, Dorothy (Dorothy Gottlieb), 1, 3, 7, 13, 44–45, 68, 82–83, 111n60, 116, 162–163, 166–168, 191n99
Day Book, The, 41, 64n85
Day's Pleasure, A (1922), 198
Day with John Burroughs, A (1921), 179
Dean, Daisy, 12
Dean, Priscilla, 229, 247n127
Debs, Eugene, 35
Deception (1921), 129, 135, 186n30, 187n55
DeKoven, John, 12
DeMille, Cecil B., 4, 23, 31, 40, 59n33, 70, 71, 81n53, 126, 183, 211–212, 220, 221, 235, 241n54, 246n114, 249n140, 251
DeMille, William, 18, 37, 40, 60n41, 181
Denver Republican, 52
Des Moines Capital, 111n58, 195, 238n5
Des Moines News, 116, 180
Des Moines Register, 166, 195
Des Moines theater (Des Moines), 163, 181
Des Moines Tribune, 13, 44, 82, 162, 166
Destruction (1915), 43–44
Detroit Journal, 116, 117
Detroit News-Tribune, 12
Devil, The (1921), 129, 187n40
Devil's Double, The (1916), 52
Dexter, Elliot, 164, 190n93, 206, 209
Diamond in the Sky, The (1915), 64n81
Dickens, Charles, 163
Disraeli (1921), 128
Ditmars, Raymond L., 134, 187n52
Divine, E. C., 39
Dixon, Thomas F., 36, 37, 57n16, 63n75
Doll's House, A (1922), 67n123
Don't Change Your Husband (1919), 110n46, 163–164
Don't Change Your Wife (1920), 249n140
Double Trouble (1915), 44, 65n96, 153
Dowling, Joseph J., 121, 185n19
Down to Earth (1918), 70
Draft 258 (1918), 218
"Dream of Eugene Aram," 98
Dream Street (1921), 169, 188n64, 227
Drew, Mrs. Sidney, 3, 91, 123, 135–136, 144, 153, 155, 188n61, 251
Drew, Sidney, 91, 144, 153, 155, 189n81
DuBarry (1915), 57n17
Dulcy (1923), 234

Dumas, Alexandre, 120, 130, 143
Dumb Girl of Portici (1916), 62n61
Dumo, Evelyn, 178
Duncan, Bud, 239n15
Duncan, William, 89, 113n80
Dupont, Miss, 223, 247n118
Durand, Leah, 190n86, 195, 238n5
Durfee, Minta, 165, 191n96

Eau Claire Leader, 114n94, 219
Eckel theater (Syracuse), 43
Éclair (France, Fort Lee), 108, 113
Edison, Thomas, 111, 230, 248n130
Edison Manufacturing, 112n70, 112n72, 230
Edwards, Snitz, 236, 249n146
Eltinge, Julian, 217
Emerson, John, 221, 246n116
Emery, Gilbert, 123, 185n23
Empey, Arthur, 113n79
Enemies of Women (1923), 234, 236–237
L'Enfant Roi (1923), 220, 223, 246n112
Escape, The (1914), 21
Essanay Film, 36, 59n34, 63n68, 64n86, 65n94, 65n95, 67n121, 135, 224, 244n82, 244n89
Exhibitors Herald, 97
Exhibitors Herald and Motography, 168, 191n101
Eyes of the World, The (1919), 168

Fabian, Warner, 206, 209, 241n46
Fairbanks, Douglas, 4, 6, 42, 44, 65n96, 70, 83, 89, 90, 92, 94, 97, 110n54, 114n93, 117, 118–119, 120, 130, 131, 145–149, 153, 172, 173–174, 176–177, 192n121, 196, 207, 213, 216, 227, 234, 235–236, 246n116, 248n135, 249n145
Faith of Her Fathers, The (1915), 26
Family Theater (Forest City, PA), 113–114n84
Famous Players-Lasky, 5, 13, 58n17, 60n41, 61n46, 61n52, 62n60, 65n99, 98, 100, 108–109n28, 109n36, 115n101, 185n18, 186n37, 192n114, 192n122, 193–194n134, 218
Farm Ballads, 140
Farnum, Dustin, 18, 58n17, 58n25, 147, 217
Farnum, William, 94, 114n88, 143, 147, 169, 170, 192n107, 217
Farrar, Geraldine, 30, 37, 40, 61n49, 61n51, 70, 71, 108n24
Fascinating Widow, The, 217

Favorite Players, 20
Fawcett, George, 76, 109n34, 175
Fazenda, Louise, 197, 239n14
Ferguson, Elsie, 83, 129
Field, George, 226, 247n123
Fields, Eleanor, 79, 80
Fight for Millions, A (1918), 89, 113n80
Figman, Max, 20, 58n24
Film Daily, 12, 193n126, 199
Film Daily Yearbook, 7, 195
Film Girl, The (Marjorie Dunmore Tooke), 3, 4, 5, 12, 41–42, 68, 83, 90
Fires of Youth, The (1918), 70
First National Pictures, 209, 242n61
Flaherty, Robert J., 219, 227, 247n124
Flame of Life, The (1923), 229
Flaming Youth (1923), 5, 202, 206–207, 208–209, 211, 234, 241n45
Flanner, Janet, 2, 4, 5, 6, 68, 90, 113n82
Flinn, John E., 81
Flint Journal, 116
Foolish Wives (1922), 4, 199–200, 211, 219, 222–223, 239–240n21, 241n44
Fool There Was, A (1915), 37, 38–39, 64n81
Footlights (1921), 129, 187n40
For Better, For Worse (1919), 163
Forbidden Fruit (1921), 183
Ford, Harrison, 201, 210, 214, 240n22
Fords, Hal, 43
Fort Wayne Sunday News, 168
Fort Worth Star-Telegram, 12, 68
Foundling, The (1916), 114n92
Four Horsemen of the Apocalypse, The (1921), 120, 124, 128, 134, 141–142, 185–186n27, 187n54, 204, 216, 225, 234, 236
Fox, William, 64n80, 171, 192n108
Fox Film, 38, 64n80, 67n122, 114n87, 114n88, 135, 143, 144, 186n37, 189n72, 192n108, 224
Francis, Alec B., 201, 240n24
Franklin, Sydney, 201, 240n26
Frederick, Pauline, 217, 245n96
Friends of the Seventh Art, 220, 227
Frisco, Albert, 178
Fuller, Dale, 223, 247n119

Gail, Alice, 72
Garden of Allah, The (1917), 98
Garden theater (Des Moines), 65n97
Garson, Harry, 109n29
Gauntier, Gene, 60–61n45

INDEX   261

Gelthorn, a Rustic Venice (1915), 30
George, Maude, 223, 247n118
Gerard, James, 81, 111n56
Gilded Cage, The (1922), 214
Giles, Corliss, 75
Ginzburg, Carlo, 252
Girl of the Golden West, The (1915), 22
Gish, Dorothy, 70, 107n9, 109n33, 166
Gish, Lillian, 70, 75, 107n9, 109n32, 117, 118, 134, 137, 158, 234
Glass, Gaston, 175, 192n117
Glendon, Frank, 180, 193n128
Glyn, Elinor, 37, 62n60
Going Some, 217
Golden Chance, The (1916), 45–46
Goldfish, Samuel, 59n33, 81, 98, 101–102, 115n103
Goldwyn Pictures, 67n119, 101, 113n75, 113n76, 114n85, 115n103, 115n104, 115n112, 185n16, 190n95, 213, 218, 244n83
Golem, The (1921), 135, 187n55
Goodrich, Edna, 47
Goose Girl, The (1915), 58n17
Gordon, Margorie, 86
Grand Guignol, 150, 189n79
Grandma's Boy (1922), 198, 239n11
Grand Rapids Herald, 116
Graustark (1915), 65n95
Graves, George W., 97
Gravina, Cesare, 223
Great Secret, The (1917), 66n116
Great Train Robbery, The (1903), 220, 230
Great War/World War I, 7, 42, 62n56, 68, 113n79, 116, 120, 252
Griffith, D.W., 4, 13, 18, 19, 21, 22, 28–29, 35, 37, 38, 50, 52, 57n16, 58nn19–21, 61n46, 61n53, 62n61, 64n79, 70, 75–76, 80, 82, 83, 109n32, 117, 118, 134, 136–137, 145, 155–162, 169, 184n10, 188n64, 188n66, 190n82–83, 202, 213, 220, 227, 230, 247nn121–122, 248n134, 251
Gunning, "Wid," 5, 12, 60n36, 69, 179, 193n126

Hackathorne, George, 180, 193n128
Hackett, James K., 217
Hairy Ape, The, 243n68
Half Breed, The (1916), 153
Hall, F. W. Mordaunt, 195, 238n3
Hall, Prunella, 195

Hamilton, Cosmo, 73, 108n26, 181
Hamilton, Lloyd "Ham," 197, 239n15
Hamilton, Mahlon, 210, 243n68
Hammerstein, Elaine, 230, 248n129
Hammond, Percy, 70, 107n9
Hampton, Hope, 230, 248n129
Hanson, Juanita, 78, 79, 110n45
Harron, Johnny, 213, 244n81
Harron, Robert, 70, 76, 118, 213
Hart, William S., 52, 83, 89, 90, 92, 93, 94, 105, 111–112n61, 114n87, 115n102, 115n107, 115n111, 147, 166, 185, 217, 245n94, 248n135
Hartley, Alberta, 2, 3, 4, 5, 116, 180–181
Hartman, Ruth, 20, 58n25
Hatton, Raymond, 71, 107n19
Haver, Phyllis, 197, 239n13
Hawley, Wanda, 127, 186n37
Hayakawa, Sessue, 22–23, 59n36, 61n46, 145, 149, 152, 189n78
Hayes, Frank, 77, 99
Haynes, Aldura, 111n58
Healy, R. A., 89–90
Hearst, William Randolph, 77, 85, 243n67
Heartbreak House, 179
Heart of Humanity, The (1919), 131, 187n47
Heart of Maryland, The (1915), 57n17
Hearts of the World (1918), 70, 75–76, 82, 83–85, 109n33, 111n58, 131, 136, 137, 190n82
Hearts Up (1921), 120
Hecht, Ben, 37, 186n33
Hefferman, Harold, 113n78, 252
Hell's Hinges (1916), 111–112n61, 192n120
Hergesheimer, Joseph, 196, 238n8
Her Greatest Love (1918), 72
Her One Mistake (1918), 90, 95–97, 114n90
Hickman, Wilbur, 130
High Road, The (1915), 26
Hilliard, Harry, 52, 54, 67n122
His Picture in the Papers (1916), 153, 174
Hodgdon, Barbara, xiv, 7
Hoffman, Esther, 4, 41
Hollander, W. K., 12, 69, 109n39, 112n69, 134, 252
Hollywood (1923), 234–235
Holmes, E. Burton, 87, 113n74
Holt, Jack, 182, 193–194n134
Home Sweet Home (1914), 61n46, 109n32, 230
Hoosier Romance, A (1918), 70, 76–77, 98–99, 115n98

Horsely, William, 17
House of Glass, The (1918), 70, 74–75
How to Write for the Movies (1915), 36
Hoyt, Harry O., 209, 242n58
Hulette, Gladys, 197
Humoresque (1921), 181
Hunter, Glenn, 201, 240n23
Hypocrites (1915), 62n61

Ibañez, Vincent Blasco, 124, 128, 141, 186n27, 203, 218, 225, 228, 234, 236
Ibsen, Henrik, 66n110, 67n123
Idle Wives (1916), 52, 56
IMP, 58n23, 62n57, 230
Impossible Mrs. Bellew, The (1922), 207
Inauguration of William McKinley (1897), 230
Ince, Thomas H., 58n23, 81, 209
Indianapolis News, 130
Indianapolis Star, 4, 68, 69, 90, 102
Indianapolis Times, 116
Influenza pandemic of 1918, 70, 111n60, 112n70, 252
Ingram, Rex, 120, 124, 135, 141, 142, 185n27, 187n54, 218
International News, 207, 230
In the Days of the Thundering Herd (1914), 114n87
In the Palace of the King (?), 218
Intolerance (1916), 52, 66n111, 66n114, 75, 108n25, 136, 190n82, 239–240n21
Iron Trail, The (1921), 115n100
Italian, The (1915), 58n23

Jannings, Emil, 135
Janowitz, Hans, 178, 193n124
Jazz Singer, The (1927), 109n38
Jean Doré (1915), 108n23, 114n92
Jefferson, Thomas, 77, 99
Joan the Woman (1917), 61n49, 70–71, 108n24, 221
Jobson, Edward, 99
Joclyn, Mildred, 2, 3, 13, 47–48
Johnson, Edward, 77
Johnson, Julian, 81
Johnson, Mr. and Mrs. Martin, 207, 208, 242n56
Johnson, Noble, 69
Jones, Aaron, 81
Jones, Juli (William Foster), 12, 57n5
Jones, Mrs. Flossie A., 114n93

Jose, Edward, 39, 64n83
Joy, Leatrice, 212
Joyce, Alice, 60–61n45, 120, 122–123, 185n22
Judith of Bethulia (1914), 42, 61n46
Julian, Rupert, 205, 211, 219, 241n43
Julius Caesar (1914), 248n133
Just Tony (1922), 219
Juvenile Protective Association (Chicago), 33, 63n76

Kalem Film, 26, 43, 59n32, 60n40, 60n45, 65n99, 110n53, 185n22, 189n81, 239n15, 243n70
Karzas, Andrew, 169
Keaton, Buster, 197, 239n12, 239n17
Keenen, Frank, 147, 189n76, 217
Kelly, Charlotte S., 2, 4, 5, 102–103, 130–131, 173
Kelly, Kitty (Audrie Alspaugh), 1, 2, 3, 4, 5, 6, 7, 12, 21–24, 37, 45, 52, 57n12, 59n32, 60n37, 68, 82, 83, 85–86, 89, 169, 207, 252
Kendall, Ezra, 217
Kennedy, A. M., 14
Kennedy, Thomas C., 97
Kern, Elizabeth, 2, 3, 5, 195, 196, 207
Kerry, Norman, 205, 206, 241n44
Kessler, Edith, 180
Keystone Film, 57n14, 65n94, 77–80, 110n44–53, 190n95, 191n96, 220, 230, 239n 7, 247n119, 248n134
Kick in High Life, A (1920), 176
Kid, The (1921), 128, 129, 187n42, 198, 227
Kimball, Edward, 75
Kinema Theater (Los Angeles), 196
kinetoscope, 230, 248n130
King, Bradley, 207, 209, 242n63
King, Henry, 196, 238n9
Kingsley, Grace, 5, 12, 13, 57n12, 196
Kipling, Rudyard, 117, 142, 184n7, 203
Kleine F.B.O., 230, 248n133
Kosloff, Theodore, 208, 242n55
Ku Klux Klan, 21, 38

La Crosse Tribune, 12, 117
Laemmle, Carl, 58n23, 62n57, 80, 199, 200
Lamb, The (1916), 145, 146
Lane, Lupino, 213, 244n84
Langston, Tony, 116, 184n3
Lanvorigt, W., 116
Lardner, Ring, 70, 107n13
La Salle theater (Chicago), 33

Lasky, Jesse L., 59n33, 81
Lasky Company, 17, 30, 61n53, 101, 115n103
Latham, Woodville, 230, 248n131
Lavender and Old Lace, 112
Lawrence, Oma Moody, 2, 13, 48–49, 68, 97
Lee, Lila, 182, 193nn133–134, 204, 225
Leffler, Mary B., 68
Leighton, Lillian, 71, 107n19
Le Saint, Edward J., 114n90
Lewis, Senator J. Hamilton, 81, 111n56
Liberty Loan bonds, 83, 85
License No. 13/The Hoodoo Auto (1905), 230, 248n132
Lieber & Company, 217
Lincoln, Abraham, 49, 156
Lincoln Motion Picture, 69, 107n6
Linder, Max, 213, 244n82
Lindsay, Vachel, 64n79
Little Doll's Dressmaker, The (1915), 42
Little Girl Next Door, The (1916), 33, 35, 47, 62n58
Little Lord Fauntleroy (1921), 128, 129, 185n19
Little Old New York (1923), 207, 210, 234, 243n71
Little Orphan Annie (1918), 109n36
"Little Orphan Annie," 109n36
Lloyd, Harold, 186n37, 197, 239n11
Lockwood, Harold, 67n119, 167
Loew, Marcus, 67n119, 115n104
Lois Weber Productions, 62n61
Lonely Villa, The (1909), 230
Long, Walter, 225, 247n122
Loos, Anita, 146, 174, 221, 246n116
Los Angeles Herald, 13, 116
Los Angeles Times, 12, 13, 196
Lost and Found (1922), 213
Love Light, The (1921), 120, 123–124, 172, 177–178, 251
Loves of Pharaoh, The (1922), 211
Lubitsch, Ernst, 5, 110n48, 120, 125, 129, 186nn29–30, 211, 220, 249n140
Lumière company, 230, 248n130, 248n131
Lussier, Richard F., 12
Lyric Theater (New York), 179

MacDonald, Margaret I., 59n28
MacGrath, Harold, 166, 191n98
Mack, Gardner, 11
MacLaren, Mary, 21, 47, 58n27, 62n61
MacPherson, Jeannie, 183, 219, 220–221, 246n114

Madame Peacock (1920), 172
Maeterlinck, Maurice, 86, 87, 113n76, 113n77, 159
Mae Tinee (Frances Peck), 1, 2, 4, 6, 7, 12, 13, 22, 52, 53, 66n114, 68, 69–70, 107n17, 116, 120–121, 134, 172, 184n13, 188n62, 189n73, 196, 201–203, 249n141
Majestic Film, 13, 19, 26, 58n19, 58n20, 61n46, 248n134, 248n135
Maker of Dreams, The (1915), 43
Male and Female (1919), 110n46, 185n18, 186n37
Manhattan Madness (1918), 145, 147–148
Mantle, Burns, 108n23, 210
Marcin, Max, 74, 109n30
Marion, Frances, 10n17, 177–178, 192–193n122
Marion, George, 209, 243n65
Marmont, Percy, 174–175, 192n115
Marriage Circle, The (1924), 110n48, 186n30, 249n140
Marsh, Mae, 76, 109n33
Marshall, Tully, 71, 107n19
Martin, Allen Langdon, 201
Martin, Beth, 123
Martin, Quinn, 117
Mason City Globe Gazette, 116
Master and the Man, The (1911), 230, 248n132
Masterpiece Film, 20
Mathis, June, 211, 217–218, 226, 245n95
Matin, Le, 220, 233
Mayer, Carl/Karl, 178, 193n124
Mayer, Louis B., 67n119, 191n97
Mayo, Edna, 41, 42, 64n86
McAvoy, May, 230, 248n129
McCardell, Roy, 39, 64n81
McCoy, Harry, 77, 99, 109n37
McDowell, Claire, 236, 249n146
McKim, Robert, 177, 192n120, 236
McRae, Rae, 6, 166
McWade, Margaret, 140, 188n69
Meighan, Tom, 121, 185n18, 235
Melford, George C., 25, 27, 60n40
Meredith, Lois, 25, 60n42
Mérimée, Prosper, 40, 64n84
Merry Go Round, The (1923), 202, 205–206, 211, 219, 234, 241nn43–44
Metro Film, 26, 52–54, 66n116, 67nn119–123, 86, 112n70, 112n72, 144, 185n27, 186n28, 188n61, 189n81, 208, 218

Michaux, Oscar, 116, 184n3
Mickey (1919), 163, 164–165, 190n92, 191n96
Midsummer Madness (1920), 181–182
Millionaire's Double, The (?), 218
Milwaukee Journal, 116
Minneapolis Journal, 116
Minneapolis Tribune, 12, 116
Minnie Ha Ha, 191
Miracle Man, The (1919), 120, 121, 145, 185nn16–21
Miracle of Life, The (1915), 34
Mix, Tom, 92, 114n87, 117, 219
Moline Dispatch, 117
Monogram Theater (Chicago), 89–90
Moore, Colleen, 70, 77, 98, 99, 109n36, 202, 206, 209, 211, 234
Moran, Polly, 79, 110n50
Morgan, Gene, 11
Morosco, Oliver, 18, 20, 47, 58n18
Mothers of France (1917), 69, 72–73, 108nn21–22
Motion Picture News, 3, 7, 42, 68, 116, 195
Motography, 97
Motte, Marguerite de la, 177, 192n121, 236
Moulton, Professor Ray, 137, 188n67
Münsterberg, Hugo, 6, 24, 31–33, 62n56
Muse, W., 116
Mussolini, Benito, 234, 235, 249n145
Mutt and Jeff, 73
Mutual Film, 19, 58n19, 63n68, 230, 248nn134–135

NAACP, 35
Nagel, Conrad, 182, 193n134, 212
Naldi, Nita, 204, 225, 235, 241n38
Nanook of the North (1922), 202, 204–205, 219, 226–227, 241n40, 247n124
Narrow Trail, The (1917), 111–112n61
National Committee for Better Films, 6
National Film (Indianapolis), 113
Naughty Marietta, 243n70
Nazimova, Alla, 52, 54–56, 67nn123–124, 83, 163, 172, 188n65, 204
Ne'er Do Well (1916), 98
Negri, Pola, 5, 66n115, 120, 125, 129, 134, 172, 186n29, 219, 220, 234, 235, 239n 20
Neilan, Marshall, 60, 109n36, 216
Neptune's Daughter (1914), 66n115
Nero (1922), 144
New Governor, The (1915), 28, 61n47
New Orleans Item, 12
New York Age, 12, 56n1, 59, 116

New York American, 195
New York Evening Mail, 5, 12, 126
New York Film Arts Guild, xiii, 3
New York Herald, 199
New York Herald-Tribune, 199
New York Journal, 195, 236n2
New York Morning Telegraph, 77, 110n43
New York Motion Picture, 58n23
New York Times, 5, 57n6, 61n51, 66n114, 66n117, 67n124, 108n23, 111n59, 113n77, 185n25, 186n32, 187n39, 190n83, 192n112, 193n127, 193n133, 195, 240n37, 242n57, 243n71, 249n148, 252
New York Tribune, 4, 69, 116, 144, 171, 199, 239n18
New York World, 117
New York Zoological Society, 134
Niblo, Fred, 176, 192n119, 213
Nicholas, Prudence, 195
Nichols, George, 165, 191n96
Nigger, The, 28, 61n47
Night Life in Hollywood (1922), 202
Noble, John W., 67n120
Normand, Mabel, 110nn44–45, 115n112, 163, 165, 190n92, 190n95, 191n96, 196, 197, 239n17
North, Tom, 81
Novak, Jane, 130
Novelty (Syracuse), 43

Oakley, Laura, 15, 57n14
Oakman, Wheeler, 165, 191n96
Olcott, Sidney, 60n45, 185n22, 210, 243n70
Old Wives for New (1918), 163, 164
Oliphant, T. 69
Olympic theater (Chicago), 75
Omaha World-Herald, 195, 207
O'Neill, Eugene, 207, 209, 242n62, 243n68
One Week (1921), 128
Orchestra Hall (Chicago), 26, 86, 87, 125, 205
Orphans of the Storm (1921), 109n32
Orpheum theater (Chicago), 234, 237
Othello, 145, 148
Otto, Ona, 11
Over the Hill (1921), 128, 140–141, 187n40
"Over the Hill to the Poorhouse," 187n41
Over the Top (1918), 89, 113n79

Pages from Life (1915), 26
Paramount, 29, 59n33, 89, 110n46, 113nn74–75, 115nn101–102, 163, 185n17, 186n29, 188n61, 193n134, 239nn17–19, 243n67

Paramount-Artcraft, 100, 111–112n61, 115n102, 118
Paramount Pictograph, 87
Paramount-Post Nature Pictures, 174, 192n114
Parsons, Louella O., 1, 3, 13, 36–37, 60n37, 62n58, 63n72, 68, 77, 195
Parsons, William, 91, 114n85
Passin' Through (1916), 153
Passion Flower, The (1921), 129, 187n40
Passion/Madame Du Barry (1921), 6, 120, 125, 129, 134, 172, 186nn29–30
Pathé Exchange, 58n26, 187n48, 188n61
Pathé-Frères, 30, 133, 134, 184n10, 187n50, 190, 244n82
Pathé News, 187n48
Pathé Review, 130, 134, 187n48
Pay Day (1922), 202
Pearce, Peggy, 79, 110n51
Peel, Robert, 96
Peer Gynt, 66n110
Pelléas and Mélisande, 113n76
Pelswick, Rose, 195, 238n2
Peppy Polly (1919), 109
Percy, Eileen, 182, 194n135
Pershing's Crusaders (1918), 82, 89
Peter Pan (1904), 57–58n17
Peter Pan (1924), 66n115
Philbin, Mary, 205, 206, 241n44
Pickford, Mary, 4, 10n17, 41, 83, 89, 92, 111n60, 120, 123–124, 129, 131, 155, 166, 177–178, 185n18, 216, 237, 251
Pittsburgh Press, 85
Plummer, J., 116
Poe, Edgar Allan, 18, 125, 126, 186n33
Polly of the Follies (1922), 219, 221–222
Polo, Eddie, 223
Polo, Malvina, 223, 247n119
Poor Little Peppina (1916), 243n70
Poor Little Rich Girl, A (1917), 112n72, 113n76
Poppy Girl's Husband (1919), 115n111
Porten, Henny, 135
Powell, David, 214, 244n88
Power, Tyrone, 34, 47, 62n59
Prevost, Marie, 78, 80, 110n48, 197
Price, Gertrude, 3, 11, 41, 48
Price, Guy, 116
Price, Oscar, 230
Price of Fame, The (1916), 52
Pritchard, R. E., 12
Prizma Color, 179
programming, 5–6, 90, 91, 135, 230

Queen Elizabeth (1912), 66n111, 108n22
Queen of Sheba, The (1921), 129–130, 144, 178, 187n40
Quirk, James, 81
Quo Vadis? (1912), 61n48, 220, 230, 248n133

Rae, Isabelle, 43
Rainey's African Pictures (1912), 22
Randolph theater (Chicago), 136
Rawlinson, Herbert, 83, 111–112n61
Ray, Charles, 185n19, 230
Real Adventure, The (1922), 213, 244n85
Rebecca of Sunnybrook Farm, 57n17
Red Cross, 73, 104, 150
Red Lantern, The (1919), 67n123, 163
Red Lights (1923), 234
Reed, Luther, 210
Reed, Myrtle, 86, 112n71
Reid, Wallace, 30, 45, 61n52, 71, 147, 217
Reinhardt, Max, 186
Reliance Film, 13, 19, 58nn19–20, 61n46, 230, 248nn134–135
Rene Haggard Journey On (1915), 27
Return of Draw Egan, The (1916), 115n107
Rialto theater (Des Moines), 84, 163, 182
Rialto theater (New York), 90, 101, 113–114n84
Rialto theater (Omaha), 209, 210
Riaume, Helen, 34, 47
Riders of the Purple Sage (1918), 114n88
Ridgley, Cleo, 45, 65n99
Riley, James Whitcomb, 76, 98, 99, 109n35
Rival Railroad's Plot, The (1914), 59n32
River's End, The (1920), 130
Rivoli Theater (New York), 90, 91, 101, 173
Roberts, Edith, 212, 244n80
Roberts, Theodore, 25, 60n43, 71, 183
Robertson, Lolita, 20, 58n24
Robin Hood (1922), 4, 202, 211, 235
Rob Reel, 6, 249n141
Rock, W., 117
Rogers, Rene, 47
Roland, Ruth, 58n26, 60–61n45
Romance of Tarzan, The (1918), 107n17
Romeo and Juliet (1916), 52–54, 64n82, 66n116, 143
Romeo et Juliette, 61n49
Roosevelt theater (Chicago), 226, 236
Rosanova, Rosa, 226
Rose of the Rancho (1914), 18
Rose theater (Chicago), 108n24
Rosita (1923), 186n30, 189n76, 234, 237

Ross, Harold, 90, 113n81
Ross, Ishbel, 1, 2, 172, 196, 203
Rothacker, Watterson, 216, 244n90
Rothacker Film Manufacturing, 211, 215, 216, 244n90
Rothapfel, S. L., 6, 90–91, 98, 101–102, 113–114n84, 179
Rowland, Richard, 67n119
Rowland, W., 116
Russell, William, 209, 242n64

Salisbury, Edward A., 22, 24, 60nn38–39
Salomé (1919), 163
Salomé (1923), 67n123
"Salon du cinéma," 6, 8, 220, 227
Sandberg, Carl, 5, 116, 186n33, 241n41, 249n141, 252
San Francisco Bulletin, 11
Sardou, Victorien, 150
Saturday Night (1922), 211–212, 221
Saunders, C., 116
Saxe brothers, 113–114n84
Sayre, J. Willis, 56n1
Scandal (1918), 70, 73–74, 108n25
Schenck, Joseph, 174
Schnitzler, Arthur, 127, 186n36
Scorsese, Martin, 8
Scrambled Lives (1921), 58n17
Scrap Iron (1921), 128
Scripps-McRae newspaper chain, 11, 41, 48, 56n3
"See America First," 93
Selby, Norman, 75
Selig, William, 19, 20, 57n15, 99
Selig Polyscope, 13, 18, 19, 21, 27, 57n15, 58n22, 59n34, 113n80, 114n87, 115n99, 194n137, 224
Selwyn, Clarissa, 87
Selwyn brothers, 115n103
Selznick, Lewis J., 81
Semon, Larry, 197, 213, 239n12
Sennett, Mack, 78, 110n44, 110n45, 110n47, 174, 190n95, 197, 239nn13–14, 239n17
Sentimental Tommy (1921), 128
Serrano, Vincent, 175, 192n116
Seventh Heaven (1927), 108–109n28
Seymour, Clairine, 118, 184n10
Shakespeare, William, 53, 54, 66n117, 67n118, 130, 132, 189n76, 200
Shaw, George Bernard, 179

Shaw, Peggy, 143
Sheehan, Winfield, 81
Sheik, The (1921), 60n40, 186n35
Shepherd King, The (1923), 144
Sherrill, William, 81
Shipman, Nell, 11
Shoes (1916), 13, 21, 57n11, 59nn27–28, 62n61
Sills, Milton, 206, 209, 241n47
Simpson, Russell, 87
Sins of the Mothers, The (1915), 42
Skerritt, N., 117
Smalley, Phillips, 62n61, 209, 242n59
Smilin' Through (1922), 199, 200–201, 211, 214
Snow White (1916), 58n17
Society for Visual Education, 135, 137–138, 188n60
Solano, Solita, 90
Soldier's Oath, A (1915), 114n88
Soldiers of Fortune (1914), 58n25
S.O.S. (1917), 70
Spanish Dancer, The (1923), 66n115, 234
Speakeasy, The (1919), 174
Spoilers, The (1914), 21, 57n15, 98, 114n88, 115n100, 241n54
Spoor, George, 68
Squaw Man, The (1914), 58n17, 60n42
Squaw Man, The (1918), 131, 187n47
Standing, Wydham, 201, 214, 240n22
Stanley, Forrest, 183, 194n138
Stark, George W., 12
Starr, Frances, 18, 57–58n17
Stedman, Myrtle, 209, 242n59
Stedman, Vera, 79, 110n52
Stern, Herman, 229
Stewart, Anita, 4, 10n17, 42, 163, 165, 191n97
Stillman theater (Cleveland), 118
Stoddard, Ralph P., 56n1
Stolen Goods (1915), 22, 27–28
Stolte, Arthur C., 12
Stone, Lewis, 130
Storm, The (1922), 227
Strand Theater (Chicago), 23, 27, 29, 30, 37, 39
Strand Theater (Des Moines), 181, 182
Strand Theater (New York), 6, 113–114n84, 174, 200
Strand Theater (Syracuse), 44
Studdiford, Grace, 175
Studebaker theater (Chicago), 25
Successful Adventure, A (1918), 218

Swanson, Gloria, 62n60, 78, 79, 80, 110nn46–47, 127, 185n18, 204, 207, 214, 215, 243n70
Sweet, Blanche, 27–28, 42, 61n46, 202, 209

Taliaferro, Edith, 18, 57n17
Taliaferro, Mabel, 57n17
Talmadge, Constance, 10n16, 70, 73, 108n25, 123, 219, 222, 234, 246n116
Talmadge, Norma, 4, 61n52, 83, 108n25, 129, 172, 174, 175, 199, 200–201, 211, 214, 219, 231, 234
Tarzan of the Apes (1918), 57n13, 107n17
Taylor, Bert Leyton, 62n55
Taylor, Bertram, 130
Taylor, William Desmond, 191n95, 216, 245n92
Teare, Ethel, 79, 110n53
Tearle, Conway, 232
Teddy at the Throttle (1917), 110n46
teleview, 230, 248n130
Tevis, N. D., 12, 117
Thanhouser, 67n120
Their Social Splash (1915), 26
Thief of Bagdad, The (1924), 207, 237
Thomas, Olive, 211, 2216, 45n92
Thomas H. Ince Film, 13, 20, 111n61
Three Musketeers, The (1921), 120, 128, 130, 192n119, 192n121, 235
Three Weeks (1907), 62n60
Three Weeks (1914), 37
Thurman, Mary, 79, 110n49, 197
tinting and toning, 145, 187n51
To Hell with the Kaiser (1918), 218
Tol'able David (1921), 196–197
Toll Gate, The (1920), 111–112n61
Torrence, Ernest, 197, 238n10
Tourneur, Maurice, 86, 87, 113nn76–77
Tracy, Virginia, 3, 4, 116, 144–145, 149, 168, 172, 189n73
Trailing African Wild Animals (1923), 207, 208
Trail of the Lonesome Pine, The, 111–112n61
Treat 'Em Rough (1919), 114n87, 117
Trenton, Pell, 75
Triangle Corporation, 58n19, 58n23, 65n96, 109n36, 110n44, 190n95, 248nn134–135
Trilby (1915), 113n76
True Heart Susie (1919), 109n32, 117, 118, 145, 159–162
Tucker, George Loane, 120, 121, 145, 185n16

Turnbull, Margaret, 27, 61n46
Turner, Florence, 61n52
Two Natures Within Him, The (1915), 27
Two Orphans, The (1922), 227

Unborn, The (1916), 52
Under Four Flags (1919), 117
Underhill, Harriette, 4, 6, 69, 116, 171–173, 181, 186n32, 199, 239n20
United Press, 11
Universal City, 5, 13, 14–17, 57nn12–13, 62n57, 119–120
Universal Film, 13, 14, 17, 18, 19, 62n57, 62n61, 65n100, 185n20, 194n134, 205, 222, 227, 229, 230, 239n19, 241n44, 246n114, 247n125
University of California, 60n38
University of Chicago, 49, 90, 137, 188n67
Upstream (1927), 108–109n28

Valentino, Rodolf/Rudolph, 60n40, 186n35, 202, 203–204, 208, 218, 219, 225, 240–241n37, 243n70
Valk, Edith, 79
Van Buren, Mabel, 25, 60n42
Verdi, Freddie, 123
Victim, The (1915), 26
Vidor, Florence, 213, 244n86
Vidor, King, 244n86
Vinson, Ruth, 12
Virginian, The (1914), 58n17, 60n42, 61n53, 111–112n61
Vitagraph Film, 42, 43, 58n25, 61n52, 65n93, 70, 89, 108n25, 108n29, 113n80, 144, 185n22, 188n61, 189n81, 191n97, 230, 239n12, 244n89
Von Stroheim, Erich, 199–200, 202, 205, 219, 222–223, 234, 239–240n21, 241nn43–44, 247n118

Walcamp, Marie, 47, 65n100
Walker, Johnny, 141
Walker, Lillian, 42, 65n93
Walsh, George, 147, 189n76
Walthall, Henry B./Harry, 38, 64n79, 215
Walton, Lester A., 12, 56n1, 116
Wanderer's Pledge, The, 43
War Brides (1916), 52, 54–56, 66n115, 67n123, 188n65
Ward, Fannie, 59n36, 145, 149, 189n78

Warfield, David, 18
Warrens of Virginia, The, 60n41
Washington Star, 107n8
Washington Times, 11
Washburn, Bryant, 43, 65n95, 215, 244n89
Waterloo Reporter, 12
Way Down East (1921), 134, 190, 227
Wayne, Maude, 79
Weaver of Dreams (1918), 85, 86–87
Weber, Lois, 3, 11, 13, 21, 23, 35, 47, 48, 52, 57n14, 61n53, 62n61, 120, 127, 139–140, 179, 242n59, 251
Webster, Harry MacRae, 81
Welch, Philip H., 12, 59n28
Welch, William, 140, 189n70
Western Blood (1918), 114n87
What Do Men Want? (1921), 172, 179–180, 181, 188n68
Wheeling Register, 116
When Knighthood Was in Flower (1922), 210, 243n67
When the Clouds Roll By (1919), 110n54, 172, 173–174
Where Are My Children? (1916), 4, 23, 33–35, 37, 45, 46–47, 62n61, 251
White, Pearl, 105
White Sister, The (1923), 234
Whittaker, Charles, 31, 62n55
Why Trust Your Husband? (1921), 181, 182
Wid's Daily, 12, 193n126
Wild Animal Life in America (1915), 22, 24–25, 60n39

Williams, Kathlyn, 183, 194n137, 215
Wilson, Lois, 182, 193n134
Wilson, President Woodrow, 81, 111
Windsor, Claire, 139, 180, 188n68
Winston, Harry, 210
Wise, H., 116
Wishing Ring, The (1914), 113n76
With Serb and Austrian (1915), 26
Wolheim, Louis, 210, 243n68
Woman, The (1915), 25–26, 60n41
Woman God Forgot, The (1917), 61n49
Woman's Place (1921), 128
Woman Thou Gavest Me, The (1919), 241n47
Wood, Polly, 2, 3, 195, 196, 211, 234, 249n142
Worcester Gazette, 116
Work (1915), 42
World Film, 108nn28–29, 192–193n122
Wray, John Griffith, 209
Wrightman, Ruth, 213, 244n83
Wynn, Ed, 214, 244n87

Yellow Typhoon, The (1920), 166
YMCA, 42
Young, Clara Kimball, 61n52, 70, 74–75, 109n29, 155
Young, Rida Johnson, 210, 243n70
Youngstown Vindicator, 117

Ziegfeld theater (Chicago), 38
Zukor, Adolph, 59n33, 80, 101, 181, 193n131

Richard Abel is Professor Emeritus of International Cinema and Media Studies at the University of Michigan. His recent books include *Menus for Movie Land: Newspapers and the Emergence of American Film Culture, 1913–1916*, and *Motor City Movie Culture, 1916–1925*. In 2017, the Giornate del cinema muto (Pordeone, Italy) honored him with its Jean Mitry Award. With Peter Holland he edited a collection of Barbara C. Hodgdon's writings, *Ghostly Fragments*.

WOMEN AND FILM HISTORY INTERNATIONAL

A Great Big Girl Like Me: The Films of Marie Dressler   *Victoria Sturtevant*
The Uncanny Gaze: The Drama of Early German Cinema   *Heide Schlüpmann*
Universal Women: Filmmaking and Institutional Change in Early
    Hollywood   *Mark Garrett Cooper*
Exporting Perilous Pauline: Pearl White and the Serial Film Craze
    Edited by Marina Dahlquist
Germaine Dulac: A Cinema of Sensations   *Tami Williams*
Seeing Sarah Bernhardt: Performance and Silent Film   *Victoria Duckett*
Doing Women's Film History: Reframing Cinemas, Past and Future
    Edited by Christine Gledhill and Julia Knight
Pink Slipped: What Happened to Women in the Silent Film Industries?
    Jane M. Gaines
Queer Timing: The Emergence of Lesbian Sexuality in Early Cinema
    Susan Potter
Subject to Reality: Women and Documentary Film   *Shilyh Warren*
Movie Workers: The Women Who Made British Cinema   *Melanie Bell*
Movie Mavens: US Newspaper Women Take On the Movies, 1914–1923
    Richard Abel

The University of Illinois Press
is a founding member of the
Association of University Presses.

University of Illinois Press
1325 South Oak Street
Champaign, IL 61820-6903
www.press.uillinois.edu